THE INSTITUTIONAL VEIL IN PUBLIC INTERNATIONAL LAW

This book deals with the nature of international organisations and the tension between their legal nature and the system of classic, state-based international law. This tension is important in theory and practice, particularly when organisations are brought under the rule of international law and have to be conceptualised as legal subjects. The position is complicated by what the author terms 'the institutional veil', comparable to the corporate veil found in corporate law. The book focuses on the law of treaties, as this pre-eminently 'horizontal' branch of international law brings out the problem particularly clearly. The first part of the book addresses the legal phenomenon of international organisations, their legal features as independent concepts, the history of international organisations and of legal thought in respect of them, and the development of contemporary law on international organisations. The second part deals with the practice of international organisations and treaty-making. It discusses treaty-making practice within organisations, judicial practice in interpretation of organisations' constitutive treaties, and the practice of treaty-making by organisations. The third and final part analyses the process by which international organisations have been brought under the rule of the written law of treaties, offering a practical application of the conceptual framework as previously set out. Part three is at the same time an analytic overview of the drafting history of the 1986 Vienna Convention on the Law of Treaties between States and International Organisations or between International Organisations. This is a profound and penetrating examination of the character of international organisations and their place in international law, and will be an important source for anyone interested in the future role of organisations in the international legal system.

Hart Monographs in Transnational and International Law

Series Editor: Craig Scott, Professor of Law, Osgoode Hall Law School of York University, Toronto

The objective of this series is to publish high-quality scholarship in public international law and private international law, as well as work that adopts 'transnational law' as its thematic, theoretical or doctrinal focus. The series strives to be a leading venue for work of the following sort:

* critical reappraisals of foundational concepts and core doctrinal principles of both public and private international law, and their operation in practice, including insights drawn from general legal theory;

* analysis and development of conceptions of 'transnational law', including in relation to the role of unofficial law and informal processes in transnational regulation and in relation to theories and studies of 'governance' in transnational spheres; and

* empirical studies of the emergence, evolution and transformation of international and/or transnational legal orders, including accounts and explanations of how law is constructed within different communities of interpretation and practice.

The series will also be home to monographs that explore the interactions between the ever-integrating fields of public and private international law. Of special interest are explorations of the extent to which these interactions are structured by higher-order principles and policies, on the one hand, and by politics and the exercise of various forms of power, on the other hand.

The series is open to work not only by law scholars but also by scholars from cognate disciplines.

Titles in this series

Volume 1: Terrorism and the State: Rethinking the Rules of State Responsibility

Tal Becker

Volume 2: Transnational Law and Local Struggles: Mining, Communities and the World Bank

David Szablowski

The Institutional Veil in Public International Law

International Organisations and the Law of Treaties

CATHERINE BRÖLMANN

•HART•
PUBLISHING
OXFORD AND PORTLAND, OREGON
2007

Published in North America (US and Canada)
by Hart Publishing
c/o International Specialized Book Services
920 NE 58th Avenue, Suite 300
Portland, OR 97213-3786
USA
Tel: +1 503 287 3093 or toll-free: (1) 800 944 6190
Fax: +1 503 280 8832
E-mail: orders@isbs.com
Website: www.isbs.com

Hart Publishing16c Worcester Place, Oxford, OX1 2JW
Telephone: +44 (0)1865 517530 Fax: +44 (0) 1865 510710
E-mail: mail@hartpub.co.uk
Website: http://www.hartpub.co.uk

British Library Cataloguing in Publication Data

Data Available

ISBN-13: 978-1-84113-634-9 (hardback)

Typeset by Columns Design Ltd, Reading
Printed and bound in Great Britain by
TJ International Ltd, Padstow, Cornwall

For J. and H.

Acknowledgments

Many people have contributed to the completion of this book, both in an academic and in a personal context. The basis of this book is a PhD project; I confirm my heartfelt gratitude to the persons named in the preface of the edition concluding that project.

In relation to the present book some names have to be mentioned in particular. I am indebted to Jan Klabbers, for a generous exchange of ideas on treaties and organisations over the years; and to Susan Marks for valuable advice on conceptualisation and on final drafting of the text.

I am especially grateful to Niels Blokker, Martti Koskenniemi, André Nollkaemper and Nigel White, for acute comments and critical observations to the text at various stages.

The making of this book has furthermore benefitted from the opportunities of academic collaboration with Malgosia Fitzmaurice, and from the valuable insights on publication of Erika de Wet.

I thank my colleagues of the International Law Department of the *Universiteit van Amsterdam* for stimulating discussions; and the Lauterpacht Centre for Research in International Law of the University of Cambridge, as well as Queen Mary College of the University of London, for offering the archetypal research environment during a period of writing.

Many thanks go to Murat Aydemir for his friendship and advice on matters including academic law and cultural analysis. Finally, I thank Janne Nijman for a substantive intellectual and personal contribution to this book.

Amsterdam
1st September 2006

Summary Contents

List of Abbreviations xv

1 Introduction 1

Part One International Organisations as International Legal Actors 9

2 The Nature of International Organisations 11

3 Conceptions of a New Legal Actor 35

4 The United Nations Era 65

Concluding Remarks to Part One

Part Two International Organisations and Treaty Practice 99

5 International Organisations as a Forum for Treaty-making 101

6 Constitutive Treaties of International Organisations 113

7 Treaty-Making by International Organisations 125

Concluding Remarks to Part Two

Part Three International Organisations and the Conventional Law of Treaties 141

8 Towards a Codified Law of Treaties for International Organisations 143

9 The 1986 Vienna Convention: Preliminary Questions and Procedural Aspects 181

10 The 1986 Vienna Convention on the Law of Treaties Between States and International Organizations or Between International Organizations 197

Concluding Remarks to Part Three

11 The Invisible Continent: Concluding Remarks 251

Annexes

Annex I. Table of comparison: Articles 1986 Convention and Articles 1969 Convention 274

Annex II. Table of comparison: Articles 1986 Convention and draft Articles 1982 274

Annex III. Articles of the 1969 Convention marked as 'problematic' for the purpose of the 1986 Vienna Conference 275

Annex IV. Some parallel provisions of the 1986 Convention and the 1969 Convention 277

Select Bibliography of Authors 283
Index 305

Contents

List of Abbreviations xv

1 Introduction 1

Part One International Organisations as International Legal Actors 9

2 The Nature of International Organisations 11
- 2.1 Preliminary Remarks 12
- 2.2 Formal Aspects 13
  - 2.2.1 Definition 13
  - 2.2.2 Classification 22
- 2.3 Material aspects 24
  - 2.3.1 Functionality 25
  - 2.3.2 Centralisation 27
  - 2.3.3 Transparency 29

3 Conceptions of a New Legal Actor 35
- 3.1 The State 35
- 3.2 The Rise of International Organisations: The Nineteenth Century 39
  - 3.2.1 Institutions 39
  - 3.2.2 Legal Images 44
- 3.3 The League of Nations Era 48
  - 3.3.1 Institutions 48
  - 3.3.2 Legal Images 54

4 The United Nations Era 65
- 4.1 Institutions 65
- 4.2 Legal Images 67
  - 4.2.1 The International Organisation as a Legal Person 68
    - *Legal Personality in International Law* 68
    - *Legal Personality in Relation to International Organisations* 71
  - 4.2.2 Legal Personality of International Organisations: Attribution and Effects 78
  - 4.2.3 Legal Personality of International Organisations: Foundation 83
  - 4.2.4 Objective Legal Personality 88
  - 4.2.5 Capacities and Competences 90

Concluding Remarks to Part One 95

Part Two International Organisations and Treaty Practice 99

5 International Organisations as a Forum for Treaty-making 101
5.1 Centralisation in United Nations Practice 102
5.2 Centralisation in Technical Organisations 107

6 Constitutive Treaties of International Organisations 113
6.1 Treaty or Constitution? 113
6.2 The Law of Treaties Applied to Constitutive Instruments 116

7 Treaty-Making by International Organisations 125
7.1 IGO Treaties in Practice 125
7.1.1 A Quantitative Perspective 125
7.1.2 A Qualitative Perspective 128
7.2 IGO Treaties in Doctrine 132
7.2.1 The Status of IGO Agreements 132
7.2.2 The Treaty-making Powers of International Organisations 134

Concluding Remarks to Part Two 139

Part Three International Organisations and the Conventional Law of Treaties 141

8 Towards a Codified Law of Treaties for International Organisations 143
8.1 Preparatory Work by the International Law Commission 144
8.1.1 IGO Treaty-making Capacity: 1950–1952 145
8.1.2 'Organisations of States': 1953–1954 150
8.1.3 A General Law of Treaties Code: 1955–1960 152
8.1.4 Involving the Law of the Organisation: 1961–1966 155
Definition 158
Capacity 158
Other Provisions 160
8.1.5 The Final ILC Draft Articles 162
8.2 Reception of the ILC Draft and the 1968–1969 Vienna Conference 165
8.2.1 Comments of Governments and International Organisations and Discussion in the Sixth Committee 165
8.2.2 The Vienna Conference (1968–1969) 168
8.3 International Organisations in the First Stage of the Codification Process 173

9 The 1986 Vienna Convention: Preliminary Questions and Procedural Aspects 181
9.1 Questions of Methodology 182
9.1.1 Drafting Methodology 182
9.1.2 Form 185
9.2 The Procedural Position of International Organisations 186

9.2.1 The Participation of International Organisations in the Diplomatic Conference 186
Participants 187
Status 189
9.2.2 Final Clauses of the Second Vienna Convention 190
Becoming Bound to the Convention 190
Entry into Force of the Convention 191
9.3 Diplomatic Fortune of the Convention 192
9.4 Conclusion: The Status of Organisations in Method and Procedure 193

10 The 1986 Vienna Convention on the Law of Treaties Between States and International Organizations or Between International Organizations 197
10.1 Issues of Doctrine 200
10.1.1 The Classification of Treaties by Party 200
10.1.2 Treaty-Making Capacity 203
10.1.3 Expressing the Juridical Will 205
Consent, Assent and Acquiescence 206
Reservations 210
10.1.4 Member States and Third States 212
The Drafting History of Article 36bis 213
Issues of Article 36bis 219
10.1.5 'Internal Law' 225
Invoking the Rules of the Organisation 226
Reserving the Rules of the Organisation 229
10.1.6 Terminology 230
10.2 Issues of Practice 233
10.2.1 Territory 233
10.2.2 Dispute Settlement 234
10.2.3 Descriptive Force 235
10.3 Issues of Principle 237
10.3.1 The International Organisation as a Moral Person 237
10.3.2 The International Community of States 242

Concluding Remarks to Part Three 245

General Conclusions 249

11 The Invisible Continent: Concluding Remarks 251
11.1 Propositions on the Institutional Veil 253
Organisations are Semi-closed 253
Organisations are Semi-open 254
The Inherent Transparency of Organisations 255
The One-dimensional Character of International Law 256
Organisations as Independent Actors 257
The Legal Order Overrides the Setup of the Subject 258

11.2 The Institutional Veil in the Conventional Law of Treaties 260
11.3 The Institutional Veil and International Responsibility 262
11.4 The Institutional Veil in General International Law 267
International Organisations and International Law 267
The Nature of International Law 268
Other Legal Subjects 269
11.5 The Positivist Perspective on the Institutional Veil 269

Annexes 273
Annex I. Table of comparison: Articles 1986 Convention and Articles 1969 Convention 274
1986 Convention Articles 274
Annex II. Table of comparison: Articles 1986 Convention and draft Articles 1982 274
1986 Convention Articles 274
Annex III. Articles of the 1969 Convention marked as 'problematic' for the purpose of the 1986 Vienna Conference 275
Annex IV. Some parallel provisions of the 1986 Convention and the 1969 Convention 277

Select Bibliography of Authors 283
Index 305

List of Abbreviations

ACC	Administrative Committee on Coordination (now the United Nations System Chief Executives Board (CEB) for Coordination)
AFDI	Annuaire Français de droit international
American JIL	American Journal of International Law
ARIEL	Austrian Review of International and European Law
ASIL	American Society of International Law
British YIL	British Yearbook of International Law
Cardozo LR	Cardozo Law Review
CMLRev	Common Market Law Review
Columbia LR	Columbia Law Review
CTS	Consolidated Treaty Series (Oceana)
CW	Committee on the Whole (UN diplomatic conference)
EBRD	European Bank for Reconstruction and Development
EC	European Community
ECHR	European Court for Human Rights
ECOSOC	Economic and Social Council
EPIL	Encyclopedia of Public International Law
EU	European Union
European JIL	European Journal of International Law
FAO	Food and Agricultiral Organization
GAOR	General Assembly Official Records (UN)
German YIL	German Yearbook of International Law
Harvard ILJ	Harvard International Law Journal
IAEA	International Atomic Energy Agency
IBRD	International Bank for Reconstruction and Development
ICAO	International Civil Aviation Organization
ICCPR	International Covenant on Civil and Political Rights
ICLQ	International and Comparative Law Quarterly
IDI	Institut de droit international
IFC	International Finance Corporation
IGO	(International) Intergovernmental Organization
ILC	International Law Commission
ILO	International Labour Organization
IMF	International Monetary Fund
ITU	International Telegraphic Union

Journal HIL	Journal for the History of International Law
LNTS	League of Nations Treaty Series
LoN	League of Nations
Martens NRG	Martens Nouveau Recueil Generale
NATO	North Atlantic Treaty Organization
NGO	Non-Governmental Organization
Nordic JIL	Nordic Journal of International Law
NVIR	Nederlandse Vereniging voor Internationaal Recht
OAS	Organization of American States
OECD	Organization for Economic Cooperation and Development
OPCW	Organization for the Prohibition of Chemical Weapons
OSCE	Organization for Security and Cooperation in Europe
ÖZöRV	Österreichisches Zeitschrift für öffentliches Recht und Völkerrecht
PCIJ	Permanent Court of International Justice
RdC	Recueil des Cours
RDI	Rivista di Diritto Internazionale
RGDIP	Révue générale de droit international public
UNCLOS	United Nations Convention on the Law of the Sea
UNDP	United Nations Development Programme
UNESCO	United Nations Educational, Scientific and Cultural Organization
UN(GA)	United Nations (General Assembly)
UNHCR	United Nations High Commissioner for Refugees
UNIDO	United Nations Industrial Development Organization
UNTS	United Nations Treaty Series
UPU	Universal Postal Union
Virginia JIL	Virginia Journal of International Law
WHO	World Health Organization
WMO	World Metereological Organization
YILC	Yearbook of the International Law Commission
ZaöRV	Zeitschrift für ausländisches öffentliches Recht und Völkerrecht
ZöR	Zeitschrift für öffentliches Recht

1

Introduction

THE MOST CONSPICUOUS non-state actors in international law since World War Two are international intergovernmental organisations. Organisations are involved in almost all fields of human cooperation, where they present themselves not only as institutional fora for states, but also as independent international actors.

This book looks at the role of international organisations in international law, and their conceptualisation as legal actors. It proposes that the dual image of organisations – open structures that are vehicles for states and at the same time closed structures that are independent legal actors – has resulted in a transparent legal set-up (symbolised by what is termed the 'institutional veil') with member states and other component elements of the organisation to some extent legally visible behind the legal veil that clothes it. This particular condition of organisations has not been fully acknowledged and, moreover, cannot fully be accommodated in the current one-dimensional system of international law. This set-up is a factor in several contemporary debates, with the legal responsibility of organisations in the context of military operations as a topical example. The complexity of these debates is however, difficult to grasp without taking account of the conceptualisation of organisations as legal subjects generally.

The conceptualisation of international organisations as legal subjects is best examined in the context of a branch of international law which counts as 'classic' and fundamental. The law of treaties eminently qualifies in that respect. It has added practical relevance since international actors conduct a large part of their formal international relations through the conclusion of treaties.

The codification of international law with respect to treaties concluded by international organisations (IGO treaties) in the '1986 Vienna Convention' is a landmark of the canonisation of organisations as international subjects. It has, however, been a notoriously difficult process. IGO treaties were a recurring subject of discussion in the course of preparation of the 1969 Vienna Convention on the Law of Treaties, and when this Convention had its scope definitively limited to inter-state treaties, it was the topic of another seventeen years of work before resulting in a final text.

Why has this process been so problematic? Incidental references to that question mention the 'special nature' of agreements concluded by international organisations, or the functional character of organisations, but without much detail. This book takes a closer look at the 'legal nature' of international organisations and examines on that basis their compatibility with the law of treaties and with international law in general. It turns out that the answer to the question posed above is more complex than it may seem at first sight. As is argued, the 'transparency' of international organisations as legal actors, and their ensuing layered character, makes them less than well-suited for the law of treaties system (or any classic voluntarist system for creating legal norms).

This book takes a threefold approach. It surveys the often counteracting principles that have complicated and shaped the conceptualisation of international organisations as subjects of international law. It looks at the different ways in which organisations are involved in treaty practice. And, finally, it examines the place which is accorded to international organisations in the law of treaties – this examination takes the form of an analysis of the 1986 *Convention on the Law of Treaties Between States and International Organizations or Between International Organizations* in relation to the classic inter-state law of treaties. The last Part is therefore at the same time an analytic overview of the drafting (hi)story of the law of treaties of organisations.

****

The logical point of departure for an assessment of IGO treaty-making is treaty-making by states. In fact, this frame of reference was explicitly chosen for the second law of treaties convention. The stated aim of the International Law Commission was to bring IGO treaties under the *existing* system, established by the 1969 Convention. It means that the drafting process of the 1986 Convention, even more so than academic debate, essentially revolved around the question as to what extent international organisations could be equated with states – the traditionally closed, billiard ball subject of international law.

That question, it will be argued, brings out the fundamental tension between the layered nature of international organisations and the one-dimensional law of treaties system. The law of treaties, given the nature of the contractual instrument, is strictly based on the principle of consensualism and by consequence is geared to equal legal partners. International organisations, however, 'are neither sovereign nor equal', as it was put in one lapidary statement by ILC Rapporteur Paul Reuter.[1]

[1] YILC 1977, Vol II (Part One), at 120, § 6.

What does this mean exactly? To be sure, the 'inequality' of states and organisations, both as a philosophical conviction and as a legal construct, is part of the framework of classic international law doctrine, in which the territorial state holds a central position and the international organisation has a servicing and functional role. However, this perspective has lost some of its power over the years. The ending of the Cold War is one reason why the idea of international organisations conducting relations on an equal footing with states no longer makes feelings run as high as in the 1960s and 1970s. At that time, as one commentator put it, an important factor in the failure to include IGO treaties in the 1969 Vienna Convention was uncertainty as 'to what extent . . . international organizations *should* be able to participate as equal units within the international legal system'.[2] This question has lost its edge with the political and doctrinal changes of the 1990s – notably the turn of events in the former socialist states and the attenuation of the doctrine of state sovereignty – but not its substance.

The problem of organisations as subject of the law of treaties is less yielding when approached in terms of the legal system itself. On a systemic level, the tension between the transparent nature of organisations and the binary set-up of international law (the tension between sovereignty and law) remains. The law of treaties, as with certain other branches of international law, proceeds from the legal equality of actors. The primary condition for upholding this equality is legal impermeability. This allows for the application of objective, 'external' criteria, while divergent institutional characteristics and factual circumstances are rendered invisible to the general legal order. This is how in international law Liechtenstein and the United States are construed as being equal; or how a Western-style parliamentary democracy and an absolute monarchy can reach formal agreement on mutually applied conditions notwithstanding different domestic legal requirements.

Apart from the obvious functional delimitation of international organisations, it is not certain that they vary more strongly in their institutional structures than do states. Rather, the fundamental difference between IGOs and states seems to be that international organisations lack the *legal* impermeability of states. To the late-modern lawyer the state may appear as a corporate entity in the same way as an international organisation, but from a formal perspective the state's internal structure is screened off from international law until it opens up of its own accord.

For international organisations, on the other hand, that is not the case. As mentioned above, this particular condition may be summarised as legal transparency, and is expressed by the metaphor of the 'institutional veil'. It

[2] Günther Hartmann, 'The Capacity of International Organisations to Conclude Treaties' in Karl Zemanek (ed), *Agreements of International Organisations and the Vienna Convention on the Law of Treaties*, 1971, 127-163, at 129 (emphasis in the original text).

can be traced to a number of factors, which are partly of a systemic nature (for example, the IGO's sectoral design, or the dictate of a dualist vision of the law, in which every rule must be either national or international); partly doctrinal (for example, the view that an organisation is a treaty, which is ruled by the will of the parties); and partly political or philosophical (for example, the argument that organisations should not assume too many powers because of a democratic deficit. The most important factor is perhaps the oscillation between the organisation's open and closed images and in a general sense the functionalist tendency towards the 'open' view of organisations as vehicles for state action. This is expressed for example in the statement by Professor Alvarez that:

> ...IOs are not intended to be proto-states or governments in the making. They were and are established for limited purposes – primarily, to facilitate the making of some treaties, to focus debate and make recommendations to governments and to serve as venues for settling disputes on closely circumscribed topics. They are institutions of limited and delegated powers, lacking the plenary rights of sovereigns under international law ....[3]

The layered character of organisations ensuing from the organisation's transparent nature is at odds with the one-dimensional structure of the law of treaties system. It will be argued that this tension, while never quite acknowledged or rendered explicit, is the primary factor to have animated discussions and shaped their outcome. This process is embodied in the 1986 Vienna Convention.

****

How has the law of treaties in relation to international organisations been addressed by legal scholarship? In general, the treaty-making practice of states *within* the framework of an international organisation has received the most attention; that is, treaties in regard of which the organisation fulfills a forum role but to which it is not itself a party. In the case of prominent political organisations such as the United Nations, the Council of Europe, the Organization of African Unity or the Organization of American States, this function has resulted in a wealth of 'law-making' multilateral instruments. These have generally overshadowed the discrete number of treaties, mostly with a more mundane content, concluded *by* those same organisations.

Scholarly interest in treaties concluded by organisations has been concentrated in roughly two periods: the 1960s, when the International Law Commission was grappling with the place of IGO treaties in the draft articles for the first Law of Treaties Convention; and in the 1980s, around the conclusion of the second Vienna Convention. Writings on the 1986

[3] José Alvarez, *International Organisations as Law-Makers*, 2005, at 15.

Vienna Convention mostly have the form of a textual commentary to the Convention, leaving scope for further thought on the background and systemics of the text. The 1960s, on the other hand, produced several monographic studies on the question of treaty-making by international organisations and its legal basis in particular. These works generally took the perspective of international institutional law or, more broadly, the law of international organisation. As this field of study proceeds from the internal structure of the organisation, it tends to regard international organisations as 'open' structures and to disregard the tension that comes into play when it comes to the external relations of organisations and concomitant legal fictions such as treaty-making capacity.

By contrast, this book considers international organisations from an external perspective and analyses the conceptualisation of organisations as actors in general international law, notably in the law of treaties. It does so by proceeding *within* the positivist framework that is the frame of reference for the majority of international lawyers and policy-makers. The aim is thus to give an immanent critique of international law and doctrine, and of the way in which these have included organisations.

For the purpose of clarity and analytical stability, the 'positivist paradigm' may at times be portrayed as more monolithic than would be warranted from a general point of view. 'The' positivist paradigm is not entirely closed off and is in constant movement; the identities of 'the' state and 'the' international organisation are continuously being re-negotiated. What matters in the present context is the *modus operandi* of the positivist system – voluntarist and based on state sovereignty. It is a system which may be unravelling at the seams, but which at present still sets the parameters for international legal relations. This 'continuing hold of legal positivism' (as referred to by Alvarez),[4] including its bearing on legal practice, is precisely why it is worthwhile to take the formal system as a point of departure in an examination of the concept and role of international organisations. At a more fundamental level, it makes clear how that formal system, while pressing organisations in the classic one-dimensional mould, is having its voluntarist premises gradually undermined by a tension of its own making.

* * * *

As argued above, the oscillation between the open and closed image of international organisations, and the tension between the transparent nature of organisations and the one-dimensional set-up of international law

[4] Alvarez, above, note 3, at 586.

amount to a systemic condition. This is a topical issue, for more reasons than just the formative effect of opposing convictions about the role of the state.

Next to the necessity to fill a conceptual lacuna regarding international organisations, the central issue in practice is that the flexible institutional veil creates uncertainties about accountability at the various levels of decision-making authority. The ultimate formal setting for problems of accountability, addressed in a brief *excursus* in the final chapter of this book, is the machinery of international legal *responsibility* as applied to organisations, currently under study by the International Law Commission. However, the challenges posed by the participation of organisations in the international system extend to the mechanisms of accountability in the broad sense. This includes the question of a possible binding effect of the organisation's obligations upon member states; or conversely, of the member states' obligations upon the organisation; or the question of the locus of accountability in the case of human rights violations – to name but a few recurring points of debate.

****

This book is divided into three parts. Part One proposes a theoretical framework for the consideration of international organisations as actors in international law. Chapter 2 seeks to outline the nature of international organisations as legal entities. It addresses the definition of an 'international organisation' and three material characteristics that arguably render a core of the legal manifestation of organisations from an external perspective. Chapter 3 examines, from the point of view of doctrine and practice, the legal image of IGOs as legal actors in pre-United Nations international life. This is done by way of a brief survey of intellectual and doctrinal history up until World War Two. Chapter 4 then aims to do the same for the United Nations era, while putting less emphasis on the history of institutions – well-documented and well-known as it is – and more on the legal image of organisations as this emerges from several well-known points of doctrinal and theoretical debate revolving around the tenet of legal personality.

Part Two addresses the involvement of international organisations with treaty-making in the broad sense. It makes clear how the institutional veil changes appearance depending on the context. With some simplification one can say that when the organisation acts as a forum for treaty-making by states, the organisation manifests itself as an open system (Chapter 5). When the constituent treaty of an organisation is under review, the organisation appears as partly open and partly closed (Chapter 6). When the organisation is itself party to a treaty, it manifests almost entirely as a closed system in the way of a state (Chapter 7). These cases neatly illustrate the separate institutional order of organisations – posing a boundary to, and exerting influence on, general international law, *in casu* the law of treaties, in various ways. They also show that the legal boundary of the organisation is never entirely open or entirely closed, but always more fuzzy than that of states. Chapter 7 then also provides the practical and doctrinal context for Part Three.

This final Part examines the law of treaties as applicable to treaties concluded by international organisations on the basis of the 1986 Vienna Convention. Chapter 8 describes the preliminary stage, which revolved around the question of whether treaties concluded by international organisations were to be included in the general law of treaties at all. This was a recurrent question during the preparatory work for the first Vienna Convention, until it was decided by the final vote to limit its scope to inter-state treaties. Chapter 9 addresses the collateral aspects of the second Vienna Convention – the organisation of the diplomatic conference, the method of drafting and the final clauses – on the points where these reflect the (ambiguous) role that was accorded to international organisations in the process. The text of the 1986 Convention and its *travaux préparatoires* are then considered in Chapter 10.

The work strategy of the International Law Commission, and later of the Diplomatic Conference, was to limit substantive review and discussion to the provisions of the 1969 Convention that had been specifically marked as 'problematic' for transposition to the new Convention. Combined with the drafters' objective to create one integral body of rules, this means that the preparatory work for the 1986 Convention was concerned only with those parts of the law of treaties in which the equation of organisations to states was considered difficult or controversial.

Chapter 10 focuses on these provisions. They constitute the essence of the 1986 Convention, in whichever form they have ended up in the final text, because they render the essence of the proces sof inclusion of organisations in the international law canon. As with the preparatory work for the 1969 Convention, discussion on these provisions can almost entirely be traced back to the specific features of organisations outlined in Part One, and to the contrast between the transparent nature of international organisations and the one-dimensional framework of the law of treaties. The economic drafting strategy chosen by the International Law Commission also means that, although not a classic article-by-article commentary, Chapter 10 may serve as a reasonably inclusive analysis of the 1986 Convention.

Chapter 11 – together with the Summarising Remarks to Parts One, Two and Three – contains concluding remarks. It puts together the main propositions of the book, and seeks to place these in a broader framework.

Part One

International Organisations as International Legal Actors

2

The Nature of International Organisations

THIS CHAPTER AIMS to describe the 'nature' of international intergovernmental organisations ('international organisations', 'organisations' or 'IGOs')[1] as legal entities by looking at three formal characteristics (viz used for the purposes of definition) as well as three material traits. The chapter proceeds in some detail, in order to provide the necessary formal and conceptual background to the rest of the book. After a set of preliminary remarks in the first section, which serve to set the parameters for this book and clarify its structure, the second section addresses the question of definition, as a set of formal(ised) features, and briefly discusses the related issue of classification.

The third section considers three material characteristics: functionality, centralisation and transparency. These are referred to as 'material' because they are not for the purpose of international law formally defining features. 'Functionality' refers to the fact that organisations are designed and defined on the basis of function rather than territory. 'Centralisation' denotes the degree of centralisation, or vertical dynamic, which each international organisation displays with respect to the general international legal order. 'Transparency', finally, is an endemic condition of intergovernmental organisations in general international law, partly due to the other two features counteracting: it indicates that organisations are neither entirely closed-off to international law in the way of states, nor entirely open, as instances of non-institutionalised inter-state cooperation would be.

[1] 'Institution' and 'institutionalised' are used in this book to denote all forms of association other than states, including IGOs and NGOs, which have some form of centralisation.

2.1 PRELIMINARY REMARKS

A few preliminary remarks are in order. In a general vein, the *caveat* in the previous chapter must be recalled: the voluntarist premises of current international law are at times somewhat overdrawn for reasons of clarity and analytical stability.

First, references to the 'closed' character of states are are made with the obvious qualification that the impermeability of the state's legal order has diminished since World War Two, notably through the individual becoming an addressee of international legal norms. That topic lies outside the scope of the following chapters and will not be addressed. At the same time this book to some extent positions itself in the debate, as it proceeds from the view that, while states are 'opening up' more and more, in a positivist perspective this happens on their own accord – by assuming treaty-based obligations, by (unwittingly) participating in the process of formation of customary law, or even by becoming bound to higher norms imposed by the international community – a community of which states are perceived as the ultimate building blocks.[2] Even though such a process may lead to a centralised legal order where in practice the voluntarist principle has withdrawn from sight (as for example in Western-style democratic states), in the formal framework this is essentially different from the top-down dynamic which lawyers resort to – as will be clear from the following chapters – when international organisations are brought under the rule of international law.

Second, a legal feature is, according to the contemporary majority view, not a natural phenomenon.[3] Therefore, apart from the fact that it cannot be detached from its relationship with other elements in the same system, in a sense it also does not exist outside its social and doctrinal contexts. For the purposes of this chapter, however, legal features are presented as much as possible as isolated traits.

Third, the outline given in sections 2.2 and 2.3 aims to delimit the object of study as well as, to some extent, to set out its theoretical premises. It is therefore fair to recall that like any other this description is based on a choice. However, it is submitted that the characteristics listed in this chapter comprise the core of organisations' legal identity in general international law.

Fourth, this study proceeds from the perspective of general international law, not international institutional law. The institutional variety among international organisations is taken into consideration only insofar as

[2] See section 10.3.2 below.

[3] Leaving aside the thorny issue of essential characteristics in general, the conventional character of *legal* phenomena is not controversial, as the fictional and situational character of law is generally undisputed.

general international law attaches legal consequences to it. This clearly proceeds from the idea that there is a distinction between these two branches of the law – related in turn to the assumption that the institutional law of an organisation constitutes a separate legal order. This is by no means a bold proposition, but one which is worth bearing in mind since it also implies an 'internal' (from within the organisation) and 'external' (from general international law) perspective.[4]

Finally, as the analysis in this book aims to operate within the positivist paradigm, it takes a black and white approach. It therefore does not do justice to the continuum of institutional forms (and the grey areas in which it may be uncertain whether an international creature is an IGO *vel non*), nor to the fluency of rule-making and norm-setting processes, nor to the blurring of external and internal operation of organisations.[5]

2.2 FORMAL ASPECTS

2.2.1 Definition

A specific definition may have limited usefulness for gaining 'a systemic or contextual understanding' of international organisations.[6] This said, a brief look at the familiar listings of definitional properties seems useful in several respects. It serves to identify the object of study and to increase analytical and conceptual clarity in its treatment. Such a definition may also contribute to an understanding of the legal nature of international organisations, all the more so because it is clearly tied in with doctrinal perspectives (addressed in Chapters 3 and 4) on organisations.

The claim that a definition could say anything about the 'nature' of organisations is problematic, considering their acknowledged conventional nature as creatures of law. Still, the practice of addressing legal constructs as objective social phenomena leaves room for both the nominal and the explanatory (or ontological) type of definition.[7] The institutional autonomy of organisations, which figures in all definitions of 'organisation', serves in both roles.

[4] Elaborated below in sections 2.3.2 and 2.3.3, and in ch 4. To mark this distinction, at times the term '*general* international law' is used to refer to 'international law'.

[5] Although these undoubtedly exist – see section 2.2.2 and cf eg José Alvarez, *International Organizations as Law-Makers*, 2005, at 11, 12.

[6] Cf White's observation regarding the relative usefulness of 'descriptive analyses' of international organisations (Nigel White, *The Law of International Organization* (2nd edn), 2005, at 1–2).

[7] Cf the *Oxford English Dictionary* (2nd edn 1989, s.v.) on the ontological and the semiotic (or explanatory versus nominal) type of definition: '6. a. To state exactly what (a thing) is; to set forth or explain the essential nature of. [...] b. To set forth or explain what (a word or expression) means; to declare the signification of (a word)'; cf above note 3.

Likewise it is awkward to apply the distinction between a descriptive (describing what appears to be in reality) and a normative (stating what ought to be in order to qualify) definition in the traditional sense.[8] This is both because all legal phenomena have a normative basis to begin with, in the sense that they are brought about by some *rule*, and because any identification on the basis of a description of practice *or* a postulated set of conditions (or a combination of both) may have legal consequences, which are normative as such. In the case of legal phenomena – including regimes with 'objective' status such as organisations – it is therefore more useful to take any *legal* definition as 'normative'. Such a definition circumscribes a category (eg 'legal person') for the purpose of attaching certain legal consequences to it. In contrast, a descriptive definition would be of a purely nominal or explanatory character.[9]

As to the content, it has been stated that '[t]here is no legal or generally accepted definition of an international organization,[10] but this seems overtly pessimistic. Although the wording may vary, there does appear to be agreement on a set of core definitional elements, sufficient for the identification of an 'international organisation'.

Generally, definitions designed for international legal practice[11] do not enter into great detail, as they mostly have the single purpose of excluding non-governmental organisations. An example is the frugal Article 2(1)i common to the Law of Treaties Conventions of 1969 and 1986.[12] Likewise, implicitly, the UN Economic and Social Council with regard to the implementation of Article 71 of the United Nations Charter on consultative status of non-governmental organisations: 'Any international organisation which is not established by intergovernmental agreement shall be considered as a non-governmental organisation for the purpose of these arrangements'.[13]

[8] Compare the predominantly normative element of autonomy as a necessary condition for the quality of 'organisation', and the more descriptive element of inter-state creation, which has changed to include other subjects as this appeared in practice (see below).

[9] See above note 7.

[10] Eg Robin Churchill and Geir Ulfstein, ' Autonomous Institutional Arrangements in Multilateral Environmental Agreements: A Little-Noticed Phenomenon in International Law', 94 *American JIL* 2000, 623–659, at 632.

[11] 'Practice' refers to the practice of international relations as well as to conventional rules geared to regulating such relations – as opposed to primarily 'doctrinal' considerations.

[12] The provision reads '"International organization" means an intergovernmental organization.' See ILC Commentary to the (identical) final draft article, YILC 1966, Vol II, § 14, at 190; see also Commentary to the final draft articles for the second Vienna Convention,YILC 1982, Vol II (Part Two), at 21 (cf ch 10 below). Similar provisions in Art I(1)(1) of the 1975 Vienna Convention on the Representation of States in their Relations with International Organizations of a Universal Character (A/CONF.67/16) and Art 2(1)(n) of the 1978 Vienna Convention on Succession of States in respect of Treaties of 23 August 1978, 1946 UNTS, at 3.

[13] Resolution 288 (X) of 27 February 1950; amplified by Resolution 1296 (XLIV) of 25 June 1968: ' . . .[non-governmental organizations] . . .includ[e] organizations which accept

The encyclopedic *Yearbook of International Organizations* uses an equally scant standard combined with the subjective criterion of self-identification to identify intergovernmental organisations.[14]

The study on Responsibility of International Organizations taken up by the International Law Commission in 2000[15] is a notable exception. It envisages a rather detailed working definition, which is atypical but not surprising, since, as argued by the Special Rapporteur, for the establishment of responsibility it is especially important that the category be determined very precisely.[16] Article 2 reads: 'For the purposes of the present draft articles, the term "international organization" refers to an organization established by a treaty or other instrument governed by international law and possessing its own international legal personality. International organizations may include as members, in addition to States, other entities.'[17]

Otherwise, it is possible that international practice in general simply has no need for a definition which specifies more than the organisation's intergovernmental nature. In this respect it is significant that the definition of international organisation has not been put to the (judicial) test. The present author is not aware of any cases before international courts or tribunals in which the (legal) qualification of an institution has been at issue. A recent, 'radically empirical' study[18] on the position of organisations before national courts tells us that this is little different in national law. When the question does arise, it concerns the distinction between intergovernmental and non-governmental organisations – in which cases, the author suggests, national judges are inclined to designate an institution as an 'intergovernmental organisation', as this allows for the attribution of immunity.[19]

members designated by government authorities, provided that such membership does not interfere with the free expression of views of the organizations'.

[14] See in *Yearbook of International Organizations* 2001 (Criteria for Types A to D: Conventional organisations): 'In practice therefore, the editors assume that an organization is intergovernmental if it is established by signature of an agreement engendering obligations between governments, whether or not that agreement is eventually published. If any organisation declares itself to be non-governmental, it is accepted as such by the editors. All organizations established by agreements to which three states or more are parties are therefore included' (http://www.uia.org//.htm). Following the adoption of ECOSOC Resolution 334 (XI) of 20 July 1950, it was agreed with the UN Secretariat in New York that bodies arising out of bilateral agreements should not be included in the *Yearbook*.

[15] Included by the Commission in its long-term programme of work on occasion of the fifty-second session, in 2000 (*Official Records of the General Assembly, Fifty-fifth session, Supplement No 10* (A/55/10), ch IX.1, para 729).

[16] The first draft articles adopted by the Commission and extensive commentary in YILC 2003, Vol II (Part Two) at 38–45, §§ 1–14; see also Henry Schermers and Niels Blokker, *International Institutional Law*, 1995, § 29A.

[17] See below note 37 and accompanying text.

[18] August Reinisch, *International Organizations before National Courts*, 2000, at 1.

[19] *Ibid*, at 170–171.

The definitions developed in doctrine have more facets, arguably for the aim of a normative and ontological scope. Michel Virally was one of the first scholars who took a general, systematic approach to international organisations from the viewpoint of 'the science of law,' with the aim to 'clarify the significance and bearing of the concepts that it employs'.[20] His definition, which remains authoritative,[21] presents an international organisation as 'an association of States, established by agreement among its members and possessing a permanent system or set of organs, whose task it is to pursue objectives of common interest, by means of cooperation among its members'.[22] Virally specifically distinguished five core traits in organisations: 'their inter-State basis, their voluntaristic basis, their possession of a permanent system of organs, their autonomy and their cooperative function'.[23]

In order to maximise the definition as a tool for identification in general international law, it is possible to focus on criteria that are a condition *sine qua non*. For example, within the framework of positive international law ('international law' meaning 'the law of peace') the 'inter-state basis' of organisations can be said to comprise all aspects of the 'voluntaristic basis' relevant in the context of the creation of an organisation. Since the reverse is not necessarily true, and both criteria are not needed in one definition, the inter-state basis will be taken as a core element. It may be noted that at the time of Professor Virally's writing, there was probably no evidence of other legal subjects establishing organisations.

From the external perspective, the 'cooperative function' also seems less distinctive, as the aim of cooperation inspires a whole range of international legal relationships, whether institutionalised or not.[24] Alternatively, the realist critic might argue that, once the organisation is in existence, if an 'objective of common interest' was shared by a minority of member states only this would not affect the association's identity of 'international organisation'. Professor Virally was of the view that only the 'cooperative function [...] is the subject of controversy.'[25] This controversy, however, pertained to the field of international institutional law rather than general international law, and revolved around the question whether organisations

[20] Michel Virally, 'Definition and Classification of International Organizations: A Legal Approach' (1977), in Georges Abi-Saab (ed), *The Concept of International Organization*, 1981, 50–66, at 51.

[21] Quoted for example by White in the introductory section of his textbook; see above, note 6, at 2.

[22] Virally, 'Definition and Classification...', above note 20, at 51.

[23] *Ibid*.

[24] Although this element may be mentioned in the constitutive treaty. Cf the 1998 Rome Statute, by which the States parties established the permanent organ of the ICC whose task is to pursue their common interest 'to put an end to impunity for the perpetrators of [the] crimes and thus to contribute to the prevention of such crimes.' (Preamble, § 5).

[25] Virally, above, note 20, at 54 et passim.

aimed at 'integration' should be studied alongside classic organisations aimed at 'cooperation' as being of the same genus.[26]

What remains is a core definition of 'organisations' that i) have been created by states; ii) possess a degree of permanency; and iii) possess a degree of autonomy with respect to member states. The absence of the criterion 'created under international law' – both in the sense of 'based in' and 'governed by' international law – may be explained from the fact that in Virally's analysis this was considered a given because of the inter-state nature of the establishing act.

The criterion of autonomy reflects the independent status of the organisation vis-à-vis its member states, to which we will return later on. The element of permanency reflects the institutionalised character as opposed to other forms of international cooperation. Arguably this was a more meaningful criterion at the time of writing, when the dividing line between a diplomatic conference and an international organisation was less fuzzy than it has become in later years.[27] It is uncertain whether in the light of present-day practice 'a permanent system of organs' is to be considered an essential element of the definition of international organisation. Moreover, 'autonomy' is difficult to conceive without some form of permanency.

Definitions proposed in more recent writings essentially revolve around the same concepts. For example Klabbers, who proceeds from a purposely traditional formulation, subsequently to put it in perspective, mentions three defining elements: organisations are i) created between states; ii) are created by treaty; and iii) possess an independent will. Schermers and Blokker propose a definition of 'international organisation' which also contains three defining elements: an organisation is i) created by international agreement; ii) has at least one organ 'with a will of its own'; and iii) is established under international law.[28]

The latter definition is conceptually similar to the ones mentioned before and differs mainly in its flexible formulation. The 'agreement' mentioned first is not limited to the category of treaties proper; it may also be

[26] Virally, who considered the EC to be a particular kind of institution on the basis of its aim of 'integration' (rather than the 'cooperation' of regular international organisations), was of the opinion they should not be considered as being of the same genus (at 53–55); but see the opposite view, eg in Henry Schermers and Niels Blokker, *International Institutional Law*, 1995, §§ 27, 28. Incidentally, the drafting process of the second Vienna Convention – in which examples relating to the EC and to other organisations generally figure side by side without a principled distinction being made – seems to confirm the latter view (ch 10 below). Cf also Michel Virally, 'La notion de fonction dans la théorie de l'organisation internationale' in Suzanne Bastid (ed), *Mélanges offerts à Rousseau*, 1974, 277–300, at 288–290.

[27] On 'new' types of international organisations, see below note 52 and accompanying text.

[28] Schermers and Blokker, above, note 26, §§ 29–47.

expressed in other ways. This appears to reflect practice.[29] The formal treaty basis, meant to safeguard and underscore the consensual basis of the organisation, was stipulated in, for example, Article 24 of the LoN Covenant (which limited association of technical organisations with the League to those institutions that were 'intergovernmental' and 'established by general treaties'), but abandoned in Article 57 of the UN Charter. Although no reference is made to the juristic device of 'tacit consent' as a basis for the creation of an organisation by customary law, this may also come into play, as some associations or régimes seem *unwittingly* to assume the status of an international organisation and consequential legal personality.[30] A reference to the creators of the organisation is absent. These are however present through the notion of 'international agreement', which leaves way for an open category of 'subjects of international law'.

The criterion of the independent 'will' of the organisation is refined by the condition of 'at least one organ'. Again, the element of permanency is absent, although it may be implied by the reference to an 'organ'.

The new edition of Bowett's textbook on the law of international institutions proposes five 'definitional aspects' of international organisations. These operate predominantly in the internal perspective of international institutional law: i) 'its membership must be composed of states and/or other international organisations; ii) it must be established by treaty; iii) it must have an autonomous will distinct from that of its members; iv) it must be vested with legal personality; and iv) it must be capable of adopting norms addressed to its members'.[31]

A set of basic criteria can thus be distilled from the perspective of general international law. The first element is comparable to the inter-state basis mentioned by Virally. The notion of 'membership', as opposed to 'creators', may be taken to reflect the internal perspective of international institutional law.

The second criterion stipulates that an international organisation must have its basis in a treaty. Only one of the two elements is needed for a basic definition. For a form of institutionalised cooperation, states or international organisations as subjects of international law would *per se* ultimately rely on an international agreement in either written or unwritten form – even if it was an agreement between states subsequently to enact

[29] As confirmed by § 4 of the commentary to definition Art 2 of the 2003 ILC draft Articles, above, note 16, which mentions inter alia the *Pan American Institute of Geography and History and the Organization of the Petroleum Exporting Countries* created not by treaty but by resolution of the UNGA or a diplomatic conference. See also Schermers and Blokker, above note 26, § 34 for examples.

[30] See ch 4 below.

[31] Philippe Sands and Pierre Klein, Bowett's *Law of International Institutions* (5th edn), 2001, at 16.

'parallel legislation' by way of a constituent instrument.[32] In this particular case, the notion of 'treaty' has the disadvantage that it would exclude organisations of undisputed status which are not based on a written agreement.[33] A treaty would be concluded *per se* by subjects of international law (where the formula 'states and/or [...] international organisations' has the disadvantage that it would exclude other prospective international actors which *de jure* or *de facto* may come to display the legal capacity to participate in the creation of an international organisation of undisputed status).

The 'autonomous will' of the organisation can be taken as a classical formulation of the criterion of 'autonomy', which we find in all definitions.

The element of legal personality, finally, represents an interesting turn in the discussion about the position of international organisations in the international legal order. In practice, legal personality seems to accrue to all entities that qualify as 'international organisations', and in that sense legal personality may be considered as a characteristic. However, this is not to say that it is a prerequisite for the existence of an international organisation. It appears that doctrine, analogously to the treatment of states, separates the stage of identification of an organisation from that of the attribution of legal personality. As will be argued, legal personality is attributed by the legal order in which the organisation is a prospective actor. It is an 'external' attribute (which is why it will be discussed at a later stage),[34] not part of the institutional make-up which turns the entity into an 'organisation' in the first place. To include the requirement of 'legal personality' in a definition which is then used to determine whether an institution qualifies as an organisation so it can be accorded legal personality, may raise a problem of circularity (reminiscent of the awkwardness of the fourth 'Montevideo criterion').[35]

This is different when the definition is used purely for identification of existing legal actors, as in the ILC draft Articles on Responsibility of International Organizations.[36] It may be noted that the definition initially proposed by Special Rapporteur Gaja concentrates more on the organisation's institutional independence vis-à-vis the member states ('...insofar as

[32] See examples in note 29 above– cf the 'voluntaristic' basis in the definition proposed by Virally, above note 23 and accompanying text.

[33] Such as eg the *Asian-African Legal Consultative Committee*; see Schermers and Blokker, above note 26, § 34, for examples of creation of an organisation by means other than a treaty.

[34] Chapter 4 below deals extensively with legal personality.

[35] The fourth 'Montevideo criterion' reads 'capacity to enter into relations with the other states' (1933 *Convention On Rights And Duties Of States, 49 stat. 3097; treaty series 881)*, application of which is problematic when the 'Montevideo criteria' are brought in not to identify an existing state, but – as often the case – to decide whether an entity qualifies to become a state.

[36] Cf above notes 15 and 16 and accompanying text. See also Schermers and Blokker, above note 26, § 29A.

it exercises in its own capacity certain governmental functions'),[37] whereas the definition adopted by the Drafting Committee relates to the external legal quality ('...possessing its own international legal personality').[38]

In a slightly different vein still, authors such as Seidl-Hohenveldern and Brownlie propose a definition, not of 'international organizations' but rather of 'international organizations with legal personality'.[39] Interestingly, their criteria suggest that all organisations have legal personality, as essentially the only difference with the definition of 'organisation' as proposed for example by Schermers and Blokker is 'the ability independently to conduct international relations'.

Summing up, the core aspects seem to be that an international organisation is established by international law, or by subjects of international law; that it is governed by international law, rather than incorporated in a national legal order; and that it has a degree of autonomy. What does this tell us about what doctrine perceives to be the essence of an international organisation? Its existence is based on the act of uncontested international actors, and it has independence vis-à-vis its component elements (member states). As a tool for legal designation, the definition by Schermers and Blokker seems to be the most serviceable, as it is concise, flexible and, buttressed by several examples, appears adequately to cover practice[40] (including recent practice, as the working definition of the ILC draft

[37] The definition proposed by Special Rapporteur Gaja in his first report read: '[f]or the purposes of the present draft articles, the term 'international organization" refers to an organization which includes States among its members insofar it exercises in its own capacity certain governmental functions' (UN Doc A/CN.4/532 (2003)); see also above note 17.

[38] The draft article 2 adopted by the Drafting Committee at the same 55th session reads: '[f]or the purposes of the present draft articles, the term "international organization" refers to an organization established by a treaty or other instrument governed by international law and possessing its own international legal personality. International organizations may include as members, in addition to States, other entities.' (UN Doc A/CN.4/L.632 (2003)).

[39] Ian Brownlie, *Principles of Public International Law* (6th edn), 2003, at 649, refers to 'the criteria' of legal personality in organisations, which he summarises as follows: '1. Permanent associations of states, with lawful objects, equipped with organs; 2. A distinction, in terms of legal powers and purposes, between the organization and its member states; 3. *The existence of legal powers exercisable on the international plane and not solely within the national systems of one or more states*' (emphasis added); Ignaz Seidl-Hohenveldern and Gerhard Loibl, *Das Recht der Internationalen Organisationen einschliesslich der Supranationalen Gemeinschaften*, 1996, at 4–6: an organisation with international legal personality has the following characteristics: 1. aimed at duration; 2. established by agreement; 3. established between states – (or 'between states and other subjects of international law, respectively'); 4. constituent partners renounce to a part of their sovereign rights; 5. has a lawful objective; 6. constituent partners allow the structure (*Gebilde*) a will of its own; 7. at least one organ is competent to represent this separate will; 8. '*[constituent partners] in this manner enable the structure to be in its own name bearer of rights and duties in the field of international law and of domestic law.*' (emphasis added, translation by the present author); White (above note 6) implicitly takes a similar approach. See ch 4 below on legal personality.

[40] Being widely relied on (see eg reference in note 58 below), in addition it may have a considerable degree of the self-fulfilling power proper to international law writing.

Articles on responsibility of international organisations is quite similar).[41] It also meets with the general agreement of experts on institutions such as Alvarez.[42]

Of this core definition, then, institutional autonomy or 'independent will' appears as a central feature in the discussion. This may be because it is the most elusive trait to establish, or because intuitively we take it as more than a formal-legal requirement alone:[43] (from an ontological perspective) it would be first of all the autonomy of an institution in respect of its component elements which turns it into an 'international organisation'. From the early days of international organisation doctrine the institutional feature of autonomy has indeed served as a foundation for the external attribution of a separate legal identity of sorts – formalised as legal personality – to such an extent that these have been (erroneously) assimilated.[44]

The *volonté distincte* is admittedly of a somewhat metaphysical character, and how it should be identified is not generally elaborated upon by writers.[45] It is mostly – and rightly – construed from the internal affairs of the organisation: a particular decision-making procedure, by which the organisation may, for example, determine the extent of its own powers, or issue rules, however modest in purport, binding the member states in their totality. Recently the question has been addressed more systematically by White; he mentions certain institutional features as indicia for the existence of a separate 'will', and distinguishes the *extent* of such autonomy, which will, for example, be dependent on whether the organisation has contractual or constitutional foundations.[46]

In all cases, if an organisation maintains anything like external relations, the institutional autonomy will display both an internal aspect (competence to take majority decisions binding on the member states) and an external one (competence legally to interact with non-member states in its

[41] Cf. above notes 15 and 16 and accompanying text.

[42] Alvarez, above, note 5, at 4–17.

[43] Cf Paul Reuter, *Institutions internationales*, 1954, at 195, 'En tant qu'*organisation* il ne peut que s'agir d'un groupe susceptible de manifester d'une manière permanente une volonté juridiquement distincte de celle de ces membres.' According to White, who does not elaborate on a formal definition of IGOs, 'one of the key features and consequences of personality is *autonomy from the member States*' (White, above, note 6, at 47, emphasis added). Likewise, Ramses Wessel, 'Revisiting the International Legal Status of the EU', 5 *European Foreign Affairs Review* 2000, 507–537, at 514, 515.

[44] Ch 3, and section 4.2.1 below.

[45] Schermers and Blokker do not elaborate. Cf Jan Klabbers, 'The Changing Image of International Organisations,' in Jean-Marc Coicaud and Veijo Heiskanen, *The Legitimacy of International Organizations*, 2001, 221–255, at 226–227. See ch 3 below on the concept of the 'will' of international organisations in 19th and early 20th century legal writing.

[46] Nigel White, 'Discerning Separate Will', in Wybo Heere (ed), *From Government to Governance: The Growing Impact of Non-State Actors on the International and European Legal System* (Proceedings of the 2004 Hague Joint ASIL/NVIR Conference), 2004, 31–38.

own name). A relation with a member state may also be 'external' when the organisation does not use internal decision-making or other competences which have been envisaged in the constituent instrument. Even the external effect of institutional autonomy, however, is not identical to legal personality, which, as mentioned, is a different concept that is connected to the legal order in which the organisation is to function.[47]

2.2.2 Classification

Once non-governmental organisations are excluded, international organisations can be classified according to several sub-divisions. International institutional law employs categories based for example on membership (universal versus closed organisations); and purpose (general/political versus functional/technical organisations). Also, although not common, treaty bodies can be set apart from classic inter-governmental organisations. In political science, classifications include those on the basis of scope (eg functional or geographic), competence (limited versus general) and function (eg security or economic), or integration (low versus high).[48]

Special mention should be made of the classification based on institutional competences (international versus supranational organisations).[49] The controversy of whether 'supranational' organisations should be studied alongside regular international organisations or, on the contrary, be set apart,[50] cannot be entered into here. From a non-comparativist, general international law perspective it seems legitimate to put them in one category. This is all the more so because even this sub-division – which perhaps has the most dramatic ring of all in the law of international organisations – appears to have no autonomous effect in general international law. The difference in legal operation between the European Community and the Council of Europe stems from the institutional make-up of the respective organisations, not from general international law.

So, while these categorisations provide a valuable analytical tool for the comparative study of international organisations, general international law does not attach legal consequences to the institutional varieties to which they refer. As such, these varieties fall outside the scope of this study.

[47] White in 'Discerning Separate Will', above note 46. On legal personality and its attribution to international organisations see ch 4 below.

[48] Werner Feld and Robert Jordan, *International Organizations: A Comparative Approach* (2nd edn), 1988, at 9–13.

[49] Cf. Schermers and Blokker, above, note 26, §§ 58–62; Bowett–Sands, above, note 31, at 18–19. Schermers and Blokker, §§ 48–65, come to a similar (general) classification on the basis of the functionality principle as identified by Virally (above note 26).

[50] See above note 26 and accompanying text.

Essentially it would be different only if a formalised distinction was made between international organisations with legal personality, and international organisations without. There is, however, no known successful attempt at such a classification[51] – which, incidentally, goes to underscore the argument made for objective personality and general capacity in section 4.2 below.

Finally, it has been suggested that 'international organisations' should not be viewed as a closed category, but rather as part of a continuum to which a variety of treaty régimes belong.[52] This would be in line with a general trend that the class of international organisations is becoming more varied. However, the definition of 'international organisation' is primarily used as a normative or legal definition – which by nature leaves little room for fuzzy boundaries. The practical relevance of such legal categorisation is illustrated for example by the 1992 *Case Concerning Certain Phosphate Lands in Nauru*, in which the International Court held explicitly that the Authority which administered Nauru 'did not have an international legal personality distinct from those of the states thus designated'.[53] This had the consequence – as pointed out by ILC Special Rapporteur Crawford[54] – that no responsibility of an organisation was at issue and that only the states involved with the governance of Nauru could be addressed. In other words, the Authority was not an organisation, and there was no institutional veil screening off the member states from general international law.

Thus, by the Schermers and Blokker definition, certain fora for intergovernmental cooperation are excluded, whereas certain régimes that in form do not appear as classic international organisations are included. The Conference on Disarmament, a traditional negotiation forum that shows no signs of a *volonté distincte*,[55] is an example of the former, while the Ozone Secretariat, a one-organ treaty body in which binding rules may be adopted by majority, is an example of the latter.[56] The Ozone Secretariat belongs to the class of régimes set up by multilateral treaties to monitor the

[51] Cf above note 39 and accompanying text.

[52] Cf Denis Simon: '[T]oute convention affectant un ensemble de moyens organisés à la réalisation d'un objectif commun [. . .] engendre un ordre juridique propre destiné à mettre en forme juridique la coordination des instruments normatifs permettant la poursuite des finalités collectives.' (*L'interpretation judiciaire des traités d'organizations internationales: morphologie des conventions et fonction jurisdictionelle*, 1981, at 488). Cf also Alvarez, above, note 5, at 11, 12 and the accompanying text to that note.

[53] 1992 *Case Concerning Certain Phosphate Lands in Nauru* (Nauru v Australia), 1992 ICJ Reports 240, at 258.

[54] UN Doc A/CN.4/498 Add 1, §160 at 4 (Second Report on the Law of State Responsibility).

[55] On the Conference on Disarmament see section 5.1 below.

[56] The Ozone Secretariat was established by the 1985 Montreal Convention (1513 UNTS 3); see section 3.2.1 below on the Bureaux. The Secretariat is an example of an independent 'treaty body', ie one that after creation is not incorporated as organ in an existing organisation.

parties' compliance.[57] These régimes have been described as 'treaty bodies' and recently – in relation to post-1970s environmental treaties in particular – have been termed 'Autonomous Institutional Arrangements'.[58] When such treaty bodies have competence to stipulate new rules, as in the case of the Ozone Secretariat, they may be considered international organisations. If they solely monitor compliance in an executive manner, they are not.

In the scheme of Schermers and Blokker, bodies created by a treaty separate from the constitutive treaty of an international organisation, but subsequently incorporated in the organisation, are considered 'treaty organs', and not separate international organisations.[59] An example is the Human Rights Committee, established by the ICCPR and closely linked to the UN.[60] Finally, (economic) integration organisations such as the European Community are covered alongside other organisations. For example the European Union for some time would not have been covered by the definition, as the question of whether the EU as a whole met the above-mentioned criteria (notably on autonomy) seemed undecided. In recent years, however, the EU appears to have unequivocally taken on the shape of a fully-fledged international organisation and accepted the concomitant presumption of legal personality.[61]

2.3 MATERIAL ASPECTS

Three features should be mentioned which do not generally figure in normative or even descriptive definitions, but which characterise international organisations as actors in general international law: functionality, centralisation and transparency.

[57] The Ozone Secretariat qualifies as a 'treaty body' even if it co-exists with, and facilitates, a Conference of the Parties. The 1985 Vienna Convention for the Protection of the Ozone Layer has not created an organisation, with the Conference and the Secretariat as organs, but it has created two separate bodies (in arts 6 and 7, respectively). The Convention is available at http://www.unep.ch/ozone/index.asp.

[58] Churchill and Ulfstein, above, note 10.

[59] The phenomenon of 'treaty organs' (Schermers and Blokker, above, note 26, §§ 386–387) raises questions which fall outside the scope of this study, viz of delegation and liability.

[60] Schermers and Blokker, above, note 26, §§ 386–387.

[61] See section 4.2.3 below on the Union and its legal personality *vel non*.

2.3.1 Functionality

International organisations are functionally defined. Notwithstanding challenges posed to the classic international system,[62] it is safe to say that for the purpose of positive international law, states are still the primary form of political and legal organisation.[63] It follows that on the international plane the state operates as an aim in itself, whereas an organisation exists for a particular purpose, or area of operation, that has been (initially) determined by its creators.[64] Even an organisation of unprecedented comprehensiveness such as the European Union is functionally defined, unlike a state. Such functionality – with no particular reference intended to either the 'functionalist' theory of international organisation or the 'functional necessity' argument in international institutional law – has a doctrinal and a formal-institutional aspect. Not only are organisations ultimately perceived and legitimised as service institutions for states, but their very legal form is determined by function rather than, for example, territory. 'Functionality' in this broad sense is similar to the notion used by Virally: ' . . .it is an organization's function that constitutes its true *raison d'etre* [. . .]. Moreover, the organization's structure is directly determined by this function or purpose'.[65]

The organisation's functional limitation entails that its 'powers' are an issue. What are generally referred to as 'powers' may denote both the capacity of the organisation to act in general international law and its competence to act within its institutional order vis-à-vis the member states. A distinction, on the basis of source or scope of powers, between 'capacity' and 'competence' could add some clarity, although here the domestic law analogy is not unproblematic.[66] It is in any event instrumental to set apart

[62] Cf Martti Koskenniemi, 'The Future of Statehood', 32 *Harvard ILJ* 1991, 397–410. Among lawyers this is not a generally shared concern; while international relations scholars have, eg in the framework of regime theory, shifted away their focus from the state as a basic unit of analysis (cf. Frederic Kratochwil and Edward Mansfield (eds), *International Organization*, 1994), international lawyers – operating within a formal(ist) system moulded on sovereign states – in general seem less inclined to do so. On the fact that 'constitutional norms relating to formal sources remain essentially state-based', while 'political processes within the international system have undergone profound changes' eg Gennady Danilenko, *Law-Making in the International Community*, 1993, at 193–197 (citation at 194), and references.

[63] Cf Ignaz Seidl-Hohenveldern and Torsten Stein, *Völkerrecht*, 2000, at 133: 'In der Praxis völlig *unbestritten* is *nur* die Völkerrechtssubjektivität der *souveränen Staaten*.' (emphasis in the original).

[64] Cf the distinction made by Virally between the *finalité integrée* of states and the *finalité fonctionelle* of international organisations in 'La notion de fonction dans ... ' above, note 26, at 282 in particular. See also section 4.2.5 below.

[65] Virally, above, note 20, at 59; also quoted in Schermers and Blokker, above, note 26, § 48; Michel Virally, *L'organization mondiale*, 1972. When viewed in terms of legal personality (ch 4 below), the functional role of IGOs is implied by the notion (which has no clear legal implications) of 'functional' personality.

[66] This point is elaborated upon below in section 4.2.5.

the 'competence' which relates to the degree of power (in the case of a *no* vote of a permanent member, the UN Security Council can take binding decisions on procedural matters, but not on non-procedural matters) from the 'competence', which refers to the material field in which the organisation can operate (the European Community can conclude a treaty on textiles but not on disarmament). Almost fifty years after the International Court of Justice famously addressed the '(implied) powers' of the organisation, it specifically referred to the latter notion as the 'area of competence' (to be defined by the 'principle of speciality').[67]

Finally, it may be recalled that the functional design of international organisations entails a fundamental difference between the position of an organisation and that of a (con)federal entity in international law. Functionality (competence with regard to a particular function – varying among individual organisations – without *a priori* territorial limitation) and territoriality (competence with regard to all functions in a legal order with territorial limitation)[68] are different parameters. Organisations and states therefore do not 'overlap' in the same way as for example the parts and the whole of a federal structure, nor are they simply interchangeable as international legal entities.[69] A simple example is that a party may reach an understanding with an organisation, while it is the member states that are to provide the pecuniary or human resources necessary for the organisation to meet its obligations – such as would be the case with the deployment of troops for a peace-keeping mission by the UN and the agreement reached with the 'host state'.

[67] *Reparation for Injuries*, ICJ Rep1949, at 179; *Legality of the Use by a State of Nuclear Weapons in Armed Conflict* (Advisory Opinion), 1996, §§ 19 and 25 respectively – see section 4.2 below.

[68] Cf the classic international law setting based on territoriality eg in Christian Tomuschat: 'Traditionally, international law rested on the principle of territoriality. Every State enjoyed exclusive competence for developments within its territory.' (Obligations for States, 241 *RdC* 1993, at 210).

[69] It is significant that the tentative analogy between treaties concluded by organisations and treaties concluded by federal states was not maintained. In 1962 it was decided to exclude organisations from the scope of the draft Articles (ILC Report, YILC 1962, Vol II, § 21 at 161), whereas the paragraph on treaty making capacity of 'states members of a federal union' was retained until rejection at the Vienna Conference in 1969 (8th meeting of the Plenary Conference, 28 April, §§ 50 and 51). On the preparatory work of the 1969 Vienna Convention ch 8 below.

2.3.2 Centralisation

From the perspective of general international law, a prime feature of an international organisation is its centralised character.[70] The term 'centralisation' refers to an institutional structure which even to a minimal degree performs a function in lieu of (the sum total of) its members. This is also the feature that separates the law of the organisation to some extent from general international law, thus creating an 'internal order' of the organisation.

That the establishment of an international organisation always involves an element of centralisation – not only in the political sense, but also in the formal-institutional sense – is to some extent a truism. As mentioned above, the autonomy or independent 'will' of the organisation is generally taken as a core element in the definition of international organisations as opposed to other instances of inter-state co-operation.[71] Centralisation is related to the formal-institutional characteristic of 'autonomy', but it is a broader notion. For example the treaty-making process within the framework of an international organisation may come by several instances of centralisation. These range from a preliminary stage in the negotiation process in which the organisation prepares a proposal *en petit comité*, to adoption of a treaty text by the organisation rather than by the negotiating parties.[72]

Whereas in formal terms the autonomy or *volonté distincte* of the organisation takes precedence – if only to a minimal extent – over the sovereignty of the individual states,[73] 'centralisation' refers to a material aspect of the nature of international organisations. Put in somewhat stale, but apposite terms, this is the vertical dynamic in contrast to the horizontal, consensual, structure of the international legal order in its classic manifestation.[74]

[70] Cf Kelsen who uses the notion of centralisation as a precondition for the differentiation between the 'duties, rights and competences' of the organisation and those of the member states, and attributes such centralisation to the UN (Hans Kelsen, *The Law of the United Nations: A Critical Analysis of its Fundamental Problems*, 1950, at 329.

[71] See section 2.2.1 above.

[72] Cf Paul Reuter (*Introduction to the Law of Treaties*, 1995, at 4): '[o]n the international level, the basic principles are very simple: only final consent is legally binding but agreed formalities may act as milestones marking the procedural stages leading up to the final consent'. On treaty-making practice within the framework of international organisations, see ch 5 below.

[73] Cf Seidl-Hohenveldern and Loibl, above, note 39, at 5): states 'renounce to the exercise of an, if only infinitesimal, part of their sovereign rights' for the benefit of the organisation; cf also Christof Schreuer, 'The Waning of the Sovereign State: Towards a New Paradigm for International Law?', 4 *European JIL* 1993, 447–471, at 451.

[74] Described by Kelsen from a formal standpoint (above note 70) and by Alvarez from the (rich) perspective of legal practice (above, note 5, at 273–414).

The degree of centralisation may vary – this is dependent on the IGO's institutional make-up as designed by its creators[75] – but centralisation itself as such can be taken as a common characteristic.

It follows from the centralised character of organisations that these have an internal legal order which stands apart from general international law. This is not a daring conclusion; it seems undisputed in legal writing[76] and in positive international law, which in several instances accords an autonomous status to the internal law of organisations.[77] In the *Certain Expenses* case the International Court observed:

> If it is agreed that the action in question is within the scope of the functions of the Organization but it is alleged that it has been initiated or carried out in a manner not in conformity with the division of functions among the several organs which the Charter prescribes, *one moves to the internal plane, to the internal structure of the Organization.* If the action was taken by the wrong organ, it was irregular *as a matter of that internal structure*, but this would not necessarily mean that the expense incurred was not an expense of the Organization. Both national and international law contemplate cases in which the body corporate or politic may be bound, as to third parties, by an ultra vires act of an agent.[78]

The separate status can clearly be traced to the consensual basis of the act establishing the organisation, and to the *pacta tertiis* principle in relation to this establishing act (which is to be dissociated from the subsequent (objective) legal existence of the organism thus created).[79]

[75] Virally spoke of a 'dialectic relationship' between the functions of the organisation and its structural elements; 'the relationship between the objective and its means' (Virally, *L'organisation mondiale*, above, note 65, at 26). This is regardless of the doctrinal stance taken with regard to the legal basis of 'capacities' or 'legal personality'; see ch 5 below.

[76] As for general texts, note that for example Brownlie when listing instances of 'law-making' by international organisations, reserves a special category for 'internal law-making'. Otherwise, eg René-Jean Dupuy, *Manuel sur les organisations internationales /A Handbook on International Organizations*, 1998, at 377–398 (by Philippe Cahier); cf White, above, note 6, at 104, on the fact that in the *Expenses* case [at 168] the International Court implicitly accepted that action taken by the wrong organ within an organisation would not necessarily invalidate the act in relation to third parties. Cf also Eckart Klein and Matthias Pechstein, *Das Vertragsrecht internationaler Organisationen*, 1985, at 39; Günther Hartmann, 'The Capacity of International Organizations to Conclude Treaties', in Karl Zemanek (ed), *Agreements of International Organizations and the Vienna Convention on the Law of Treaties*, 1971; Hermann Mosler, The International Society as a Legal Community – Part 3: Institutionalised International Co-operation, in *RdC*, 1974, 11–320, at 210.

[77] Cf the general reservation clause in Art 5 of the 1969 Vienna Convention on the law of Treaties: 'The present Convention applies to any treaty which is the constituent instrument of an international organization and to any treaty adopted within an international organization without prejudice to any relevant rules of the organization"; see ch 10 below.

[78] *Certain Expenses of the United Nations (Article 17, Paragraph 2, of the Charter)*, ICJ Reports 1962, 151, at 168 (emphasis added).

[79] Cf Paul Reuter, *Introduction to the Law of Treaties*, 1995, at 126–129, who convincingly argues that 'objective regimes' created by treaty should remain outside the scope of the law of treaties.

The legal discipline of international institutional law bears out this separation. *Qua* substantive international law, 'the law of international organisations' presents a rather slender body of rules, its main tenet being perhaps the principle of *implied powers*, which is a principle rather than a legal norm. The larger part of international institutional law consists of 'rules' in the sense of 'regularities', distilled from the various institutional systems, which may have legal effect but no normative force in general international law. As the World Bank Tribunal stated in its first decision: 'The Tribunal does not overlook the fact that each international organisation has its own constituent instrument; its own membership; its own institutional structure; its own functions; its own measure of legal personality ...'.[80] In the words of Bowett-Sands: 'Each organisation may therefore be considered as *something of a sub-system*.'[81]

The assumption that organisations have an internal legal order inevitably leads to a question of sources. As mentioned above, elements of a legal order which is 'separate' do not of themselves have normative force in general international law – that is, they do not have the *Normadressaten* in that legal order and cannot confer rights or obligations. In addition, the binary character of the law makes it impossible to envisage these institutional norms as a *little bit* binding. This boils down to the classic statement on state law made by the Permanent Court in the 1926 *Case concerning certain German interests in Polish Upper Silesia*: 'From the standpoint of international law [. . .] municipal laws are merely facts which express the will and constitute the activities of states'.[82]

2.3.3 Transparency

The most particular and complex feature of international organisations as actors in international law is their transparent quality. In a strictly positivist vein, the legal appearance of organisations has been described as follows: '[a]vec les organizations internationales, [. . .] le voile de la personnalité morale est transparent, et nul effort n'est nécessaire pour apercevoir la nudité des Etats derrière ce voile immatériel'.[83] But it is not that clear-cut.

[80] *Holidays Inns v Morocco*, no 89/1, 1979, quoted in Bowett–Sands, above, note 31, at 17.

[81] *Ibid* (emphasis added).

[82] PCIJ, No. 7 (Merits); Judgments. Nos 1–24.

[83] Prosper Weil, Cours general de droit international public, *RdC* 1992, at 104; on the concept of legal personality from a 'functional' perspective cf. Hermann Mosler, 'Subjects of International Law', *Encyclopedia of Public International Law*, Vol 7, 1984, 442–459, at 444; and Special Rapporteur Paul Reuter in his *Sixth Report on the Question of Treaties Concluded between States and International Organizations or Between Two or More*

International organisations present a structure that is neither entirely 'open', in the sense that it blends with general international law, nor entirely 'closed', in the way of states.[84] This quality is partly due to the interaction of the two features mentioned above: the organisation's functional character, on the one hand, and its centralised structure, on the other – or, put differently, the sovereignty of member states versus the legal independence of the organisation. In a general sense, the legal identity of international organisations is shaped by two competing images: the organisation as a forum for states and the organisation as an independent actor.

This dual imagery – which results in a degree of transparency in the institutional veil that clothes organisations – exists in the minds of international lawyers and politicians. It also exists in social reality, as on the international scene organisations actually perform both roles.[85] Finally, it is reflected in the institutional structure of organisations. While international organisations have a separate internal legal order, as argued above, this legal order does not possess the 'closeness and impermeability'[86] of the domestic law of states. Organisations appear to some extent as open structures: that is, member states remain visible behind the corporate veil and may be included in processes of decision-making and law-making which involve the organisation.[87]

The openness of organisations, which is not shared by other international legal subjects, seems to be brought about by several interrelated factors. First, the component elements of international organisations – states – are eminent legal persons in their own right. Second, organisations are defined on a functional, rather than on a territorial basis (see section 2.3.2 above).

Next to these systemic factors (which, incidentally, suggest two reasons why organisations may not readily bring about the demise of the nation

International Organizations: 'International organisations are neither sovereign nor equal; all their powers are strictly at the service of their member states [. . .].' (YILC 1977, Vol II (Part One), at 120, para 6).

[84] On the 'closed' legal order of states, see section 2.1 above.

[85] On organisations as a forum for states' treaty-making on the one hand and independent treaty-makers on the other, Catherine Brölmann, 'The Legal Nature of International Organisations and the Law of Treaties', 4 *Austrian Review of International and European Law* (2000), 85–125. See also ch 5 below.

[86] Cf the terminology in Wilhelm Grewe, *Epochen der Völkerrechtsgeschichte*, 1984, at 233 – the classic notion of 'impermeability' is matched by the 'Billiard Ball' in international relations theory. On the 'closed' legal order of states, see section 2.1 above.

[87] Cf Special Rapporteur Reuter, who in the context of the law of treaties considered that 'the affirmation of the legal personality of the organization, must be modified by *factual* considerations' such as 'the fact that in practice the "effective performance" of their obligations often could be secured only through resources of the member states' (Sixth Report, YILC 1977, Vol. II (Part One), at 126).

state, envisioned by some[88] in connection with the process of globalisation), doctrine has favoured an open appearance of international organisations. The prevailing dualist view of the law envisions national law and international law as making up the complete legal universe.[89] The ensuing conception of a unitary system of international law has no room for a separate legal order that is not municipal law.

Although positive law indicates a different course, the doctrinal perspective on the organisation's institutional law as an integral part of general international law can be found with some contemporary writers.[90] It is present in the general view, as it was formulated some decades before by Kooijmans, that only the sovereign state truly 'places itself between man and the law'.[91] It is also implied in the dictum of the International Court in the 1980 WHO Advisory Opinion, where it found both the obligations stemming from the constitution and those stemming from international agreements (the organisation's internal affairs and its 'external relations') to be binding on organisations on the basis of general international law: 'International organisations are *subjects of international law* and, *as such, are bound by any obligations* incumbent upon them under general rules of international law, *under their constitutions* or under international agreements to which they are parties.'[92]

Indeed, while the idea of a separation between the legal order of an organisation and that of its member states dates back to the *interbellum*,[93] the idea of a separation between the organisation's internal law and general international law has never quite settled[94] – paradoxically so, because, as was mentioned above, at the same time doctrine and practice seem to proceed from a general assumption to the contrary.

[88] L Ali Khan, *The Extinction of Nation-States: A World without Borders*, 1996 (notably Part II).

[89] Cf Julio Barberis, 'Nouvelles questions concernant la personnalite juridique internationale', in *179 RdC I* 1983, 145–304, at 171: 'le droit interne des états et le droit interétatique formeraient le cadre complet de l'ordre juridique universel.' It has been pointed out that the conceptual framework of an overarching 'unitary international law' is 'implicitly perpetuate[d]' by contemporary theorists such as McDougal, Falk and Kennedy (Philip Trimble, 'International Law, World Order and Critical Legal Studies', 42 *Stanford Law Review* 1990, 811–845, at 835).

[90] Eg Bindschedler: '[. . .] this internal [administrative] law of associations of states ranks as international law in the same way as the other provisions' (Rudolf Bindschedler, 'International Organizations: General Aspects', in *Encyclopedia of Public International Law*, Vol II, 1995, at 1290).

[91] Peter Kooijmans, *The Doctrine of the Legal Equality of States*, 1964, at 36.

[92] Opinion concerning *The Interpretation of the Agreement of 25 March 1951 between the WHO and Egypt*; ICJ Rep. 1980, 73, at 89–90 (italics added).

[93] See ch 3 below on this period, in which the related notion of separate legal personality took shape.

[94] Cf Schermers and Blokker, above note 26, §§ 1142–1148.

This range of counteracting images – both in institutional make-up and in legal doctrine, as well as 'outside' the legal paradigm – gives international organisations their particular quality: on the one hand, organisations are open and their internal structures are partly visible on the general international plane; on the other, organisations are distinct entities with a separate legal order which is not completely accessible. The result is a structure that is neither open nor closed, but 'transparent'. This means that member states are visible, or expected to be visible (which in doctrine may at times amount to the same thing), but that the institutional veil prevents them from being directly and exclusively addressed by international law, as they would be if the organisation had no separate identity.

The transparency of international organisations, finally, is sustained by the fact that in practice an important role of organisations is that of a forum for the activities and actions of states – a prominent role of organisations such as the United Nations, the Council of Europe and the Organization of American States.[95]

That in these situations technically speaking states act mostly *within* the internal legal order of the organisation, in the quality of member states, is often left out of account – something which is undoubtedly inspired, in turn, by the tendency to regard the organisation's legal order preponderantly as an open system, part of general international law. But the separate layer of the institutional legal order is recognised by practice, as appears eg from Article 9 the 1969 Vienna Convention on the Law of Treaties.[96] Conversely, a *dédoublement fonctionnel* of sorts occurs when an organisation maintains external relations with a state that is also a member state, something which is often the case with universal organisations.[97]

The transparency of organisations is thus a systemic condition, resulting from the continuous tension between the organisation's servicing, functional, open aspect on the one hand, and its independent, centralised, closed aspect on the other. It is reflected in the characteristic struggle of the parties to an IGO constituent treaty to remain *Herren der Verträge* – a struggle which is visible for example in the (scholarly) discussion on the UN Security Council's interpretation of its own powers with regard to rule-making and the establishment of subsidiary organs;[98] or in the

95 See ch 5 below.

96 Article 9 makes a distinction between states in a treaty-making process using the infrastructure of an organisation and states being part of that infrastructure in the sense that they act according to the rules envisaged in the institutional law of the organisation. See ch 10 below.

97 Cf Rosalyn Higgins (Rapporteur), 'The Legal Consequences for Member States of the Non-Fulfilment by International Organizations of their Obligations Toward Third Parties', *Yearbook of the Institute of International Law* 1995, at 260.

98 Be it with a (contested) administrative function, such as the UN Compensation Commission in 1991 (eg Bernhard Graefrath, 'Iraqi Reparations and the Security Council', 55 ZaöRV 1995, 1–68), or with a semi-judicial function, such as the International Criminal

discussion on the conclusion of a treaty by five international organisations for the establishment of another international organisation, the Joint Vienna Institute;[99] or in the doctrinal grapple with the constituent treaty of an international organisation, which may be viewed at the same time as a treaty and as a constitution,[100] with concomitant implications for the choice of legal discourse and the applicability of general international law.

One aspect of the transparency of organisations is that they are 'layered' legal subjects with their internal structures partly visible. It has been stated that 'because of the institutionalised back-coupling between the IO and its member states, IOs as organisms are not comparable to states'.[101] But the more fundamental issue seems to be that the back-coupling between an organisation and its member states is more accessible from the international legal plane than the back-coupling between states and their subjects, because of the transparent quality of the institutional veil, in comparison with the impermeable quality attributed to the sovereign veil of states.

Tribunal for the Former Yugoslavia in 1993 (George Politakis, 'Enforcing International Humanitarian Law: The Decision of the Appeals Chamber of the War crimes Tribunal on the Duško Tadič Case (Jurisdiction)', 52 ZöR 1997, 283–329).

[99] The Joint Vienna Institute came into being at 29 July 1994, established by the BIS, the EBRD, the IBRD, the IMF and the OECD. See François Rousseau, 'Joint Vienna Institute': brèves remarques relatives à la creation de l'institut commun de Vienne', 1995 RGDIP, No 3, 639–650.

[100] Cf ch 6 below.

[101] Klein and Pechstein, above, note 76, at 35.

3

Conceptions of a New Legal Actor

THIS CHAPTER ADDRESSES the history of international organisations up until the era of the United Nations. This period spans the second half of the nineteenth century (section 3.2) and the first half of the twentieth century (section 3.3). The beginning of the twentieth century, in line with historiographic convention, is set at the end of the World War I. Both sections consider the advance of organisations and their role as international actors (in the sub-sections '*Institutions*'), as well as the development of legal thought in their regard, notably with respect to their independent indentity (in the sub-sections '*Legal Images*'). As the state is the primary point of reference for the history of international organisations, this chapter starts out with a separate paragraph (section 3.1) on the position of the state in eighteenth- and nineteenth-century legal thought.

3.1 THE STATE

Modern intergovernmental organisations date back to the mid-nineteenth century. For an understanding of the climate in which the prototypes of contemporary institutions came about, we have to look at the state, which by that time was the unchallenged focal point of political authority.

Which moment in history should best be taken as marking the advent of the state is a matter of some debate,[1] but it is certain that by the eighteenth century it was a well-established form of political organisation, occupying a central place in political thought. While the state was a well-established

[1] See eg this question mentioned, with references, in Martti Koskenniemi, 'The Politics of International Law', 1 *European Journal of International Law* 1990, 4–32, at 5. In the context of international law, the question is often formulated in terms of when the state came to occupy its exclusive position on the international scene; eg a recent endeavour to 'deconstruct the Westphalian model' with useful references in Stéphane Beaulac, 'The Westphalian Legal Orthodoxy – Myth or Reality?', 2 *Journal HIL* 2000, 148–177, with the hypothesis that, 'contrary to the overwhelmingly accepted view, 1648 does not close the final chapter of the multilayered system of authority in Europe.' (at 150); Cf eg Bernard Gilson, *The Conceptual System of Sovereign Equality*, 1984, at 6–15; David Raic, *Statehood and the Law of Self-Determination*, 2002, at 20–28; and in general, Peter Rietbergen, *Europe: A Cultural History*, 1998, at 194–226.

concept, a considerable part of the intellectual energy of the time was still put into its *legitimation*. An obvious illustration is the concern with contract-theories, proposing a basis for a state made up of free and equal individuals.[2]

The sensitivity to the corporate and fictional nature of the state remained when the independent 'personality' of the state, primarily in its internal implications, came to be an issue.[3] Theories on the state's personality were accordingly construed from that perspective and based on 'a concept of "moral person" in a purely mechanical and atomistic fashion [. . .], built up of nothing but free and equal individuals and cemented only by obligations'.[4]

Meanwhile, the locus of sovereignty was shifting. Originally used by rulers as a 'slogan'[5] against the re-establishment of imperial or papal power, 'sovereignty' came to refer to the people or 'the state' as such,[6] rather than to the monarch. This development, too, was explored at first in connection to the internal organisation of the state,[7] but it had obvious external implications. The notion of state sovereignty entailed the principle of state equality,[8] which, in turn, was associated with the liberal vision of equality of individuals.[9]

The sovereignty tenet notwithstanding, a large part of eighteenth-century 'international'[10] doctrine was conducive to a relative perspective on the state. Influential trends of enlightened natural law thought[11] envisaged the state as subject to superior rules, as for example in the system of Christian Wolff. In this respect, it has been pointed out that Wolff's *civitas maxima* appears not as a precursor of the League of Nations, but rather as a portent to Kelsen's *Stufenbau*[12] – that is, as a 'monistic' rather than a state-based construction.

[2] Michael Harry Lessnoff (ed), Social Contract Theory, 1990; one starting point for the liberal theory that would be transposed to the international plane as well (cf Roberto Unger, *Knowledge and Politics*, 1975).

[3] Cf the conclusions in Francis Ruddy, *International Law in the Enlightenment*, 1975, at 311–316.

[4] Otto von Gierke, *The development of Political Theory* (trans Bernard Freyd), 1966, at 179 (cited in Ruddy, above, note 3, at 135).

[5] Helmut Steinberger, 'Sovereignty' in *EPIL* 10, 1981, 397–418, at 399–400.

[6] *Ibid*; a 'conceptual approach' in Nicholas Onuf, 'Sovereignty: Outline of a conceptual history', 16 Alternatives 1991, 425–446.

[7] An abstraction incorporated in the European constitutions of the late 18th century; eg Dietmar Willoweit and Ulrike Seif (eds), *Europäische Verfassungsgeschichte*, 2003.

[8] Ruddy, above, note 3, at 55–57.

[9] Juan Manuel Castro Rial, 'States, Sovereign Equality', EPIL 10, 1981, 477-481, at 478.

[10] Mark Janis, 'Jeremy Bentham and the Fashioning of 'International Law'', 78 *American JIL* 1984, 405–418.

[11] Cf Ruddy, above, note 3, at 33–58.

[12] Arthur Nussbaum, *A Concise History of the Law of Nations*, 1961, at 144.

In schools of thought that did not recognise natural law for the international sphere – which implied that any international order would necessarily be based on consent – the state, too, appeared as an entity less self-evident and sacrosanct than it would in later times. For example Rousseau based the law of nations on, if anything, a form of 'contract' between states, but at the same time he stressed the natural goodness of man as a building stone.[13]

Vattel, who rejected Leibnitz's idea of a universal authority and Wolff's postulate of a *civitas maxima*, nevertheless endeavoured to reconcile the notions of international order and state independence by making a distinction between 'imperfect' and 'perfect rights', where the latter would have a jusnaturalist indefeasibility of sorts.[14]

Even Kant's treatise on *perpetual peace,* clearly proceeding from the idea of a contract between free and equal states in a Hobbesian state of nature, gives the impression of being ultimately more concerned with individuals than with the states in which they live, as his global federation of states is only a transitional stage on the way to an (if perhaps unattainable) *civitas gentium* of individuals.[15]

The relative perspective on the state changed radically in the course of the nineteenth century. Natural law thought made way for an almost exclusively positivist approach,[16] while the preoccupation with the state's corporate character and the basis of its moral personality disappeared.

Sovereignty had become 'an artificial and abstract idea located in the state', and doctrinal attention turned to its external implications. Linked to territory, sovereignty became exclusive and absolute, strengthening the tenet of legal equality of states.[17] This was the rise of what has been called the 'closeness and impermeability' of the state,[18] reinforced by the rise of nationalism. Now the state assumed an almost axiomatic character, and came to occupy a position much like that of an 'original subject', presumably pre-existing the legal order in which it operates, comparable to the individual in municipal law. The absolute position of the state entailed

[13] Cornelius Murphy, *The Search for World Order*, 1985, at 58–60; Ruddy, above, note 3, at 55 (who does not quite agree) and John Barton ('Two Ideas of International Organization', in Michigan Law Review Association (ed), *Two Ideas of International Organization*, 1987, 382–394), who for that reason characterises Rousseau's view on international order as 'organic' rather than truly 'contractual'.

[14] Chapter III in Ruddy, above, note 3, entirely on De Vattel.

[15] Immanuel Kant, 'To Perpetual Peace (1795)', in *Perpetual Peace and Other Essays* (translation and introduction by T Humphrey), 1983, § 357. For an elaboration of the view that Kant essentially saw states as 'transparent' collectives of individuals, see Fernando Teson, 'The Kantian Theory of International Law', in 92 *Columbia L Rev* 1992, 53–102, at 70–72.

[16] Antonio Truyol y Serra, *Histoire du droit international public*, 1995, at 115–127.

[17] David Kennedy, 'International Law and the Nineteenth Century: History of an Illusion', 65 *Nordic JIL* 1996, 385-420, at 406 ff, quote at 407.

[18] Cf terminology in Wilhelm Grewe, *Epochen der Völkerrechtsgeschichte*, 1984, at 233; Rudolf Bindschedler, 'International Organizations: General Aspects' in EPIL 5, 1983, at 124.

a division of the law in two: national and international[19] – which in turn reinforced the image of the state as an 'original subject'.

In 1821 Hegel referred to states as 'completely autonomous totalities in themselves' and as 'the absolute power on earth (in which the world spirit unfolds itself)'.[20] This was a philosophical-idealist expression of the viewpoint that would be predominant also in nineteenth-century legal thought.[21] It was reflected for instance in the 'duty of self-preservation' of the state.[22] It inspired an emphasis on the 'will' of the state, and a theory of 'self-limitation' of states as the basis of legal obligation.[23]

At the beginning of the twentieth century, the 'real personality theory' lost its leading role. The *legal* identity of the state was no longer linked to a pre-existing metaphysical identity, but seen as a fictional and conventional understanding.[24] The social and political identity of the state, however, remained to a large extent unscathed.

In short, the immediate precursors of modern organisations were bred in a climate of absolute state sovereignty and voluntarist positivism.[25] These institutions were not aimed at transcending the state but, on the contrary, rooted in a rigorously state-based system. Meanwhile, the perspective on

[19] See also section 2.3.3 above.

[20] *Grundlinien der Philosophie des Rechts* (1821 -Knox translation of 1821), Suhrkamp, 1986, §§ 330 and 331, respectively. But for Hegel the state was not a power above and outside the human individual; rather it was the sum total of all human relationships, the only framework in which the individual could function and develop (Franz Rosenzweig, *Hegel und der Staat*, 1921 (1982 edn)).

[21] In particular the German positivist school; see Peter Kooijmans, *The Doctrine of the Legal Equality of States*, 1964, 126–151; at 131 on the reception of Hegel up until the First World War.

[22] Eg Georg Jellinek, *Die Lehre von den Staatenverbindungen*, 1882, at 102: ' . . .da es nun die höchste Pflicht des Staates ist, sich selbst zu erhalten, uns zwar nicht als ruhende ordnung, sondern auch als bewegende Kraft des Volkslebens'.

[23] Also Jellinek (above, note 22), and Bergbohm; see references in Kooijmans, above, note 21, at 126–151; Bernard Gilson, *The Conceptual System of Sovereign Equality*, 1984, at 44–52. Cf Kelsen on the view (not shared by him) of the state as a sociological entity – the state respectively as a body constituted by human interaction, by a common will, as an 'organism' or as a social system defined by domination (Hans Kelsen, *General Theory of Law and State (transl Anders Wedberg)*, 1945, at 183–188).

[24] Cf DP O'Connell, *International Law*, 1965, at 90, on 'the tremendous pressures of Hegelian or positivist philosophies underlying each of these positions'. See Gilson, above, note 23, at 24–38 on the intricate varieties in this respect, such as 'real corporate entity' (proposed eg by Schelling, Fichte – the state as a corporate whole); the 'real corporate person' (Gierke being the main proponent, equating the state entirely with a physical person); the 'fictitious person' view (the other extreme, propagated primarily by Von Savigny, taken further by Duguit); and the state as a 'relatively real person' ('legal corporations [including the state] ... are real "with a difference". They are not organic but dialectically organized.') Gilson, above, note 23, at 35.

[25] Although probably at no point in time the 'classic' vision of a horizontal legal order with sovereign and equal monadic state-entities has existed in a pure form; see David Kennedy, 'International Law and the Nineteenth Century: History of an Illusion', 65 *Nordic JIL* 1996, 385–420.

non-state entities was undoubtedly informed by the 'atomistic and mechanical' image of the state in the previous century, when it was itself perceived as a body corporate.

3.2 THE RISE OF INTERNATIONAL ORGANISATIONS: THE NINETEENTH CENTURY

3.2.1 Institutions

Contemporary organisations are generally traced back to two nineteenth-century trends:[26] first, a novel kind, or level, of political cooperation, reflected in the development of the conference system of the Concert of Europe; and second, an increasing need for technical cooperation, met by the public international unions.[27] While the conference system[28] 'foreshadowed the goals and orientations of international co-operation within the major international organisations still to come',[29] the technical organisations presented an institutional framework.[30] The Hague Conferences of 1899 and 1907 may be singled out as a third factor. This system of collective diplomacy, brought to an untimely end by World War I, can be set apart from the European conference system for its pursuance of universality,[31] in both the geographical and the political sense, and for innovative conference techniques such as the use of chairmen, committees

[26] Pierre Gerbet, 'Rise and Development of International Organization: a Synthesis', in Georges Abi-Saab, *The Concept of International Organization*, 1981, 27–49, at 31.

[27] Paul Reuter, *Institutions internationales*, 1954, from a general legal and institutional perspective. On the history of international institutions from an institutional perspective, Philippe Sands and Pierre Klein, *Bowett's Law of International Institutions* (5th edn), 2001, at 1–13; Clive Archer, *International Organizations*, 1992, 1–37; from a general legal perspective, Rudolf Bindschedler, 'International Organizations: General Aspects', EPIL 5, 1983, 119-140; related to different theoretical perspectives on IGOs: Nigel White, *The Law of International Organizations*, 2005, at 2–23.

[28] See Inis Claude, *Swords into Ploughshares: The Problems and Progress of International Organization*, 1971, at 24–28 on the fact that 'diplomacy by conference became an established fact of life in the nineteenth century' (at 25). The 'system' included the 1815 Congress of Vienna (plus four sequels until 1822), the Congress of Paris of 1856, the London Conferences (1871 and 1912–1913), the Berlin Congresses (1878, 1884–1885) and the Algeciras Conference of 1906.

[29] Georges Abi-Saab, 'Introduction', in Abi-Saab (ed), above, note 26, at 11; see also Bindschedler, above, note 27; Mark Janis, *An Introduction to International Law* (4th edn), 2003, at 203–207.

[30] See Claude, above, note 28, at 36–37, on institutional novelties brought by the 19th century non-political internatio-nal bodies, such as the secretariat, and the dichotomy between the general policy making body with full membership and the governing body, composed of selected members.

[31] Claude, above, note 28, at 21–40; but see Archer, above, note 27, at 11 who explicitly disagrees with Claude on this point. A detailed survey in Joseph Choate, *The Two Hague Conferences*, 1913.

and roll calls. The tradition of projects for global peace (extending from the fourteenth century well into the nineteenth century),[32] on the other hand, appears to have been less relevant for the development of modern international organisations, as these 'never reflected or appealed to a strong sense of current need',[33] and consequently did not breed much institutionalisation.

The European conference system, which for its smooth functioning has been likened to 'a de facto international organization',[34] developed a practice of fostering the adoption and conclusion of international conventions. This practice is closely linked to the technique of the multilateral treaty,[35] the most important development of modern treaty-making thus coinciding with the dawn of the international organisation itself. An important 'centralising' development in its wake was the institution of a single depositary for the treaty instrument, which tended to functions previously performed in the framework of separate bilateral treaty-relations.[36] The European system, however, lacked a permanent *and* centralised institutional structure.

The public unions, on the other hand, presented a degree of formalisation and centralisation that, according to most modern criteria, would have them qualify as intergovernmental organisations. At the time, there was no generally accepted definition of 'public international union',[37] nor an agreed classification. 'Union' is used here as a generic term, but initially these institutions seem to have been called by various names, which in a sense relate to different aspects.

The term 'bureau' refers to the permanent secretariats, which, as governing bodies, turned institutions from mere 'treaty regimes' into 'organisations';[38] it was also used as a *pars pro toto* for the union as a

[32] Jacob ter Meulen, *Der Gedanke der internationalen Organization in seiner Entwicklung*, 1917; Murphy, above, note 13.

[33] Claude, above, note 28, at 24.

[34] Eg Paul Reuter, *Introduction to the Law of Treaties*, 1995, at 8, who remarks that it 'in practical terms often compares rather favourably with the League of Nations or the United Nations'.

[35] See Krystyna Marek, 'Contribution a l'étude de l'histoire du traité multilateral', in Emanuel Diez et al (eds), *Festschrift für Rudolf Bindschedler*, 1980, 17–39, with an account of instances of treaty-making practice preceding the Final Act of the 1815 Congress of Vienna, which, as a cluster of bilateral treaties, was famous for being the onset of 'multilateralism'; cf Manfred Lachs, 'Le développement et les fonctions des traités multilateraux', 1957 RdC 92/II, 228–341.

[36] Eg Reuter, *Introduction*... above note 34, at 5–6.

[37] Bowett-Sands, above, note 27, at 6, 7; Andrea Rapisardi-Mirabelli, 'Théorie générale des unions internationales', 1925 RdC/I, 345–391; and Michel Dendias, 'Les principaux services internationaux administratifs', 63 RdC/1 1938, 247–366, for references.

[38] Some 257 'law-making' treaties have been counted for the period between 1864–1914 (Hudson, International Legislation, Vol I, p XIX); approximately 50 of these established actual 'bureaux' (cf Reuter, *Institutions*... above note 27, at 31–32).

whole. The term 'administrative union' points to the aspect of 'administration' as opposed to the traditional subjects of international diplomacy. It stressed the element of communality in the administration of international affairs, as opposed to the management of international affairs by individual states.[39] The designation 'public' then served to contrast these institutions to the 'private unions' of the time.[40] This was a significant label because the relationship between these two categories was more intricate than is the case at present – due to, among other things, the gradual transition of initiatives for 'international administration' from the private to the public sphere.[41] Finally, the notion of 'international organ' was in fashion, associated with an internationalist outlook.[42]

Some writers were concerned with a distinction between 'administrative unions' and other associations on the basis of function or field of operation, rather than institutional structure.[43] Thus for example Anzilotti set apart the River Commissions from the administrative unions in general.[44] However, since in our time, organisations – by the sheer width of the issue areas they cover – are considered primarily on the basis of *formal* institutional features,[45] these are also the most relevant in older organisations,[46] as they allow us to trace a line of development. In the general sense, some 50 public international organisations or unions were established before 1914.[47]

The principles for a régime for international rivers contained in the Final Act of the 1815 Congress of Vienna[48] resulted in various river commissions, of which the Rhine Commission and, later, the European Danube

[39] Pierre Kazansky, 'Théorie de l'administration internationale, IX RGDIP 1902, at 366 *et passim*; Dendias, above, note 37, at 249. See section 3.2.2 below for differences of opinion on (legal) nature of such 'administration'.

[40] Between 1840 and 1914 approximately 400 permanent private associations came into being. Well-known examples are the International Committee of the Red Cross (1863), the International Law Association (1873), the Inter-Parliamentary Union (1889); Sands-Bowett, above, note 27, at 4–9.

[41] Claude, above, note 28, at 38.

[42] However, the 'organ' was mostly associated with the states collectively and less readily with an 'international community' – see section 3.3.2 below on the inter-war period. At the time these were not established analytical categories, so to some extent a distinction has to be read into the text – Kazansky (above, note 39) probably proceeded from the 'community' view.

[43] See section 3.2.2 below.

[44] Dionisio Anzilotti, *Corso di Diritto Internazionale* (3rd edn), 1928, at 281 ff; followed by Julio Barberis, 'Nouvelles questions concernant la personnalité juridique internationale', 179 RdC 1983, 145–304, at 215–217.

[45] Cf section 2.2.1 above.

[46] Indeed, contemporary institutional law seems to put the River Commissions and technical organisations in one general category of 'unions', without the sort of discussion raised by a possible distinction between surpranational and international institutions. For example Bowett-Sands (above, note 27, at 6, 7) and Claude (above, note 28, at 34).

[47] Gerbet, above, note 26, at 36.

[48] Articles 96, 108–118.

Commission are the best-known.[49] These were, in contemporary terms restricted organisations, membership being limited to the riparian states. Also, they dealt with comparatively politicised matters.

Other public institutions, sometimes set apart as the genuine administrative bodies and mostly with open membership, were concerned with the administration of technical matters, such as the International Telegraphic Union (1868),[50] the Universal Postal Union (1874),[51] the International Committee of Weights and Measures (1875) and the Union of Railway Freight Transportation (1890).[52] Reuter mentions the existence of some fourteen *bureaux* at the outbreak of the first World War.[53] Somewhat outside regular categorisation was the International Commission for the Cape Spartel Light,[54] which existed from 1865 until 1958. An early attempt at European integration is found in the German *Zollverein* (1834–1871). Opinion is divided, however, as to whether it qualifies as an early intergovernmental organisation;[55] for one thing, it lacked a permanent organ or even a decision-making organ. On a regional level, the Pan-American Conference system (set up in 1826, prior to the European system, and consolidated at the Washington Conference of 1889) had been formalised in 1912 with a Bureau that was named the Pan-American Union.[56]

Generally, the institutional make-up of these organisations hinged on the principle of unanimity, neatly reflecting the tenet of state sovereignty and the strictly functional perspective on international organisations.[57] This is most clear in the international conferences which dealt with political matters – it was only at the Hague Conferences that recommendations

[49] Central Commission for navigation on the Rhine River, Annex 16 to the Final Act of the Congress of Vienna (2 Martens NRG 427–430; Annexes are not reproduced in the CTS). For its initially less economic importance the principles for a régime for international rivers established by the Congress of Vienna in 1815 were not applied to the Danube. The European Danube Commission was established by the Paris Peace Treaty of 1856; its privileges were increased at the Paris Conference of 1965 (18 Martens NRG 143).

[50] Originally the 'International Telegraphic Bureau'; 130 CTS 198.

[51] Originally the 'General Postal Union'; 147 CTS 136.

[52] 174 CTS 1.

[53] Reuter, above, note 27, at 32.

[54] Convention Concerning the Administration and Upholding of the Lighthouse at Cape Spartel (31–5-1865), 131 CTS 203. Parties were the Netherlands, Belgium, Portugal, Spain, Austria, Sweden-Norway, France, Italy, the United States and Great-Britain. See David Bederman, 'The Souls of International Organizations: Legal Personality and the Lighthouse at Cape Spartel', 36 *Virginia JIL* 1996, 275–377; see also section 3.3.2 below.

[55] Hungdah Chiu (*The Capacity of International Organizations to Conclude Treaties, and the Special Legal Aspects of the Treaties so Concluded*, 1966, at 6) is of the opinion it does not, since its 'General Conference' would lack permanency and decision-making powers; Werner Meng ('Zollverein', EPIL 7, 1984, 542–544, at 542) on the contrary holds that the General Conference would qualify as a permanent body.

[56] Reuter, above, note 27, at 34, 314–315.

[57] See section 2.2.2 above.

(*vœux)* would be passed by a majority vote.[58] Also in the more formalised framework of the Unions, unanimity was the rule, although practice shows an occasional departure therefrom.[59] This view of practice is refined by Tammes, who pointed out that such majority decisions almost never entailed legal obligations for the member states.[60] Likewise, each member state would normally have one vote. Rare exceptions are found in some of the River Commissions, where certain administrative matters were decided by way of an early form of weighted voting related to the length of the riverbank.[61]

The international organisations of this time displayed activity mainly in relation to their member states and *within* their institutional framework. This may explain why according to one writer the European Rhine Commission 'was not an example of an international body acting on its own initiative'.[62]

The legislative and judicial powers of certain River Commissions were nonetheless considerable – Seidl-Hohenveldern held the powers of the European Danube Commission to be 'so far-reaching that they may well be compared to those enjoyed by *supra*national organizations, especially the European Communities'.[63] But these competences, again, asserted themselves in the internal order of the organisation.[64] There was little scope for the organisation to have 'external relations', and it is uncertain how its institutional powers operated outside the institutional framework. In that period generally headquarters arrangements were regulated by oral agreement or by a treaty between the member states and the host state,[65] where the institution would not enter as a party. An exception is the agreement concluded by the International Committee of Weights and Measures with France on the Committee's headquarters.[66]

The *Zollverein* did make agreements, but apart from the doubts concerning the status of the institution (viz its independence vis-à-vis the

[58] Archer, above, note 27, at 10–11; Claude, above, note 28, at 31; Shabtai Rosenne, 'International Conferences and Congresses', EPIL 1992, 739–746.

[59] See Bowett-Sands, above, note 27, at 6–9; and Reuter, above, note 27, at 30–36. This practice may be seen as a prelude to the majority decision-making in later technical organisations.

[60] Arnold Tammes, *Hoofdstukken van Internationale Organisatie*, 1951, at 39–45.

[61] Bowett-Sands, above, note 27, at 6.

[62] JP Chamberlain (1923) cited in Bederman, above, note 54, at 346; see also the references in footnote 404 at the same page.

[63] Ignaz Seidl-Hohenveldern, 'Danube River', *EPIL* 12 , 1990, 80–83, at 80 (emphasis in the original).

[64] Cf Tammes, above, note 60, at 44, 45.

[65] From Chiu (above, note 55, at 8–17) it appears that of the 50-something organisations of that time (above note 47), few had concluded an agreement for the purposes of headquarters arrangements. On contemporary practice in this respect, ch 4 below.

[66] 4-X-1875, ICWM archive; reported in Chiu, above, note 55, at 6. According to this author it is the earliest example of an IGO treaty.

member states and hence its quality of 'organisation' to begin with) mentioned above,[67] these agreements in reality seem to have been concluded by the heads of state of certain *Zollverein* member states representing other members via the legal device of delegation (*Vertretung*). Although such agreements would contain a reference to the members united in the framework of the *Zollverein*, there would be no allusion to an independent character of the institution.[68]

3.2.2 Legal Images

The nineteenth-century institutions were created by 'statesmen who sought new arrangements and devices whereby the sovereign units of the old system could pursue their interests and manage their affairs in the altered circumstances of the age of communication and industrialism'.[69] Where states counted as the supreme political bodies, organisations had a purely functional role.

This is in a general sense reflected in the notion 'international organisation', which started making an appearance in pre-War writings. In 1911 Paul Reinsch held that 'the realm of international organization is an accomplished fact.'[70] At that point he seemed to be referring to a concept of world organisation, or rather 'public administration', by states through collective institutions ('organs') which had some permanency, but which lacked the independent 'will' or even 'identity' that later would become central. The origin of the term 'international organisation' was traced by Pitman Potter to writings of James Lorimer in the 1860s and 1870s. But although Lorimer was known to continental lawyers, the term did not catch on until some forty years later when German and Austrian scholars moved from 'the vaguer and less conscious terminology of the 1900s [...] to a more specific and deliberate reference [...]', with later PCIJ judge Walther Schücking as a leading figure.[71] It would then take until the establishment of the League of Nations for the concept to become ('after much educational agony'[72]) widely accepted. Writing in late 1945, Potter gave expression to the hopes and expectations of his own time when he explained: 'Indeed [the expression "international organization"] became obvious and admitted then ... only because in the League effort adequate

[67] Above note 55.
[68] See eg the Treaty of Commerce of 26–1-1856 between Prussia, Hannover and the Hessen electorate 'for themselves and in the name of the other states of the Zollverein' on the one hand and the Hanseatic city of Bremen on the other (114 CTS 193–223).
[69] Claude, above, note 28, at 24.
[70] Paul Reinsch, Public International Unions, 1911, at 4.
[71] Pitman Potter, 'Origin of the Term International Organization', 39 *American JIL* 1945, 803–806, citation at 805.
[72] *Ibid*, at 806.

emphasis was placed, beyond sentiments and ideas and rules of law, upon permanent institutions, organization, and the structure, albeit rudimentary, of the international federal state'.[73]

The European Congress had raised various questions of diplomatic law and the law of treaties with respect to states,[74] but few or none about the legal nature of the conference system as such. In contrast, the comparatively centralised structure of the 'technical organisations' gave more cause for discussion – a discussion that was 'fairly arid' and mostly focused on the question of whether international institutions could have 'a legal existence separate and distinct from their member states' at all.[75]

It is significant that the great nineteenth-century authority on corporate legal personality, Otto von Gierke, was also an adherent of the 'organic theory', in which the state is equated to a natural organism.[76] With respect to the administrative unions, Gierke wrote in 1868 that '[those organisations] which exist for example for railways and the postal and telegraph systems, cannot be regarded as corporations under existing law. They are merely contractual relationships'.[77] This is in line with the established view of the time in which an organisation was completely equated with its constitutive treaty as a vehicle for concerted state action.[78]

Some authors, however, perceived the international administrative unions as having a degree of independence. For Jellinek the distinctive feature of the unions was the ability to act through organs and not merely through the agreement of their members.[79] Kazansky, who in an internationalist vein saw organisations as 'organs' of the international community, in 1897 stressed the 'voluntary and mutual consent' of states underlying the organisation,[80] but in his more comprehensive analysis of 'international administration' of 1902 he also pointed at the 'independent will' of the organisation.[81]

[73] *Ibid* (emphasis added).
[74] See above notes 28, 35, 49.
[75] Bederman, above, note 54, at 343.
[76] Cf Kelsen, above, note 23, at 185–186 on the different theories.
[77] Otto von Gierke, *Community in Historical Perspective*, (A Black (ed) and M Fischer (trans); includes much of *Das Deutsche Genossenschaftsrecht*, originally published in 1868), 1990. On the reception of Gierke at the previous turn of the century, see Bederman, above, note 54, at 354–356.
[78] As eg Jellinek, above, note 22; see also references in Rapisardi-Mirabelli, above, note 37, at 346 et passim. To some extent this remains topical: cf the dual approach to IGO constitutive treaties. Section 4.2 below, on the organisation as a treaty and the organisation as a legal organism (with objective personality); ch 6 below, on interpretation of the organisation's constitutive treaty as a regular treaty or as a 'constitution'.
[79] Jellinek, above, note 22, at 158; cf Gilson, above, note 23, at 480.
[80] Referred to in Bederman, above, note 54, at 344.
[81] Kazansky (1902), above, note 39, at 361, 366; cf also Bederman, above, note 54, at 343–363, on the concept of the 'will' of international organisations in 19th and early 20th century legal writing.

The idea of a separate legal identity for organisations gradually gained ground. Continental legal scholarschip and notably the German positivist school had an active role in shaping the necessary doctrinal context. This context was entirely set within the law of treaties framework and strictly consensualist in character. Some developments in this field, however, were vital for the advance of international organisation. A procedural novelty was the multilateral treaty,[82] a valuable tool for the creation of international institutions.[83] On a conceptual level the idea of the *Gemeinwillen* took root, famously introduced by Triepel: a separate 'will' distinct from the sum of wills combined in an association of states.[84] This common will was related to, and could be embodied in, the *Vereinbarung*, the early concept of a 'law-making treaty'.[85]

It is doubtful that the separate identity of organisations at the time amounted to an image of 'legal personality', that is to say, of an external legal identity accorded by the international legal order.[86] It is even unlikely that the organisation's employment of its institutional independence vis-à-vis the member states had an external dimension – the focus was on the interaction between organisation and member states,[87] and mainly *within* the institutional framework of the organisation, ie as envisaged in the constituent instrument.[88] This was possible because, as stated above, the organisations of the time were relatively self-contained in their fields of operation, with little need for prominent 'external relations'.

Some activities possibly amounted to 'external' legal acts, such as the agreements concluded by the International Congo Association or by the German *Zollverein*. However, their significance is unclear because the

[82] The onset of which is commonly marked by the Final Act of the 1915 Congress of Vienna (concluding multilateral procedure) and by the 1856 Paris Treaty, which had a multilateral form from the first stages onwards (cf Reuter, above, note 34, at 4–9; Abdullah El-Erian, *First report on Relations between States and Inter-Governmental Organizations*, YILC 1963, UN Doc A/CN.4/161 and Add 1, §§ 24 and 25).

[83] See above, note 34 and accompanying text. The constituent treaties of ITU and UPU are examples of 'modern' multilateral treaties.

[84] Heinrich Triepel, *Völkerrecht und Landesrecht*, 1899 – the basis for the binding force of the Gemeinwillen, Triepel himself admitted, had to be found in an extra-legal context. Cf Alfred Verdross, *Die Verfassung der Völkerrechtsgemeinschaft*, 1926, at 20 ('...als grundlage des Völkerrechts'); Kooijmans, above, note 21, at 133, 134; and Gilson, above, note 23; cf below, note 173 and accompanying text.

[85] The Vereinbarung, which figured already in the writings of Bergbohm and Jellinek, is mostly translated as an 'agreement', as opposed to 'legal transaction' (Rechtsgeschäft); cf Kooijmans, above, note 21, at 133, 134.

[86] On the difference between 'autonomy' (an institutional characteristic), and 'legal personality' (a general legal qualification) eg ch 2 above.

[87] With Pasquale Fiore and perhaps Kazansky as a rare exception. See Pasquale Fiore, Il diritto internazionale codificato, 1890, recapitulated and elaborated in 'L'organization juridique de la société internationale', 1899 RDI, 105. See also section 3.3.2 below. As Bederman (above, note 54, at 345) points out, Fiore was one of the first, and at this point perhaps the only one, to outline a general functional theory of international organisations.

[88] Cf Bederman, above, note 54, at 344–347 (on pre-war doctrine).

status of the *Zollverein* as such was uncertain,[89] while the International Congo Association was unquestionably not an intergovernmental organisation but a Belgian initiative (preparing the way for the Congo Free State). These institutions are therefore commonly left out of account in studies observing a formal perspective.[90] All the same, it seems that at the time the agreements entered into by them carried some weight. They were presented, for example by Fiore, as evidence of a possible independent legal personality or at least a legal capacity for treaty-making on the part of international organisations.[91]

The legal struggle with international organisations is epitomised by the International Commission for the Cape Spartel Lighthouse, which appeared as an 'international servitude' and an 'internationalised territory' before taking the shape of an 'international organisation'.[92] It is no coincidence that the first interpretations of the Lighthouse Commission had a territorial component. The premise of states as the sole subjects of international law[93] had established the principle of territoriality,[94] and therefrom territorial jurisdiction, as a condition for the participation in international law (reinforcing the central position of the state in a circular manner).

The territoriality principle thus posed additional limitations to the conceptualisation of organisations as international legal subjects.[95] It is also one reason why the legal existence of an organisation would need a continuous basis in the agreement of the member states; and such a basis indeed appears from the institutional set-up of the organisations of the time (for instance in the unanimity rule – see section 3.2.1 above), coupled with a strictly voluntarist perspective. Otherwise – and equally unsurprising – there are no signs that lawyers perceived of organisations constituting

[89] Section 3.2.1 above.

[90] Cf Chiu, above, note 55, at 6–7.

[91] Fiore, *Codice*... above, note 87, at 329.

[92] As described by Bederman; see section 3.3 below, on the interwar period in which the status of the Commission was formally at issue. The eventful story of the Lighthouse Commission (1865–1958) is recounted in the first part of Bederman, above, note 54. The seminal second part of the essay proposes 'the outlines of an intellectual history' for international organisations in the late nineteenth and early twentieth centuries.

[93] Bederman, above, note 54, at 333–335 and references.

[94] Cf Alexander Murphy ('The Sovereign State System as Political-Territorial Ideal: Historical and Contemporary Considerations', in Thomas Biersteker and Cynthia Weber (eds), *The Sovereign State System as Political-Territorial Ideal: Historical and Contemporary Considerations*, 1996, 81–120), who argues that, while the sovereignty of actual states may have been challenged, the ideal of territorial sovereignty never was.

[95] Cf Hermann Mosler, 'Subjects of International Law', in EPIL 7, 1984, 442-459, at 447.

a separate legal order apart from the sphere of general international law.[96] Put in terms of this book, organisations were predominantly 'open' structures.[97]

3.3 THE LEAGUE OF NATIONS ERA

3.3.1 Institutions

The twentieth century has been described as 'the era of establishment of international organization,' as opposed to 'the era of preparation [. . .]' that was the nineteenth century.[98] The League of Nations and the International Labour Organization (ILO), their constitutive instruments being included in the Versailles treaties,[99] were the most prominent new intergovernmental institutions. They can indeed be seen as a consolidation of earlier trends, both in form and effect. Form-wise, the ILO built on the model of the nineteenth-century technical organisations.[100] The League of Nations relied, more loosely, on the examples of the international Bureaux (for its Secretariat), the Concert of Europe (for its Council) and the Hague Conferences (for its Assembly).[101] What was new about it was 'the idea ... to force the coalescence of pre-1914 relations into a "system"'.[102]

In general terms both organisations were more influential in the international arena than their predecessors had been. In the case of the ILO this occurred primarily *within* the legal order of the organisation, which displayed an unprecedented degree of centralisation.[103] The League was

[96] Cf Bederman, above, note 54, at 344–347 (on pre-war doctrine).

[97] See ch 2 above – this is a perspective conveyed by the then common denomination 'association of states'; see eg Pasquale Fiore's *Codice* of 1889, § 681; cf the terminology later employed by Lauterpacht (section 8.1.2 below); and the argument advanced by the International Law Commission in relation to the 1986 Convention that the definition of 'group of states' include 'international organisation' (section 10.3.1 below, s.v. arts 52 and 76).

[98] Claude, above, note 28, at 41.

[99] Treaty of Peace between the Allied and Associated Powers and Germany, and Protocol [Treaty of Versailles] (incorporating the Covenant of the League of Nations – Part I and the Constitution of the International Labour Organisation – Part XIII) (Versailles, 28 June 1919), 225 CTS 189, 225 CTS 195.

[100] Apart from the fact that part of its work could build on that of the International Labour Office, which had been established in 1901.

[101] Claude, above, note 28, at 43; clearly this leaves room for discussion (which exceeds the present scope) – Archer (above, note 27, at 18–20) convincingly argues that although the models may be from the previous century, the reason why certain structures rather than others were chosen can be directly traced to the war-time experience; see also ch 1 on Virally's dialectic relationship between form and function.

[102] Alvarez, *International Organizations as Law-Makers*, 2005, at 19.

[103] Cf section 2.3.2 above.

more prominent in its external appearance. The universality of its membership, combined with the generality of its purposes,[104] made it a more pervasive factor in international life than any other institution had been so far. The League was probably the first organisation to be clearly visible as an independent international actor, and to some extent to manifest as a *legal* actor as well. Meanwhile the League's internal legal order had a rather traditional and not highly centralised design (usually connected by commentators to its broad scope) compared to that of the functional organisations. These two organisations may serve to give an impression of the legal activity of organisations in the interwar period. This activity had now clearly assumed an internal and an external dimension (although such terms are still something of an anachronism – see section 2.3.2 below). Both are visible in the treaty-making practice of the time.

The internal dimension of organisations may be illustrated by the operation of their institutional order as a forum for treaty-making states. Both the ILO and the League of Nations actively furthered the conclusion of treaties by their member states. The League especially, because of its (mostly unrewarding) endeavours at codification of international law,[105] was involved in the conclusion of many of the multilateral treaties of that era.[106] Among other things it established a practice of systematically convening diplomatic conferences for this purpose. Contemporaries noted a new tendency towards majority rule-making,[107] but in general the treaty-making process of the time is characterised by the unanimity rule observed from the earliest stages up to adoption of the text.[108] The principle of unanimity was firmly established in the League – formally in the Rules of Procedure of the plenary organ,[109] and informally in the decision-making practice of diplomatic conferences convened by the Organization.[110] Only on rare occasions would a treaty be adopted by the League's Assembly rather than in a conference convened for the purpose,

[104] Background on the League in Claude, above, note 29, at 43 *et passim*, and Archer, above, note 27, at 15–23.

[105] See, on the 1930 Codification Conference, Shabtai Rosenne, *League of Nations Conference for the Codification of International Law*, 1975.

[106] On the 'initiatives or interventions' by the League which had a bearing on the law of treaties, see Reuter, above, note 27, at 9–12.

[107] Bederman, above, note 54, at 358–363.

[108] See David Kennedy, 'The Move to Institutions', 8 *Cardozo Law Review* 1987, 841–988, at 962–963.

[109] No 19 of the Rules of Procedure of the Assembly; cf also Tammes, above, note 60, at 74–85.

[110] Either by implication from the League system in general, or explicitly envisaged; see examples of the Rules of Procedure of several conferences mentioned in Shabtai Rosenne, 'UN Treaty Practice', RdC 1954, at 312.

and then it would usually be followed by signature subject to ratification.[111] Otherwise the League introduced some important innovations in the general treaty-making process, such as the obligation to register treaties with the League Secretariat (Article 18 of the Covenant), and the frequent transfer of depository functions to the Secretary-General or the Bureau of the Organization.[112] While the institutional framework of the League was decidedly more solid than the framework of the European conference system, it mainly reflected on the stage of negotiations rather than on the formal-legal aspects of the treaty-making process.[113]

The International Labour Organization (ILO), with a relatively centralised institutional structure, may be put at the other end of the scale. The ILO appears ahead of its time with a strong executive secretariat and a constitutional mandate to prepare and adopt conventions in its plenary organ by a two-thirds majority.[114] The ILO constitution further stipulates that the adopted text, *without* additional signature by the states, within a fixed period of time be submitted by the government to the competent national legislative body, whose eventual acceptance of the convention then entails an *obligation* for the state to ratify.[115]

Other organisations of that period include the unions already in existence, as well as a few new ones such as the Health Organization (established on the basis of Article 23(f) of the League Covenant). Article 24 of the League Convenant provided for an association between the

[111] The distinction between conventions concluded 'under the auspices' of the organisation and those concluded 'within' the organisation is addressed in ch 5 below; cf Reuter, above, note 27, at 10–11. A noteworthy exception is the case of the 1928 General Act for the Pacific Settlement of International Disputes which was 'adopted' in a conclusive manner similar to the ILO procedure (below). (Reuter, above, note 34, at 43). Adoption of the Act (93 LNTS 343) by the Assembly was preceded by authentication by means of the sole signature of the Secretary-General and the President of the Assembly. No further signature subject to ratification on the part of states was needed, only the final expression of consent to be bound.

[112] The function may have held more legal aspects than it would later, under the United Nations which after the crisis concerning the many reservations to the 1948 Genocide Convention explicitly renounced any task of legal asessment on the part of the depositary; see Shabtai Rosenne, 'The Depository of International Treaties', 61 *American JIL* 1967, 923–945, references to the relevant UNGA resolutions at 928. See, on League practice in general, Shabtai Rosenne, *Developments in the Law of Treaties (1945–1986)*, 1989, at 353–359.

[113] Wilfred Jenks, 'The Legal Personality of International Organizations', 22 *British YIL* 1945, 267–275, at 47. On institutional aspects of League practice see eg Rosenne, *UN Treaty Practice*, above, note 110, at 311–313.

[114] ILO Constitution Art 19; the International Labour Conference, due to its composition of tripartite national delegations, was in itself a novelty; on the ILO in general, KT Samson, 'International Labour Organization', EPIL Vol II, 1995, 1150–1159.

[115] See Charles Rousseau, *Droit international public*, 1953, at 39; and Reuter, above, note 34, at 43, who mention subsequent 'notification' by the Minister for Foreign Affairs to the Organization, taking the place of deposit or even ratification. The direct address to the national legislature was considered far-reaching and it was eg by the French government not accepted until 1926.

League and the 'international bureaux', old and new.[116] By the reference in Article 24 to 'general treaties' as a legal basis, candidate *associées* were limited to intergovernmental institutions, something which, incidentally, further clarified and sharpened the line between private and public institutions. The fact that only five newly created organisations were admitted to be 'placed under the direction' of the League,[117] gives some insight into the focus of international activity during the interwar period. Some fifty 'intergovernmental' organisations with a technical scope had been set up before 1914;[118] not many entered into a subsequent association with the League, however.[119]

The constitutive instruments of these organisations would vary according to the needs posed by the organisations' fields of operation, but these in any event envisaged less far-reaching competences than the ILO constitution. Only the new Health Organization was, as a relative exception, fitted with a procedure for the adoption of treaties by a two-thirds majority in the plenary organ, which was similar to that of the ILO, with the difference that conventions then would be transmitted to governments through the Council of the League, where again the unanimity rule prevailed.[120]

An organisation such as the Cape Spartel Lighthouse Commission, present already in the legal landscape of the nineteenth century,[121] remained outside the system or even the sphere of influence of the League of Nations. In this body (of limited membership), the principle of state sovereignty and equality asserted itself more strongly, as is visible from what Bederman summarises as the absence of any provision on decision-making in the 1865 Convention, the tendency to turn to consensus as 'a strong antidote to majority-ruling tendencies' and the preoccupation with diplomatic protocol.[122]

[116] Article 24 reads: 'There shall be placed under the direction of the League all international bureaux already established by general treaties if the parties of such treaties consent. All such international bureaux and all commissions for the regulation of matters of international interest hereafter constituted shall be placed under the direction of the League.'

[117] For example, the application of the International Agricultural Committee in 1923 was rejected on the ground that it was 'not a purely intergovernmental organization'; Derek Bowett, *The Law of International Institutions*, 1982, at 9–10.

[118] Gerbet, above, note 26, at 36.

[119] This was for a well-known argument of principle (the undesirability of politicising technical organisations) and for an immediate practical reason (association with the League could jeopardise US membership of the technical organisation in question) – cf Archer, above, note 21, at 20–21; Bowett-Sands, above, note 27, at 9–10.

[120] Resolution of 10/12/1920 (LoN Sp.Sup. Jan. 1921, at 18); part of the procedure was later enshrined in aArts 19 and 20 of the WHO Constitution.

[121] See above note 92, and accompanying text. The Lighthouse Commission was established by the Convention of 31 May 1865; parties were the Netherlands, Belgium, Portugal, Spain, Austria, Sweden-Norway, France, Italy, the United States and Great-Britain.

[122] Bederman, above, note 54, at 301.

Next to a degree of independence vis-à-vis the member states within the institutional order, organisations developed an external legal identity. Some organisations undoubtedly maintained 'external relations', albeit on a modest scale, and did so notably through the conclusion of international agreements.

Especially in the case of the League of Nations this amounted to a 'treaty-making practice' of sorts. Chiu distinguishes the following categories: i) agreements with mem-ber states (two agreements containing a *modus vivendi* – the first one (of 1921) is often presented as the first IGO treaty[123] – and an operational agreement with Switzerland); ii) agreements with non-member states (only one, an exchange of notes with the United States on registration of treaties with the LoN Secretariat); iii) agreements with other international organisations (a 1925 agreement with the International Institute for Agriculture and some 10 agreements with the UN in 1946 and 1947 connected to the transfer of certain assets and responsibilities); iv) the mandates; and v) the minority treaties.[124]

Curiously, it is the mandates and the minority treaties that have given the League its reputation for an early unstoppable rise to independent legal capacity,[125] which is why these may be looked at in some detail. This reputation can probably be partly explained from their role in decisions of the PCIJ and the ICJ. In reality the mandate procedures represent atypical if not controversial examples of treaty-making activity.

Minority protection by the League of Nations took the form of either declarations made by states before the League Council[126] or 'guarantees' assumed by the League in respect of minority protection treaties.[127] The Mandates had been drafted by the Mandatory (Principal Allied and Associated) States, after territories had been allocated at the 1919 Paris Conference and the 1920 San Remo Conference, and they were accepted by an official declaration of the Council of the League. Contrary to current doctrine there seems to have been a tendency to interpret these unilateral

[123] But see above note 66. Incidentally, the *modus vivendi* is particular in that Switzerland explicitly recognised the international legal personality of the League, see section 3.3.2 below.

[124] The most in depth survey of IGO treaty-making in this period is probably found in Chiu, above, note 55, at 8–13. See also Jean Huber, *Le droit de conclure des traités internationaux*, 1951; Renata Sonnenfeld, 'International Organizations as Parties to Treaties', XI *Polish YIL* 1981-1982, 177-200.

[125] Cf El-Erian, *First report...* above, note 82, at 180.

[126] Such 'minority declarations' were made by Albania (1921); Lithuania (1922); Latvia (1923); Estonia (1923); Bulgaria (1924); Greece (1924); Iraq (1932); see Chiu, above, note 55, at 10.

[127] Some 11 such treaties (either entirely or in part concerned with minority protection) were concluded; a listing in Chiu, above, note 55, at 10–11.

declarations, paralleled by a reactive declaration by the League, as treaties[128] (which would be possible for instance under the theory of 'disjunctive exchange of notes').[129] Presumably the Mandates were canonised as international agreements by the PCIJ in its 1924 *Mavrommatis* decision,[130] and in any event they were expressly qualified as agreements between the League and the declarant state in a 1950 report of the UN Secretariat.[131] Likewise, a 'guarantee' in respect of minority treaties or chapters on minority protection – in each case formally assumed by the League after a decision of the Council – was apperently viewed as a 'collateral' treaty.[132] Although form-wise very different from regular treaties, these acts have – in a comparatively formalist period – made a substantive contribution to the notion of 'external relations' by international organisations.

(The few) examples of other organisations that have become party to international agreements include the Health Organization (one agreement concluded in 1922 with the Soviet Union on privileges and immunities of staffmembers);[133] the Saar Governing Commission (several agreements with France and Germany);[134] the International Institute of Intellectual Co-operation (an agreement with UNESCO in 1946 and a competence for the director to conclude 'all necessary agreements with the competent administrations');[135] the Nansen International Refugees Office (the League Council had made acceptance of the clause in the Covenant regarding privileges and immunities conditional upon the conclusion of additional

[128] For example the Albanian declaration (registered with the League Secretariat) was (implicitly) treated by the PCIJ as if it were a treaty rather than a unilateral statement (*Minority Schools in Albania*, Ser. A/B, No 62 (1935)); cf Chiu, above, note 55, at 58.

[129] This seems to accord with the views of Lauterpacht and Rosenne; see Chiu, above, note 55, at 55–56; see also Myers, 'The Names and Scope of Treaties', 51 *American JIL* 1957, 574–604, at 579.

[130] In the 1924 Mavrommatis Palestine Concession case the PCIJ held that 'the Mandate falls within the category of 'matters especially provided for in Treaties and Conventions in force' under the terms of Article 36 of the Statute' (Ser A, No 2, 1924, at 12). This statement has been taken to mean (eg by Chiu, above, note 55, at 35) that the Court considered the mandate to be a treaty, if somewhat illogically, since grammatically 'mandate' is co-ordinated with 'matters provided for in Treaties' and not with 'Treaties' as such. In its 1925 Annual report the Court however seems to explicitly equate the mandates with treaties (quoted in Chiu, above, note 55, at 36), and therefore to have considered the League an independent treaty-party. See also below note 185 and accompanying text on the South West Africa cases where the question was raised before the ICJ.

[131] Chiu, above, note 55, at 10.

[132] In the terms of Reuter, *Introduction*, above, note 34, at 104–105); cf Chiu, above, note 55, at 11 ('these acceptances of extra functions by the LN are in a sense equivalent to concluding treaties').

[133] Quoted in Chiu, above, note 55, at 14.

[134] Eg with France in 1920 (23 LNTS 242) and with Germany in 1923 (27 LNTS 290); see Chiu, above, note 55, at 15.

[135] UNESCO Doc C/30 (1946), at 241; 'Revised Staff Regulations' of the IIIC quoted in Chiu, above, note 55, at 15.

'agreement[s] between the Office and the governments of the countries concerned' other than Switzerland. It is unclear whether such agreements have ever been concluded).[136]

Of bodies not formally affiliated with the League, the Permanent Court of International Justice concluded a status-agreement with the Netherlands.[137] The Reparation Commission, set up under Article 223 of the Versailles Treaty, concluded an agreement with Germany;[138] the International Commission of the Danube concluded an agreement with two riparian states, Romania and Yugoslavia.[139] The Cape Spartel Lighthouse Commission was a signatory to the multilateral 1934 *Regional Arrangement Concerning Maritime Radio Beacons*, clearly in its own right and not as an agent for the member states.[140]

Although some organisations thus performed juristic acts in general international law, this ability was not formalised in their constituent instruments, nor put to the test in a judicial context. It is illustrative that Article 24 of the League Covenant (in association with 'international bureaux') did not refer in any way to 'agreements' between the League and the pertinent organisation, contrary to the 'relationship agreements' envisaged in Article 63(1) of the UN Charter.

3.3.2 Legal Images

The experiences of World War I presented new challenges to voluntarist positivism and the absolute status of state sovereignty.[141] One example from a 'dualist' perspective is the foundation of the binding force of international law, which Anzilotti came to situate not in the will of sovereign states but rather in the objective, extra-juridical norm of *pacta sunt servanda*.[142] In this he went further than Triepel[143] and departed

[136] Cf Art 19. The Statute of the Office (an autonomous body) was approved by the League Council on 19 January 1931 (LoN Off J, 12th year 157 (1931).

[137] Approved by the LoN Council on 5 June 1928, PCIJ, Ser E, No 4, at 57 (1928).

[138] On 9 August 1924, 41 LNTS 432.

[139] On 28 June 1932, 140 LNTS 191. The International Commission of the Danube was the successor to the European Commission of the Danube (above, note 49); it was established 23 July 1921.

[140] 6 Hudson 1937, 851; see Bederman, above, note 54, at 296; Chiu, above, note 55, at 17.

[141] Kooijmans speaks of a 'revolution' in this respect (above, note 21, at 152).

[142] *Corso di diritto internazionale*, 1923, at 26 (agreements), 27 (custom, by tacit consent), also 42. Cf the concise article by Giorgio Gaja, 'Positivism and Dualism in Dionisio Anzilotti', 3 *European JIL* 1992, 123–138.

[143] Cf Triepel, above, note 84, at 81–90 (at 82: 'Immer und überall wird man an den Punkt gelangen, an dem eine rechtliche Erklärung der Verbindlicheit des Rechtes selbst unmöglich werd.'); an outline of 'classic' dualism embodied by eg Triepel and Anzilotti, in

altogether from the stance taken by for example Jellinek.[144] More far-reaching propositions came from the 'monist'[145] and the 'sociological'[146] visions of law.

The notion of 'international organs', which in the interwar period was fairly common, can present an ambiguous image. Obviously the term reflects an international(ist) perspective, but its implications may vary. The term 'organ' would by definition refer to an entity *part of* another entity and as such endowed with an independent identity at the institutional level, but not with legal personality at the general level.[147] Presently an 'international organ' would in the formal sense be a state organ or an organ of an organisation, and by *dédoublement fonctionnel* also be considered as an organ of the international community as a whole.[148] At the time of the writing of Kazansky and Anzilotti, an 'international organ' denoted an international institution in its entirity. The significance then depended on how the 'international' was defined: as a collective of states or as a community (that dual meaning also being present in pre-War writing),[149] but the choice of terms in itself – 'organ' with the connotation of dependence – is telling.

Kazansky, however, stressed the international community identity of the organs.[150] Anzilotti, on the other hand, saw 'international organs' as collective organs of states (rather than of the 'international community') and strongly emphasised the underlying inter-state agreement. Moreover, the single 'will' expressed by such an organ would not be *its* will, but rather the 'common will' of the states, for which it would be acting as an agent[151] – and as such it would be no sign of a separate identity. In his writings Anzilotti treated 'international organs' alongside state organs and

Gaetano Arangio-Ruiz, 'dualism revisited: international law and inter-individual law,' LXXXVI *Rivista di Diritto Internazionale* 2003, 909–999, at 928–945.

144 See above note 23 and accompanying text; the unilateral voluntarism proposed by Jellinek ultimately implies that a state can change its obligation by its individual will.

145 As proposed by Kelsen – cf above note 23 and below notes 153 and 194.

146 Nussbaum, above, note 12, 276–285; in relation to Georges Scelle in particular, cf Hubert Thierry, 'The Thought of Georges Scelle', 1 *European JIL* 1990, 193–209, at 194: 'Scelle was led during a period of 'legal regression' to construct a system of legal thought opposed to 'the dogmas and mystical beliefs of collective personality', to 'state tyrannies', to 'medieval anarchy'; on this epoch in general Martti Koskenniemi, *The Gentle Civilizer of Nations*, 2002, at 266–352 ('International Law as Sociology: France 1871–1930').

147 Hence the position of 'treaty organs' (section 2.2.1 above) in the general system is problematic, as is the conclusion of treaties by formal UN organs, such as the UNHCR and the UNDP (before that became a specialised agency).

148 Cf Seidl-Hohenveldern and Stein, below, note 155, at 181, who use the expression 'Organe der Völkerrechtsgemeinschaft.'

149 Both, in contemporary terms, the 'society' and the 'community' view; section 3.2.2 above, note 42.

150 Above note 42.

151 As pointed out by El-Erian, *First report*... above, note 82, at 164.

pertinent legal tenets such as agency.[152] Kelsen spoke of 'organs of the international community', and although he did recognise an international community established by treaty (in fact several, depending on different treaties) which would be equipped with organs, he made no mention of a separate legal identity.[153]

Otherwise, the League of Nations, created as an organisation with universal aspirations both in membership and field of operation, raised entirely new questions as to legal status and classification. While these questions were never judicially examined, as they were in relation to the United Nations shortly after its establishment, they did engage legal scholarship of the time.[154]

For a valuation of the League a limited number of categories could serve as a frame of reference: alliances, administrative unions (*Zweckverbände*), and (con)federations.[155] Several authors considerd the League to be a confederation, on the basis of an accepted definition, formulated by Jellinek, which seemed neatly to cover the new organisation.[156] This had the advantage of safeguarding the territorial parameter. However, in the view of Oppenheim, who analyzed the League of Nations in one of his last writings, the League qualified neither as 'a super-state, nor a confederation of States, nor an Alliance'; and by a process of elimination he reached the conclusion that it was an entity *sui generis*.[157]

For the League, its separate identity at an institutional level was undisputed, in both an internal and an external[158] context. But because of its pervasive role in international life, the need for a general legal interpretation of the League (and in its wake that of other international organisations) now became more urgent. Thus the question of the organisation's position and status in the international legal order – the question of 'legal personality'[159] – became explicit. Although no explict distinction was made between institutional independence and legal personality, there

[152] Dionisio Anzilotti, *Cours de droit international*, 1929, at 283, 284.

[153] Hans Kelsen, *Principles of International Law*, 1952, at 172; see El-Erian, *First report...* above, note 82, at 164, for a brief overview.

[154] See eg Lassa Oppenheim, 'Le caractère essentiel de la société des nations', 26 *RGDIP* 1919, 234–244; Percy Corbett, 'What is the League of Nations?', 5 *British YIL* 1924, 119-148. Cf also Johannes Verzijl, *International Law in Historical Perspective*, Part VI, 1973, at 303.

[155] These classic models eg in the survey of subjects in Ignaz Seidl-Hohenveldern and Torsten Stein, *Völkerrecht*, 2000, at 133–180.

[156] Georg Jellinek, *Allgemeine Staatslehre*, 1890, chapter XXI ('permanent union of independent states, based on agreement, and having for its object the protection of the territory of those statesand the preservation of peace between them'); see Corbett, above, note 154, at 121, for references to writers who refer to Jellinek.

[157] Oppenheim, above, note 154, at 241; Corbett: '[M]ust we, like Oppenheim, ... accept the surrender of his sui generis?' (above, note 154, at 119).

[158] See section 3.3.1 above for the League's treaty-making practice.

[159] Previously addressed systematically by very few, such as Fiore; see above, note 87.

was now clearly a different take on the matter – witness the attempts to identify the League with recognised legal persons in international law.

The question was approached in various ways, reflecting the range of opinions on legal personality in general.[160] These can be roughly divided into the school which sees states as *a priori* the sole subjects of international law and employs a 'threshold definition' of legal personality, on the one hand, and the school which proceeds from an open class of international law subjects (with an ensuing inclination to *infer* legal personality from factual juristic acts), on the other. Oppenheim eventually attributed a degree of legal personality to the Organization, apparently inferring such from rights and obligations *de facto* present in the Organization.[161] Jellinek, on the other hand, *a priori* dismissed the possibility of personality for entities other than states.[162] The general climate for the appreciation of international institutions was increasingly favourable, but the image of legal personality for non-state entities remained controversial. Percy Corbett, writing in 1924, noted that Continental lawyers showed great interest in the matter but displayed 'an extraordinary diversity of views on the subject'. Anglo-Saxon scholars, on the other hand, 'practically ignored' the debate.[163] Bederman has also pointed to this trend, which is something of a cliché in legal history: Continental scholars generally were attempting to fit international organisations in the existing matrix, while Anglo-American scholars were adopting a pragmatic approach.[164]

If and when legal personality in relation to non-state entities was considered, doctrine borrowed from domestic law to describe the new developments. Next to the distinction between original and derived legal subjects, this engendered a distinction between the 'natural' (or physical) person and the artificial or 'corporate' person.[165] On the international plane the natural person could be said to have its counterpart in the state, the primary subject of international law,[166] whereas legal or corporate

[160] See for authors pro (Oppenheim, Bonfils and Fauchile, and Schucking and Wehberg) and contra (Huber and Rolin) personality of the League, Corbett, above, note 154, at 120, 121 in his footnote 3.

[161] Oppenheim, above, note 154: at 239: 'Les droits et les devoirs respectifs de la Societé et des États qui en sont membres sont par la plupart définis par le pacte de la Societé.' – see section 4.2.2 below on the dialectic relation between de facto capacities and 'legal personality'.

[162] Jellinek, above, note 22, at 49 ('Völkerrechtliche Subjecte sind nur Staaten.'); Cf El-Erian, *First report…* above, note 82, at 180, for a reference to several authors pro and contra organisations' legal personality.

[163] Corbett, above, note 154, at 120 and references.

[164] Bederman, above, note 54, at 278.

[165] See eg Alexander Nekam, *The Personality Conception of the Legal Entity*, 1938; Mosler, 'Subjects…', above, note 95. NB. that in accordance with usage in international law in the present text 'legal person', as synonymous with 'legal subject', is meant to refer to any subject, biological and corporate, 'original' and 'derived' alike.

[166] See section 3.1 above.

persons (or, in the words of Gierke,[167] 'collective personalities') would be the secondary subjects of international law with 'derived' personality. This was the starting point for any discussion on legal personality of organisations, notwithstanding a by that time articulate critique of the concept of legal person[168] and of the state as a legal person.[169]

The Cape Spartel Lighthouse Commission mentioned above[170] became a test case when it had to be established whether the Commission possessed civil personality for the purpose of concluding contracts with the administration of the Tangier Zone.[171] Because of the limited membership of the Lighthouse Commission, the Cape Spartel case more poignantly put the question of legal personality. The Legal Advisor of the International Zone of Tangier was charged with an examination of the Commission's legal status in 1929. His analysis reached a comparatively large readership, as an English summary of his report appeared in the *American Journal of International Law* in 1931:

> Is the International Commission of Cape Spartel Lighthouse, in the first place, a juristic person in public international law? This very delicate question is related to the somewhat debatable theory as to the existence of international personalities, other than states.[172]

It is significant that for Counselor Marchegiano, as a learned practioner, the *Vereinbarung* and the *Gemeinwille*,[173] and the notion of international legal personality of organisations as conceived by Pasquale Fiore,[174] seem to have been central concepts.[175] After considering the different legal

[167] See section 3.2.2 above.

[168] Cf, in general, Nekam, above, note 165; cf section 4.2.1 below.

[169] Eg Kelsen, above, note 23, at 181–188 (the state is not an organic nor even a social reality), at 377 (on the false analogy between individuals and states). For Kelsen the entire notion of 'legal personality' lacked legal reality and was an auxiliary concept at best: Kelsen, *General theory*... above, note 23, at 185–186; cf Gilson, above, note 23, at 31–32.

[170] Sections 3.2.2 and 3.3.1 above.

[171] The story of the Commission asserting independence can be found in Bederman, above, note 54, at 331 in particular.

[172] Giuseppe Marchegiano, 'The Juristic Character of the International Commission of Cape Spartel Lighthouse', 25 *American JIL* 1931, 339–347, at 339.

[173] Above notes 84 and 85; cf eg Dendias, above, note 37. Apart from references to, in particular, Jellinek (eg at 248), Marchegiano's conclusions on an overriding collective 'will' of international administrative unions clearly follow up on the ideas of Triepel. It should be noted that Triepel's *Völkerrecht und Landesrecht*, 1890 was translated into French only 30 years later (*Droit international et droit interne*, 1920).

[174] Note that Fiore takes into consideration 'associations of states' as subject of the law of treaties, in a quite modern wording: 'Capacité sera également reconnue aux associations qui se sont vu attribuer la personalité internationale. Elle ne leur appartiendra toutefois que dans les limites résultant de la fin et du but pour lesquels leur personalité a été reconnue [. . .]' (Pasquale Fiore, *Le droit international codifié et sa sanction juridique*, 1890, § 681 at 243; cf § 36 at 90). See section 3.2.2 above; see below note 197.

[175] Explicitly elaborated upon by Marchegiano in his original study of the Cape Spartel Lighthouse Commission, as recounted in detail by Bederman, above, note 54, at 343–349.

appearances of the Commission ('international servitude' and an 'internationalised territory' – inspired by the territorial element in the Lighthouse regime, related to the Tangier zone), Marchegiano did conclude that the Lighthouse Commission was an 'international organisation', and with separate legal personality. Interestingly, he seemingly based this conclusion on *de facto* legal capacities (inferred from factual independent activity) on the part of the Commission.[176]

Although at this point perhaps no general agreement existed – an impression reinforced by the fact that analytical categories were not always clear – doctrine was opening up. An institutional independent identity, both for internal and external purposes, was now an acceptable image. In addition the idea of legal personality – as in the case of the Cape Spartel – took root, although it remained controversial. The debate on the legal identity of organisations as a whole proceeded from the law of treaties paradigm, and therewith a strictly consensualist basis. Also Pasquale Fiore (who, as Bederman points out, had been the first to outline a general functional theory of international organisations)[177] saw the possible legal personality of international organisations ('associations') as strictly subjective and effective only vis-à-vis states that recognised it.[178]

Otherwise, the state of international law in general posed some barriers to the new developments. The doctrinal division between primary and secundary legal persons underscored the functional nature of organisations for the benefit of states – whose own functional and fictional nature had disappeared from view in the nineteenth century.[179] The dichotomy of national-international law made it difficult to envisage an international organisation as being anything else but an essentially open structure, belonging entirely to the realm of general international law. Finally, the nature and the cohesion of the international legal order was a cause for debate in itself.[180] For instance Dendias saw only an 'administrative order', while Heller saw no order at all but a 'vacuum' in which equals deal with each other.[181]

Nonetheless, it seems that the League was a catalyst in the conceptualisation of legal personality for non-state entities. El-Erian, writing his Report in 1963, mentions Anzilotti as a conspicuous example of a change

[176] 'From another point of view also the juristic personality of the Commisison in the domain of international law is clearly manifested in its relations with the Shereefian government, and with those of the powers represented in Morocco [...]' (Marchegiano, above, note 172, at 342.

[177] Above, note 54, at 345.

[178] Pasquale Fiore, *Il diritto internazionale codificato*, 1890, § 82.

[179] See also section 3.1. Cf Martti Koskenniemi, 'The Wonderful Artificiality of States', in *American Society of International Law Proceedings* 1994, 1995, 22–29.

[180] Cf above, note 42, and notes 148 and 149 and accompanying text.

[181] Dendias, above, note 37.

of heart in this respect. In 1904 the author categorically repudiated the possibility of organisations' personality; in 1929 he cautioned against limiting legal personality to states.[182] El-Erian also recalls the 'guarded pronouncement' in the Oppenheim-McNair edition of 1928,[183] next to the 'categorical pronouncement' in the Oppenheim-Lauterpacht edition of 1955 – in which Lauterpacht wrote that 'the predominant opinion was that the League of Nations [...] was a subject of international law'.[184]

Some time after judges Spender and Fitzmaurice in their Joint Dissenting Opinion in the South West Africa cases would state that:

> [...] it is by no means certain that in 1920 . . . international legal opinion would have accepted the conclusion arrived at by the present Court in the Injuries to United Nations Servants case . . . that international organizations could have legal personality separate and distinct from that of their Members, and rank as entities 'subjects of international law.[185]

The Court, in its judgment in the Second Phase, made the proviso that:

> [t]he foregoing conclusions hold good whether the League is regarded as having possessed the kind of corporate legal personality that the Court . . . found the United Nations to be invested with, – or whether the League is regarded as a collectivity of States functioning on an institutional basis, whose collective rights in respect of League matters were, as in Article 2 of the Covenant implied, exercisable only through the appropriate League organs, and not independently of these.[186]

Some aspects of the early twentieth-century scholarly debate on the legal nature of international organisations, notably of the League, are especially noteworthy in the present context. First, a somewhat elusive trait of the discussion on legal personality is the lack of distinction between the internal and the external manifestations of an organisation. The organisation *is* recognised as a centralised, independent structure – hence the interest in the category of the 'law-making treaty' or *Vereinbarung* and in the *Gemeinwillen* in connection with international institutions. But the logical next step of a distinction between the internal order of the organisation and the general legal order in which it conducts its 'external relations', is not taken. Competences of the organisation with regard to

[182] El-Erian, *First report...* above, note 82, at 179, 180, § 152.
[183] Oppenheim-McNair, *International Law* (4th edn), Vol I, 1928, at 321.
[184] Oppenheim-Lauterpacht, *International Law* (8th edn), Vol I, 1955, at 384. A similar development in the view on individuals as objects/subjects; cf the well-known transition in the Oppenheim editions from a category of international legal subjects that is limited to states (1912 edn) to one which may also include individuals (1958 edition); relevant pages of the two editions reproduced in: Louis Sohn and Thomas Buergenthal (eds), *International Protection of Human Rights*, 1973, at 1–8.
[185] *South West Africa cases* (Preliminary Objections), ICJ Rep 1962, 318, at 475.
[186] ICJ Reports 1966, 5, at 30.

member states (Danube Commission) and legal acts vis-à-vis third states (the agreements concluded *by* the League) are treated without differentiation, as they apparently are conceptualised as part of the same set of rules. The inherent contradictions in this line of argument led to a somewhat circular discussion. If organisations were *not* considered to constitute a separate legal order (the semi-closed aspect of the institutional veil), they would be equated with their constitutive treaty. This would bring in the precept of *pacta tertiis*, which meant that organisations such as the League would not be able to conclude treaties with non-member states. For the system to explain that the League *did* conclude such treaties (see section 3.3.1 above) the institutional rules of the organisation would have to be designated as to some extent separate from international, inter-state law. But doctrine was not ready to accept this premise, so that institutional rules were regarded as general international law, etc. This stalemate during the interbellum gave rise to intense scholarly discussion. When it came up again for the UN in the *Reparation case* of 1949 the International Court of Justice chose a drastic way out by establishing objective personality on the basis of an unprecedented 'constitutional' line of argument (see section 4.2.4 below).

Second, a distinction between institutional independence and 'legal personality' is not made explicit, although at the same time 'legal personality' is clearly set apart as a legal qualification – perhaps even more so than in later years (see Chapter 4 below) because any line of argument taking organisations beyond their form of state-based, open structures, would be a conscious decision.

Third, it appears that 'organisations' were not considered as one formal category in the same way as they are now. Rather than concentrating on the formal characteristics of an institution as a determining factor, observers took a material and casuistic approach. The League was perceived as an entirely new phenomenon. Whereas it would now be common to trace back the League of Nations to nineteenth-century institutions,[187] clearly this was not self-evident for writers of the period. Rather, they focused on the political roots of the League, in the inter-state co-operation of the Allied Forces during World War I.[188] Thus, Oppenheim did not turn to examine the institutional traits of the nineteenth-century public unions, since '[the League's] constitutional organs as well as its functions are

[187] See eg Claude (above, note 27), Archer (above, note 27), Bowett-Sands (above, note 27).

[188] '. . .the institutions of the League were fashioned by the immediate experience of war-time co-operation rather than by seventeenth-century writers . . .' as put by Archer (above, note 21, at 21) – who is more radical in his valuation of influence of the War period than eg Claude (above, note 27).

equally without precedent'.[189] Likewise Corbett held that the League could not be compared to the administrative unions (*Zweckverbände*) both in the variety and the nature of its tasks.[190]

Legal personality can be linked to specific legal capacities in various ways (see section 4.2.2 below). The fact that organisations – notably the League of Nations – actually performed independent legal acts (in particular, concluded international agreements (see section 3.3.1 above)), caused a new interest in the legal capacity to conclude treaties. This shift of focus also made it possible to bypass the dilemma of legal personality.[191] Individual 'capacities' were more convenient as an analytical tool, because they seemed more susceptible to inductive reasoning; they were – and are – usually *presumed* in case of concrete acts, such as the conclusion of agreements, unless rebutted (as is shown in the *Reparation case*, where the Court argues that because the UN has performed certain legal acts, it must be deemed to have the capacity to do so – see section 4.2.4 below).

But a powerful counteracting image was of course that of legal capacity, and the capacity to conclude international agreements in particular, being strictly linked to sovereignty and thereby reserved to states. This was expressed by the Permanent Court of International Justice in the *Wimbledon* Case: '[. . .] la faculté de contracter des engagements internationaux est *précisement* un attribut de la souverainété de l'Etat'.[192]

In general, however, in the interwar period the tenet of sovereignty was extenuated.[193] For example Anzilotti presented an alternative construct in which legal capacity is not an attribute of sovereignty but an attribute of international legal subjectivity.[194] This may be taken as the seed of an 'objective theory' of attribution,[195] which opened up international law for other legal actors. The spirit of the time is also reflected in the Advisory Opinion on the *Jurisdiction of the Courts of Danzig*, in which the

189 Oppenheim, above, note 154, at 238.

190 Corbett, above, note 154, at 147.

191 Cf Clive Parry, 'The Treaty-Making Power of the United Nations', 26 *British YIL* 1949, 108–150, at 108.

192 Although the possibility of non-sovereign entities having this *faculté* is not excluded, especially the French formula strongly suggests as much (the English text is less assertive: '[. . .] the right of entering into international engagements is an attribute of State sovereignty.'); PCIJ, Ser A, No 1, 1923, at 25 (emphasis added). Reaffirmed in the Advisory Opinion on the *Exchange of Greek and Turkish Populations*, PCIJ, Ser. B, No. 10, 1925, at p 21. For the view of writers, see eg Karl Strupp, 'Les règles générales du droit de la paix', 47 RdC 1934, at p 420.

193 Which is where section 3.1 above, on the state, left off.

194 See Dionisio Anzilotti, *Corso di Diritto Internazionale*, 1929, at 122, 339, 340, 352–356; cf on the relativity, or the coventionality of the concept of state sovereignty, in that period Hans Kelsen, *Das Problem der Souveränität*, 1928 ('...daβ Souveränität eine 'historische Kategorie'sei,' at 4); Verdross, above, note 85, in particular at 118. See also Hermann Mosler, 'Völkerrecht als Rechtsordnung', 6–46, in Hermann Mosler (ed) *Völkerrecht als rechtsordnung: Grundlagen und Quellen*, 1976, at 8–11.

195 See sections 4.2.1 and 4.2.2 below.

Permanent Court held that an international agreement might contain 'some definite rules creating individual rights and obligations.'[196]

The question of treaty-making capacity in particular was addressed by those concerned with codification of the law of treaties. Around the turn of the century there were several public and private initiatives in this field.[197] Some years after the unrewarding endeavours of the Committee of Experts of the League of Nations,[198] a widely acclaimed attempt at the codification of the law of treaties was presented by the Harvard Law School.[199] The 1935 Harvard *Draft Convention on the Law of Treaties* excludes from its scope subjects of international law other than states.[200] This was achieved by limiting the (working) definition of 'treaty', rather than the scope of the Draft as a whole (as was done in the 1969 Vienna Convention). The Commentary explains:

'Since the League of Nations is not a State, an instrument to which it is a party *would not be a treaty* as the term is used in this Convention. [. . .] Because of their abnormal character and the difficulty of formulating general rules which would seem applicable to a class of instruments which are distinctly *sui generis*, it seems desirable that they should be excluded from the scope of this Convention [. . .].'[201]

This approach aimed to reconcile the imperative of a state-based international system with the practice of international relations in a different manner. It allowed for non-state institutions to perform *legal* acts (and for the possible inference of 'legal personality'), but it gave these acts a different status from acts performed by states. This view found wide

[196] Dantzig case in PCIJ, Ser B, No 15, 1928, at 17.

[197] See eg Field's Draft Code of 1876, Bluntschli's Draft Code of 1881, the 1889 Draft Code by Pasquale Fiore, the 1927 draft (on treaties) of the International Commission of American Jurists, the 1928 Havana Convention on Treaties; sections of these texts are reproduced in the Appendices to the Harvard Draft, see below note 199. See also Reuter, *Introduction...*, above, note 34, at 29–30.

[198] The question of (the procedural aspect of) 'international conferences and the conclusion and drafting of international treaties', which initially figured on the list of subjects 'ripe for codification' prepared by the Committee (LoN Doc C198 M.72) for purposes of the 1930 Codification Conference, was eventually abandoned by the Assembly of the League; several states, such as Germany, Japan and the United States, had expressed doubts as to the feasibility of codification of the law of treaties altogether; see minutes reproduced in Shabtai Rosenne (ed), *League of Nations: Committee of experts for the Progressive Codification of International Law [1925–1928]*, 1973, Vol. I, at 236, 266, 285, 335, 346; and Documents in Vol. II, at p 313 (governments' replies to a questionnaire on the matter at pp 153–308); and Rosenne, above, note 105 (Resolution adopted by the LoN Assembly at 27/IX/1927, reproduced at p ix).

[199] Harvard Law School, Research in International Law, III (Law of Treaties), the 36 draft Articles are reproduced in a Supplement to 29 *American JIL* 1935, pp 655–1226.

[200] Article 1 reads: 'As the term is used in this Convention: (a) A 'Treaty' is a formal instrument of agreement by which two or more States establish or seek to establish a relation under international law between themselves. [. . .] (c) The term 'Treaty' does not include an instrument to which a person other than a State is or may be a party.'

[201] Commentary to Art 1(a), above, note 199, at 692, emphasis added.

acceptance, judging from the fact that most lawyers carefully observed a terminological distinction between 'agreements' concluded by organisations, and 'treaties' or 'conventions' concluded by states, insisting that this reflect a formal difference.[202]

This distinction was en vogue for some time after World War II, and traces are found in the Vienna Conventions. But, as Corbett observed already in 1924, 'there is a point in the examination of any institution where it becomes impossible even for the lawyer to dismiss an inelegant development with the familiar distinction between the law and the fact'.[203]

[202] Professor Parry modified his views on the matter with the rise of UN practice (above, note 191).

[203] Corbett, above, note 154, at 119.

4

The United Nations Era

THE PRESENT CHAPTER looks at the position of international organisations in the period after 1945. The post-war international organisations and their role in international legal relations are briefly addressed in section 4.1. Section 4.2 treats different legal perspectives on the image of international organisations as independent actors. This chapter takes a more technical approach than Chapter 3 does with respect to the pre-war period, focusing on the concept of legal personality and the way it has been construed in relation to international organisations. 'Legal personality' is the vehicle for conceptualising any entity – an individual, organisation, corporation – as a legal actor. With the separate identity of organisations becoming more prominent, legal personality has become a focal point of doctrinal and theoretical discussion (which, however, does not include the philosophical foundations of the concept and use of legal personality[1]). As is clear from the following, this discussion is shaped all along by the transparent appearance of organisations – as both 'open' and 'closed' – and by the limitations of international law to address such transparency, although this is never rendered explicit. This chapter gives a detailed analysis of this discussion,

4.1 INSTITUTIONS

This chapter does not aim to give a taxonomy of contemporary international organisations, as these are documented and analysed in several outstanding sources.[2] A good overview may be gained from the *Yearbook*

[1] For an examination of the philosophical foundations of 'international legal personality', including the various moral perspectives which determine the meaning attributed to this concept by different authors from Leibniz onwards, see Janne E Nijman, *The Concept of International Legal Personality: An Inquiry into the History and the Theory of International Law*, 2004.

[2] See, for general textbooks on the law of international organisation(s), Inis L Claude, *Swords into Ploughshares: The Problems and Progress of International Organization*, 1971; CF Amerasinghe, *Principles of Institutional Law of International Organizations*, 1996; Ignaz Seidl-Hohenveldern and Gerhard Loibl, *Das Recht der Internationalen Organisationen einschließlich der Supranationalen Gemeinschaften*, 2000; Philippe Sands and Pierre Klein,

of International Organization, which in 2005 (on the basis of the criteria mentioned above)[3] listed 246 intergovernmental organisations, one of which is a federation of international organisations; 34 of which are universal membership organisations; 33 of which are intercontinental membership organisations; and 178 of which are organisations of regionally oriented membership.[4] Of course, these 246 institutions can be classified in any of the ways mentioned above (see section 2.2.2); but such classifications will not reflect differences in the position of organisations in general international law.

In the United Nations era, which for the present purpose may (as yet) be taken as a 'period', international organisations have become more prominent as international legal actors. This is apparent from the fact that organisations are now performing legal acts in various fields – they bring claims (with the 1949 *Reparation* case as a hallmark); they dispatch diplomatic delegations; they send out military missions *and* assume independent responsibility for damage arising in the course of these missions.[5] It is also clear from the fact that organisations are explicitly considered addressees of (prospective) conventional legal norms, such as in the field of immunities[6] and of international responsibility,[7] as well as of customary norms.[8] Arguably the conclusion of treaties can count as the most

Bowett's Law of International Institutions, 2001; Jan Klabbers, *An Introduction to International Institutional Law*, 2002; Henry Schermers and Niels Blokker, *International Intitutional Law*, 2003; Nigel White, *The Law of International Organizations*, 2005; a comprehensive study, in which IGOs are considered from an institutional ('open') viewpoint, but studied as to their effect on normative processes in general international law, is José Alvarez, *International Organizations as Law-Makers*, 2006.

[3] Section 2.2.1 above.

[4] The *Yearbook of International Organization 2004-2005*, München, Saur, 2005; http://www.uia.org/ and https://www.diversitas.org/db/x.php; the *Yearbook*'s statistical section in Vol. 5 contains a wealth of information on IGOs, NGOs, multilateral arrangements, national bodies, etc., and as such does justice to the notorious variety of structures and levels of governance in current international life. The numbers reported here are comparatively low, as they relate to the UIA group of 'conventional international bodies', which is slightly stricter than the definition proposed in this book.

[5] Eg NATO has compensated approximately $40,000 to a Bulgarian family for damage to their house by a deflected missile during the Kosovo campaign (*Trouw* 3-VIII-2000). See Schermers and Blokker, above, note 2, §§ 1582–1583; also Marten Zwanenburg, *Accountability under International Humanitarian Law for UN and NATO Peace Support Operations*, 2003.

[6] 'Status, privileges and immunities of international organizations...'. The decision of the Commission to commence 'the second part of the topic of Relations with International Organizations' was taken in 1976. The topic was discontinued in 1992 (endorsed by UNGA Res.47/33 of 25 November 1992).

[7] YILC 2003, Vol II (Part Two), at 29 ff. In 2000 the Commission has decided to include the topic 'Responsibility of international organisations' in its long-term programme of work.

[8] 'Organizations are subjects of international law and, as such, are bound by any obligations incumbent upon them under general rules of international law...'. (Opinion concerning *The Interpretation of the Agreement of 25 March 1951 between the WHO and Egypt*; ICJ Rep 1980, 73, at 89–90).

significant expression of an independent legal identity, as in the pre-War period. This is so, not only because organisations conclude many treaties, but also because almost all organisations conclude at least one treaty, namely a headquarters agreement.[9] The treaty-making practice of organisations will be addressed separately in Chapter 7. The codification of legal rules regarding such treaties is the subject of Part Three of this book.

4.2 LEGAL IMAGES

The growing importance of organisations has been accompanied by a progressively intricate doctrinal debate. The image of organisations as having a separate legal order has been cause for a new interest in the institutional characteristics of international organisations, which in turn has lead to the birth of the 'law of international organisations', or 'international institutional law', as a branch of legal studies.[10] However, the developing role of organisations as independent international actors has entailed some complex questions which need to be addressed from the perspective of general international law. Within the positivist paradigm such a role is inextricably linked to the legal fiction of 'personality'.[11] While the term has connotations of sterile academic discussion, it is also the vehicle for the conceptualisation of actors, especially new actors, in international law and as such a powerful trope (to use Bederman's reference) and analytical tool.

The present section discusses the concept of legal personality as it is generally used in relation to international organisations (section 4.2.1); the different approaches, or 'theories', with regard to the attribution of legal personality to organisations (section 4.2.2); and the specific question of the legal foundation of such personality (section 4.2.3). Finally, it treats the tenet of objective legal personality (section 4.2.4); and the notions of capacity and competence as used in relation to IGOs (section 4.2.5).

It is helpful to separate these issues, which represent different aspects of the creation of a legal identity. It also brings out clearly how the particular

[9] Whereas it is not the only legal framework possible; sometimes the member states will conclude an agreement with the host state for the benefit of the organisation. Benelux and the Danube Committee are examples of IGOs without a host state agreement; see Schermers and Blokker, above, note 2, § 1690. An example of (parallel) national legislation functioning in lieu of a host state agreement is the statute law adopted in the Netherlands, in the same way as in 'host state' Austria, to ensure the staff of the OSCE with certain international privileges and immunities within the national legal order (mainly because OSCE as yet 'has' no legal personality (section 4.2.3 below)). See ch 7 below.

[10] See references above in note 2.

[11] Whatever the philosophical underpinnings (eg 'real' or 'fictitious' personality) may be – see section 3.1 above.

features of organisations as sketched in Chapter 2 (functionality, centralisation and transparency) are important factors in that process. In the practice of post-War international relations, organisations *are* participating on a wide scale. But at the same time, doctrine reveals how it is problematic to situate this participation in classic international law. The transparent image of organisations – an image shifting between open and closed – becomes more marked as the organisations' manifestation as an open forum for states, self-evident in the League of Nations era, now is squarely at odds with the organisations' separate legal identity.

4.2.1 The International Organisation as a Legal Person

Legal Personality in International Law

As a preliminary point, we recall that inside the system 'legal personality' is the attire which enables an entity to function in a legal order; more importantly, this attire is awarded by that same legal order, which determines which entities participate in its sphere and which do not. Legal personality cannot, by a candidate actor, unilaterally be bestowed upon itself.[12] If we take international law as a 'system'[13] or an 'order' – and most people in the legal trade do – in spite of its internal contradiction and fragmentation, this must also be how it works in international law.[14] Any legal order will decide which actors are allowed to participate *in jure* and which are not – whether this be done by written law or by a complex process of crystallisation of unwritten norms. This is how, for example, in Dutch law it is established that a group of people can perform juristic acts when assuming the shape of a co-operative society, but not when acting as a group of neighbours from the same street. Or in international law that the Holy See is a legal person, whereas Greenpeace – for now – is not.

The term and concept of 'legal personality' have generated a wealth of literature, proceeding from the theory of (international) bodies corporate,

[12] A basic tenet, expressed for example by Karl Zemanek – be it in a slightly different context: 'Keine Erscheinung der Tatsachenwelt ist a priori Person im Rechtssinn. Sie wird es erst dadurch, daß eine bestimmte Rechtsordnung sie als solche bezeichnet'. (*Das Vertragsrecht der internationalen Organizationen*, 1957, at 20); also eg Daniel O'Connell, *International Law*, 1965, at 89: 'Only the rules of law can determine this, and they may select different entities…'.

[13] In the generic sense of 'a set or assemblage of things connected, associated, or interdependent, so as to form a complex unity' (*Oxford English Dictionary*, 2nd edn, 1989).

[14] In a general sense, Philip Allott, *The Health of Nations: Society and Law beyond the State,* 2002, at 297: '[international constitutional law] confers on artificial persons, including the state-societies, the capacity to act as parties to international legal relations'.

or from a catalogue of 'legal subjects' in the system of international law; or from the study of specific legal 'capacities', such as treaty-making or the right to bring a claim.[15]

The definition of 'legal person', used as synonymous with 'legal subject', has been couched in terms of an actual condition – 'bearer of rights and duties in (international) law' – or, more often, in terms of a predisposition – 'possessing the quality of being endowed with legal capacity'.[16]

The term 'legal personality' in international law has been rightly described as 'nebulous',[17] but as a basic, nominal definition it is apparently employed without difficulty. As a more extensive, explanatory definition, the term appears to have different meanings. On the one hand it is used to imply specific legal capacities. Legal personality would for example always imply 'capacity to conclude treaties'. On the other hand it is used as an abstract quality or an empty predicate. Any actor bearing any legal rights or duties would be a 'legal person'. The term seems to be used most generally in the latter sense.[18] It is difficult to see how this could be otherwise, if only because in international law parlance 'legal person' has come to refer also to individuals.[19]

Legal personality in this sense is often *inferred from* the apparent presence of concrete legal capacities, which then serve as indicia. More generally the predicate 'legal personality' in international law carries a complication – arguably because the dual function of normativity and descriptivity presents itself more clearly in international law than in centralised national law (most domestic legal systems will set out by law explicitly which entities qualify as (corporate) legal persons). At times

[15] An example of the first is Alexander Nekam, *The Personality Conception of the Legal Entity*, 1938; of the second eg Chris Okeke, *Controversial Subjects of Contemporary International Law: An Examination of the New Entities of International Law and Their Treaty-Making Capacity*, 1974; of the third, Jean Huber, *Le droit de conclure des traités internationaux*, 1951; Jan Willem Schneider, *Treaty-Making Power of International Organizations*, 1959; Hungdah Chiu, *The Capacity of International Organizations to Conclude Treaties, and the Special Legal Aspects of the Treaties so Concluded*, 1966, who proceed from the treaty-making capacity of IGOs, however largely treat the same legal questions as those who concentrate on 'personality'.

[16] Hermann Mosler, 'Subjects of International Law', 7 *EPIL* 1984, 442–459, at 443 on synonymity of 'subject' and 'person' in post-war doctrine. Cf also Malcolm Shaw, *International Law*, 2003, at 177: 'territorial entities [...] treated as possessing the *capacity to become* international persons' (emphasis added). With regard to IGOs in particular, the 1949 Opinion in the *Reparation* case, below note 43 and accompanying text.

[17] Cf White, above, note 2 (1st edn), ch 3.

[18] In the following, 'legal personality' will be used in the latter sense, unless another meaning is clear from the text. The term 'limited legal personality' indicates a limitation on the full range of capacities found in a state, but it does not clarify the double meaning.

[19] In most textbooks the fact that individuals are directly addressed by international legal norms is expressed with the term 'legal personality'. A well-known milestone was the change in legal assesment of individuals in the Oppenheim editions since 1912 (above, section 3.3.2, notes 183 and 184).

'legal personality' works as a threshold – proceeding from an established catalogue of international legal subjects, which keeps actors from being considered as a subject of international law regardless of their actions at the international plane – and at others it merely is an *ex post* qualification on the basis of apparently performed legal acts.

Currently there seems to be agreement on adopting the threshold approach vis-à-vis NGOs – whatever signs of international legal practice these may show[20] – and these are thus generally excluded from the catalogue of international legal persons. With respect to private companies, on the other hand, doctrine appears to be in a state of flux, with some authors *a priori* excluding companies from the list of legal subjects,[21] and others taking a pragmatic, inductive approach, describing companies as 'international legal persons' to the degree these perform legally relevant acts in international practice.[22]

Both approaches have at some stage played a role with respect to international organisations,[23] but the first one became instantly obsolete when the UN was declared an international legal person in the *Reparation* case.

As to the *idea* of personality, the 'real personality theory' lost its leading role at the beginning of the twentieth century[24] – that is, before the development of international organisation truly took off.[25] Legal personality thus was no longer regarded as the flip side of a metaphysical identity, but as a fictional and conventional understanding.[26] Even though the acknowledgement of the fictional character of the 'legal personality' of the

[20] Cf the external relations of prominent NGOs such as Amnesty International, and of *sui generis* entities such as the Red Cross. There is a practice of concluding agreements which could be seen as 'international(ised)', but which are generally phrased to remain outside both national law and international law; cf the agreements concluded by FAO with Greenpeace (on file with the author), which are 'governed by general principles of law'.

[21] Cf Shaw, who excludes 'transnational corporations' but does mention them as potential candidates for 'acquiring' international legal personality. Cf the attempts to set up international directives to this effect such as the OECD Guidelines for Multinational Enterprises (see Shaw, above, note 16, at 224, footnote 238 for the Guidelines).

[22] See for example the general textbook by Martin Dixon (*Textbook on International Law* (5th edn), 2005), who on the basis of the fact that legal relations between states and corporations can be 'internationalised' (as was at issue in the 1976 *Texaco v Lybia* case) concludes that such multinational enterprises have a certain degree of 'functional' legal personality (at 116, 117). Likewise, he holds that internationalised contracts 'should properly be regarded as a treaty' (at 54, 55). But see the description of the oil concessions case in EPIL I 1992, 715–721. Cf also White, above, note 2, at 57–58, on 'factual' and 'legal' personality (referring to the de facto power to influence *versus* legal powers to exercise), and the desirability of the two coinciding.

[23] See on the inter-war period, section 3.3 above.

[24] See Bernard Gilson, *The Conceptual System of Sovereign Equality*, 1984, at 23–38; cf section 3.1 above, note 24; cf also O'Connell, above, note 12, at 89–91.

[25] Section 3.2 above.

[26] Cf O'Connell, above, note 12, at 90, on 'the tremendous pressures of Hegelian or positivist philosophies underlying each of these positions;' cf section 3.1 above, note 24.

state was not taken to challenge the social reality of the state, it did bring some flexibility into legal subjects doctrine – thus creating a more open climate for the conceptualisation of organisations as subjects of international law.

At the same time, the concept of legal personality as such sets a rather rigid framework. For one thing it operates on the rights–duties construal – which has been criticised in various quarters, for example because the vision of law as a 'dynamic process' would leave no room for the subject–object dichotomy,[27] or because the very distinction cannot be upheld on epistemological grounds.[28] Second, the 'legal person' is an anthropomorphous concept – envisaging a 'bearer' of rights and duties. This notion has been subject to criticism for being a logical fallacy[29] and with the argument that 'social science explanations should only be made in terms of [human] individuals'.[30] A third factor, and perhaps the most practically relevant in the present context, is that current doctrine maintains the traditional distinction between 'original' legal persons (that is creatures presumed to exist in a social reality preceding the law subsequently created by them) and 'derived' or 'secondary' legal persons. In international law, this distinction has fixed the hierarchy of states and other legal subjects, including international organisations.

Legal Personality in Relation to International Organisations

The concept of international legal personality is not the only, nor necessarily the central, notion in the study of international organisations.[31] Various fields of debate – on the role of organisations as infrastructures for the decision-making of states; on organisations as institutional structures; on organisations as part of a diffuse network and process of policy-making

[27] Cf Higgins, on the positivist distinction between subjects and objects and the construct of subjects 'possessing rights and duties': 'we have erected an intellectual prison of our own choosing and then declared it to be an unalterable constraint' (Rosalyn Higgins, *Problems and Process: International Law And How We Use It*, 1994, at 50).

[28] A point pressed by critical theory; these critiques have been mostly focussed on the problematic concept of the 'object' – eg James Boyle, 'Is Subjectivity Possible? The Postmodern Subject In Legal Theory' (62 *University of Colorado Law Review* 1991, 489–517) concentrates on the 'subject' (and concludes that already a multi-faced, 'post-modern' concept exists).

[29] Nekam, above, note 15 ('pseudo-logical mind of man').

[30] Hans Kelsen, *General Theory of the Law and the State*, 1945, at 93–109 ('animism'); a definition of 'methodological individualism' eg in Fernando Teson, 'The Kantian Theory of International Law', in 92 *Columbia L Rev* 1992, 53–102, at 54, footnote 5. See also above, ch 3, notes 23 and 168, 169 and accompanying text. A comprehensive study of the *concept* of international legal personality from a historical-theoretical perspective in Nijman, above, note 1.

[31] See in general White, above, note 2, at 1–22, and Alvarez, above, note 2, at 17–57, for a survey of how different theories of law address international organisation(s).

and law-creation; or on organisations as possible rivals of states and tools for global governance – may call for a different approach.

For example David Bederman proposes a more flexible outlook: 'While international lawyers continue to describe international institutions with the tired, traditional metaphor of "personality", the states that are members of those institutions, the people who staff and serve them, and the empirical and theoretical scholars who study them have come to see them in terms of "communities".'[32] This is a reference to the 'community of interest', a term employed by the Permanent Court when it referred to a collectivity of riparian states – *in casu* not an organisation – bound by a communal régime for international river law.[33]

The view that legal personality may, as 'a powerful legal trope',[34] obfuscate analysis is clearly a valid point. When the aim is to examine organisations as actors within the positive law framework, however, it has to be given a central place, as law firmly couples the ability independently to perform juristic acts with the fiction of legal personality.

To reiterate a point stated earlier, it is the legal order in which a candidate subject is to function which attributes legal personality. If we accept the presumption that international law qualifies as a 'legal order',[35] if we accept that it is that unified legal order in which different subjects are to co-exist and interact, and if we accept that the law of an international organisation is to some extent 'internal' (that is, distinct from general international law),[36] this is how the creation of legal personality for an international organisation would have to be imagined – however *legal* the process which created the organisation, and however prominent the constituent states as members of 'the international community' in their own right.

Thus Brownlie has observed: '[w]here there is no constitutional provision for, as it were, recognizing and registering associations as legal persons, the primary test is functional'.[37] This is not to say that it would be thus for the institution, or for the states which have created it, to decide on its legal capacity. Rather, it means that in absence of a formal test provided

[32] David Bederman, 'The Souls of International Organizations: Legal Personality and the Lighthouse at Cape Spartel', 36 *Virginia JIL* 1996, 275–377 at 371.

[33] Bederman, above, note 32, at 277–278; Territorial Jurisdiction of the International Commission of the River Oder, PCIJ 1929 (Ser A, No 23), No 16, at 27. Interestingly, the term used by the Permanent Court to refer to a community of independent states by Bederman is used for the purpose of deconstructing both the organisation and the state.

[34] Bederman, above, note 32, at 371.

[35] Above, note 13 and accompanying text.

[36] Section 2.3.2 above.

[37] Brownlie, below, note 51; quote, in relation to IGOs, at 648.

by the legal system, the (material) test is whether it appears from practice that the international legal order has accorded such legal personality to organisations.

One consequence of the division between 'original' and 'secondary' subjects is that in the case of original subjects – states – the *scope* of legal personality is a matter of relative interest. The important thing for an independent state is to be identified as such; the legal consequences are generally agreed upon. On the basis of such identification, the legal order accords 'full' personality, the legal system being construed as tailored to the original subjects that are entities pre-existing the law. The recognition of states, and whatever legal effect is attached to that act, is essentially concerned with a factual concept of statehood. The creation of a state is not a normative act in international law, although international law may pose certain limiting conditions (in addition to the Montevideo criteria) for the acceptance of an entity as a state.[38] The creation of a state may no longer be only a 'matter of fact' (Montevideo criteria), but also 'a matter of law'; the fact remains that legal personality is attributed *subsequently* by international law. Although there is only a split second between them, these constitute separate legal moments. 'Thus, a State is not a legal person *because* it satisfies the criteria for statehood, but because *international law* attributes full international personality to such a factual situation.'[39]

This two-stage mechanism is no different when the 'secondary' subjects of a legal order are at issue, but the matter of legal personality is more important as these subjects do not necessarily have the power to perform all legal acts envisaged in the system. It is one reason why, with respect to international organisations, the discussion on the foundation and scope of legal personality has been particularly lively (and sometimes nebulous). It also explains why initially lawyers concentrated on the question as to whether an organisation possessed legal personality, rather than on the question of what exactly constituted an 'international organisation'.[40]

After World War II the *possibility* of non-state entities possessing legal personality came to be generally accepted.[41] International organisations were the prime beneficiaries of this change in climate. For this, the 1949 *Reparation* case is a hallmark, as the Opinion made, if perhaps inspired by

[38] Eg a democratic system, or human rights safeguards in national law (as eg in the *EC Guidelines on the Recognition of New States in Eastern Europe and in the Soviet Union* of 16 December 1991) are construed as a condition for recognition of new states as 'state', not as 'legal person'. Cf mention of legal constructions as objective phenomena above, in section 2.2.1 above. Cf Gaetano Arangio-Ruiz ('Dualism revisited: international law and interindividual law', LXXXVI *Rivista di Diritto Internazionale* 2003, 909–999, at 964–971) on the state as a non-legal entity ('the factual nature of the state') in international law.

[39] David Raič, *Statehood and the Law of Self-Determination*, 2002, at 38.

[40] Sections 3.2 and 3.3 above.

[41] See section 3.1 above on the period before WWII.

political necessity, several far-reaching statements on the legal identity of organisations.[42] This identity, however, was a precarious issue. The well-known reference to the 'super-state'[43] echoed a concern that had been voiced during the San Francisco conference,[44] while the notion as such had come up already in relation to the League of Nations, as mentioned for example by Oppenheim and Corbett.[45]

In the 1980 *WHO* Advisory Opinion, the Court expressed itself in similarly reassuring terms, and without making an attempt to differentiate between organisations ('there is nothing in the character of international organizations to justify their being considered as some form of "super-state"').[46] That the role and identity of international organisations would also be a public concern, appears from the United Nations website 'Questions and Answers about the UN: Image & Reality', which emphatically responds to what are presumably a layperson's FAQs: 'Is the United Nations a world government?' ('The UN is not, and was never intended to be, a world government. As an organization of sovereign and independent States, it does only what Member States have agreed it can do. It is their instrument...') and 'Do countries surrender their sovereignty at the UN?' ('The members of the UN are sovereign nations, and the UN Charter is one of the strongest safeguards of sovereignty, enshrining that principle as one of its central pillars. ...').[47]

The acceptance of possible legal personality for organisations did not mean that international law was prepared to identify 'international organisations' and on that basis automatically attribute legal personality, as in the case of states.[48] The *Repertory of United Nations Practice* of the 1950s envisaged – without giving examples – member states concluding international agreements with 'an international organisation that is not a subject

[42] Cf section 4.2.4 below.

[43] *ICJ Reports* 1949, at 179: '[...] the Organization is an international person. That is not the same thing as saying that it is a State[...] Still less it is the same as saying that it is a 'super-State' whatever that expression may mean'.

[44] The Committee which discussed the matter was anxious to avoid any implication that the to-be-created United Nations would in any sense be a 'super-state' (Report to the [US] president on the results of the San Francisco Conference, Dept of State Publication 2349 (1945)). It was concluded that international personality of the UN would '[i]n effect, ... be determined implicitly from the provisions of the Charter taken as a whole'(12 UNCIO 703, at 710); see section 6.2 below.

[45] Cf Corbett ('What is the League of Nations?', 5 *British YIL* 1924, 119-148), who mentions the 'invariably repudiated 'super-State" at 142. See also section 3.1 above.

[46] Interpretation of Peace Agreement of 25 March 1951 between the WHO and Egypt, ICJ Reports 1980, at 89.

[47] http://www.un.org/geninfo/ir/ch1/ch1.htm, as at 1 Jan 2006.

[48] See section 4.2.2 below.

of international law' (in which case there would be no duty of registration).[49] Extension to other organisations of the course set by the International Court in the *Reparation* case was not self-evident, but it seems that after initial attempts to distinguish between organisations with legal personality and those without, it came to be applied to organisations as a general category. It is significant that the textbooks of, for example, Seidl-Hohenveldern[50] and Brownlie[51] do not give a definition of 'international organisation' but rather of 'international organisation with legal personality'. As mentioned above, these definitions differ from the definition of 'international organisation' as proposed for example by Schermers and Blokker, essentially only in the addition of one legal feature: the possession of some form of international legal capacity.[52]

Since organisations will have such 'capacity' only if they possess 'legal personality' – whether that term be used as a threshold or as a predicate *ex post*[53] – this definition, to the extent it is used to determine legal personality *vel non*, is circular. More importantly, the fact that the extra-legal[54] elements in a definition of 'organisation with legal personality' (organs, autonomy, etc) match those in the definitions of 'organisation' as such, points to the difficulty of conceptualising an intergovernmental organisation *without* legal personality.[55]

That difficulty is reinforced by the fact that the core element of an 'international organisation' appears to be the institutional characteristic of

[49] See *Repertory of Practice of United Nations Organs*, Vol 5 (1955), at 292–297; quoted in Wilhelm Geck, 'Treaties: Registration and Publication', in 7 EPIL 1984, 490–496, at 491; interestingly the author does not appear to attach consequences to the legal status (or lack thereof) of the international organisation for the legal status of the agreement.

[50] Seidl-Hohenveldern and Loibl, above, note 2, at 5, point 8: '[constituent partners] in this manner enable the structure to be in its own name bearer of rights and duties in the field of international law and of domestic law'. (emphasis added, translation by the present author). On definitions see section 2.2.1 above.

[51] Ian Brownlie, *Principles of Public International Law* (6th edn), 2003, at 649; Professor Brownlie refers to 'the criteria' of legal personality in organisations, and mentions as a third point : '3. The existence of legal powers exercisable on the international plane and not solely within the national systems of one or more states'. On definitions see section 2.2.1 above.

[52] Section 2.2.1 above.

[53] Cf section 4.2.1 above.

[54] 'Extra-legal' intended as 'without normative force in *international* law'.

[55] Note that the 2003 draft Articles on Responsibility of International Organizations by the ILC does include a separate element of legal personality in the definition, but the commentary does not give examples of organisations without (YILC 2003, Vol II (Part Two) at 38–45, §§ 1–14). This is a-typical and may be *ex abundante cautela*, given the increasing variety among international institutions which could at some point make it difficult to agree upon a sufficiently clear-cut definition. Additional limiting conditions as we find posed by international law to the recognition of states *as such* (not as 'legal persons' cf above), note 38 are difficult to formulate for organisations since they would be concerned with the ability of the organisation to sustain its institutional independence also when an obligation is breached and responsibility is triggered.

'autonomy' vis-à-vis the member states.[56] This means that any institution displaying that feature will basically qualify as an 'international organisation'. And 'autonomy' clearly is closely linked to the legal quality of 'personality', although it is part of the institutional make-up of the organisation. Without autonomy, independent legal personality is difficult to conceive – but in terms of source and normative force they are not the same: autonomy vis-à-vis the member states is based on the IGO's institutional rules; personality is accorded by general international law. For many scholars however, the legal personality of an organisation seems to stem directly from its institutional autonomy. According to Higgins, 'an international association lacking legal personality, and possessing no *volonté distincte*, remains the creature of the states members who are thus liable for its acts'.[57] Article 2(b) of the Draft resolution of the *Institut de droit international* on international responsibility of IGO member states stipulates that '[t]he existence of a *volonté distincte* [...] is *evidence* of international legal personality'.[58] When an institutional law scholar such as White discusses the independent legal identity of international organisations, he stresses the internal aspect of 'autonomy' by referring to the constituent instruments of organisations for determining international legal personality.[59] Another example of the institutional perspective is given by Ramses Wessel. His model accords with practice in that legal personality is envisaged for all international organisations, but it is constructed entirely from an internal, institutional angle.[60]

Such an institutional perspective can of course be traced back to the transparent image of organisations. On the one hand lawyers look to international law which would accord, as any legal system, personality to entities that can be objectively identified as belonging to a certain class.[61] And this is in fact what happens, as there are essentially no institutions which have been qualified as 'international organisations' while lacking

[56] Section 2.2.1 above.

[57] Rosalyn Higgins (Rapporteur), 'The Legal Consequences for Member States of the Non-Fulfilment by International Organizations of their Obligations Toward Third Parties', *Yearbook of the Institute of International Law*, 1995, 251–469 (Final Report, pp 461–465), at 254

[58] Draft resolution (October 1994) at 465 (emphasis added).

[59] White, above, note 2, ch 2.

[60] 'Contrary to the way in which it is dealt with in most studies, the concept of legal personality in international institutional law does not find its primary value in the explanation of what international organizations may do on the international scene, but rather in the possibility of demarcating them from their Member States. Thus, legal personality is first and foremost a concept that can be used whenever international institutional law addresses the form of cooperation between the participating states. This implies that whenever there is an international legal entity, it is a legal person'. (Ramses Wessel, 'Revisiting the International Legal Status of the EU', 5 *European Foreign Affairs Review* 2000, 507–537, at 510).

[61] Section 4.2.1 above.

legal personality.[62] On the other hand lawyers are inclined to regard organisations as open structures and to look to institutional features, such as 'permanency of organs' or 'autonomy', for the finding of legal personality. Such features, however, operate internally to the institutional structure and have turned the entity into an 'international organisation' for the purpose of international law. The legal personality necessary to function in that law cannot be derived from the internal law of the organisation itself.

Clearly we do not find this approach with other subjects of international law, such as states or insurgent groups, or any of the legal subjects that figure in contemporary narratives of the law. From the perspective of international law, these subjects, and especially the state, tend to be described in sociological or ontological terms, while their internal-constitutive sphere is not taken into account.[63] Requirements put by international law in relation to states – respect for human rights, democracy,[64] but also the classic 'effective control' (which has been paralleled to the requirement of autonomy in organisations)[65] – are concerned with the recognition of the state as such, not with the recognition of its legal personality. Thus the effect may be the same, but the construct is very different.[66]

International organisations, in contrast, seem to be regarded as transparent legal constructs and their constitutive law as a special branch of public international law rather than as 'internal' law (although at the same time positive law confirms it is just that).[67] This has left room for a discussion that unwittingly moves between two poles – the will of the member states (the organisation as an open structure) and the dictates of the legal system (the organisation as a closed structure). The institutional features of the organisation and the systemic features of international law operate side by side in one discourse.

[62] See section 4.2.3 below on EU and OCSE.

[63] Cf above, note 38.

[64] Cf eg the EC Guidelines on the Recognition of New States in Eastern Europe and in the Soviet Union (16 December 1991).

[65] Francesca Martines, 'Legal Status and Powers of the Court', in Antonio Cassese, Paolo Gaeta and John Jones (eds), *The Rome Statute of the International Criminal Court: A Commentary*, 2002 (Vol I).

[66] Cf above, notes 38 and 39 and accompanying text.

[67] Section 2.3.3 above.

4.2.2 Legal Personality of International Organisations: Attribution and Effects

The threshold definition of 'personality' and the *a priori* exclusion of organisations from the catalogue of international legal subjects[68] played a role in the League of Nations era, but lost its place with the *Reparation* case. This was visible also in otherwise strongly state-oriented legal thought, as illustrated by El-Erian with a reference to the 1947 Hague lectures by Professor Krylov: 'les organismes internationaux ne sont pas non plus sujets de droit internationaux' (note the implicit distinction between institutional autonomy and legal personality); and to the 1956 treatise by Professor Tunkin ('at the same time international law does not preclude that this or that international organization may be given a certain measure of international personality').[69]

The classic pronouncement on the legal personality of international organisations, the 1949 *Reparation* Opinion, carefully steers a middle way between the traditional meaning of the term, moulded on the 'full personality' of states,[70] and a new, pragmatic application. Although it appears that legal personality is inferred from the *de facto* existence of legal capacity, at times the Court gives a contrary suggestion, thus taking a seemingly circular line of argument. First the Court suggests something of a causal relationship:

> But, in the international sphere, has the Organization such a nature as involves the capacity to bring an international claim? In order to answer this question, the Court must first enquire whether the Charter has given the Organization such a position that it possesses, in regard to its Members, rights which it is entitled to ask them to respect. In other words, does the Organization possess international personality?[71]

The Court then reaches an affirmative answer to this question, which is based, however, on the apparent existence of certain capacities that are taken as indicia for, rather than as consequences of, international legal personality. The Court seems clearly to indicate that the concept of 'legal personality' should be understood as an *in principio* disposition, rather than a status that generates particular capacities:

[68] Above, note 23 and accompanying text.

[69] Abdullah El-Erian, Relations between States and Inter-Governmental Organisations (First Report), UN Doc A/CN.4/161 and Add 1, 1963, at 180, § 153.

[70] Above, note 38 and accompanying text.

[71] Above, note 43 at 178; cf critical observations on consistency of the line of reasoning in Derek Bowett, *The Law of International Institutions*, 1982, at 336, 337.

> the Court has come to the conclusion that the Organization is an international person. [. . .] What it does mean is that it is a subject of international law and capable of possessing international rights and duties.[72]

It concludes the phrase, however, by suggesting that the right to bring a claim is a logical *consequence* of the Organization's legal personality: ' . . . and that it has capacity to maintain its rights by bringing international claims'.

In 1949, legal personality for international organisations was a new if not controversial concept.[73] It thus seems logical that the Court proceeded from the traditional notion of legal personality as attributed a priori and carrying concrete implications as to legal capacity. However, if legal personality had to be established for the United Nations, this could be done only inductively by proceeding from *de facto* present capacities, which at least could be relegated clearly to the 'will' of the founding states.[74] This led to an oscillating argument in which the Court 'made a pragmatic and teleological assessment of the basis of international personality'.[75]

The difficulties that the Court encountered in the *Reparation* case in constructing legal personality to this day re-emerge in international law discussions. Even if in practice it seems that legal personality was attached to any institution with certain objective characteristics[76] (found in a definition of 'international organisation'), doctrine construed the attribution of legal personality to organisations as well as its concrete implications in different ways. These differences are connected partly to the different meanings attached to the notion of 'personality' as such (section 4.2.1. above), and partly to the different opinions on the legal foundation of organisations (section 4.2.3 below).[77]

[72] Above, note 43, at 179.

[73] Above, note 23 and accompanying text.

[74] On the issue of 'objective personality' – which is in turn linked to the objective approach to attribution – see section 4.2.4 below.

[75] Oscar Schachter, 'Review of J Schneider: Treaty-making Power of International Organisations', 54 *American JIL* 1960, 201–202; Amerasinghe, above, note 2, at 129.

[76] White (above, note 2, at 40–43) dedicates a separate paragraph to the (practical) 'consequences'of personality.

[77] For a survey of traditional opinions on IGOs and legal personality eg Julio Barberis, *Nouvelles questions concernant la personnalite juridique internationale*, 179 RdC I, 179, 1983, 145–304; and Abdullah El-Erian, Relations between States and Inter-Governmental Organizations (First Report), UN Doc A/CN.4/161 and Add 1, 1963; as well as Ian Scobbie (revising Abdullah El-Erian), International organizations and international relations in René-Jean Dupuy (ed), *A Handbook on International Organizations*, Hague Academy of International Law, 1998, 831–896.

A range of possible approaches is described in the classification proposed by Rama-Montaldo,[78] which has become something of a classic. The author distinguishes between an 'objective' and an 'inductive' approach to establish the existence of legal personality, and between a 'formal' and a 'material' approach to determine the consequences of such establishment. In the objective approach, every entity that meets certain objective criteria in terms of extra-legal[79] characteristics is considered to have legal personality. According to the inductive approach, legal personality is established on the basis of certain *de facto* existing capacities.

As to the implications, the formal approach then attaches to 'legal personality' no particular legal capacities – those are deemed to depend on the subject concerned; it is essentially an empty, context-sensitive predicate. In contrast, in the material approach, the qualification 'legal personality' would imply particular legal capacities, or a 'core' thereof. For example, in the objective approach, if the International Lead and Zinc Study Group meets the definition of 'international organisation', this would render it an international 'person'. In the inductive approach, the fact that the Study Group has concluded an agreement with the Common Fund for Commodities which is accepted as an international legal instrument (*in casu* because it is registered in the UNTS),[80] would imply that the Study Group has treaty-making capacity;[81] and legal personality would be established from there.[82]

The 'material approach' was unproblematic on implications of personality, when states were considered the sole subjects of international law, while other (territorial) entities would have legal personality subsequently 'limited' by delegation of powers from or to sovereign states. However, as mentioned above (see section 4.2.1), at present 'legal personality' tends to be used as an empty (or, in Rama-Montaldo's terms, 'formal') predicate – inevitably, because its implications are obviously not identical for all legal subjects. This must have also been the thought underlying the suggestion made some forty years ago by one of the first scholars to address the

[78] Manuel Rama-Montaldo, 'International Legal Personality and Implied Powers of International Organizations' in 1970 *British YIL* 44, 111–155; referred to by Schermers and Blokker, above, note 2, § 1565, as 'a somewhat different approach'.

[79] Above, note 54.

[80] Grant Agreement– Transfer of Technology and Promotion of Demand: Zinc Die Casting (with Regulations and Rules for Second Account Operations); signed at Amsterdam on 23 April and at London on 6 May 1993. Filed and recorded at the request of the Common Fund for Commodities on 27 July 1994.

[81] The possibility that an institution concludes an international agreement *without* capacity, or – in institutional terms: *ultra vires* – is left out of account. This may be an issue where agreements made by organs of organisations are concerned; cf § 3.4.1 in Marjoleine Zieck, *UNHCR's World-Wide Presence in the Field: A Legal analysis of UNHCR's Cooperation Agreements,* 2006; cf ch 3 above, note 147 and accompanying text.

[82] This seems to be the approach of eg Amerasinghe, above, note 2, at 83.

question of treaty-making capacity ('power') of organisations: that a law-making convention be concluded explicitly to set out the legal capacities of international organisations, such as on treaty-making power and the ability to bring a claim.[83]

If we want to stay with the classic notion of 'legal personality' as a material qualification, in the way it could be used for states (which have an unchallenged, 'full' set of capacities), a new variable must be introduced to account for the differences in scope and effect. For example, White in the first edition of his textbook – which took a more formal analytical approach – concluded that the most adequate theory would be offered by the 'objective material approach'.[84] The full range of capacities would then be restricted by the 'functional limitation' of organisations. This appears as an institutional argument – apart from practical circumstances, such as the fact that most organisations do not have territory, it refers to the function of the organisation, which is determined by the institutional law of the organisation, not by general international law – but it is not really, if it does not claim normative force in general international law (which seems to be in accordance with White's argument). In that case the functional limitation of an organisation must be construed as a set of extra-legal features, in addition to the ones (part of the 'definition') that turn the institution into an 'international organisation' for the purposes of international law.

The close connection between attribution and effect of the legal personality qualification may be a reason to employ a more basic distinction which combines the two. Thus, the ILA Committee on international organisations distinguishes between the 'status approach', 'whereby an international organization must be deemed to possess personality, which then implies a range of competences' on the one hand, and the 'function approach', 'whereby personality may be derived from the list of rights and obligations of the organization, or indeed its tasks and functions, as constitutionally provided [or] as a form of necessary intendment', on the other.[85]

[83] Jan Willem Schneider, *Treaty-Making Power of International Organizations*, 1959, at 141; from the practical point of view it would have presented a middle way: more control of member states as they would be able to participate in establishing a conventional regime, rather than watching the growth of customary law on the matter (as has happened in fact), and on the other hand there would not have been the perceived need for an ad hoc assessment of the international organisation's capacity for treaty-making each time the case presents itself.

[84] White, above, note 2 (1st edn), at 36.

[85] 1998 ILA Taipei Conference, Committee on the Accountability of International Organizations, *First Report*, at 605. The second (2000) and third (2002) reports do not specifically address this question.

While the 'function approach' is not at odds with practice (when needed, every organisation can be presumed to have capacities, either 'constitutionally provided', or 'as a form of necessary intendment'), it has the disadvantage of introducing institutional features in external international law discourse.[86] In this case it does amount to an 'institutional argument', as these features are claimed to have normative force.

It would therefore seem more sound, and equally adequate in relation to practice, to follow White and proceed from the 'objective approach'. We could then say that, while the 'inductive approach' may serve to introduce a new category of legal subjects (as the International Court did fifty years ago in the *Reparation* case), the 'objective approach' to personality attribution has since then come to prevail. It makes sense that international law would operate in relation to organisations in the same way as in relation to states and other legal subjects. It also makes sense that the technique for personality attribution would be in line with the general dynamic in law, that it is 'applied' by an objective approach and 'changed' by an inductive approach.

As to the implications of legal personality, the degree to which legal capacities will become effective is determined by the institutional make-up of the organisation. This is a slightly awkward mechanism which in some form or other is unavoidable because of the functional, rather than territorial, design of organisations.[87] The 'functional limitation', however, is part of the internal set-up of the organisation; it has no normative force in international law.[88] By the 'functional limitation', the practical distinction between the 'formal approach' (personality as an empty predicate) and the 'material approach' (personality as implying specific capacities) is cancelled out.

Thus the focus of legal interest has shifted away from the attribution of legal personality on a case-by-case basis, as in the early days of international organisation,[89] to the establishment of personality on the basis of objective institutional features. As put by Higgins, '[i]f the attributes are there, personality exists'.[90] In this respect international organisations have been equated to states. Meanwhile, doctrine insists on looking to the internal institutional order of organisations – ie the 'will' of the founding states – to establish legal effect in general international law.

[86] Likewise the approach proposed by Schermers and Blokker for attribution and foundation of legal personality of organisations; below, note 111.

[87] Section 2.3.1 above.

[88] On normative force of institutional law in international law, see section 2.3.2 above.

[89] Sections 3.2.2 and 3.3.2 above.

[90] Cf Higgins, *Problems and Process*..., above, note 27, at 47.

4.2.3 Legal Personality of International Organisations: Foundation

The next issue is that of the *foundation* of organisations' legal personality. The question is related, but not identical, to that of attribution. Whatever the mechanism for attribution of 'legal personality' and its presumed relationship with concrete legal capacities, in positivist doctrine the legal foundation of an organisation's personality remains to be determined. The basic question then is whether that foundation lies in the 'will' (the *Willensereinigung*) of the states constituting the organisation or, on the contrary, in general international law.

This question has more than any other animated doctrinal discussion. One reason is undoubtedly that it involves choosing between the member states (sovereign states parties to the constituent treaty) and the international legal order (international community) as the ultimate source of authority, thereby touching at the heart of post-War international law debate.[91]

However, at the root lies still the same oscillation between the 'open' and the 'closed' manifestation of international organisations. Clearly the very possibility of a dilemma on legal foundation is linked to the dual perspective on organisations. If, as other legal subjects, organisations were considered only from an external perspective, the question would not present itself to begin with. Since only the legal order can accord legal personality to candidate legal actors,[92] as a matter of principle, the legal basis for that personality would be in general international law.

When this tenet is upheld, if only in an implicit manner (for example by proceeding from the 'domestic law analogy'), thc legal personality of organisations must be based on international (customary) law. When we proceed from the sovereignty of member states, however, a logical course is to found an organisation's personality on the will of the member states. Following Klabbers, we may call this the 'objective theory' and the 'will theory', respectively.[93] These amount to an 'external' and an 'internal' perspective.

In line with the state-centric set-up of international law, attempts to interpret the independent role of organisations have proceeded from the

[91] Which partly revolves around the identity of an international community which would transcend the sum of states (cf Bruno Simma and Andreas Paulus, 'The 'International Community': Facing the Challenge of Globalization,' 9 *European JIL* 1998, 266–277); and the related question of the requirement of consent for being bound by an international obligation (eg Gennady Danilenko, *Law-Making in the International Community*, 1993, esp at 58–68).

[92] Section 4.2.1 above.

[93] Klabbers, above, note 2, at 52–57; also Jan Klabbers, 'Presumptive Personality: The European Union in International Law', in Martti Koskenniemi (ed), *International Law Aspects of the European Union*, 1998, 231–253.

latter, internal perspective. Consequently, doctrine has held the source of 'legal personality' – as represented (in whichever causal relationship) for example by treaty-making 'capacity' – to be located in the organisation's constitution, as the embodiment of the 'will' of the founding states.[94]

The will theory may still be 'by far the more popular of the two'.[95] Meanwhile it seems that, as with respect to attribution (section 4.2.2 above), the 'objective theory' is the more efficient tool. For one thing, it is the most adequate description of practice. Essentially all international organisations (that is, institutions which meet 'the' definition) appear to have legal personality, if only because they all conclude headquarters agreements. But up until the 1990s almost *no* IGO constituent treaties contained a provision on international legal personality[96] (in the UN Charter it was purposely omitted),[97] or on general legal capacities.

In the last decade, provisions on self-declared international personality in the constituent treaty of organisations have become more common.[98] An example is Article 4(1) of the 1998 Rome Statute, which states that the Court shall have 'such international legal personality and such legal capacity as may be necessary for the exercise of its functions and the fulfilment of its purposes'. Likewise, the European Community is explicitly envisaged as having international personality,[99] as well as – on the basis of a pertinent provision in the prospective European Constitution – the European Union.[100] But, if the absence of a provision on legal personality in an IGO constituent treaty does not have legal effect in general international law, it means that the explicit attribution of legal personality (or any specific capacity) to an organisation by its founding states has equally little consequence. The only thing it can mean is that these states have had the intention to bring to life a particular entity with particular features – features which in international law qualify it as a 'legal person'.[101]

[94] Karl Zemanek, 'International Organizations: Treaty-Making Power' in 5 *EPIL* 1983, 168-171.

[95] Klabbers, above, note 2, at 53.

[96] Schermers and Blokker, above, note 2, § 1564, footnote 9 for some exceptions.

[97] Cf Bruno Simma et al (eds), *The Charter of the United Nations: A Commentary*, 2002, at 1302–1314 on Art 104 of the Charter ('legal capacity' in the territory of its members).

[98] Schermers and Blokker, above, note 2, § 1564, footnote 10 for some examples.

[99] Article 281: 'The Community shall have legal personality'. (Consolidated Version Of The Treaty Establishing The European Community, Official Journal C 325, 24 December 2002).

[100] Cf Treaty establishing a Constitution for Europe, CIG 87/2/04 Rev 2, Article I-7: 'The Union shall have legal personality', which is to be interpreted as implying both national and international (subjective and objective) legal personality.

[101] The same conclusion, via a different line of argument (see below, note 116 and accompanying text), in Klabbers, above, note 2, at 53; also Amerasinghe, above, note 2, at 68–70; the opinion in Schermers and Blokker, above, note 2, § 1564 that a statement in the

A further case in point is the fact that organisations which have a self-proclaimed *lack* of personality seem to incur a legal identity even against their will (or that of the founders) if they meet the criteria of an 'organisation'. This may have been the case for the EU, and currently for the OSCE. The EU has for some time repudiated the predicate of legal person (while commentators have been in doubt),[102] but in recent years it has unequivocally taken on legal personality.[103] The OSCE has, notwithstanding its explicitly non-formal design,[104] now felt compelled to consider the question of legal capacity of the Organization[105] – even if there is a definite lack of agreement on the matter among the 'participating states' (who for this reason are not designated as 'member states').[106] Along the same lines it may be recalled that the legal strategy of the Soviet Union for many years to deny the existence of the European Community (and hence refuse to accept the EC as a treaty partner) was based on the objective approach. The Soviet Union, as it was not a party to the constituent treaty, challenged the objective existence of the EC *tout court*, not its legal personality.[107]

The great proponent of the objective theory on organisations' legal personality since the 1960s has been Finn Seyerstedt.[108] Seyersted's writing

IGO constituent treaty of self-declared *international* personality 'clarify the status of the organization for non-members', should perhaps be read from this perspective.

[102] Klabbers, 'Presumptive Personality'...above, note 93, EU legal acts at 250; Wessel, above, note 60.

[103] Notably by concluding agreements (http://ue.eu.int/), and by including a provision in the prospective European Constitution on legal personality; cf above, note 100.

[104] Although the *Conference for Security and Cooperation in Europe* adopted the name of 'organisation' (at the Budapest session in 1995, 34 ILM 1995, 773), '[t]he OSCE has a unique status. On the one hand, it has no legal status under international law and all its decisions are politically but not legally binding. Nevertheless, it possesses most of the normal attributes of an international organization [...].'(*OSCE Handbook Online* –http://www.osce.org /publications /handbook).

[105] Cf eg the Report on OSCE Legal Capacity and on Privileges and Immunities to the Ministerial Council PC.JOUR/383 (26 November 2000), endorsed by the Permanent Council ('Acknowledging the intensive negotiations held in order to solve the open question of legal capacity of the OSCE and the granting of privileges and immunities, [...]') by Decision No 383, at the 312th Plenary Meeting – to the knowledge of this author, that process is still ongoing.

[106] Cf Also Ige Dekker and Ramses Wessel, 'Van CVSE naar OVSE: De sluipende institutionalisering en onvermijdelijke juridisering van een internationale conferentie', 31 *Vrede En Veiligheid* 2002, 425–438, who suggest (at 236), that it is difficult for the OSCE to 'deny' a separate legal identity.

[107] Cf Hans Blix, 'Contemporary aspects of recognition' 130 RdC 1970, 587–704, at 621, quoted in Klabbers, 'Presumptive Personality'...above, note 93, at 242. See also section 4.2.4 below.

[108] Finn Seyersted, *Objective International Personality of Intergovernmental Organisations: Do Their Capacities Really Depend upon Their Constitutions?*, 1963. See also Finn Seyersted, 'Treaty-Making Capacity of International Organizati-ons: Article 6 of the International Law Commission's Draft Articles on the Law of Treaties Between States and Internati-onal Organizations or Between International Organizations', 34 ÖZöRV 1983, 261-267.

on the topic in 1963 may be considered prophetic, as it seems international doctrine and practice are moving increasingly along the lines of his point of view. Thus Professor Karl Zemanek, law of treaties expert and for many years an unfailing adherent of the 'will theory',[109] in the late 1980s conceded that it would be 'a more convincing interpretation [. . .] to suppose that IOs possess treaty-making capacity by virtue of general (customary) international law'.[110]

Two authoritative textbooks on international institutional law may be cited for their approach to the foundation of legal personality. Either book presents a model for explaining current practice – which is that essentially all organisations, once qualified as such, are deemed to have personality – and both aim to safeguard the internal, institutional perspective and the external, public international law perspective at the same time.

Schermers and Blokker identify three approaches with respect to the legal personality of organizations:[111] the school that recognises legal personality only if this is expressly attributed in the IGO constituent instrument; the school that considers legal personality to attach automatically to an institution which by certain objective criteria qualifies as an 'organisation'; and a third school, which traces the legal basis of IGO personality to the 'will' of the member states via specific legal capacities (such as treaty-making), which, even if not expressly mentioned, can be derived from the constitutive instrument via the 'implied powers' doctrine. According to the authors, the latter view is currently the prevailing one.

At root, this is a twofold division, amounting to a choice between the objective theory and the will theory. The third alternative is the 'will theory' made flexible by the additional application of the implied powers doctrine. It is true to say that this construction – which proceeds from the internal perspective – will have the same net result as application of the objective theory. It can easily be argued that all organisations possess legal personality on the basis of the will of the founding states, because even if personality has not expressly been stipulated, it must be considered to have been implied because the creators of an organisation presumably will it to be fully functional.

However, it may be noted that this presents an 'institutional argument', in the sense that it claims normative force in international law for

[109] See above, note 94.

[110] Karl Zemanek, 'The United Nations Conference on the Law of Treaties Between States and International Organizations or Between International Organizations: The unrecorded history of its 'general agreement" in Karl Heinz Böckstiegel et al (eds), *Völkerrecht, Recht der Internationalen Organizationen, Weltwirtschaftsrecht* (Festschrift für Ignaz Seidl-Hohenveldern), 1988, 665–679, at 671.

[111] A division which draws partly on the question of legal foundation and partly on that of objectivity of IGO personality; Schermers and Blokker, above, note 2, §§ 1565–1567. See also above, note 78 and accompanying text.

institutional features.[112] Otherwise, the argument made in Schermers and Blokker *against* the objective theory as advocated by Seyersted is a complicated one. Whether Seyersted actually proposes 'original' personality for organisations[113] is debatable. It seems that he is not so much concerned with the original *versus* derived subjects paradigm (the primary role of states is not challenged even by Seyersted), but rather with the legal foundation of IGO personality in general international law, which would amount to the 'objective theory' outlined above.[114]

Another way out of the dilemma is proposed by Jan Klabbers.[115] He proposes a middle way between the will theory and the objective theory, with the 'theory of presumptive personality'. Contrary to Schermers and Blokker he does not proceed from the institutional frame of reference, but rather from general international law. The 'theory of presumptive personality' amounts to the objective approach – all institutions which qualify as 'organisations' are presumed to have legal personality – but with a possibility of rebuttal of the presumption (rebuttal, it is suggested, by the member states). This, too, appears as an elegant solution which covers existing practice.

However, here it is not entirely clear either why the objective theory would not serve the latter purpose. According to Klabbers, the major weak point of the theory is that it overrides the will of the member states.[116] But that is not felt to be a problem for the component elements of states and other legal subjects, in regard to which international law invariably operates according to the 'objective theory'. Otherwise, the fact that some institutions appear to incur legal personality against their will – an illustrative point specifically made by the author – makes sense from a general law perspective. If an institution meets the criteria of an 'organisation', and especially if it actually performs legal acts *in externo*,[117] it seems logical that the institution would assume a legal shape. The member states have created an entity with certain characteristics, as individuals would, to which the legal system subsequently attributes the ability to act and to be held responsible, *vel non*. Finally, the 'theory of presumptive personality' envisages the possibility of rebuttal by the member states. This theory thus introduces what above has been called an 'institutional argument', which detracts from its power.

[112] As does the 'function approach' of the ILA – cf above, note 85.

[113] Argued in Schermers and Blokker, above, note 2, § 1562.

[114] Seyersted, above, note 108, references and accompanying text.

[115] Klabbers, above, note 2, and Klabbers, 'Presumptive Personality:...' above, note 93.

[116] Klabbers, above, note 2, at 55. On objective legal personality of organisations, see section 4.2.4 below.

[117] Which seems to be the case for the EU; cf Klabbers, 'Presumptive Personality:...' above, note 93, at 250.

Obviously the 'objective theory' on foundation is linked to the 'objective theory' on attribution of legal personality. In both cases the objective approach seems elegant, simple and befitting of the international law sytem. The arguments made above in relation to 'theories' on personality attribution equally apply here.[118] Adopting the objective approach to organisations would not need to be qualified as a 'pragmatic solution',[119] or a case of 'practice' (as opposed to doctrine);[120] it is on the contrary the most logical course to take.

In fact, the arguments for the will theory appear to be based primarily on the tacit premise that the sovereign will of the founding states be safeguarded. Thus, next to the objective approach or the external perspective, the 'will theory' or the internal, institutional perspective is maintained in one frame of reference, although these two strands of argument would be mutually exclusive. Unaware because of the transparent quality of organisations and the fuzzy contours of the international legal order, doctrine uses institutional and international arguments side by side.

4.2.4 Objective Legal Personality

Once an organisation's legal personality is established, the question remains whether this is opposable to states or other subjects who are not members. In addressing the question of whether organisations have an objective existence, doctrine again shows both an internal and an external perspective.

In the first view, legal personality of an organisation is subjective, and opposable only to member states.[121] This amounts by definition to an open view of organisations, which are seen as a set of legal relations between the member states, yielding an independent regime only as between themselves. No objective legal phenomenon has been created, and probably not even an objective 'social phenomenon', as (according to many) a state would be. This is also in line with the 'will theory' on the foundation of legal personality.

Higgins has stated, of the subjective personality view, that it is 'to ignore the objective legal reality of international personality. [...] It is not a matter of recognition. It is a matter of objective reality'.[122] The view of legal personality as an 'objective legal reality' is easily linked to the objective

[118] Above, text accompanying notes 84 and 85.
[119] Klabbers, above, note 2, at 55.
[120] As does White, see above, note 76 and accompanying text.
[121] Cf Higgins, *Problems and Process...* above, note 27, at 47, footnote 27 in particular on adherents (such as Schwarzenberger, Mosler and Seidl-Hohenveldern) to subjective personality.
[122] Higgins, above, note 27, at 47.

approach to legal personality's attribution (on the basis of objective features) and foundation (in general international law), and it may be considered the least controversial of the three. An example is Article 2(c) of the 1994 IDI Draft resolution, which reads: 'The international personality of international organization is, as a matter of international law, opposable to third parties, and is not dependent upon any recognition by them'.[123]

One particular feature of the debate on objective legal personality is that, because of the terms in which it is cast ('the position of non-member states'), the issue is readily brought within the law of treaties framework. The organisation is equated with a treaty (or with a 'treaty regime', at most), and objective personality would then amount to opposability of the constitutive treaty against third states. This can of course be rejected as a breach of the *pacta tertiis* rule. The subjective personality of an entity created by treaty can easily be explained by the law of treaties, but the only way to accommodate objective personality would be to bring IGO constituent treaties within a *sui generis* category ('treaties akin to charters of incorporation') as done by McNair;[124] or the established regime in the contemporary category of 'objective regimes', which is what Reuter seems to read in the *Reparations* case.[125] These tenets, however, only explain the independence of the treaty regime, not its legal foundation.

A vital development, which to some extent leaves the treaty framework and its voluntarist basis intact, has been the idea of a constitutive instrument as a constitution rather than as a treaty. This implies that a separate legal order is created, which would in part become detached from the establishing instrument and its governing rules. At the same time the 'constitution' is an international treaty, and this is probably the most convincing argument positive international law has to offer to penetrate the internal law of a legal subject. Interestingly, in cases where the law of treaties is applied to constitutive treaties, a 'constitutional variant' has developed next to the traditional approach.[126]

The *Reparation* Opinion, again, is famous for a pronouncement on the matter. There was a legitimate interest in attributing objective personality to the United Nations, but the Court was not prepared to adopt an objective approach to the attribution and foundation of legal personality, which would mean that legal personality is by definition 'objective'. Hence

[123] IDI Draft resolution (October 1994) above, note 58, at 465).

[124] 'The Function and the Differing Legal Character of Treaties', XI *British YIL* 1930, 100–118, at 117. McNair's 'dispositive treaties' and 'constitutive treaties' are not a useful analytical tool in this respect because of their strong territorial element (Lord Arnold McNair, *The Law of treaties*, 1961, at 256–271).

[125] Paul Reuter, *Introduction to the Law of Treaties*, 1995, at 124.

[126] In the law of treatics constitutive treaties appear relatively closed-off in comparison to 'regular' treaties, and resistant to traditional interpretive exercise. See ch 6 below on constituent treaties as treaties, on the one hand, and as constitutions, on the other.

the Court proceeded from the institutional perspective, or the 'will theory', and then arrived, 'by some unorthodox reasoning',[127] at the desired outcome:

> [T]he Court's opinion is that fifty States, representing the vast majority of the members of the international community, had the power, in conformity with international law, to bring into being an entity possessing objective international personality, and not merely personality recognized by them alone, together with capacity to bring international claims.[128]

By declaring the United Nations an objective legal person, the Court set a course for international organisations in general, and the scope of IGO personality has not been subject of particularly intense discussion since. However, it appears, for instance from the debate on the International Criminal Court, that the use of the law of treaties paradigm as a vehicle for opening up an organisation and imposing a strictly voluntarist setting remains topical.[129]

4.2.5 Capacities and Competences

Already Wilfred Jenks has suggested that it may not be necessary to 'invoke the concept of legal personality for the purpose of defining the legal capacity of international organizations'.[130] Nevertheless the two notions have been frequently connected, albeit often in a circular manner (see also section 4.2.2 above). Leaving the relationship between legal personality and legal capacity aside, the 'powers' of organisations may be addressed briefly as they are an element of the legal interpretation of organisations.[131]

Most (national) systems of law distinguish between 'capacity' and 'competence', where the first is an *in principio* legal disposition conferred by the law (eg a corporate person which has the capacity to buy and sell property, but not the capacity to marry), and the latter is an ability to perform legal acts bestowed (by the law or by another person) upon the

[127] In the words of Shabtai Rosenne, *Developments in the Law of Treaties (1945–1986)*, 1989, at 238.

[128] *Reparation for Injuries*, above, note 43, at 179.

[129] The issue of jurisdiction vis-à-vis nationals of non-parties to the Statute was initially debated predominantly in a law of treaties paradigm, but later put more in terms of delegation and transfer of national jurisdictional powers. Eg Dapo Akande, 'The Jurisdiction of the International Criminal Court over Nationals of Non-Parties: Legal Basis and Limits', in 1 *Journal of International Criminal Justice* 2003, pp 618–650.

[130] Cf Wilfred Jenks, 'The Legal Personality of International Organisations', 22 *British YIL* 1945, 267–275, at 271. See also section 7.2 below on treaty-making capacity in particular.

[131] Different kinds of IGO power distinguished in section 2.3.1 above.

person for a particular purpose (eg a person who has the competence to represent the state, or other persons in law).[132]

Transposed to the international plane, within the state these two types of power, which may be equally called capacity and competence, coincide completely (in the words of Virally, they are the *finalité integrée* of the state).[133] Classic international law doctrine thus had little need for a development of this distinction.[134] With respect to international organisations, however, it is relevant: given its *finalité fonctionelle*,[135] or in the words of White, 'functional limitation'[136] an organisation's capacity and competence do not overlap.

In international law the use of terms is inconsistent, but the conceptual distinction plays a role, as appears for example from the (somewhat unwieldy) distinctions proposed by Huber, between *jouissance* and *exercise* of *jus tractatuum*,[137] or by Bekker, between 'treaty-making capacity' and 'the *extent* of the treaty-making capacity of an individual organization'.[138] There is general agreement that capacity is a general condition, for example to conclude treaties, while competence is a 'more concrete and specific' power.[139]

[132] Capacité – Compétence; Fähigkeit – Befugnis or Zuständigkeit; Bekwaamheid – Bevoegdheid; cf *Dictionnaire de la terminologie du Droit International Sirey*, 1960 (s.v. 'compétence' and 'capacité'); David Walker, *The Oxford Companion to Law*, 1980 (s.v. 'capacity').

[133] Michel Virally, 'La notion de fonction dans la théorie de l'organization internationale,', in Suzanne Bastid (ed), *Mélanges offerts à Rousseau*, 1974, 277–300, at 282 in particular; cf Charles Rousseau, RdC 1948/II, at 248, about the unlimited competence of states.

[134] With regard to sovereign states this distinction has not come up, but in the context of 'non-sovereign states' it has: Oppenheim/Lauterpacht, above, note 39, at 494: 'A State possesses the treaty-making power only in so far as it is sovereign. States which are not fully sovereign can become parties only to such treaties as they are competent to conclude' (emphasis added). The theory of federative states played a role in the conceptualisation of organisations as legal entities. In the context of the law of treaties the ILC maintained for some time the tentative analogy between treaties concluded by organisations and treaties concluded by federal states, but it was abandoned in 1962 with the decision to exclude organisations from the scope of the draft Articles on the Law of Treaties (ILC Report, YILC 1962, Vol II, § 21 at 161).

[135] Cf Virally who, in 'La notion....above, note 133 (at 282 in particular) compares the 'finalité integrée' of a state with the 'finalité fonctionelle' of an international organisation.

[136] A term which includes next to the institutional make-up of an organisation also factual circumstances, such as that most organisations do not 'have' territory; cf above, note 84 and accompanying text.

[137] Jean Huber, *Le droit de conclure des traités internationaux*, 1951, at 22; these notions arguably can be equated to the capacity – competence distinction.

[138] Pieter Bekker, *The Legal Position of Intergovernmental Organisations: A Functional Necessity Analysis of Their Legal Status and Immunities*, 1994, at 65 (emphasis in the original); see in general 63–71 and 75–85 on capacity and competence. Wessel (above, note 60, at 150) takes Bekkers distinction as one between legal personality 'as a quality' and capacity 'as an asset'.

[139] Klabbers, above, note 2, at 279, and references.

Furthermore, 'competence' tends to be used in a dual sense: to denote the legal acts an organisation may perform, and to denote the *area* in which an organisation may operate. Nearly 50 years after the *Reparation* case, the Court offered some terminological clarification by referring to the 'area of competence' of an organisation.[140] This is delimited by the 'principle of speciality': 'The Court need hardly point out that international organisations are subjects of international law which do not, unlike States, possess a general [area of] competence'.[141] This area of competence , then, accounts for the fact that the European Community can conclude a treaty on fibre but not on military alliance (unless it changes its institutional mission statement).

'Competence', on the other hand, should be used to refer to all other aspects of the 'powers' of the organisation (essentially this revolves around the relation between the organisation and its member states); and to the degree to which the organisation can take binding measures. Competence may account for a prohibition on parrot imports issued by the International Committee for Bird Preservation (to use a notorious example from the ILC discussions in the 1950s)[142] to a customs agreement concluded by the European Community in lieu of its member states. But this is allegedly a question of degree and belongs to the realm of the organisation's institutional law.[143]

In the light of this distinction it becomes clearer why the early attempts to limit the attribution of international personality and legal capacities to for example 'the most important organisations',[144] were fruitless. Practice confirms that, although an organisation's political importance may be proportional to its competence or area of competence, the latter has no bearing on the organisation's capacity for, for example, treaty-making *within* the delimited field of activity. Likewise, as was pointed out on the basis of empirical research in the 1950s and 1960s, the size of an organisation's membership does not appear to affect its treaty-making capacity.[145]

140 International Court of Justice, *Legality of the Use by a State of Nuclear Weapons in Armed Conflict* (Advisory Opinion), General List, No 93, 1996, § 19: 'In order to delineate the field of activity or the area of competence of an international organization...'

141 Above, note 140, § 25.

142 Eg Sandström, YILC 1950, Vol I, § 62 at 79.

143 Some writers have distinguished 'area of competence' and 'competence' also before the *(WHO) Nuclear Weapons* pronouncement; eg Rudolf Bindschedler ('International Organizations: General Aspects', *EPIL* 5, 1983, 119-140) who refers to it as to 'material' and 'formal division of competences', respectively.

144 See above, note 49 and accompanying text.

145 Günther Hartmann, 'The Capacity of International Organizations to Conclude Treaties', in Karl Zemanek (ed.), *The Capacity of International Organizations to Conclude Treaties*, 1971, 127–163, at 159.

In the same vein, the observation that '[t]he contrast in competence and significance between the United Nations on the one hand and a body like the International Institute of Refrigeration on the other could hardly be more striking', coupled with the suggestion that such a difference would have consequences for the endowment with legal personality and capacity,[146] arguably does not lay accent correctly. The contrast between Liechtenstein and the United States is in many respects just as striking. An organisation's competences, however modest, do not prejudice the fact that, if the need for co-operation with states or other organisations arises, it possesses 'full' treaty-making capacity, and not for instance the capacity to conclude only bilateral treaties, or oral agreements.

Apart from terminology, a conceptual distinction is helpful for two reasons, neither of which applies in the case of states. First, the above-mentioned interplay between the legal personality of an organisation and its functional limitation, which accounts for its capability to act in practice, can be concisely put in terms of an interplay between capacity and competence. The capacities of an organisation are limited by its competence and area of comptence.[147]

The second reason is the legal basis of capacity and competence. It appears relatively uncontroversial *in principle* to found capacity in international law.[148] But then the construction of legal capacity in general international law – unsurprisingly – shows the same difficulties as that of the foundation of 'legal personality' in general.[149] The competence and area of competence, in contrast, are generally traced to the institutional make-up of the organisation. As the organisation's (*area* of) competence is delimited by the constituent treaty, it is based on the will of the member states.

Klabbers mentions a 'doctrinal debate' on capacity and competence[150] but leaves uncertain where and how this has played out. Considering the terminological and conceptual confusion – arguably related to the transparency of the organisations' institutional veil – it may also be considered that there has been too little debate on the matter. The distinction between capacity, competence and area of competence can be instrumentalised for the purpose of capturing the tension between the internal and external perspective, which has been described in the previous paragraphs. Here the *Reparation* case may once more serve as an example, in that the 'implied

[146] Donald Greig, *International Law*, 1976, at 109 (emphasis added).

[147] This is what notions such as 'functionally limited personality' or 'limited capacity' ultimately refer to.

[148] See Klabbers, above, note 2, at 279, which arguably skims over the old debates of principle somewhat swiftly.

[149] Sections 4.2.2 and 4.2.3 above. The specific legal capacity for treaty-making will be addressed in ch 7 below.

[150] Klabbers, above, note 2, at 280.

powers doctrine' as formulated in relation to the United Nations appears to be concerned with both capacities and competences (that is, powers assigned by the legal order and powers assigned by the member states; or a quality attributed by the general legal order and a quality attributed by the internal, institutional legal order) simultaneously.[151]

[151] Cf eg 'Under international law, the Organization must be deemed to have those powers which, though not expressly provided in the Charter, are conferred upon it by necessary implication as being essential to the performance of its duties' and '[t]he capacity of the organization ...arises by necessary intendment out of the Charter' (above, note 43, 184).

Concluding Remarks to Part One

PART ONE DESCRIBES the image of international organisations in international law. In particular, it aims to show that organisations as international actors are transparent legal entities. This is to say that organisations are not legally impermeable in the way of states, and that their institutional orders – the member states and organs at various levels – are to some extent (willed) visible and (willed) accessible from the plane of general international law. The inquiry in Part One takes the form of an skeletal history of ideas regarding the legal image of international organisations in the nineteenth and early twentieth centuries and a detailed analysis of the doctrinal debates on the (more formal) legal image of organisations in the UN era.

The transparent character of organisations is brought about by a number of factors.[1] First, the organisation's component elements are sovereign states, the prime international legal persons. Second, the legal universe is traditionally divided in two; it can thus accommodate only law that is either 'international' or 'domestic'. In addition there are two inherent features: the functionality of international organisations[2] (which distinguishes them from most other legal subjects, as it entails a varying area of competence) and their centralised structure[3] (which distinguishes them from ordinary inter-state relations, as these are 'horizontal').

Finally, the transparency of organisations is favoured by historical continuity. International organisations started out as completely open structures which served as vehicles for states. This was the starting point for legal thought on organisations in the late nineteenth and early twentieth centuries. At that time the institutional autonomy of organisations was not obvious, as decisions were generally taken by unanimity, but it was a topic of discussion from the early days onwards. Even when autonomy of the organisation vis-à-vis the member states at the institutional level was conceded (an early example are the river commissions), this autonomy for a long time had no external dimension: organisations did not yet conduct 'external relations', and where they did, it was interpreted in terms of agency on behalf of the member states.

[1] See section 2.3.3.
[2] See section 2.3.1.
[3] See section 2.3.2.

By the time the United Nations and many other subsequent organisations were operational, international organisations displayed extensive legal activity on their own accord. This meant that international law has to clothe these institutions with the ability to perform legal acts, which brought in the tenet of legal personality. While for the League it could be left implicit, in relation to the UN it had to be addressed at an early stage. A catalyst in the process was the *Reparation* opinion of 1949, in which the International Court of Justice declared the United Nations to be a legal person, and an 'objective' legal person at that.

The idea of legal independence thus hinges on the notion of personality. For this reason the image of organisations in the last fifty years can be described by way of the grapple of international law doctrine with the question of legal personality for organisations.[4]

The construction of such personality could seem self-evident when proceeding from a few perfectly uncontroversial assumptions. The first is that legal personality is conferred by the legal system, not by a candidate legal person upon itself. Identification of that candidate may be a question of legal and not just factual criteria. However, subsequently the entity is assessed as an objective, social phenomenon. The identification of a social entity and the attribution of legal personality to it constitute two separate legal moments (even if in time they may be a split second apart). This is readily apparent in the case of states: note that 'recognition' (even on the basis of legal criteria, as nowadays happens in addition to the 'Montevideo criteria') is construed as recognition of the existence of the state as such, not of its legal personality.

The second assumption is that international law is perceived as a unified legal 'system' or 'order' in which different legal subjects, including international organisations, function and interact. Logically they are governed by common systemic rules of that legal order.

The third is that international organisations are separate legal entities and thus constitute a legal order which is to some extent separate. One consequence is that the legal features of that order do not *per se* have normative force in general international law.

On the basis of these assumptions, the legal personality of organisations would have to be construed in the same way as that of other legal subjects. However, an interesting fact emerges. Doctrine presents essentially two schools, which parallel the two perspectives on international organisations in general. The one takes an external perspective and approaches organisations from the plane of general international law, as closed entities. The other proceeds from an internal, open perspective on organisations and resorts to the 'will' of the constituent states to establish legal personality.

[4] See ch 3.

The latter approach leaves room for confusion about the 'autonomy' of organisations vis-à-vis their member states. Often this has been more or less equated with legal personality. A look at the host of contemporary definitions shows that autonomy is indeed a core element in the definition of 'international organisation'. But it is also an institutional (or internal) feature, brought about by agreement of the constituent states, not by general international law. It may be a necessary condition set by international law for an institution to become an 'international organisation,' but it does not have of itself normative force in general international law.

The external approach (which in the various classifications is usually called 'objective') undoubtedly appears as the more logical one, since the question of personality pertains to the level of general international law. Nonetheless, the internal perspective seems to be prevailing. While this may reflect the transparent nature of organisations, in the system of general international law, the internal perspective is difficult consistently to maintain, as was argued above. This is confirmed by the fact that 50 years have brought no general agreement on the matter – even if, possibly in the wake of general developments in international law, a growing trend towards the 'objective' is visible.

Part Two

International Organisations and Treaty Practice

5

International Organisations as a Forum for Treaty-making

THIS CHAPTER LOOKS at the institutional order of international organisations by considering their role as a forum and their facilitation of other actors (notably states) in concluding treaties.[1] It takes an external, international law perspective, rather than an institutional perspective, by comparing the law and practice of treaty-making within the organisation to that in the classic international setting. As it turns out, in its forum function, the organisation appears as an open legal structure – but not entirely so, as the institutional legal order is to some extent centralised with respect to international law, with the institutional veil becoming ever so slightly opaque to international law.[2]

This becomes clear, both from barriers posed by the IGO framework to the applicability of the general law of treaties, and from developments in treaty-making practice *within* the IGO framework which are made possible by its centralised character. The material for this chapter is taken from the treaty practice within the United Nations system – for its global scope, extensiveness and historical continuity. The many instances of regional treaty-making practice, such as in the Council of Europe,[3] are not considered here.

[1] 'Treaty-making', as treaty-making power', refers to the process of becoming a formal party to a treaty. In contrast, American legal writing especially uses 'treaty-making' in the literal sense of 'taking action, such as repairing a text, to make for a treaty regime to come into being' (cf José Alvarez, *International Organizations as Law-Makers*, 2005, at 274). An early version of this chapter has appeared in 'The Legal Nature of International Organisations and the Law of Treaties', 4 *Austrian Review of International and European Law* 2000, 85–125, § 3

[2] Section 2.3.2 above. For formal signs of centralisation, obviously related to 'autonomy', see eg Nigel White, *The Law of International Organizations*, 2005, at 70–107 on the 'powers' of international organisations; a rich account of IGO (often UN and WTO) practice in a less formal-legal discourse in Alvarez, above, note 1, at 274–337; in terms of the present book it shows clear signs of centralisation in the treaty-making process.

[3] See Jörg Polakiewicz, *Treaty-making in the Council of Europe*, 1999 and http://conventions.coe.int/; and a general survey of Conventions concluded in the framework of organisations in Henry Schermers and Niels Blokker, *International Institutional Law*, 2003, §§1262–1317.

5.1 CENTRALISATION IN UNITED NATIONS PRACTICE

The increasingly important position of international organisations after World War II[4] is exemplified by their role in the treaty-making practice of states. The treaty-making process within the ILO had already been a 'valuable rationalisation' of the traditionally 'cumbersome' procedure for conclusion and entry into force of treaties, but it had had 'relatively little effect on the practice of the League of Nations'.[5] A prominent writer on international institutions in the early days of the UN expressed the hope that the power of the ECOSOC enshrined in Article 62(3) of the UN Charter to 'prepare draft conventions [. . .] within its competence' would be 'used with imagination and vigour' for the benefit of 'a far-reaching rationalisation of the technique of the multipartite instrument'.[6]

The United Nations has only partly lived up to these expectations.[7] Rosenne has summarised the changes brought into the treaty-making process under the United Nations system as: the abolition of the unanimity rule; the extension of the ILO system[8] to some of the Specialized Agencies; and 'the decentralization and dissipation of the functional competence through various organs'.[9]

The first two developments can count as an instance of centralisation of international norm-setting processes through the use of the institutional order of the organisation. The treaty-making process within the framework of the UN has indeed been 'rationalised' insofar as for instance the adoption of the text by a two-thirds majority in a UN conference-framework has become established practice.[10] In addition adoption of the text within the General Assembly in lieu of a diplomatic conference has

[4] Cf above ch 4, note 2.

[5] Wilfred Jenks, 'Some Constitutional problems of International Organisations', 22 *British YIL* 1945, 11–72, at 48.

[6] *Ibid.*

[7] A rich account of the practice of 'treaty-making' (in the meaning of 'preparing the conclusion of treaties by states') in notably the UN System in Alvarez, above, note 1, chs 5 and 6; the author does not take a formal-legal perspective, but addresses the interplay between negotiating venues, negotiating procedures and interstate cooperation to assess the impact on treaty-making processes according to various criteria.

[8] Section 3.3.1 above on the plenary organ's competence to adopt conventions by a two thirds majority.

[9] Shabtai Rosenne, *United Nations Treaty Practice*, RdC 1954/II, 281–444, at 313; an overview also in Rosalyn Higgins, *The development of international law through the political organs of the United Nations*, 1963.

[10] Tullio Treves, 'Innovations dans la technique de codification du droit international: la préparation de la conference de Vienne sur les traités passés par les organisations internationales', XXXII AFDI 1986, 474–494. The procedural aspect of 'rationalisation' of course leaves out of account that the practice of adoption by majority has left way for the development of a complex, time-consuming and otherwise sometimes undesirable practice with regard to treaty reservations.

become relatively common,[11] in which cases acceptance of the text requires only a simple majority.[12] In either case, however, the minority is overruled only with regard to the stage of adoption proper and is not brought into the grey zone between signature and ratification (covered by Article 18 VCLT I). Extension of the ILO system – in which 'adoption' in the plenary organ has the legal effect of signature subject to ratification by the states' plenipotentiaries – to the United Nations was expressly rejected at the San Francisco Conference.[13]

The decentralisation of the United Nations' competence through its organs mentioned by Rosenne is another innovation from the League of Nations era. It relates to a decentralisation of competences *within* the organisational structure.[14] For several stages of the treaty-making process it is no longer the main plenary organ or the main executive organ that represents the Organization, but a subordinate body connected to the main organs in a sometimes intricate manner. This development has had a strong impact on the multilateral treaty-making processes in the framework of the Organization and has given rise to multifarious practices.[15] Generally, it

[11] From the publication *Multilateral Treaties Deposited with the Secretary-General* (UN Doc. St/Leg/Ser.E/–) it seems that, leaving aside a number of hybrid procedures, treaties adopted by the General Assembly and other permanent institutional bodies are in a ratio of 1 to 4 to treaties adopted at an *ad hoc* conference or meeting. In contrast, for instance in the Council of Europe framework conventions are adopted by the Committee of Ministers. These conventions have been drafted in a Steering Committee or a Committee of Experts under supervision of a Steering Committee. Although its members are apointed by governments, the Committee is answerable to the Committee of Ministers directly (cf Polakiewicz, above, note 3, at 22–24 and http://www.coe.fr/eng/legaltxt/treaties.htm).

[12] Unless the subject is such as to warrant a two-thirds majority vote (Art 18(2) of the UN Charter); cf Paul Reuter, *Introduction to the Law of Treaties*, 1995, at 87.

[13] UNCIO, Vol 9, at 79–81. A method similar to the ILO procedure, though without the element of 'willingness to pursue the treaty-making procedure' implied by signature subject to ratification or a similar legal moment, is found eg in the case of the 1946 Convention on the Privileges and Immunities of the United Nations (1 UNTS 15; 90 UNTS 327) and the 1947 Convention on the Privileges and Immunities of the Specialized Agencies (33 UNTS 261 *et seq*), which were 'adopted' and 'approved', respectively, by the UN General Assembly and subsequently envisaged a single legal act on the part of states, accession or succession, as the immediate expression of consent to be bound. When states nonetheless communicated their accession 'subject to ratification', this was interpreted by the Secretary-General as a declaration of intention (see the 1959 *Summary of the Practice of the Secretary-General as Depository of Multilateral Agreements* (ST/-LEG/7), §48).

[14] Cf section 6.2 below.

[15] An examination of the different UN organs and bodies involved in the treaty-making process falls outside the scope of this article, as does a doctrinal discussion on delegation and the role of IGO organs (Henry Schermers and Niels Blokker, *International Institutional Law*, 2003, §§ 217–235). A extensive survey of the various combinations and interactions is found in *Review of the Multilateral Treaty-Making Process*, UN Doc ST/Leg/Ser B/2; see also Rosenne, *UN Treaty Practice...*, above, note 9, at 321–326; Shabtai Rosenne, *Developments in the Law of Treaties (1945–1986)*, 1989, at 390–394; and Reuter, *Introduction*, above, note 12, at 60–66.

relates to the earlier stages of the treaty-making process, but instances of institutional decentralisation are also found at the stage of the adoption of the text.[16]

On a general note it can be said that in the 50 years since Rosenne's time of writing, these still count as the three new features in treaty practice within the United Nations – although there may be differences in degree, such as in the case of internal decentralisation which has since greatly expanded, and also in relation to the increase in subsidiary organs and the expansion of the 'UN family'.[17] Notwithstanding advantages of time and finance gained from the use of a centralised IGO framework, however, the multilateral treaty-making process is still perceived by many as 'cumbersome'. In 1976 UN treaty-making practice was described as 'varied, chancy, frequently experimental and often inefficient'.[18] New factors, however, have to be taken into account, such as the complex processes of decentralisation *within* the Organization, mentioned above, and the general fact that the number of member states has more than tripled since the creation of the United Nations.

In the present context it should be noted that the centralised institutional framework of the Organization, though predominantly 'open' in its role as a forum for (mostly) states, ever so discreetly poses a barrier to the operation of the general law of treaties. This is most conspicuous when it comes to treaties the text of which is *adopted* in an organisation.[19] In this case the reservation clause in Article 5 of the two Vienna Conventions gives precedence to the institutional law of the organisation over general international law.[20] But also in the practice of treaties which are 'merely drawn up under the auspices of an organisation or through use of its facilities' – a prominent example being the 1998 ICC Statute, adopted by

[16] Eg the 1982 Charter of the Asian and Pacific Development Centre, adopted by the UN ECOSOC's Economic and Social Commission for Asia and the Pacific (Resolution 225 (XXXVIII); UN Docs. E/198/20 and E/ESCAP/287).

[17] See Oscar Schachter and Chistopher Joyner (eds), *United Nations Legal Order,* 1995 in general; and Paul Szasz, General Law-Making Processes', in Christopher Joyner (ed), *The United Nations and International Law,* 1997, 27–64.

[18] See Part One, *Rationale*, of the *Review of the Multilateral Treaty-Making Process, above,* note 15, at 7–12 (citation of the Australian Foreign Minister at 7); the burden placed on the states' national systems, not all of which have extensive governmental machineries for the conduct of external relations, also becomes clear from the UNITAR commissioned study by Oscar Schachter et al, *Towards Wider Acceptance of UN Treaties*, 1971.

[19] This goes for most UN-fostered human rights treaties, starting with the 1948 Convention on the Prevention and Punishment of the Crime of Genocide (adopted by UNGA Resolution 260(III) which was unanimously adopted; see above, note 11 and see below note 25 and accompanying text.

[20] Article 5: 'The present Convention applies to any treaty *[between one or more States and one or more international organisations]* which is the constituent instrument of an international organisation and to any treaty adopted within an international organisation, without prejudice to any relevant rules of the organisation'. (in the 1986 Convention, bracketed text was added to the text of Art 5 of the 1969 Convention).

the United Nations Diplomatic Conference of Plenipotentiaries on the Establishment of an International Criminal Court – the institutional framework has had a centralising effect. This in turn has left its mark on the general law of treaties, as appears from the preparatory work of the 1969 Vienna Convention.

Thus the International Law Commission reportedly gave 'particular attention' to UN practice, for instance with regard to the function of the depository.[21] Another example is the provision in Article 9(2) of the 1969 Vienna Convention ('Adoption of the text')[22] – first, because of the (acknowledged) reference to UN conference practice, and second because of the very fact that, although UN conference practice is far from universally observed, the Commission did not insert a general reservation clause with regard to the 'internal rules of the organisation', but chose to set out a defined norm instead. Meanwhile, Article 9(1) envisages the traditional unanimity rule for adoption of a treaty *outside* a conference framework, a provision by no means relevant for bilateral treaties only.[23]

The drafters of Article 9 distinguished, in effect, between different levels of centralisation: they respected the structure of a diplomatic conference as opposed to a genuine 'horizontal' forum by stipulating a particular rule instead of the regular unanimity rule;[24] but they did not equate this structure to a proper IGO framework, in which case the law of treaties is, by way of a general reservation clause (Article 5 VCLT I), precluded from operating at all. The ILC commentary confirms that Article 5 (final draft Article 4) on *inter alia* 'treaties [. . .] which are adopted within international organisations' was expressly 'intended to exclude treaties merely drawn up under the auspices of an organisation or through use of its facilities and to confine the reservation to treaties the text of which is drawn up and adopted within an organ of the organisation'.[25] Thus the 1969 Vienna Convention itself, even if it had been endowed with retroactive effect, would not have been governed by the IGO reservation clause of Article 5, however closely the process of conclusion was tied in with the infrastructure of the United Nations.

An influence by the institutional framework can be traced in general conference practice as well. Certain developments – such as the trend to do

[21] Cf the ILC's reference to the 1959 *Summary of the Practice. . .* , above, note 13, in its commentary to Art 72 on the functions of the depository (YILC 1966, Vol II, § 1, at 269).

[22] Article 9(2) reads: 'The adoption of the text of a treaty at an international conference takes place by the vote of two thirds of the States present and voting, unless by the same majority they shall decide to apply a different rule'.

[23] Article 9(1) reads: 'The adoption of the text of a treaty takes place by the consent of all the States participating in its drawing up except as provided in paragraph 2'. Article 9(1) was drafted inter alia with a view to 'restricted' multilateral treaties.

[24] This is in line with a tendency, noted by Reuter, to 'institutionalize international conferences and turn them into entities' (*Introduction*, above, note 12, at 87).

[25] Commentary to final Draft Art 4, YILC 1966, Vol II, § 3, at 191.

as much work as possible in committees, where decisions are normally made by a simple rather than a qualified majority[26] – could be taken as a sign that, as in the League era,[27] conference practice has developed along the lines of the general institutional features of the organisations which in many cases are host to these conferences.[28] This includes the tendency in diplomatic conferences to avoid voting altogether and to aim for consensus (an outstanding example being the Third United Nations Conference on the Law of the Sea). Voting practice 'has come full circle'[29] – from unanimous voting through majority voting to consensus procedures. Indeed, when a consensus procedure, even if it does not formally amount to voting, is made obligatory in the Rules of Procedure (as in the case of the Conference on Disarmament, described below), in the broad sense it becomes part of 'voting practice'.

A politically high-profile event in treaty practice may be taken as an example of the difference between a relatively centralised and self-contained international organisation on the one hand and a genuine 'forum', albeit a permanent one, for inter-state co-operation on the other. The Conference on Disarmament (CD) is a traditional platform or, in its own words, 'negotiating forum,'[30] in which treaty texts are negotiated and adopted (obligatorily) by consensus.[31] It would not have 'autonomy' according to a formal definition of 'organisation'.[32] When in 1996 the CD did not succeed in reaching consensus on the adoption of the text of the Comprehensive Nuclear Test-Ban Treaty, Australia sent the text as an attachment to a letter to the UN General Assembly. It was then submitted to the General Assembly as a Draft resolution with the sponsorship of more than 120 states[33] and could subsequently be adopted with wide

[26] If the subject of the conference does not easily allow for a division of work over different committees on the basis of substantive criteria, negotiating parties gain this procedural advantage by working in a Committee on the Whole rather than in the Plenary; one example is the 1968–69 Vienna Conference itself (Rule 50 of the Rules of Procedure, reproduced in UN Doc A/Conf.39/11, at XXV).

[27] See section 3.3.1 above.

[28] Cf in general, Treves, above, note 10, and Shabtai Rosenne, 'International Conferences and Congresses', EPIL, Vol I, 1992, 739–746.

[29] David Kennedy, 'The Move to Institutions', 8 *Cardozo Law Review* 1987, 841–988, at 967, and references to voting literature therein; cf also Louis Sohn, 'Voting Procedures in United Nations Conferences for the Codification of International Law', 69 *American JIL* 1975 310–353, with a survey of practice between 1944 and 1975.

[30] No. I of the Rules of Procedure (CD/8/Rev 7, 27 June 1996 – www.unog.ch/frames/disarm/disdoc.htm). The CD dates back to the 1950s and is open to the nuclear weapon States and, presently, 56 other States. It is only loosely connected to the United Nations. Cf Reuter, *Introduction. . .*, above, note 12, at 12, on the tendency to safeguard the position of the Great Powers by keeping the treaty-making process with respect to certain politically sensitive matters 'outside the organisational framework'.

[31] No 18 of the Rules of Procedure; cf above, note 29 and accompanying text.

[32] Section 2.2.1 above.

[33] UN Doc A/50/L.78 (6 September 1996).

support (exceeding the required two-thirds majority).[34] Put differently: by taking it out of a 'horizontal' framework and bringing into another – centralised – one, the collective stage of the treaty-making process could be completed.[35]

The objective of IGO 'sponsored' conventions (that is, treaties either drawn up or adopted, or even 'signed subject to ratification' via the institutional structure of the organisation) to act as a decision-making instrument *within* the organisation and as a means to realise the objectives and functions of the organisation, is not taken into account here, as the institutional life *per se* of organisations lies outside the scope of this book. Likewise, the role of IGOs in the subsequent monitoring of treaty regimes, possibly through the incorporation of 'treaty organs', is not addressed.[36] Nonetheless, in relation to compliance monitoring one example may be given in which the centralised IGO framework is resorted to as a solution for the dilemmas posed by the strict equality of the treaty parties: the (not yet successful) projects to vitalise, through the use of a centralised framework, the 'two-stage test' for reservations as envisaged in Articles 19 and 20 of the 1969 Vienna Convention and to reserve the assessment of the legality of reservations (Article 19, on admissibility) to an impartial body, be it a treaty organ that is part of an international organisation (the UN Human Rights Committee), or a treaty body that is part of a treaty regime (the European Court for Human Rights).[37]

5.2 CENTRALISATION IN TECHNICAL ORGANISATIONS

As to the centralised framework for treaty-making, the previous outline of United Nations (-related) practice would broadly describe the present state of affairs regarding general international organisations. Examples of

[34] Article 18(2) UN Charter; UN Doc A/50/1027 (10 September 1996); an analysis of the Comprehensive Nuclear Test-Ban Treaty (35 ILM 1439) and its genesis in Guido den Dekker, 'De beproeving van de Comprehensive Test Ban Treaty,' 16 *Merkourios* 50, 1996, 7–13.

[35] As at 1 September 2006 the CTBT has not yet entered into force – being conditional on the ratification of all 44 states listed in Annex 2 (10 of which have not ratified).

[36] See section 2.2.1 above.

[37] See eg Catherine Redgwell, 'Reservations to Treaties and Human Rights Committee General Comment No. 24(52)', 46 *ICLQ* 1997, 390–412; and Bruno Simma, 'Reservations to Human Rights Treaties – Some Recent Developments', in Gerhard Haffner and Gerhard Loibl et al (eds), *Liber Amicorum Professor Seidl-Hohenveldern*, 1998, 659–682. The proposal of the UN HRCommittee for it to assume authority to judge reservations made to the ICCPR met with strong opposition on the part of eg the UK and France (cf Redgwell, above); for now the ILC study on reservations does not seem take a centralising approach either (cf ILC report 2003, UN Doc A/58/10, Supplement No 10).

farther-reaching centralisation are found in several of the post-war technical organisations.[38] The International Law Commission gave particular attention to this practice when it decided on the inclusion of the Article 5 saving clause in the 1969 Vienna Convention.[39]

When serving as a framework for treaty-making, several Specialised Agencies, such as the WHO (Articles 19 and 20) and UNESCO (Article IV(B)), have adopted the ILO system;[40] this means that adoption and signature are procured on the same occasion, most often in the plenary organ, and that subsequently only one legal act on the part of the member states individually – 'ratification' – is needed for states to become bound.[41]

A more centralised form of international rule-making still – which may actually transcend the qualification 'treaty norms' – is the enactment of rules by the organisation which are binding on a resolutive condition. In the International Civil Aviation Organization, 'standards' are adopted or amended by the Council by a two-thirds majority. These become effective *unless* the majority of the members register an objection within three months. After these standards are duly promulgated, there is technically no obligation for the member states to comply: they may choose individually to 'opt out' or 'contract out' by notification to the Council. The legal effect of *failure* to notify is not clear and it has not been put to the test, which allows for opinion to be divided on whether these standards are formally binding. However, in either case, ICAO standards seem to be invariably complied with in practice, which is some indication for a customary rule on the matter. In ICAO, where the opting-out system originates, the element of centralisation is particularly apparent, as the Council is not a plenary organ. Comparable procedures for the enactment of 'regulatory acts' exist for instance in the WHO (where the law-making function resides in the plenary organ, however (see Articles 21 and 22)), and in several other Specialised Agencies.[42]

[38] A helpful survey of traits of treaty-making within organisations in §§ 1262–1317 of Schermers and Blokker (above, note 15), who from an institutional law perspective rubricate such 'conventions' under the section 'decisions of the organisation'. An overview of recent developments also in eg Christian Tietje, 'The Changing Legal Structure of International Treaties as an Aspect of an Emerging Global Governance Architecture', 42 *German YIL* 1999, 26–55.

[39] Rosenne, *Developments...*, above, note 15, at 250, and references; cf above, note 25 and accompanying text.

[40] Section 2.3.1 above.

[41] Charles Alexandrowicz, *The Law-Making Functions of the Specialised Agencies of the United Nations*, 1973, at 15–39 (on convention-making within ILO, UNESCO and FAO); Frederic Kirgis, "Specialized Law-Making Processes', in Christopher Joyner (ed), *The United Nations and International Law*, 1997, 65–94.

[42] Convention on International Civil Aviation (1944), 15 UNTS 295 (Arts. 37, 54(1), 90). See Alexandrowicz, above, note 41, at 40–69 (on 'quasi-legislative acts' of Specialised Agencies); Eckart Klein, 'United Nations, Specialized Agencies", EPIL, Vol 5, 1983, 349–368; Kirgis, above, note 41, at 70 ff.

Certain treaty regimes that present to some degree centralised structures without the classic multi-organ structure and without being based on a general constituent instrument, show a similar practice. The qualification of these one-organ treaty bodies as 'international organisations' seems generally uncontroversial.[43] For example the 1985 Vienna Convention for the Protection of the Ozone Layer envisages a procedure for amendments much like that of the ILO system. The procedure laid down in the 1987 Montreal Protocol on Substances which Deplete the Ozone Layer for the enactment of 'adjustments' to the original standards with regard to controlled substances, 'takes the developments towards the binding effect of majority decision-making within treaty regimes to its furthest point to date': such adjustments – failing consensus adopted by a two-thirds majority – are, contrary to, for instance, ICAO standards, explicitly said to be binding on all parties to the Protocol.[44]

These instances of majority rule-making as yet seem limited to particular institutions with technical fields of operation.[45] In general, as Danilenko concludes, 'there is no evidence that [. . .] members of the international community endorse legislative techniques based on majority law-making'.[46]

A more fundamental question is whether such regulatory acts should be considered under the rubric of 'treaty practice' at all. There is disagreement as to whether these are to be considered derivative treaty obligations for the organisation's member states – ie as deriving from the constituent treaty – or on the contrary legislative acts by an organisation simply

[43] It has been convincingly argued that conventional IGOs should not be viewed as a closed category, but rather as part of a fuzzy category to which 'treaty regimes' belong as well – see ch 2 above, note 52 and accompanying text. This view has much descriptive power, but is at odds with the purpose of a normative definition (cf section 2.2.1 above). A more flexible approach, however, seems to have emerged – cf eg Robin Churchill and Geir Ulfstein, 'Autonomous Institutional Arrangements in Multilateral Environmental Agreements: A Little-Noticed Phenomenon in International Law', 94 *American JIL* 2000, 623–659, who, on the basis of the definition proposed by Schermers and Blokker (above, note 15) take 'Autonomous Institutional Arrangements' such as the Ozone Secretariat to qualify as international organisations.

[44] Article 2(9)d of the Montreal Protocol stipulates that decisions (possibly taken by majority) are binding on all parties and enter into force six months after notification by the Secretariat. An analysis of the procedural aspects of the 1985 Ozone Convention (1513 UNTS 3) and the 1987 Montreal Protocol (1522 UNTS 3), in Malgosia Fitzmaurice, 'Modifications to the Principles of Consent in Relation to Certain Treaty Obligations', *ARIEL* 1997, 275–317, at 281–283 and 291–293 (citation at 291).

[45] Leaving aside the difficulty of making a meaningful classification of IGOs, in the present context the distinction between political and technical organisations, or between IGOs that mainly act as a forum for interstate negotiation on the one hand and IGOs that act primarily as a machinery for rule-making activity on the other (Thomas Mensah, 'The Practice of International Law in International Organisations', in Bin Cheng (ed), *International law: teaching and practice*, 1982, 146–163, at 147), may be relevant.

[46] Danilenko, referring to comments of states participating in the third UNCLOS (Gennady Danilenko, *Law-Making in the International Community*, 1993, at 67–68).

binding its member states.[47] Essentially the same question is whether the various systems of IGO standard-setting are covered by the existing categories of sources, or whether, on the other hand, they constitute a new source of international law.[48]

An unequivocal answer seems difficult at this point. On the one hand the binding character of these regulatory acts can in principle be construed from an expression of consent *ex ante* on the part of states.[49] On the other hand, the principle of consent is stretched to its limits, to say the least. At some point, the organisation may have the legislative paradigm prevail for reasons of practical and doctrinal necessity. An example is the European Community legal order, where obligations stemming from 'community legislation' (Article 249 (old Article 189) EC) are clearly set apart from obligations stemming from 'treaty practice' of the member states (for example Article 293 (old Article 220) EC).

But in general such regulatory acts may be, and are, viewed either way. What is important is that this view is ultimately determined by the way in which an international organisation is perceived: as a predominantly open structure to be traced to the treaty by which it was created, or as a predominantly closed structure with an independent, constitutional order. The forms of rule-making described in the last section put a strain on the *concept* of treaty, that is, on the principle of consent. Arguably these are made possible *by* the centralised IGO framework and are dependent on it. This is suggested by both theory (a centralising dynamic would be needed to change the 'horizontal' structure of internal law, which necessarily hinges on consent) and practice (one does not find similar instances of rule-making outside an IGO framework).[50] Both the stretching of the treaty concept *within* the framework of international organisations (as in

[47] Cf Malgosia Fitzmaurice, who adheres to the first view (above, note 44, at 316–317), and, contrariwise, Alexandrowicz (above, note 41, at 152), on the regulatory acts of Specialised Agencies: 'this is no doubt an extra-treaty process'. A cautious approach can be found in Krzystof Skubiszewski, 'International Legislation', EPIL, Vol II, 1995, 1255–1261. See also references below in notes 48 and 49.

[48] Cf eg White, above, note 2, at 59; and Danilenko, above, note 46, at 192 ('they hardly qualify as new formal sources of general international law existing independently of a specific treaty arrangement') and, on the other hand, Vladimir Degan, *Sources of International Law*, 1997, at 6, who considers "non-obligatory' rules' such as ICAO standards, to which, nevertheless, 'the respective states almost invariably conform themselves', as a possible newly emerging source of international law.

[49] Which was the approach of the International Court of Justice, when it treated the conflict between the 1971 Montreal Convention and SC Resolution 748 – originating in the UN Charter – as a traditional case of conflicting treaties; *Case concerning Questions on Interpretation and Application of the 1971 Montreal Convention Arising from the Aerial Incident at Lockerbie* (Provisional Measures), 14 April 1992, ICJ Rep 1992, at 126.

[50] For some elaboration of the idea that new, 'counter-consensualist' developments (such as the 'living instrument' doctrine in treaty interpretation and the practice of 'international legislation') are only possible in a centralised, 'constitutionalised' environment (be it institutionally delimited, as in the framework of an organisation, or doctrinally, as in a particular

international rule-making by 'majority legislation'), and the resistance of that framework to the general law of treaties (as with the reservation clause of Article 5 VCLT)[51] are an indication of the semi-open character of the IGO legal order, that is, the legal transparency of the organisation.

field of law such as human rights), see Catherine Brölmann, 'Limits of the Treaty Paradigm', in Matthew Craven and Malgosia Fitzmaurice (eds), *Interrogating the Treaty and the Future of Treaty Law*, 2005, at 29–39.

[51] See section 5.1 above.

6

Constitutive Treaties of International Organisations

THIS CHAPTER ADDRESSES the constitutive treaties of organisations and the application of the law of treaties in their respect.[1] It has been established that organisations have a legal order which is to some extent 'internal' and distinct from international law.[2] The applicability of the law of treaties to constituent treaties is an indication of the degree of transparency of that legal order. As it turns out, organisations appear as semi-closed constructions – more so than in the forum function which was described in the previous chapter. Even when the constituent treaty is subjected to the law of treaties, it is not accessible to the law of treaties as a regular treaty would be.

6.1 TREATY OR CONSTITUTION?

Most international organisations are created by inter-state treaty.[3] But after an organisation has come into existence, it famously takes control of that same treaty at the expense of the parties' authority, and operates on the basis of a *Kompetenz-Kompetenz* of sorts – this is the tension between the member states and the organisation and the inspiration of analogies with Goethe's sorcerer's apprentice[4] and Frankenstein.[5]

Thus the organisation's constitutional order has two faces: an open, inter-state treaty regime on the one hand, and an independent constitutional order on the other. In either case the basis is an international law agreement, which may have to be resorted to with international law tools, such as the law of treaties, as a starting point for establishing the

[1] An early version of this chapter has appeared in 'The Legal Nature of International Organisations and the Law of Treaties', 4 *Austrian Review of International and European Law* 2000, 85–125, § 5

[2] See section 2.3.2 above.

[3] See section 2.2.1 above.

[4] Henry Schermers and Niels Blokker, *International Institutional Law*, 2003, § 1885.

[5] Jan Klabbers, *An Introduction to International Institutional Law*, 2002, preliminary pages.

competences of the organisation – something which the International Court of Justice has been frequently asked to do in relation to organisations of the United Nations system.

In law of treaties doctrine, this dual appearance is reflected in the two approaches that have developed in relation to constituent treaties: one emphasises its contractual nature, while the other focuses on the constitutional aspect. The constituent instrument is seen either as a treaty (with which the organisation is equated), or as a constitution underlying the independent existence of the organisation.[6] Clearly the 'constitutionalist approach' dates back to more recent times than the 'treaty approach', but some ground was cleared already in the League era with the view of constitutive treaties as a prototypal 'objective regime': in 1930 McNair classified 'treaties creating constitutional international law' as an independent sub-category of 'law-making treaties' and in conclusion recommended that 'we free ourselves from the traditional notion that the instrument known as the treaty is governed by a single set of rules'.[7]

In recent times, the constitutionalist view has been countenanced to some extent by the independent status accorded to the 'rules of the organisation' (although mostly without normative effect)[8] in several provisions of the 1986 Vienna Convention on the Law of Treaties. Most importantly, Article 5 states that '[t]he ...Convention applies to any treaty ...which is the constituent instrument of an international organisation ...without prejudice to any relevant rules of the organisation'.[9] This is a matter of the glass being half full or half empty. It is significant that the Vienna Convention is held to apply to constituent treaties. It is equally significant that this is *without prejudice to* the rules of the organisation. Arguably, the essence of Article 5 is that of a reservation clause.[10]

[6] On what has been summarised by Rosenne as the traditionalist view and the constitutionalist view, see Shabtai Rosenne, *Developments in the Law of Treaties (1945–1986)*, 1989, at 190–200, with references to 'traditionalist' and 'constitutionalist' writing in its note 17; a summary of doctrinal views in Tetsuo Sato, *Evolving Constitutions of International Organisations*, 1996, at 4–11 (for further references footnote 1, at 3); in general also Denis Simon, *L'interpretation judiciaire des traités d'organisations internationales: morphologie des conventions et fonction jurisdictionelle*, 1981. Cf section 4.2.4 above on objective legal personality of organisations.

[7] 'The Function and the Differing Legal Character of Treaties', XI *British YIL* 1930, 100–118, at 118; in Arnold McNair, *The Law of Treaties*, 1961, at 254–259), the author grouped IGO constituent treaties with dispositive treaties under the heading of what would later be termed 'objective regimes'.

[8] Article 2(1)j of the 1986 Convention reads: '"rules of the organisation" means, in particular, the constituent instruments, decisions and resolutions adopted in accordance with them, and established practice of international organisations'. On normative force and normative effect, see section 10.1.3 below *et passim*.

[9] Cf ch 5, above, note 20 and accompanying text, on art 5 of the 1969 VCLT; cf Rosenne, *Developments...*, above, note 6, at 191.

[10] See also the commentary of the ILC to the 1966 draft art 4 (1969 Convention art 5): 'such a general reservation was desirable in case the possible impact of rules of international

In contemporary law of treaties, the concept of the 'objective regime' has developed further, according to which the treaty-based regime, once established, lies outside the scope of the law of treaties. Or, in the words of Paul Reuter, '[...] the various theoretical views followed on this point by the International Law Commission [...] regard certain legal effects not as a consequence of the treaty itself but of the *situation* established by the treaty'.[11]

This view has proven instrumental in relation to international organisations, but it is unhelpful when the law of treaties does need to come into play as the most fitting set of legal tools available, as in the case of interpretation.[12] Here there seems to be some agreement that in a general sense constitutive treaties are, as put by Jennings and Watts, of an 'intrinsically evolutionary nature'.[13] This is a practical approach that does not, however, address the underlying tension, namely that between the two conceptions mentioned before. In appearance it safeguards the law of treaties paradigm, since it is put in the classic terms of a rule of interpretation, but in reality it adds a constitutionalist element. An 'evolutionary nature' does not sit easily with the idea of a consent-based formal legal agreement, which after all is supposed to fixate rules until these are changed by equally ranked rules brought about by the same contractors. Arguably this is a reason why the notion of the treaty as 'a living instrument' is not widely applied outside ECHR case law.[14]

As becomes clear from the following paragraph, the additional legal layer posed by the institutional law of the organisation is a barrier to the applicability of the general law of treaties, but not an impermeable one. The constituent instrument can be viewed neither as an entirely self-contained constitution, nor as a regular international treaty – which may be one reason why neither the traditionalist nor the constitutionalist approach has decisively prevailed.

organisations in any particular context of the law of treaties should have been inadvertently overlooked' (YILC 1966, Vol II, at 11, §1 to art 4).

[11] Paul Reuter, *Introduction to the Law of Treaties*, 1995, at 128 (emphasis in the original); see 121–129 on some analytical alternatives to describe modern practice.

[12] Above, text after footnote number 5.

[13] Eg Sir Robert Jennings and Sir Arthur Watts, *Oppenheim's International Law* (9th edn), 1992, § 629. Cf Rudolf Bernhardt, 'Evolutive Treaty Interpretation, especially of the European Convention on Human Rights', in *German Yearbook of International Law,* 1999, 11–25, who sees limited application of the evolutive approach.

[14] Expression coined by the European Court of Human Rights, and frequently resorted to in ECHR case law (eg *Tyer v UK*, 25 April 1978, Application No 00005856/72, § 31; *Loizidou v Turkey* (Judgment – Preliminary Objections), 23 March 1995, § 71; *Selmouni v France* judgment of 28 July 1999, § 101). This argument is elaborated upon in Catherine Brölmann, 'Limits of the Treaty Paradigm', in Matthew Craven and Malgosia Fitzmaurice (eds), *Interrogating the Treaty and the Future of Treaty Law,* 2005, 29–39, § III.

6.2 THE LAW OF TREATIES APPLIED TO CONSTITUTIVE INSTRUMENTS

Where the law of treaties is applied to a constituent instrument, the main issues are interpretation and amendment.[15] In both fields, case law and the rules of the organisation show a distinct departure from the traditional law of treaties.

With respect to amendment most constituent instruments clearly contrast with the principles of consent and *pacta tertiis* underlying the general rule.[16] This contrast is more conspicuous than in the case of obligations which member states may incur from the regulatory acts issued by certain specialised organisations,[17] since several IGO constitutions unequivocally provide for amendment legally effective vis-à-vis all member states on the basis of a majority vote in the competent organ and subsequent ratification by the majority of the member states. Examples are Article 108 of the UN Charter; Article 30 of the 1964 UPU Constitution; Article 28 of the WMO Constitution; and Article 7 of the Constitution of the IFC. A variant is the termination of the treaty-participation/membership of the organisation of the state that does not accept the amendment to the treaty (Article 94(b) of the 1944 Chicago Convention). In the systems of, for example, FAO (Article XX) and UNESCO (Article XIII), amendments that do not create new obligations for the member states are effectuated by a majority decision in the competent organ only.[18]

With regard to the interpretation of constituent instruments, the practice of the International Court of Justice may be taken as authoritative and indicative of general doctrinal developments. As to the interpretation of treaties in general, it is, broadly, the textual approach and the 'intention' approach that have a central place in the practice of the Court,[19] whereas

[15] The question of reservations has less practical importance since many constituent instruments do not permit reservations. It may be noted however, that art 20(3) of the 1969 Vienna Conventions respects the dual nature of the constitutive instrument also with regard to reservations: 'When a treaty is a constituent instrument of an international organisation and unless it otherwise provides, a reservation requires the acceptance of the competent organ of that organisation;' on this matter, see Rosenne, *Developments...*, above, note 6, at 218–223. A rich and intricate account of '"Constitutional" Interpretation', with less emphasis on the formal system and more on (judicial) practice appears in José Alvarez, *International Organisations as Law-makers*, 2005, at 65–108.

[16] Cf art 40(4) of the 1969 Vienna Convention: 'The amending agreement does not bind any state already a party to the agreement which does not become a party to the amending agreement'.

[17] Section 5.2 above.

[18] Cf in general Krysztof Skubiszewski, 'International Legislation', EPIL, Vol II, 1995, 1255–1261, at 1256–1257.

[19] Cf eg the *Anglo-Iranian Oil Co.* case, ICJ Rep 1952, at 104: '[The Court] must seek the interpretation which is in harmony with a natural and reasonable way of reading the text, having due regard to the intention [of the Parties]'. See, however, for a detailed and nuanced analysis of the role of the textual and the 'subjective' approach, Santiago Torres Bernárdez,

the Court has been more reluctant to apply the teleological approach or even refer to the 'object and purpose' of the treaty.[20]

This is different for constitutive treaties. From the outset the Court has pointed to the special nature of such treaties:

> On the previous occasions when the Court has had to interpret the Charter of the United Nations, it has followed the principles and rules applicable in general to the interpretation of treaties, since it has recognised that the Charter is a multilateral treaty, albeit a treaty having certain *special characteristics*.[21]

More recently the Court has elaborated on that special nature, *in casu* in relation to the WHO constitution:

> From a formal standpoint, the constituent instruments of international organisations are multilateral treaties, to which the well-established rules of treaty interpretation apply. [. . .] But the constituent instruments of international organisations are also treaties of a particular type; their object is to create new subjects of law endowed with a certain autonomy, to which the parties entrust the task of realising common goals. Such treaties can raise specific problems of interpretation owing, *inter alia*, to their character which is conventional and at the same time institutional; the very nature of the organisation created, the objectives which have been assigned to it by its founders, the imperatives associated with the effective performance of its functions, as well as its own practice, are all elements which may deserve special attention when the time comes to interpret these constituent treaties.[22]

Nonetheless, it appears that when the legal context is such that it leaves priority to the treaty element of the constituent instrument – as in contentious cases in which acceptance of the Court's jurisdiction ex Article 36 of the Statute is at issue[23] – the Court has remained with the traditional rules for treaty interpretation and has adopted a fairly conservative approach.[24]

'Interpretation of Treaties by the International Court of Justice Following the Adoption of the 1969 Vienna Convention on the Law of Treaties', in Gerhard Haffner and Gerhard Loibl et al (eds), *Liber Amicorum Professor Seidl-Hohenveldern*, 1998, 721–748.

[20] Cf arts 31–33 of the 1969 and 1986 Vienna Conventions on the Law of Treaties. The 'object and purpose test' was applied in a moderate form, eg in the *Ambatielos* case ('the Court cannot accept an interpretation which would have a result obviously contrary to the language of the declaration..'.) – ICJ Reports 1952, 28, at 45; cf Sir Ian Sinclair ('there is also the risk that the placing of undue emphasis on the 'object and purpose' of a treaty will encourage teleological methods of interpretation'.) *The Vienna Convention on the Law of Treaties* (2nd edn), 1984, at 131.

[21] *Certain Expenses of the United Nations (Article 17, paragraph 2, of the Charter)*, Advisory Opinion, ICJ Reports 1962, 157 (emphasis added).

[22] *Legality of the Use by a State of Nuclear Weapons in Armed Conflict*, ICJ Rep 1996, § 19.

[23] Rosenne, *Developments...*, above, note 6, at 234, with case law references.

[24] Cf the 1984 *Nicaragua* case (jurisdiction and admissibility), ICJ Rep 1984, at 392.

It is different when interpretation of the constituent instrument is geared to determine the competences of the IGO.[25] In these cases interpretation is a task performed both by the organisation itself[26] and by general international law, notably through judicial processes. Moreover, the International Court of Justice must take into account both the 'rules of the organisation' and general international law.[27] Thus the legal process is stratified, involving the internal legal order of the organisation as well as the general legal order. Logically the subsumed treaty element, belonging only to the general level, would be a less important factor. Practice is consistent with this in that the Court in such cases seems inclined to depart from the traditional framework, 'proceed[ing] directly to an interpretation of the constituent instrument as it stands at the time of the interpretation',[28] with a corresponding disinterest for the intention of the parties and the *travaux préparatoires*.[29]

First of all the Court's practice seems to point at a guiding principle in the choice of interpretative methods, which is the promotion of the effectiveness of the IGO.[30] This principle, in itself of teleological inspiration, then induces a choice for, generally, either the textual approach (when the text is deemed sufficiently clear) or the teleological approach. Examples of the first approach are the *Conditions of Admission* case and the *IMCO*

[25] Here the doctrine of 'implied powers' holds a prominent place; see eg Jan Klabbers, 'Over het leerstuk van de impliciete bevoegdheden in het recht der internationale organisaties', in J Steenbergen, *Ongebogen Recht*, 1998, 1–11.

[26] Oscar Schachter, 'The UN Legal Order: An Overview', in Christopher Joyner (ed), *The United Nations and International Law*, 1997, 3–26, at 9–13; Rosenne, *Developments*, above, note 6, at 241 and references; a detailed survey (for the purposes of determining the legal effects of such interpretations) in Sato, above, note 6, at 161–226.

[27] On the basis of Art 38 of the Statute, the ICJ is held to apply both general international law and the IGO's constitution, being a 'particular' international convention. On the 'duality of function' of the ICJ itself – an advisory function as a principal UN organ, and a contentious function as an organ of international law – see also Leo Gross, The International Court of Justice and the United Nations, 120 *Recueil des cours* 1967/I, eg at 370.

[28] Rosenne, *Developments…*, above, note 6, at 234; cf his general statement – with regard to the Court's interpretation of the UN Charter – that there is 'little doubt that adherence to 'traditional' legal concepts of the law of treaties is not a prominent feature of the interpretation of those provisions by the Court, although it is not displaced entirely' (at 195).

[29] See for an in depth study of the interpretation of IGO constitutions by the ICJ Sato, above, note 6; Rosenne, *Developments…*, above, note 6; Simon, above, note 6; Elihu Lauterpacht, 'The development of the Law of International Organisation by the Decisions of International Tribunals, 135 *Recueil des Cours* 1976/IV, 379–478 (aimed however, at distilling general norms of institutional law, rather than the law of treaties).

[30] Sato, above, note 6, at 154; cf 'their [of the host state and the organisation] clear obligation to co-operate in good faith to promote the objectives and purposes of the Organisation' (*Interpretation of the Agreement of 25 March 1951 between the WHO and Egypt*, Advisory Opinion, ICJ Reports 1980, 73, at 96).

case;[31] of the second the *Reparation* case; the *Effects of Awards* case (where the Court relied on the teleological approach for the competence of the UNGA to establish the Administrative Tribunal, but on the textual approach for determining the judicial nature of the Tribunal itself); and the *Namibia* Opinion of 1971.[32] The subjective or 'intentions' approach seems to be absent in this particular context, while, in short, the degree of teleological reasoning in the interpretation of constituent instruments exceeds that of traditional exercises of treaty interpretation.[33]

The teleological approach detaches the treaty regime from its treaty, although the 'object and purpose' underlying this approach allows it to be traced back to the 'will' of the treaty parties – which makes it fundamentally different from the 'evolutionary approach' mentioned above.[34]

As Rosenne points out, in the *Reparation* case the Court decided upon the legal personality of the organisation 'by some unorthodox reasoning' (viz teleological),[35] whereas along more traditional lines it could have resorted to the *travaux préparatoires* of the Charter (part of the San Francisco Conference considered such personality to be *implied* by the Charter as a whole) in order to reach the same conclusion.[36] In that sense the *Reparation* opinion may be considered as marking the break between the 'traditionalist' and the 'constitutionalist' approach.[37]

From a detailed study of the interpretation of constituent instruments in principally the Opinions of the International Court of Justice, a 'functional interpretative framework' has emerged for the interpretation of constituent instruments as opposed to regular treaties. Sato convincingly concludes that this framework differs from traditional treaty interpretation in two

[31] *Conditions for Admission of a State to Membership in the United Nations* (Advisory Opinion, ICJ Reports 1947–48, 63); *Constitution of the Maritime Safety Committee of the Inter-Governmental Maritime Consultative Organisation* (Advisory Opinion, ICJ Reports 1960, 23).

[32] *Reparation for Injuries suffered in the service of the United Nations* (ICJ Reports 1949, 174); *Effect of Awards of Compensation made by the United Nations Administrative Tribunal* (ICJ Reports 1954, 53); *Namibia Opinion* (ICJ Reports 1971, 16).

[33] Rosenne is critical of its use also in the particular context of constituent treaties, because of its being potentially 'unproductive in the political sense and [...] prejudicial to the authority of the Court' (Rosenne, *Developments...*, above, note 6, at 237); cf the remark of Sinclair, above note 20.

[34] Above note 3 and accompanying text.

[35] Viz a constitutional line of argument, concluded by the well-known phrase 'was intended to exercise and enjoy [. . .] functions and rights which can only be explained on the basis of a large measure of international personality' (*Reparation for Injuries,* above, note 32, at 179).

[36] Committee no IV/2 of the San Francisco Conference had been of the opinion that no explicit reference to international personality of the UN needed to be included in the Charter, as '[i]n effect, it will be determined implicitly from the provisions of the Charter taken as a whole' (12 UNCIO 703, at 710; quoted in Rosenne, *Developments...*, above, note 6, at 238).

[37] Rosenne, *Developments...*, above, note 6, at 238–239.

respects: the extent of teleological interpretation admitted and the importance attached to the 'practice of the organisation'.[38]

Similar to the particular interpretive strategy, the role of the 'practice of the organisation' goes to underscore the semi-open (or semi-closed) nature of the legal order of international organisations, and the ensuing stratification of international law. The practice of the organisation, or organs thereof, is a recurring element in the reasoning of the Court (for example in the *Certain Expenses* case and in the 1971 *Namibia* opinion),[39] and even when the Court has emphatically stated that it is relying on traditional methods of interpretation, there may be additional recourse to consistent practice by (an organ of) the IGO.[40] When assessing the WHO's competence to request an Advisory Opinion on the use of nuclear weapons, the Court reaffirmed that an organisation's constituent instrument was to be '[i]nterpreted in accordance with their ordinary meaning, in their context and in the light of the object and purpose of the [...] Constitution, *as well as of the practice followed by the Organisation*'.[41]

The Court thus attributes normative value to the practice of the organisation. Such practice, however, cannot be put on the same footing as the interpretive tool envisaged in Article 31(3)b of the 1969 and 1986 Vienna Conventions – 'any subsequent practice in the application of the treaty which establishes the agreement of the parties regarding its interpretation' – for precisely the reason that the 'application' of a constitutive treaty is a stratified process and partly takes place within the IGO itself, independent of the 'will' or intention of the treaty parties.[42] While the practice of the organisation itself is thus added to the law of treaties instrumentarium (although it is not mentioned in Articles 31 and 32 of the

[38] Sato, above, note 6, (in particular 41–159), including all cases before the Court in which constituent instruments were at issue up to the 1982 *Application for Review of Judgment N. 273 of the United Nations Administrative Tribunal*. Sato's conclusions are more cautious than Simon's ('l'interprétation jurisdictionelle des traités constitutifs tend effectivement privilèger le development des finalités institutionelles') above, note 6, at 194).

[39] *Certain Expenses of the United Nations* (ICJ Reports 1962, 151, at 157); and the 1971 *Namibia* opinion, above, note 32, at 16. For other references see Sato, above, note 6, 41–159.

[40] *Competence of the General Assembly for the Admission of a State to the United Nations* case, ICJ Reports 1950, 7, at 9. A recent survey of practice of organisations (notably related to peacekeeping operations) in the framework of attribution for the purpose of establishing international responsibility, in the *Second Report on Responsibility of Organisations* of ILC Special Rapporteur Gaja (UN Doc A/CN.4/541).

[41] *Legality of the Use. . .*, above, note 22, § 21 (emphasis added).

[42] Note however the argumentation in the Written Statement submitted on behalf of the Secretary-General of the United Nations (para 45) of 2 October 1998 in the case on the *Difference relating to Immunity from Legal Process of a Special Rapporteur of the Commission on Human Rights* (Opinion of 29 April 1999), in which 'the established practice of the Organisation, as confirmed by the Mazilu opinion' is implicitly equated with the 'subsequent practice' of art 31(3)b of the 1969 and 1986 Conventions (texts at www.icj-cij.org/icj).

Vienna Conventions), references to the 'subsequent practice' of the *parties* to the constituent treaty on the other hand seem to be absent in the Court's Opinions involving interpretation of IGO constitutions.[43]

Sato's study, which appeared in 1996, does not include the 1996 WHO Advisory Opinion. This can count as an important decision in the present context, in that the Court seems to take its interpretive exercise one step beyond regular (even if teleological) treaty interpretation and to adopt a truly constitutional approach. After it determines the functions of the Organisation by reference to the classic law of treaties canon,[44] the Court moves into a constitutional discourse, proceeding from the functions of the organisation, rather than working towards establishing them. This constitutional discourse includes not only references to 'the practice followed by the Organisation . . .',[45] but also an – unprecedented – 'systemic approach':

> As these provisions [in Article 63 UN Charter] demonstrate, the Charter of the United Nations laid the basis of a 'system' designed to organise international co-operation in a coherent fashion by bringing the United Nations, invested with powers of general scope, into relationship with various autonomous and complementary organisations, invested with sectorial powers. The exercise of these powers by the organisations belonging to the 'United Nations system' is co-ordinated, notably, by the relationship agreements concluded between the United Nations and each of the specialised agencies [. . .] It follows from the various instruments mentioned above that the WHO Constitution can only be interpreted, as far as the powers conferred upon that Organisation are concerned, by taking due account not only of the general principle of speciality, but also of the *logic of the overall system* contemplated by the Charter [. . .] any other conclusion would render virtually meaningless the notion of a specialised agency.[46]

Finally, as to the organisation's transparency in relation to its organs, on occasion the Court has explicitly referred to the practice of a particular organ rather than to the practice of the organisation as a whole. It may be recalled that 'the established practice of the organisation' is mentioned as a separate element of the 'rules of the organisation' in the 1986 Vienna Convention,[47] but the internal division of competences is left entirely to the institutional law of the organisation. Decentralisation *within* the organisation[48] has a centralising effect on the general international order, as the

[43] Likewise references to the intention of the parties; cf eg Lauterpacht, and other sources mentioned above in note 29.

[44] *Legality of the Use...*, above, note 22, § 21; see above note 41, and accompanying text on 'practice of the organisation'.

[45] *Ibid.*

[46] *Ibid*, § 26; on 'functional decentralisation' see Schermers and Blokker, above, note 4, § 1692.

[47] Art 2(1)j; for its text see note 8 (see also accompanying text).

[48] See section 5.1 above.

member states are one step further removed from control over the 'practice' that may subsequently shape the treaty regime they originally established.[49] Put differently, one more level is added between the general law of treaties and the constituent treaty to which it has to apply. Judge Spender referred to this problem in his Dissenting Opinion in the *Certain Expenses* case:

> I find difficulty in accepting the proposition that a practice pursued by an *organ* of the United Nations may be equated with the subsequent conduct of parties to a bilateral agreement and thus afford evidence of intention of the parties to the Charter.[50]

It is noteworthy that the practice of the International Court of Justice in this respect does not differ substantively from that of the European Court of Justice, a judicial organ that does not have the dual function of the International Court,[51] and that is meant to operate only within the – comparatively 'constitutional' – Community legal order. In its sparse references to the general rules of interpretation as codified in the Vienna Conventions, the European Court can be seen to adopt a constitutional approach, reflected in a large degree of teleological reasoning coupled with a reluctance to use the *travaux préparatoires* as a supplementary means of interpretation.[52] In the same vein, the European Court does not recognise subsequent practice of the parties as a tool for interpretation of the EC treaty.[53]

For its highly centralised character the legal order of the European Community appears as more closed than that of other international organisations. All the same, it does not have the legal impermeability of a state: witness, for example, the fact that on the basis of Article 220 (old 164) EC the European Court is also held to apply 'law' in general, for the purpose of interpretation and application of the EC treaty. This may be one reason for a contradictory line of argument in Opinion 1/91 on the EEA Treaty, in which the European Court invoked a rule of general international law while at the same time adopting a rigorously constitutional and self-contained approach.[54] As Kuijper has put it, the Court

[49] As mentioned in the context of IGOs in a forum function (ch 5), the process of decentralisation *within* IGOs is left out of this account.

[50] Above, note 39, at 189 (italics in the original); the Court however reaffirmed the validity of practice of an IGO organ (*in casu* the Security Council) as an interpretive tool in the *Namibia* Opinion, above, note 39, at 22.

[51] Cf above note 27.

[52] Pieter Jan Kuijper, 'The Court and the tribunal of the EC and the Vienna Convention on the Law of Treaties 1969', 25 *Legal Issues of European Integration* 1999, 1–23.

[53] Explicitly in the case C-327/91 (*France v Commission*), [1994] ECR I-3641 (point 36) and opinion 1/94, [1994] ECR, I-5267 (point 52 and 61). Contrary to the International Court, however, it does not seem to accept (as yet) the subsequent practice of Community institutions for the purpose of interpretation. See Kuijper, above, note 52, especially at 9–10.

[54] Opinion 1/91, [1991] ECR, I-6079, point 14.

performed a 'von Münchhausen trick' of sorts when it relied on the object and purpose test of Article 31(1) of the Vienna Conventions in its interpretation of the EC treaty[55] to underscore the special character of that treaty, and then used its own case law by way of 'context' (Article 31(2)) to substantiate the particular character of the EC treaty as opposed to the EEA Agreement.[56]

Thus, while the law of treaties is the primary legal tool for the interpretation of IGO constitutive treaties, the limited receptiveness of such treaties to the classic law of treaties (IGO rules for revision give a similar picture)[57] reveals a semi-closed legal order on the part of the organisation. Indeed, Rosenne considered constituent treaties to be so fundamentally different that in his opinion:

> it is deceptive to see in diplomatic and legal (including judicial) incidents concerning the constituent instruments 'precedents' for the general law of treaties, and *vice versa*.[58]

[55] As it had earlier in the *Polydor* case (Case 270/80, [1982] ECR, 329).

[56] Kuijper, above, note 52, at 2–4.

[57] Amendment practice in relation to constituent instruments clearly contrasts with the principles of consent and *pacta tertiis* underlying the general rule for amendment as laid down in art 40 (4) of the 1969 Vienna Convention: 'The amending agreement does not bind any state already a party to the agreement which does not become a party to the amending agreement'. See above note 18 and accompanying text.

[58] Rosenne, *Developments*..., above, note 6, at 257–258.

7

Treaty-Making by International Organisations

THE THIRD MANNER in which organisations are involved with treaty law and practice is as independent actors. Part Two therefore closes with a brief look at contemporary treaty-making by international organisations (section 7.1), and the reception of this practice in international law doctrine and theory (section 7.2). The latter section proceeds specifically from treaty practice, and is therefore presented separately from the general survey in Chapter 4 above. As it considers international organisations as treaty-making parties on their own accord, this section also serves as a bridge to Part Three, which focuses on the conventional law of treaties for IGO subjects and its legislative history.

7.1 IGO TREATIES IN PRACTICE

7.1.1 A Quantitative Perspective

The United Nations era has seen an exponential increase in agreements concluded by international organisations (IGO treaties), due primarily to the rise in number of organisations and the intensification of international relations in general.[1]

On the question of how many treaties are concluded by international organisations, some preliminary remarks are in order. Significant quantitative data on IGO treaties are not readily available, neither from a macro- nor from a micro-perspective. The larger picture is distorted due to the dispersion of sources and the varying time-lags between conclusion or entry into force of treaties and their registration. The view of individual

[1] Paul Reuter, *Introduction to the Law of Treaties*, 1995, at 12–16 ('soaring number of agreements' at 13).

organisations' treaty-making practice, on the other hand, may be fragmented because of the limited accessibility of the material, due to, for example, a filing system based on non-legal criteria and the division of portfolios within the organisation.

The primary source for IGO treaties is the widest ranging non-national source for treaties in general: the United Nations Treaty Series (*UNTS*).[2] Treaties concluded by the United Nations or a Specialized Agency are not covered by the obligation to register under Article 102 of the UN Charter.[3] These are submitted on a voluntary basis, 'filed and recorded' by the Secretariat and published in Part II of the *UNTS*.[4]

The *UNTS* was envisioned as an 'Official Gazette' by President Wilson,[5] but it has not quite fulfilled its promise. Apart from issues of the capacity of the UN Treaty section,[6] it is certain that not nearly all treaties[7] concluded are submitted to the UN. The percentage is not clear – a clear gauge is the comparison with the global treaty project of the (no longer updated) *World Treaty Index*:[8] only 50 per cent of the treaties listed for the

[2] The UNTS is accessible as part of the digital UN Treaty Collection (www.untreaty.u-n.org).

[3] By virtue of Art 102(1) of the UN Charter, every treaty entered into by a member of the Organisation is to be 'registered with the [UN] Secretariat and published by it'.

[4] On the basis of Art 10 of the Regulations adopted by the General Assembly to give effect to Art 102 (UN Doc A/Res/97(I) of 14 December 1946 – most recently amended by GA Resolution UN Doc A/Res/52/153 (1997)). Treaties to which only organisations part of the UN system are a party therefore must be filed and recorded; treaties to which both UN member states and organisations are parties must be registered normally.

[5] Point I of the Fourteen Points Speech by President Woodrow Wilson in 1918: 'Open covenants of peace, openly arrived at, after which there shall be no private international understandings of any kind but diplomacy shall proceed always frankly and in the public view' (Arthur S Link et al (eds), *The Papers of Woodrow Wilson*, vol 45 (1984), at 536).

[6] Cf Palitha Kohona, 'Implementing Article 102 of the Charter of the United Nations and the Depositary Function of the Secretary General', 1 *Romanian Journal of International Law* 2003, 141–171.

[7] Art1(1) of the Regulations (above, note 4) specifies: 'every treaty or international agreement, whatever its form and descriptive name'. The 'agreements' are also mentioned in Art 102(1) of the Charter. The term is used a broad category, not quite in line with law of treaties definitions, covering also the acceptance of a stipulation pour autrui or declarations ex Art 36(2) of the Statute of the International Court of Justice (Anthony Aust, *Modern Treaty Law and Practice*, 2000, at 276) – they do not relate to the terminological distinction in style in the 1940s and 1950s, between 'treaties' of states and 'agreements' of IGOs (see section 7.2 below)

[8] The *Treaty Information Project* (which originated in the 1960s at the Political Science Department of the University of Washington) was designed to obtain quantitative data on treaty-making and ultimately to offer a complete and searchable index of all twentieth-century treaties in the *World Treaty Index*. The WTI, which was referred to by authors including later ILC Special Rapporteur Reuter (*Introduction...*, above, note 1, at 54 (para 86)), was based on the UNTS and the LNTS, with added information from national treaty publication series and on occasion from direct contacts with individual IGOs. On the Project see Peter Rohn, 'Introduction' in *World Treaty Index*, 5 Vols, 1984, Vol 1, 5–23; also Peter Rohn, 'The United Nations Treaty Series Project' in 12 *International Studies Quarterly* 1968, 174-195; Peter Rohn, *Institutions in Treaties: A Global Survey of Magnitudes and Trends From 1945 to 1965*, 1970.

period 1946–1975 are found in the UNTS – and vary per country, where small states with an administrative and internationalist tradition arguably are more inclined to go through the necessary operations. Considering the low profile of IGO treaty practice,[9] it is likely that at least as many IGO treaties as state treaties are not submitted for registration. In 1983 the UN Administrative Committee on Co-ordination warned that 'certain organisations, including some of the United Nations system, that conclude significant agreements have not registered these'.[10]

Several estimates of the number of IGO treaties have been made over the years. In 1960 Oscar Schachter assessed on the basis of the UNTS that approximately 200 treaties had been concluded between international organisations and 1,000 treaties concluded between international organisations and states.[11] The *World Treaty Index* reports that in the period 1946–1965 of the total of 7,885 treaties published in the UNTS (Vols 1–598), 1,686 treaties, or 27 per cent, were concluded by international organisations. These treaties had been concluded by approximately 50 IGOs – which is one-quarter of those listed in the IOs Yearbook at that time.[12] Twenty years later, Zemanek stated that 'more than 2000 treaties to which international organisations are parties, have been published in the UNTS'.[13] The number of organisations engaging in treaty-making practice had increased more dramatically: in the aforementioned 1983 Statement the UN Administrative Committee on Co-ordination mentioned 'some 140 organizations' to have registered or filed and recorded agreements with the UN.[14] For now this appears a stable figure, as the UNTS in 2005 yielded 109 'international organisations' as parties to treaties published in the UNTS, and 29 'UN-Related organs and agencies'.[15] Incidentally, agreements concluded by organs of international organisations appear not to be

[9] Section 7.1.2 below; note also the fact that the 1977 UNGA Resolution which aimed to counter the backlog in publication of registered treaties by establishing a priority, explicitly mentions as less weighty agreements 'treaties concluded by international organisations (primarily the United Nations and Specialised Agencies such as the World bank and the International Development Association)' (UN Doc A/Res/32/144, § 3).

[10] UN Doc A/C.6/38/4, § 5 (1983).

[11] Oscar Schachter, 'Review of JW Schneider, Treaty-making Power of International Organizations', 54 *American JIL* 1960, 201–202, at 201. This figure is reproduced in Special Rapporteur Reuters *First report on the question of treaties concluded between states and international organizations or between two or more international organizations* of 1972 (UN Doc. A/CN.4/258, at 173.

[12] Günther Hartmann, 'The Capacity of International Organizations to Conclude Treaties' in Karl Zemanek (ed), *Agreements of International Organizations and the Vienna Convention on the Law of Treaties*, 1971, at 155.

[13] Karl Zemanek, 'International Organisations: Treaty-Making Power', in EPIL, Vol 5, 1983, at 168–169.

[14] Above, note 10, § 5.

[15] United Nations Treaty Series (14 Dec 1946 – Feb 2005) as at Sept 2006; available at http://untreaty.un.org/.

submitted for registration. For example the numerous agreements concluded by UNHCR[16] are not included in the UNTS.

From a micro-perspective, the statement by the IBRD during consultations for the drafting of the 1969 Vienna Convention is illustrative: IBRD and IDA were in the late 1960s party to over 700 agreements.[17] From the database of the European Council[18] the EC appears to have concluded some 1,500 agreements with both states and organisations on various subjects. From the Dutch foreign affairs database[19] it appears that in 2006 the Netherlands was a party to over 1,000 treaties with, in total, some 110 international organisations.

7.1.2 A Qualitative Perspective

From a qualitative perspective IGO treaty-making practice appears to be constant over the years.[20] Organisations conclude treaties with varying designations (mostly less solemn than in state treaty practice): in the form of a unitary instrument or an exchange of instruments; and in the case of agreements with other organisations sometimes in the form – analogous to the device of parallel national legislation by states – of parallel resolutions. There is also a practice of 'gentleman's agreements', but unlike the practice in the foreign affairs of some states such as the United Kingdom and the Netherlands, these agreements are not generally labeled with the term Memorandum of Understanding (MoU).[21]

[16] See section 7.2.2 below.

[17] UN Doc A/Conf.39/7/Add 1 and Add 1/Corr 1, § 5. Cf below, note 26 and accompanying text on the OPCW.

[18] As at 1 Sept 2006 http://www.consilium.europa.eu/_applications/Applications/accords/search.asp?lang=EN&cmsID=297. See also Eur-Lex (http://europa.eu.int/-lex//_accord.do?ihmlang=en&mode=rep).

[19] The PACTA database, with the digitalised Netherlands treaty-collection, became operational under auspices of Ministry for Foreign Affairs in January 2004 and is accessible via http://www.minbuza.nl/. The author is indebted to the Treaty Division of the Legal Office of the Ministry for Foreign Affairs.

[20] Described in eg Shabtai Rosenne, *United Nations Treaty Practice*, RdC 1954, 281–444, at 394–407; early practice also in Higgins, *The Development of International Law through the Political Organs of the United Nations*, 1963, at 241–249; Hungdah Chiu, *The Capacity of International Organizations to Conclude Treaties, and the Special Legal Aspects of the Treaties so Concluded*, 1966; Kesera Karunatilleke, 'Essai d'une classification des accords conclus par les organisations internationales, entre elles ou avec des états', LXXV *Revue générale de droit international public* 1971, 16–91; Henry Schermers and Niels Blokker, *International Institutional Law*, 2003, §§ 1743–1747.

[21] The Glossary of the United Nations Treaty-Making Handbook: 'The term memorandum of understanding (M.O.U.) is often used to denote a less formal international instrument than a typical treaty or international agreement. It often sets out operational arrangements under a framework international agreement. It is also used for the regulation of technical or detailed matters. An M.O.U. typically consists of a single instrument and is entered into among States and/or international organisations. The United Nations usually concludes

This is confirmed for example by the practice of the European Community (apart from the additional range of treaty activity generated by certain exclusive competences vis-à-vis the member states)[22] and – by way of two random examples[23] – by a perusal of the archives of the FAO and the OECD. Meanwhile, the internal practice of these organisations suggests that institutions do not attach the same importance to their external agreements *qua* legal instruments as would states; up to the late 1990s the archives of neither the FAO nor the OECD kept a systematic record of treaty-based rights and obligations of the organisation as such. Filing systems tend to be based not on a legal criterion, such as binding or non-binding arrangements, but on subject matter. A factor which emerges from personal information is the importance attached to the 'freedom of practice' of the organisation.[24]

The OECD, according to an internal and informal classification, is a party to five types of agreement: a) privileges and immunities agreements (signed with new members); b) cooperation agreements (with non-members); c) memoranda of understanding (with other international organisations); d) participation in the multi-organisation agreement constituting the Joint Vienna Institute (provides training for ex-Eastern bloc civil servants); and e) exchanges of letters with a number of non-member states (providing access as observers to specified OECD Committees).

The FAO Legal Service for practical purposes distinguishes between: a) agreements with states, concerning the representation of the FAO (comprising headquarters agreements; the status of FAO representatives in different states; and any agreement regulating the participation of the FAO in Conferences); b) agreements with other international organisations (comprising 'relationship agreements' (for the purpose of an institutional

M.O.U.s with Member States in order to organise its peacekeeping operations or to arrange United Nations conferences. The United Nations also concludes M.O.U.s regarding cooperation with other international organisations. The United Nations considers M.O.U.s to be binding and registers them if submitted by a party or if the United Nations is a party. Http://untreaty.un.org/English/TreatyHandbook/hbframeset.htm.

22 Now more accessible through the publication of EC treaties: see above, note 18 and accompanying text. Cf the not so recent, but to the knowledge of the present author as yet most detailed, study by Catherine Flaesch-Mougin, *Les accords externes de la CEE: essai d'une typologie* (diss Univ Libre de Bruxelles), 1979.

23 A choice inspired also by the hospitality of the organisations in question: the author is indebted to Mr Jacques de Miramon and Mr Nicola Bonucci of the OECD, and to Mr Denis Fadda, Legal Officer in the General Legal Affairs Service of FAO, for having been granted access to the archives of the organisation. Findings on the OECD are confirmed by Jean-Pierre Puissochet, 'Organisation de coopération et de developpement économiques', Droit international, Fascicule 160-A, 8, 1983.

24 This was mentioned also in the official comment of FAO with regard to the ILC draft articles on the law of treaties in 1968 (see ch 8 below).

liaison) and 'cooperation agreements' (for the purpose of an operational liaison)); and c) (standard) operational agreements with states, on the implementation of projects.

While formal designations such as 'treaty' and 'convention' are generally avoided,[25] the binding character of agreements is not at issue. In, for example, FAO practice only the legal character, *vel non*, of the 'letter of intent' is considered to be dependent on the situation or determined by the 'intention of the parties', as this term is also used for non-binding agreements. As in state treaty practice, legal policy may be to downplay the political status of agreements by using low-key terminology, in order to accommodate the national constitutional system of a treaty partner (an MoU may bypass national parliaments more easily, especially in a constitutional system that provides for executive agreements or administrative agreements) or the institutional system of the organisation itself (in for example the FAO, an MoU may be adopted by the (plenary) Conference without passing through the Financial Committee).

As an example of a young organisation – which allows for a more comprehensive view of its treaty practice – the OPCW is estimated to have concluded some 100 international agreements since its establishment in 1994.[26] These include a Headquarters Agreement with The Netherlands;[27] Privileges and Immunities Agreements (as at 1 September 2006) with some 15 per cent of the 164 member states;[28] 'Facility Agreements', which govern the inspection of certain types of facilities and plants sites;[29] 'Agreements For The Procurement Of Assistance' in case of a chemical weapons-related threat to the security of one of the member states;[30] a Relationship Agreement with the United Nations under Article 63 of the

[25] In the FAO, the terminological hierarchy of agreements entered into by the organisation appears to be the following: agreement; memo(randum) of understanding; exchange of letters; letter of agreement; letter of understanding; note of understanding; letter of intent.

[26] Article VIII, paragraph 34(a), of the OPCW Convention mandates the Executive Council to conclude agreements or arrangements with States and international organisations on behalf of the OPCW, subject to prior approval by the Conference of the States Parties. The author is thankful to Dr. Olufemi Elias and Mrs. Lisa Tabassi, Legal Officers at the Office of the Legal Adviser, OPCW, for information on the treaty practice of the Organization.

[27] Text at http://www.opcw.org/ (Basic text | HQ agreement | OPCW Decision (C-8/Dec.12).

[28] See http://www.opcw.org/ (Home > Legal affairs).

[29] Conclusion of such agreements is obligatory in case of all chemical weapons-related facilities, Schedule I facilities, and schedule II plant sites; see Art VI of the 1993 Chemical weapons Convention, http://www.opcw.org/html/db/cwc/eng/) the *Verification Annex VI*. At the request of the UN Treaty section Facility Agreements are not sent to the UN for registration under Art 102.

[30] Article X(7)b – as at 1 September 2004 only one had been concluded, with the Republic of Iran; a little over two years later the organisation had concluded six more "procurement of assistance" agreements.

UN Charter;[31] and a signature subject to ratification to the 1986 Vienna Convention as the yet sole instance of participation in a 'law-making treaty'. Otherwise agreements are usually bilateral, expression of consent on the part of the Organisation is expressed by simplified signature, and the designation of agreements is predominantly low-profile ('arrangements').

Content-wise, IGO treaties essentially do not 'compete' with state treaty practice, as organisations tend to conclude agreements on matters that are an extension of their competences in the institutional sphere. This means that only in the case of a supranational organisation – which has taken on certain functions of the member states, mostly to the exclusion of the latter[32] – will IGO treaties *in substance* be similar to state treaties.[33]

More importantly, as to formal-legal criteria[34] IGO treaty-practice is – from the perspective of general international law – perfectly comparable to that of states. This holds valid for traditional parameters such as parties, laterality, form and designation of agreements. The scant participation of organisations in so-called 'law-making' treaties as opposed to 'contract treaties'[35] could appear as an exception. However, while this distinction is relevant in legal theory, it does not play a role as such in the black-letter law of treaties.

If and when distinctive factors of a legal nature do come in, these pertain not to public international law, but to the internal institutional law of the organisation: because of its functional rather than territorial design, due regard must always be given to the organisation's functional limitation.[36] This is at stake for instance in the (official) 'institutional' argument – lack of judicial and enforcement powers – on the part of the United Nations for not becoming a full-fledged party to the 1949 Geneva Conventions;[37] and also in Annex IX of the 1982 United Nations Convention on the Law of

[31] The Relationship Agreement between the UN and the OPCW was concluded in 2000 (approved by the OPCW Conference of the States Parties in decision C-VI/DEC.5 of 17 May 2001, and by the UNGA in A/RES/55/283 of 7 September 2001 – see http://www.opcw.org/ (Home > Legal affairs > UN-OPCW Relationship agreement).

[32] One reason of the increase of the EC treaty practice is because of its increasing external competences – eg in the framework of the WTO (eg Nikolaos Lavranos, *Legal Interaction between Decisions of International Organisations and European Law*, 2004).

[33] Cf In a similar vein Schermers and Blokker, above, note 20, §§ 1661, 1662.

[34] Which are few: cf Art 2(1)a of the 1969 VCLT: ' "treaty" means an international agreement concluded between States in written form and governed by international law, whether embodied in a single instrument or in two or more related instruments and whatever its particular designation'.

[35] A rather strict view on the practice of IGOs and law-making treaties appears in Schermers and Blokker, above, note 20, § 1773.

[36] On functional limitation and the 'area of competence' of organisations, see section 4.2.5 above.

[37] Cf René-Jean Dupuy, *Manuel sur les organisations internationales / A handbook on international organisations*, 1998, at 871.

the Sea, which provides that organisations can only become party if a majority of member states is a party as well.[38]

7.2 IGO TREATIES IN DOCTRINE

When international organisations' practice of making agreements became an undeniable factor in international relations, it had to be assessed and qualified in accordance with international law. In addition to the general treatment of doctrine in respect of organisations in Part One above, this section recalls two points of discussion which were raised specifically in the appraisal of IGO treaty-making. Both were initially used as a threshold for denying such practice the qualification of 'treaty-making' in the first place. These are the status of IGO treaties and the ability or 'powers' of organisations to conclude treaties.

7.2.1 The Status of IGO Agreements

One way of reconciling the emerging treaty-making practice of international organisations with the statist system of international law is to take the position that agreements concluded by IGOs are legally different instruments from agreements concluded by states.[39] Such was the suggestion of the Permanent Court when it said 'tout contrat qui n'est pas un contrat entre des états en tant que sujets du droit international a son fondement dans une loi nationale'.[40] Such was also the opinion of Professor Parry[41] and sole arbiter Professor Dupuy, who in the *Texaco* v *Libyan Arab Republic* case stated that states alone can be parties to a treaty, whereas agreements between, for example, states and IOs would be 'instruments of another nature'.[42] This perspective, which is geared not to the legal instrument but rather to the legal parties employing it, was also at the root of a proposal tabled in the ILC during the first stage of the law of

[38] Article 2: *Signature* – 'An international organisation may sign this Convention if a majority of its member States are signatories of this Convention. At the time of signature an international organisation shall make a declaration specifying the matters governed by this Convention in respect of which competence has been transferred to that organisation by its member States which are signatories, and the nature and extent of that competence'. (The European Community signed on 7 Dec 1984 and gave its act of formal confirmation on 1 April 1998).

[39] See the last pages of section 3.3.2 above.

[40] Serie A Nos 20/21, at 41 *Serbian Loans case* 1929. Cf the division of the legal universe in international and national law, section 2.3.3 above.

[41] Cf section 3.3.2 above; see Clive Parry, 'The Treaty-Making Power of the United Nations', 26 *British YIL* 1949, 108–150; cf Zemanek, above, note 13, at 168.

[42] International Arbitral Tribunal, *Texaco Overseas Petroleum Company v Libyan Arab Republic*, 1977, ILM 17 (1978), 1–37, § 66.

treaties codification process, to disregard treaties between organisations but to take into account treaties to which a state *and* an organisation were parties.[43]

Although the terminological distinction between states' 'treaties' and organisations' 'agreements' has persisted for a long time and to some extent still does today[44] (if only because IGO treaties can generally be set apart from state treaty practice by their politically modest purport),[45] the underlying concept was abandoned, essentially because it became untenable in the light of developing doctrine and practice. The crucial factor here is the view of international law as a unified legal order in which different legal subjects interact by definition under one set of rules.[46] These rules, moreover, proceed from the principle of equality of parties. Thus the law of treaties – in defiance of recommendations to the contrary[47] – does not, and cannot, make a legal distinction between treaties on the basis of parties, as confirmed by the two Vienna Conventions.

Likewise, the law of treaties attaches no legal consequences to the content of an agreement (an exception of legal policy, and not of a general nature, being article 75 of the 1969 Vienna Convention which ties in the operation of the Vienna Conventions with the Charter system).[48] In response to Jenks' description of IGO treaties as 'essentially treaties of amity and goodwill',[49] Lauterpacht stated, 'that feature does not deprive them of the character of treaties'.[50] Referring to comments made by Sir Gerald Fitzmaurice some twenty years earlier about IGO treaties, the Commission held that:

> There are admittedly some important differences of a juridical character between certain classes or categories of international agreements. But these differences

[43] YILC 1965, Vol I, 777th meeting, § 7.

[44] Henry Schermers and Niels Blokker, *International Institutional Law*, 2003, § 1744, observe the distinction, but without attaching (general) legal implications.

[45] Cf section 7.1.2 above.

[46] Cf 4.2.1 above.

[47] Already McNair recommended that 'we free ourselves from the traditional notion that the instrument known as the treaty is governed by a single set of rules'. ('The Function and the Differing Legal Character of Treaties', XI *British YIL* 1930, 100–118, at 118; in Lord Arnold McNair, *The Law of Treaties*, 1961, at 254–259).

[48] Article 75 (*Case of an Aggressor State*): 'The provisions of the present Convention are without prejudice to any obligation in relation to a treaty which may arise for an aggressor State in consequence of measures taken in conformity with the Charter of the United Nations with reference to that State's aggression'; *mutatis mutandis* Art 76 of the 1986 Convention.

[49] Cf Wilfred Jenks, 'Some Constitutional problems of International Organizations", 22 *British YIL* 1945, at 68.

[50] Lauterpachts second report on the law of treaties (citation in UN Doc A/CN.4/L.161 at 27).

> spring neither from the form, nor any other outward characteristic of the instrument in which they are embodied: they spring exclusively from the content of the agreement, whatever its form.[51]

As the law of treaties does not envisage a legal distinction between treaties on the basis of content, it is unsurprising that it has proven difficult to classify international agreements in a legally relevant manner.[52] There is equally little ground for setting apart IGO treaties as a legal category under the law of treaties,[53] although study may show groups of agreements dealing with a specific subject matter (see section 7.1.2 above). Arguably for the same reason it has not been possible to establish a connection between particular institutional features and a particular category of IGO treaties.[54]

A cursory glance at IGO practice thus suggests that the 'important differences of a juridical character' of IGO treaties in respect of inter-state treaties, which were reported by the International Law Commission,[55] are differences which may have relevance in legal practice, but which in a technical sense are invisible to the law of treaties.

7.2.2 The Treaty-making Powers of International Organisations

In addition to what has been said on the legal personality of international organisations in Chapter 4 above, a few points remain to be made on IGO treaty-making powers in particular. The reference to 'powers' is deliberate, as this was the unspecified term used by the first studies which aimed to interpret IGO treaty-making practice in legal terms. The following, however, will address the general legal aspect of treaty-making 'capacity' – in accordance with the distinction elaborated upon above[56] – while 'competence', based on the institutional make-up of organisations, is omitted.

Of the three forms of legal capacity traditionally associated with international organisations – capacity to conclude international agreements; capacity to bring claims in case of breaches of international law; the

[51] YILC 1974, Vol II (Part One), at 298, 299.

[52] Cf Shabtai Rosenne, Developments in the Law of Treaties (1945–1986), 1989, at 190 *et passim*.

[53] Suggested by Karunatilleke, above, note 20.

[54] Eg, Hans-Jörg Geiser, who proposes a classification ('based on a functional criterion') of 'institutional' and 'operational' treaties, which may be helpful for grasping the general image (*Les Effets des Accords conclus par les Organisations Internationales (Etude en Droit des Traités des Organisations Internationales à la lumiere de la Convention de Vienne de 1969)*, 1977, at 8–22, and references).

[55] See Chapter 8 below.

[56] In Section 4.2.5.

enjoyment of privileges and immunities from national jurisdictions[57] – the attribute of treaty-making capacity has incited the most discussion. With the growing role of non-state actors, the view that '[. . .] the right of entering into international engagements is [precisely] an attribute of State sovereignty'[58] has been gradually abandoned. In the early years of the ILC study on the law of treaties, the UN Secretariat played a prominent role in this respect, insisting strongly on the recognition of the treaty-making power of international organisations.[59]

Treaty-making practice of international organisations became a subject of considerable interest in the 1950s and 1960s, and some valuable studies on the subject have been carried out.[60] These had a particular concern with the legal foundation of IGO treaty-making. With some simplification, views on the matter can be grouped in two categories, which parallel the two main doctrinal schools with respect to international legal personality.[61] In the spirit of the time, this foundation was sought mostly in the constituent instrument, possibly with a subsidiary basis in international custom.[62]

Most studies of this period treat IGO treaty-making activity in terms of treaty-making 'capacity' or 'powers' rather than in terms of 'legal personality'. Generally, treaty-making capacity is inductively construed on the basis of actual practice and terms of the IGO constituent instrument, and read within the framework of that instrument, possibly in combination with the emerging general framework of 'international institutional law'.[63]

[57] Felice Morgenstern identifies three areas of general international law suitable to be applied to international organisations: the law of state immunity; the law of diplomatic relations; the law of treaties (*Legal Problems of International Organisations*, 1986, at 4).

[58] *Case of the SS Wimbledon*, PCIJ, Ser A, No 1, 1923, at 25 (the French text adds 'précisement'); see on the inter-war period above, ch 3. Although the possibility of non-sovereign entities having this attribute is not excluded, especially the French formula strongly suggests as much. Reaffirmed in the Advisory Opinion on the *Exchange of Greek and Turkish Populations*, PCIJ, Ser B, No 10, 1925, at p 21. For the view of contemporary writers, see eg Karl Strupp, Les règles générales du droit de la paix, 47 RdC 1934, at p 420.

[59] See references in Rosenne, *UN Treaty Practice...*, above, note 20, at 293.

[60] Jean Huber, *Le droit de conclure des traités internationaux*, 1951; Karl Zemanek, *Das Vertragsrecht der internationalen Organizationen*, 1957; Jan Willem Schneider, *Treaty-Making Power of International Organisations*, 1959; Badr Kasme, *La capacité de l'organization des Nations Unies de conclure des traités*, 1960; Chiu, above, note 20. Rosenne, *UN Treaty Practice...*, above, note 20, is a study on the system and practice of the UN, including treaty-related aspects; in this tradition, cf Michel Virally, *L'organisation mondiale*, 1972; Hans Kelsen, *The law of the United Nations : a critical analysis of its fundamental problems*, 1950.

[61] See section 4.2.3 above.

[62] Kasme, above, note 60, at 35: 'Conclusion: La capacité de l'ONU a pour fondement le droit conventionel et le droit coutumier'.

[63] See *Introduction...*, above, note 1. Cf also the first edition of White's textbook, in which treaty-making capacity is elaborated upon not in the section on legal personality but in the section on 'decision-making capacity', addressing the relation between the organisation and

The question of IGO treaties regained momentum when the first Vienna Convention on the Law of Treaties definitely limited its scope to inter-state treaties. The studies of that period resorted more clearly than before to the classic law of treaties as a reference for the consideration of IGO treaties.[64] With respect to IGO treaty-making power – an issue addressed only by Article 6 of the Convention – Rosenne had stated already in 1954 that 'a condition has now been reached wherein State practice squarely endorses what a few years ago was a matter principally for doctrinal investigation'.[65] Indeed, as with the attribution and foundation of legal personality in general, the 'objective approach' appeared as an increasingly convincing model for explaining legal practice, but it was not generally accepted in view of the transparent, functional perspective on organisations.[66]

Although not yet canonised by the law of treaties doctrine, existing IGO treaty-making practice was at least not at odds with the conventional law of treaties. The only problem that emerged, and is still unsolved, was the blooming practice of IGO *organs* concluding international agreements brought about by the internal decentralisation[67] of international organisations. Next to clear-cut cases of agency,[68] as for instance with the Enforcement of Sentences Agreements concluded by the ICTY '*for* the United Nations',[69] there are several organs that conclude treaties apparently on their own accord. Doctrine has not yet found an answer to this instance of practice. For example the UNHCR – formally a subsidiary organ of the UN General Assembly but possibly endowed with

its members (Nigel White, *The Law of International Organizations*, 1996, at 103 ff); in contrast, in the second edition, treaty-making capacity is discussed in the chapter on personality (2nd ed, 2005, ch 2).

64 A notable example is the collection of essays edited by Professor Zemanek (who had been closely involved in Vienna's host function for the diplomatic conference on the law of treaties): Karl Zemanek, *Agreements of International Organizations and the Vienna Convention on the Law of Treaties*, 1971. See in particular Günther Hartmann, 'The Capacity of International Organizations to Conclude Treaties', 127–163, and Chris Osakwe, 'The Concept and Forms of Treaties Concluded by International Organizations', 165–193.

65 Rosenne, *UN Treaty Practice...*, above, note 20, at 294

66 Cf sections 4.2.2 and 4.2.3 above.

67 On 'internal decentralisation' in IGOs see section 5.1 above.

68 See Dan Sarooshi, *International Organizations and their Exercise of Sovereign Powers*, 2005, for an elaboration on the distinction in international law between three kinds of conferral of powers to organisations: agency, delegation, transfer; in any event the first category, and possibly the second, pose no problem in the context of our present discussion in so far as the competence rests with the organisation as a whole.

69 As envisaged in the treaty between the Tribunal and eg Finland (1997); Italy (1997); Norway (1998); Austria (1999); Sweden (1999) (emphasis added); the author is indebted to Dr Alexander Muller for his information in this regard.

international capacity[70] 'by derivation and intention'[71] – has concluded numerous agreements in its own name that seem to have regular legal effect. The treaty-making activity of UNCED provides another example from the UN system.[72] These organs seem to be legally bound in their own right (although it is probable that in some cases the final responsibility rests with the organisation as such, which would ultimately suggest a form of delegation).[73]

These are forms of decentralisation in which the *de facto* institutional independence of an organ assumes an internal *and* an external dimension. In such a case, it is no longer solely an institutional matter, but becomes also a matter of public international law. Unless delegation or agency can be construed, the general legal order will inevitably come into play. As has been argued in the previous chapters, international law would then have to either respect the corporate veil of the institutional order of the organisation or presume a degree of legal personality for the pertinent organ and thus make it an independent legal entity. As is confirmed by the awkward qualifications of this phenomenon of treaty-making practice, international law and notably the law of treaties do not allow for a middle way.

The 'third wave' of writing on international organisations' treaty-making occurred in the late 1980s, with the adoption of the second Vienna Convention. Studies of this period mostly took the form of a commentary to the Convention, and are therefore addressed in Part Three.[74]

[70] The possibility that an institution concludes an international agreement outside its competence, or outside its area of competence – or, in classic institutional terms, *ultra vires* – is omitted.

[71] Guy Goodwin-Gill (1996) quoted in Marjoleine Zieck, 'The "Special Agreements" concluded by UNHCR', in Jan Klabbers and René Lefeber (eds), *Essays on the Law of Treaties*, 1998, 171–187, at 176.

[72] See Schermers and Blokker for more examples – above, note 20, § 1695 ('minors in the UN family…institutions which operate more or less autonomously…'; cf section 4.2.2 above.

[73] To determine the *Normadressat* of a primary norm on the basis of the *Normadressat* of the secondary norm is, however, not unproblematic, for one because the addressee of the secondary norm may be a collective (as in the case of concurrent responsibility) or it may shift (as in the case of secondary responsibility of member states which is triggered when the organisation cannot meet its obligations arising from responsibility). Doctrine in this respect is not unified with regard to IGOs and their member states (cf Catherine Brölmann, 'A Flat Earth? International Organisations in the System of International Law', in J Klabbers (ed), *International Organisations*, Series: Library of Essays in International Law, 2005, 183–206 (reprint from Nordic JIL 2001), § 5 and references), and seems equally uncertain on the relation between organisations and their organs.

[74] See ch 10, below, footnote 9. For the 'third wave' in international institutional law studies in general, see the references above, in ch 4, footnote 2.

Concluding Remarks to Part Two

IN THE UNITED Nations era international organisations appear, more clearly than before, in different roles: they are institutional structures which serve as a forum for states, and they appear as independent legal entities that maintain international relations on their own accord. Or, in the words of Virally, they are a social structure as well as an autonomous actor.[1] These roles are addressed in Part Two, by considering the different ways in which international organisations are involved with treaty practice.

Which role an organisation assumes is clearly dependent on the legal context. More importantly, this context also determines the degree of the organisation's legal transparency. When an organisation serves as a forum for treaty-making,[2] it presents a comparatively open structure in which states take the prime role and have their relations governed by general international law. Here it should be noted, however, that the centralised framework of an organisation is never *entirely* open in the way of a classic 'horizontal' legal setting. That it to some extent remains separate from the international legal order and resists the general law of treaties appears from the practice of majority decision-making at various levels. Also for adoption of the text, an IGO framework may be used to obtain results which are unfeasible in a strictly consensual structure (as with the text of the 1996 Nuclear Test Ban Treaty, which eventually could be adopted by majority vote in the UN General Assembly)[3]. At the level of final bindingness, in some technical organisations the process of rule-making on the basis of the constituent treaty has become centralised to such a degree that it raises the question of whether the law of treaties paradigm remains instrumental at all.

From an external perspective, a different situation arises when the organisation, and not the member states, is at the heart of an issue. This essentially only happens when the scope of an organisation, being functionally defined, is questioned. This may relate to competences, or the area of competence of an organisation. In order to have the institutional framework of an organisation reviewed by general international law, the institutional order is assimilated with the constituent treaty. The law of

[1] 'Le double visage de l'organization internationale [...] À la fois structure sociale [. . .] et acteur autonome [. . .].' (Michel Virally, *L'organisation mondiale*, 1972, at 30).

[2] Illustrated notably by the United Nations system, in ch 5.

[3] See section 5.1.

treaties can then be applied.[4] In such cases, nonetheless, the institutional order appears as partly closed and less receptive to the traditional law of treaties than would be the case for regular agreements. This becomes apparent from two atypical features in the interpretive practice of the International Court in relation to IGO constituent treaties: the emphasis on teleological interpretation and the lack of concern with the intention of the original treaty parties. Both are characteristics of a constitutional line of thinking and do not sit well with regular law of treaties doctrine. From the 1949 *Reparation* case onwards, interpretation of an organisation's constituent treaty seems in fact marked by a continuous tension between law of treaties discourse and constitutional discourse. The opposition 'treaty' *versus* 'constitution' is paralleled by the opposition treaty regime *versus* international organisation.

When an organisation itself concludes a treaty,[5] it manifests as a closed, or one-dimensional, legal actor in the same way as a state. Likewise, it appears from a cursory glance that IGO treaty-making practice, although specific for its subject matter, from a formal-legal perspective is similar to that of states.[6] This must also be the reason why early attempts to set apart IGO treaties from inter-state treaties[7] on the basis of practice were not successful. Even apart from practical considerations this could not have been different. The inherently transparent image of organisations, described in Part One, ultimately has to yield to the one-dimensional mould of the legal system, *in casu* of the law of treaties. As argued in Part Three, this tension has been a central element in the conceptualisation of IGO treaty-making.

[4] See ch 6.
[5] See section 7.1.
[6] See section 7.1.2
[7] See section 7.2.1.

Part Three

International Organisations and the Conventional Law of Treaties

8

Towards a Codified Law of Treaties for International Organisations

PART THREE OF this book gives an analysis of the codification process of the law of treaties as applicable to international organisations. It proceeds on the basis of the framework that has been set out in Part One and Part Two. From the perspective of general international law the main distinctive feature of international organisations is the transparency of the institutional veil, or the transparency of organisations as legal entities.[1] Although never quite rendered explicit, this has also been a central factor in the conceptualisation of organisations as subject to the law of treaties during a codification process of some 40 years. The complexities raised by organisations in the preparation of the law of treaties Conventions can be traced back to the issues of theory and doctrine that have been addressed in the framework of general international law in Part One above.

The inclusion of organisations in the law of treaties is illustrative of the story of international organisations as independent actors in international law. This is so both because of the voluntarist nature of the law of treaties and because of the formal and pragmatic nature of the codification process, in which conceptual tensions and fuzzy notions are brought to a head. As Special Rapporteur Paul Reuter – whose own reports are a case in point – has stated, 'the International Law Commission [. . .] cannot include unduly theoretical notions in the texts it prepares for the use of Governments, judges, administrators and practitioners', and '[i]t is for the Commission, fully cognisant of all the prospects opened up by legal writers, to find a reasonable and probably empirical course, and to provide simple and practical solutions to problems ripe for solution'.[2]

This chapter addresses the question of treaties concluded by international organisations as it emerged during the first stage of the codification process. It considers the preparatory work for the first Convention on the Law of Treaties – not the 1969 Convention itself, as IGO treaties were

[1] Section 2.3.3 above.
[2] YILC 1972, Vol II, 171–199, §§ 37 and 16.

eventually excluded from its scope – within the UN framework, notably of the International Law Commission. The caesura is not only chronological but also substantive, as until that point the question was not to what extent the general rules of the law of treaties apply to IGO treaties, but whether IGO treaties could and should be included in the law of treaties canon at all. The considerations and hesitations of the Commission are recounted in some detail, so as to bring out how the answer to this question – which could have seemed unproblematic given actual IGO treaty practice – was far from evident. This chapter proceeds chronologically rather than thematically, because at this stage of the drafting process the points of discussion are few and recurrent.

8.1 PREPARATORY WORK BY THE INTERNATIONAL LAW COMMISSION

The creation of the United Nations ushered in a new era in the project of international law codification.[3] At its first session, the International Law Commission decided to give priority to the study of the law of treaties, along with two other topics.[4] It was to take another 18 years of work, and the appointment of four Special Rapporteurs, before a first codification conference on the law of treaties could be convened.[5]

It is noteworthy that Special Rapporteurs Brierly, Lauterpacht, Fitzmaurice and Waldock, successively entrusted with the task of preparing a study on the subject,[6] all included IGO treaties in the scope of their work – in the spirit of the new climate brought by the 1949 ICJ *Reparation* Opinion, which had recognised the international legal personality of the United Nations, inter alia on the basis of apparent treaty-making capacity (and competence) of the organisation.[7]

[3] On the efforts at international law codification under the League cf section 3.3.1 above.

[4] YILC 1949, at 281: (1) Law of Treaties, (2) Arbitral procedure, (3) Régime of the High Seas; see, in general, United Nations Publication, *The Work of the International Law Commission*, Sales No E.88.V.1, and Ian Sinclair, *The International Law Commission*, 1987.

[5] For a guide to the travaux préparatoires of the first Vienna Convention, starting from the 1962 draft prepared by Sir Humphrey Waldock, see Shabtai Rosenne, *The Law of Treaties: A Guide to the Legislative History of the Vienna Convention*, 1970, and Ralf Günther Wetzel and Dietrich Rauschning, *The Vienna Convention on the Law of Treaties: Travaux Préparatoires*, 1978; a thematical summary, with regard to the question of international organisations' treaties in particular, is found in the 1970 document prepared by the Secretariat (UN Doc A/CN.4/L.161 and Add 1 and 2).

[6] Professor James Brierly was appointed in 1949 (three reports, in 1950, 1951 and, after his resignation, 1952); Sir Hersch Lauterpacht was appointed in 1952 (two reports, in 1953 and 1954); Sir Gerald Fitzmaurice was appointed in 1955 (five reports, in the years 1956–1960); Sir Humphrey Waldock was appointed in 1961 (six reports, between 1962–1966); see the corresponding issues of the ILC Yearbook.

[7] See section 4.2.5 above; *Reparation for Injuries Suffered in the Service of the United Nations*, ICJ Reports 1949, 173. Cf § 26 of Brierly's commentary to the first draft (YILC

8.1.1 IGO Treaty-making Capacity: 1950–1952

The first report, by Rapporteur Brierly',[8] contained three draft articles that had a bearing on international organisations, taking a rather straightforward and logical approach from the point of view of general international law.

Article 1(a) (*Use of the term 'treaty'*):

> [As the term is used in this convention . . .] A 'Treaty' is an agreement recorded in writing between two or more States or international organisations, which establishes a relation under international law between the parties thereto.[9]

Article 2(b):

> An 'International Organization' is an association of States with common organs which is established by treaty.

Article 3:

> [a]ll states and international organizations have the capacity to make treaties, but the capacity of some States or organizations to enter into certain treaties may be limited.[10]

Referring to the *Reparation* case as an argument for the inclusion of IGO treaties, the Commentary explained, 'This draft differs from any existing draft in recognizing the capacity of international organizations to be parties to treaties'.[11] The reasons for exclusion of IGO treaties from the

1950, Vol II, at 228); and the introduction by Fitzmaurice at the 1956 Session of the Commission (YILC 1956, 368th meeting, § 56) with regard to capacity: 'The language in which that judgment had been couched was clearly applicable to many other international organisations with treaty-making powers similar to those of the United Nations'.

[8] YILC 1950, Vol II, 222–248.

[9] *Ibid*, at 223; Article 1(b): 'A "treaty" includes an agreement effected by exchange of notes'; Article 1(c): 'The term 'treaty' does not include an agreement to which any entity other than a State or international organisation is or may be a party'.

[10] Apart from the aforementioned Art 3 on 'Capacity in general', the draft contains an Art 4, on 'Constitutional provisions as to the exercise of capacity to make treaties', and 5, on 'Exercise of capacity to make treaties', which, as they deal with the internal division of competencies, will be left out of the present study.

[11] Next to the question of IGO treaties (or the parties to 'treaties' as a species of the genus 'agreement'), the other main point of discussion (which lies outside the scope of this study) was related to the form of 'treaties' and concerned 'exchanges of notes'. These had been excluded from the scope of the *Harvard Draft*, but came to be included in the VCLT, which was enabled by a definition of 'treaty' 'as an 'agreement' rather than an instrument' (cf § 33 of the commentary; YILC 1950, Vol II, at 229).

1935 Harvard Draft (which had been rather unspecific)[12] were considered 'not insuperable'.[13]

The review of the very first set of draft articles, at the 1950 session of the Commission, raised questions which are worth recalling in some detail, as they were to prove recurring points of discussion throughout the law of treaties codification process. The Commission in principle favoured inclusion of international organisations in its draft, but had some difficulty in agreeing on the legal consequences of this approach.

In relation to the scope of the articles, on which the draft contained no general provision, different questions were discussed in a sometimes intricate manner concerning: the definition of 'international organisation' and of 'treaty'; the treaty-making capacity; and the treaty-making practice of international organisations.[14]

The treaty-making capacity of organisations was a primary subject of discussion. This discussion mirrors the doctrinal debate on legal personality for organisations in general.[15] The inclusion of a provision on the capacity of states, which at that point was not questioned,[16] appeared to necessitate a corresponding pronouncement with respect to organisations. At this point, the Commission generally felt that the draft should somehow distinguish between organisations that possessed such capacity and those that did not. The problem remained to apply this distinction in practice. It was undisputed that the United Nations, as well as some other organisations such as the ILO, possessed treaty-making capacity, but on the status of other organisations no agreement could be reached.[17] This is unsurprisingly since international law ultimately operates and attributes personality on the basis of objective features, so that it would be difficult to exclude corporate bodies which have been designated as an 'organisation'.[18]

[12] '...their abnormal character and the difficulty of formulating general rules which would seem applicable to a class of instruments which are distinctly *sui generis*'. (Harvard Law School, Research in International Law, III (Law of Treaties), the 36 draft Articles are reproduced in a Supplement to 29 *American JIL* 1935, 655–122, at 692); see section 3.3.2 above.

[13] YILC 1950, Vol II, § 26 at 228; commentary on Art 3 inter alia in § 44: 'But it is clear that the inherent treaty-making capacity of international organizations, which thus exists, is confined to capacity to make treaties compatible with the letter and spirit of their several constitutions'.

[14] These matters were discussed at length at the 49th to 52nd meetings (see Summary Records of the 1950 Session, YILC 1950, Vol I: in particular 49th meeting, §§ 68–76; 50th meeting, §§ 1–57; 51st meeting, §§ 54–77, 52nd meeting, §§ 1–72).

[15] See section 4.2 above.

[16] But see below, note 93 and accompanying text on the 1962 Session; the need for a general provision on capacity became a point of discussion again during the Vienna Conference (see note 178 below, and accompanying text).

[17] See section 4.2.1 above on the initial (fruitless) efforts to distinguish between organisations with, and organisations without legal personality.

[18] See section 4.2 above.

The question of treaty-making capacity then became linked to the definition of 'international organisation' that was proposed by the Special Rapporteur in his Article 2(b).[19] The consequence of connecting treaty-making capacity to this elementary definition (which, it may be noted, lacks the notion of autonomy which in later definitions would have a central place), however, would be to acknowledge treaty-making power of virtually every intergovernmental organisation, and the Commission was not ready to accept this conclusion.[20]

Discussion in the early years shows that the draft Articles were generally felt to have 'departed greatly from tradition'.[21] The records also suggest that the notorious trend towards 'informalisation' in international law (reflected in the eventual Vienna Convention)[22] at the time was not a received idea. This is visible for example in the discussion on the definition of 'treaty' and on its limitations *ratione materiae* and *ratione personae.* A criterion of the first kind was implied, eg in the proposed distinction between *agreements* 'dealing exclusively with administrative matters' and *treaties* 'of a political nature'.[23]

The *ratione personae* limitation of the class of 'international organisations' had a bearing on the approach to IGO treaties. Most Commission members consistently distinguished between 'agreements' and 'treaties', where the latter would be a species of the former.[24] It was maintained that

[19] Text of the article above,, accompanying text of note 9; see 50th meeting, §§ 50, 51; 52nd meeting, § 39. For the discussion see also 50th meeting, §§ 47–57; (in particular statements by Faris Bey el-Khoury, § 50; cf, likewise, 51st meeting, § 60); 52nd meeting, § 62: 'It was, of course, most difficult to define what was to be understood by "international organizations", and to establish the principles determining their capacity to make treaties. [. . .] It was surely self-evident that certain [. . .] international organisations – eg, the International Committee for Bird Preservation – most probably would not come within the category of international organisations as defined in the draft Convention;' cf also 52nd meeting, §§ 23–36.

[20] Cf 50th meeting, §§ 52, 57.

[21] Mr Amado, 1950 ILC Session, 49th meeting, § 73.

[22] Article 2(1)(a): '"Treaty" means an international agreement concluded between States in written form and governed by international law, whether embodied in single instrument or in two or more related instruments and whatever its particular designation'. Cf also above, note 11.

[23] Which raised doubt as to whether any organisation was known to have concluded agreements of the second kind (Faris Bey el-Khoury, 51st meeting, § 58). Later it would become clear that this is indeed the case – see section 7.1.2 above. In general the discussion on material criteria was notably concerned with the question of whether particular instruments, such as 'agreements effected by exchange of notes', should be covered by the definition of 'treaty' (see 1950 Session, in particular 50th meeting, §§ 16–41; 51st meeting, §§ 2–53); it also caused some apprehension with regard to the terminology in the various municipal legal systems and a possible clash with the terminology used in the draft – cf the cautionary observations of Mr François, which represent a more 'monist' view as regards national and international law (49th meeting, § 71); also Mr Sandström (50th meeting, § 10); for a preponderantly 'dualist' perspective, see Mr Hsu (50th meeting, § 13).

[24] Cf the observations of Mr François on the possible tension between the draft articles and the different constitutional systems which in many cases distinguish(ed) between 'treaties'

a 'treaty' in its proper sense could have only states as parties, and that the designation as 'treaty' of an agreement between two IGOs did not tally with the meaning of 'treaty' in international law; witness the fact that for instance the Trusteeship Agreements had always been termed 'agreements'.[25] At the time this distinction found some justification in legal writing,[26] but it was not supported by the definition of 'treaty' proposed in draft Article 1(a),[27] and did not succeed in convincing the Commission in its entirety. The UN Legal Office expressed a preference for inclusion of international organisations in the draft, with reference to the fact that the Headquarters Agreements between the UN and the US had been termed 'agreements' rather than 'treaties', 'not because anyone had questioned the capacity of the United Nations to sign a treaty, but merely because ratification was easier if the agreement were called an agreement'.[28]

The procedural argument that an international organisation could not be a party to a 'treaty' because violations of treaty obligations were to be judged by the International Court of Justice, which is competent only to adjudicate disputes between states,[29] was parried with a reference to the dispute settlement procedure by Advisory Opinion, coined in the 1946 General Convention on Privileges and Immunities of the United Nations.[30]

The Commission was then asked to decide on the fundamental point of whether IGO agreements should be included in the draft at all.[31] Again this gave rise to divergent views.[32] According to one member only organisations that come under Chapter VIII of the UN Charter, such as the OAS or the Arab League, could conclude treaties.[33] Pointing to the lack of experience with treaties concluded by international organisations, another member proposed to confine the draft to 'the essential question of agreements between States'.[34] The argument now seemed to revolve around a perceived lack of insight in the treaty-making practice of organisations in general, rather than around the problem of treaty-making capacity:

and other 'agreements' such as exchanges of notes (49th meeting, § 71); Mr Sandström (50th meeting, § 10); Mr Scelle: 'In his opinion, if an international organisation [. . .] concluded an agreement with a government, the agreement had the nature of a treaty' (50th meeting, § 49).

[25] Mr Alfaro, 50th meeting, § 8(a).

[26] With respect to IGO treaties in particular, see sections 3.3.2 and 7.2.1 above.

[27] Text of the article above, in the accompanying text of note 9.

[28] Viz under the US constitutional law it would need only a simple majority in Congress, as opposed to the two-thirds majority [in the Senate] required for the ratification of a 'treaty' (Mr Kerno, 50th meeting, § 15).

[29] Faris Bey el-Khoury, 51st meeting, §§ 16 and 41(a).

[30] Mr Kerno, 50th meeting, § 44(a).

[31] Question put by Chairman Mr Scelle, 51st meeting, § 2.

[32] For discussion of the matter in general, see the 50th meeting, §§ 54–77.

[33] Faris Bey el-Khoury, 51st meeting, § 60.

[34] Mr Hudson, 50th meeting, § 55c.

> the draft convention should not deal with agreements to which IGOs were parties. But [the Commission] could state in its report that it recognized such organizations as capable of making treaties, though it awaited more information on future developments before taking a decision on specific points.[35]

On the other hand it was stated that 'the only valid argument against the inclusion of international organisations was that of novelty, and such an argument could not be taken seriously'.[36]

According to a brief passage in the 1950 Report of the Commission:

> [a] majority of the Commission were also in favour of including in its study agreements to which international organizations are parties. There was general agreement that, while the treaty-making power of certain organizations is clear, the determination of the other organizations which possess capacity for making treaties would need further consideration.[37]

Article 3 had been partly amended to the effect that the treaty-making capacity of international organisations was no longer treated analogously to that of states, but implicitly made dependent on the constituent instrument: '[a]n international organization may be endowed with the capacity to make treaties'.[38]

This decision notwithstanding, the Special Rapporteur's 1951 report referred to treaties concluded between states only.[39]

When at the next session the same provision again came up for discussion, it was decided 'to leave aside [. . .] the question of the *capacity* of international organizations to make treaties' and to draft the articles

[35] Mr Hudson, 50th meeting, § 55b; note the reference to 'treaties' (see in general §§ 55, 56); the proposal was supported by Mr Brierly (§ 64), Mr François (§ 66), and Mr Amado, who 'in view of the lack of experience, [. . .] would vote for postponement of the question' (§ 70).

[36] Mr Hsu (50th meeting, § 73); also Mr Yepes (§ 57), Mr Alfaro (though with the caveat that, with regard to capacity, the Commission should avoid a sweeping statement on all international organisations; § 63), Mr Sandström (§ 62), Mr Scelle (though on the condition that a decision on the applicability to organisations would be taken on each particular provision; § 72) and Mr Córdova (§ 67) were of this opinion; it is interesting that for some Commission members at that stage of the discussion the basic distinction between NGOs and IGOs, notwithstanding the explicit exclusion of the former category from the draft by Rapporteur Brierly (see his comment in YILC 1950, Vol II, §§ 27, 34 at 228, 229) still played a rôle: 'In the case of an association of individual members, that capacity could not possibly be admitted' (Mr Cordova; § 67).

[37] YILC 1950, Vol II, § 162 at 381.

[38] The amended to Art 3, as proposed by Mr Hudson, read: '1. All States have the capacity to make treaties, but the capacity of a State to enter into certain treaties may be limited (by international regulation); 2. An international organisation may be endowed with the capacity to make treaties' (52nd meeting, §§ 50a and 72). Consideration of the first paragraph (note the limitation put on the treaties – 'certain treaties' – rather than on states) was postponed, whereas the second paragraph was adopted without objection (§§ 70–72a).

[39] YILC 1951, Vol II, 70–73.

'with reference to States only'.[40] Otherwise, the draft articles agreed upon in the 1951 Session contained no definition of the term 'treaty' and contained a new Article 3 in which only a reference to the treaty-making capacity of states remained.[41]

8.1.2 'Organisations of States': 1953–1954

Special Rapporteur Lauterpacht followed the course set by the Commission in 1951 insofar as his draft did not contain a general provision on treaty-making capacity, with regard to either states or international organisations.[42] The reference to international organisations in the definition of 'treaty', however, was maintained, albeit phrased to emphasise the ultimate sovereignty of states:

> Article 1: Treaties are agreements between States, including organizations of States, intended to create legal rights and obligations of the parties.[43]

The ILC commentary explains this choice by referring to the open image of organisations:

> States can exercise their capacity to conclude treaties either individually or when acting collectively as organizations created by a treaty.

[40] YILC 1951, Vol I, 98th meeting, § 1 (emphasis added). This decision taken, Mr Kerno expressed his hope that it 'would not be interpreted as casting doubt on the treaty-making capacity of certain international organisations' (§ 2).

[41] Art 3: 'Capacity to enter into treaties is possessed by all States, but the capacity of a State to enter into certain treaties may be limited'; draft articles (UN Doc A/CN.4/L.28) in YILC 1951, Vol II, 73–74, at 74. Cf the draft article on treaty-making capacity originally proposed by Rapporteur Brierly, above, notes 10, 11 and accompanying text. A revised version of the draft articles in the Third Report, equally without reference to IGO treaties, was never discussed due to the resignation of the Special Rapporteur (at 57–70, at 69, § 50; Third Report in YILC 1952, Vol II, 50–56).

[42] First report in YILC 1953, Vol II, 90–162. The Rapporteur, however, dealt with the question of treaty-making capacity (and referred to the lack of a satisfying formula to cover the existing legal situation) both in the commentary to Art 1 on the definition of 'treaty' (at 95), and in the commentary to draft Art 10 on the validity of treaties ('An instrument is void as a treaty if concluded in disregard of the international limitations upon the capacity of the parties to conclude treaties'): 'The present draft embodies [. . .] the principle that international organizations possess, in general, the capacity to conclude treaties. However, it must remain a matter for consideration whether such capacity is inherent in international organisations without any limit or whether its extent is determined by their purpose and constitution. [. . .] The general language [. . .] used by the International Court of Justice in the Reparations [. . .] case, suggests that some such general limitation of capacity must be implied in all international organizations' (§§ 1, 2 and 7 at 137–141).

[43] YILC 1953, Vol II, at 90. Lauterpacht's definition of 'treaty' is found in this article, under the heading 'essential requirements of a treaty' coupled with Art 2 ('Form and designation of a treaty'): 'Agreements, as defined in Art 1, constitute treaties regardless of their form or designation' (an alternative Art 2 included exchanges of notes and unilateral declarations following an offer or followed by acceptance); the expression 'organizations of States' also figures in draft Art 7(1) entitled 'Accession'.

This was an inoffensive approach to a controversial legal phenomenon. Its logical conclusion, already indicated by Lauterpacht, was however that if international organisations were considered to be nothing else but states in some form of cooperation, the treaties such organisations conclude should not present any problem as they would not fundamentally differ from treaties concluded by states individually – '[i]t follows that agreements concluded by international organizations must be regarded as treaties . . .'.[44]

The Commission indeed agreed that:

> [t]here appears to be no decisive reason why [. . .] the rules otherwise applicable to treaties should not apply to those concluded by or between international organizations created by and composed of States.[45]

Lauterpacht held a profoundly functional – and essentially unformalistic – view on organisations:

> ...[I]t would seem desirable to direct political and juristic effort to making available, in the interest of the progressive integration of international society on a functional basis, the experience of the law of treaties for *the collective activities of States in their manifold manifestations*.[46]

Accordingly, the draft did not contain a general article on the scope of the articles, nor a definition of 'international organisation'. However, again the Commission expressed its views in the commentary, adding that the decision of 1951 provisionally to limit the draft to inter-state treaties needed 'revision:'[47]

> The expression 'organizations of States' is here intended as synonymous with the expression 'international organizations' conceived as entities which are created by treaty between States, whose membership is composed primarily of States, which have permanent organs of their own, and whose international personality is recognized either by the terms of their constituent instrument or in virtue of express recognition by a treaty concluded by them with a State.[48]

[44] Cf also Lauterpacht's note appended to the commentary to draft Art 1: 'In fact, there would appear to be no reason why, in the sphere of the treaty-making power, States acting collectively should not be in a position to do what they can do individually' (YILC 1953, Vol II, at 99, § 2).

[45] YILC 1953, Vol II, § 3 at 96. Lauterpacht goes on to state: 'On the contrary, it would seem desirable to direct political and juristic effort to making available, in the interest of the progressive integration of international society on a functional basis, the experience of the law of treaties for the collective activities of States in their manifold manifestations'. Special provisions for such IGO treaties were envisaged in a never completed Part VII (*Rules and Principles Applicable to Particular Kinds of Treaties*); see YILC 1953, Vol II, § 1 of the commentary to Art 1, at 93.

[46] YILC 1953, Vol II, § 3 at 96 (emphasis added).

[47] *Ibid.*

[48] YILC 1953, Vol II, § 2 at 99. Lauterpacht's second report (YILC 1954, Vol II, 123–139) contained some revisions and additions which are less pertinent in the present context. The

8.1.3 A General Law of Treaties Code: 1955–1960

Sir Gerald Fitzmaurice submitted the first of his five reports on the law of treaties in 1956.[49] The subject in its entirety was taken up anew,[50] this time framed in the form of an expository code.[51] According to the Special Rapporteur's introductory statement to the Commission, '[i]t would be impossible to ignore in a modern code of treaty law the fact that many international organizations existed and most of them had a treaty-making capacity'.[52]

The general Article 1, entitled 'Scope',[53] contained an optional third paragraph:

> The provisions of the present Code relating to the powers, faculties, rights and obligations of States relative to treaties, are applicable, mutatis mutandis, to international organizations and to treaties made between them, or between one of them and a State, unless the contrary is indicated or results necessarily from the context.[54]

Commission had no opportunity to consider the law of treaties topic in its next sessions, and its opinion, notably on the Rapporteur's firm stance about inclusion of IGO treaties in the general law of treaties, was not to be known (ILC Report, YILC 1953, Vol II, § 7 at 201; ILC Report, YILC 1954, Vol II, § 8 at 141).

[49] The draft articles contained in the first report by Sir Gerald Fitzmaurice (YILC 1956, Vol II, 104–128) concerned 'Scope of the Code, definitions, general principles, framing, conclusion and entry into force of treaties'; second report (1957): Termination and suspension of treaties; third report (1958): Essential validity of treaties; fourth report (1959): Effects of treaties as between parties; fifth report (1960): Effects of treaties in relation to third States (see corresponding issues of the ILC Yearbooks).

[50] Arguments for this approach were the relatively general and fragmentary character of the previous sets of draft articles and the considerable discrepancy between the articles tentatively adopted by the Commission on the basis of the Brierly reports, and draft articles proposed by Sir Hersch Lauterpacht (YILC 1956, Vol II, §§ 2–3 at 105; a comparison of these two sets of articles is facilitated by working paper UN Doc A/CN.4/L.55 prepared by the Secretariat).

[51] In the introduction to his report, the Rapporteur expounds, 'First it seems inappropriate that a code on the law of treaties should itself take the form of a treaty [. . .] In the second place, much of the law relating to treaties is not especially suitable for framing in conventional form. It consists of enunciations and abstract rules, most easily stated in the form of a code'. (YILC 1956, Vol II, § 9 at 106). The Commission subsequently embraced these arguments (see ILC Report, YILC 1959, Vol II, § 18 at 91: 'In short, the law of treaties is not in itself dependent on treaty, but is part of general customary international law').

[52] YILC 1956, Vol I, 368th meeting, § 56.

[53] Article 1(1), referring only to the form of the instrument and not to the parties, reads: 'The present code relates to treaties and other international agreements in the nature of treaties, embodied in a single instrument [. . .]; and to international agreements embodied in other forms [. . .]; provided always that they are in writing. The present code does not, as such, apply to international agreements not in written form, the validity of which is not, however, on that account to be regarded as prejudiced'. (YILC 1956, Vol II, at 107).

[54] The optional paragraph had been placed between brackets, 'the decision to include treaties entered into by international organizations being provisional' (as stated in the commentary, YILC 1956, Vol II, § 2 at 117); the Rapporteur is obviously referring to the decision of 1950 (see above) and not to that of 1951 (which, it may be recalled, was not

A 'Treaty' was defined as inter alia:

> [...] an international agreement [. . .] made between entities both or all of which are subjects of international law possessed of international personality and treaty-making capacity, [. . .][55]

and an 'international organisation' as:

> [...] a collectivity of States established by treaty, with a constitution and common organs, having a personality distinct from that of its member-states, and being a subject of international law with treaty-making capacity.[56]

The draft contained no general provision on treaty-making capacity, as the question of capacity or lack thereof would be treated as a vitiating factor in the validity of treaties and brought under the rubric of 'essential validity'.[57]

At its 1956 Session, the Commission discussed the inclusion of IGO treaties in the scope of the draft only as a preliminary question.[58] An inconclusive debate with several cautionary observations[59] led to the

mentioned in the ILC Report). It seems however, that international organisations would be covered by the draft also without § 3; cf provisions mentioned below.

[55] Article 2, the passages omitted in the main text read 'embodied in a single formal instrument (whatever its name, title or designation)' and 'intended to create rights and obligations, or to establish relationships, governed by international law' respectively. It is noteworthy that this definition, different from previous drafts, refers to 'subjects of international law', rather than to particular parties. The phrase reproduced in the main text was not put between brackets, although it would de facto cover international organisations, a choice still 'provisional' at that point; § 2 brings exchanges of notes, letters or memoranda under the definition ('there being no general rule of law requiring any particular international agreement to be cast into the form of a "treaty", as such'). For the elaborate definition in its entirety (intended, it will be recalled, as part of an expository code and not of a convention) see YILC 1956, Vol II, § 2, at 107.

[56] Article 3(b), again between brackets, YILC 1956, Vol II, § 2 at 108; § 2(b) of Art 9, on 'The exercise of the treaty-making power', contains another 'provisional' reference (put between brackets) to international organisations (YILC 1956, Vol II, at 108), which, as the article relates to the question of internal division of competencies, will be left out of account.

[57] Part Two, under the heading of 'specific conditions for essential validity;' Art 8, YILC 1958, Vol II, at 24; the Rapporteur's commentary with respect to international organisations is brief, with a reference to the optional character of the inclusion of international organisations (*ibid*, § 23 at 32).

[58] See YILC 1956, Vol I, 368th-370th meetings.

[59] Cf MM Krylov (369th meeting, § 16) and Hsu (§ 27), who supported the course pro inclusion of treaties concluded by organisations already taken by Sir Hersch Lauterpacht; see also Mr Liang (§ 66), who was a proponent of inclusion, but was not in favour of the formula used by Lauterpacht ('States, including organizations of States'), as 'the two entities could not be dealt with as if they were identical'; on the other hand MM Spiropoulos (368th meeting, § 72), Pal (§ 16), François (§ 27), Edmonds (§ 43), Sandström (§ 48), Zourek (§ 57, who advocated limitation of the draft to treaties between states. Significant is the observation by Mr Amado that '[m]uch more thought would have to be given tot the question whether there should be a separate formulation for treaties made by and with international organizations, which obviously could not be treated on the same footing as treaties between States' (§ 59); M Faris Bey el-Khoury restated (see above, note 29) his view that treaties on the validity of which the International Court of Justice could not pronounce itself, should not be dealt with in the Code (369th meeting, § 32).

implicit decision that the study should proceed with the inclusion of IGOs.[60] When at the 1959 Session the Commission had the opportunity to take up the subject again,[61] the Rapporteur proposed to reserve discussion on the position of organisations,[62] restating his view that a code should be drafted first with regard to treaties between states only, leaving for later the question 'whether the code would apply, with some modifications, to international organisations or whether they must be dealt with in a separate section'.[63]

The 14 draft Articles subsequently adopted by the Commission no longer contained provisions relevant to IGO treaties, except for Article 2(1), which, apart from minor modifications,[64] followed the text proposed by the Special Rapporteur:

> For the purposes of the present Code, an international agreement (irrespective of its form or designation) means an agreement in written form governed by international law and concluded between two or more States, *or other subjects of international law*, possessed of treaty-making capacity. [. . .].[65]

In its annual report, however, the Commission 'reaffirmed the view that it would be preferable to defer the matter [of treaties concluded with or between international organizations] to a later stage'.[66] The reference to 'other subjects of international law' had been included since 'it always has

[60] YILC 1956, Vol I, 370th meeting, §§ 12–14; the rapporteur suggested provisionally to 'draft the code with reference to States only, but bearing constantly in mind the question of its application to international organizations" (§ 12).

[61] For discussion of Arts 1, 2 and 3 see YILC 1959, Vol I, 480th, 481st, 485th-487th meetings.

[62] Text of Art 1(3) above, note 54 and accompanying text; YILC 1959, Vol I, 480th meeting, § 9.

[63] § 27; proposal adopted without discussion (§ 28).

[64] A conspicuous, although mainly terminological, change is the employment throughout the articles of the term 'international agreement' rather than 'treaty'; the former term was preferred because it allegedly lacked the usual connotation of 'treaty', 'namely, the single formal instrument which is normally subject to ratification' (ILC Report, YILC 1959, Vol II, § 1 at 92).

[65] ILC Report, YILC 1959, Vol II, at 95 (emphasis added). Note that the reference to 'legal personality' has been omitted (see summary of rationale in § 8(a) of the Commission's Commentary to the draft articles (YILC 1959, Vol II, § 2, at 96): 'The Commission felt that the essential consideration was possession of treaty-making capacity. This involved international personality in the sense that all entities having treaty-making capacity necessarily had international personality. On the other hand, it did not follow that all international persons had treaty-making capacity'.). Note that the 'broad' formula of Art 2(1) in connection with the first paragraph of Art 1, adopted at the same occasion ('The present code relates to all forms of international agreements comprised by the definition given in Art 2 [. . .]' (ibid., at 92)), results in an inconsistency with regard to the decision to limit the scope of the draft to treaties concluded between states.

[66] *Ibid*, § 6 at 96 (see also the discussion at the 481th meeting, YILC 1959, Vol I, §§ 24–28); the commentary goes on to state that 'the Commission feels that its main principles [of treaties concluded by organisations] can most effectively and certainly be established on the basis of the traditional case of treaties between States'.

been a principle of international law that entities other than States might possess international personality and treaty-making capacity'. Although the definition would in fact cover international organisations, its main function was to refer to other treaty-making entities different from states, such as the Papacy, who were meant to be covered normally by the draft.[67]

Although the ILC Report of that year gave ample attention to the topic, comments in the Sixth Committee were scarce,[68] and the draft being obviously incomplete, the UN General Assembly undertook no action.

8.1.4 Involving the Law of the Organisation: 1961–1966

The next Special Rapporteur made his acceptance of the task more or less conditional on the choice for a convention rather than an expository code as the codification tool.[69] Without further specification, the new Rapporteur was instructed to re-examine the work previously done and possibly simplify the drafts submitted by his predecessors.[70]

On the question of IGO treaties, the first Waldock report[71] adopted a compromise approach in much the same vein as Rapporteur Lauterpacht had done before. Next to 27 articles, comprised under the heading of 'The conclusion, entry into force and registration of treaties' and divided in four chapters,[72] it proposed an optional fifth chapter, entitled 'The treaties of international organizations', which would contain the 'particular rules peculiar to these treaties' and 'specifying the extent to which the articles concerning States apply to international organizations and formulate the

[67] *Ibid*, § 7.

[68] Cf GAOR, 14th session, Sixth Committee, 604th meeting, § 5; and 605th meeting, § 51.

[69] See 1965, Sixth Committee, 851st meeting, § 43. A resumé of the rationale in YILC 1962, Vol II, § 17 at 160: 'first, an expository code [. . .] cannot in the nature of things be so effective as a convention for consolidating the law; [. . .] Secondly, the codification of the law of treaties through a multilateral convention would give all the new States the opportunity to participate directly in the formulation of the law if they so wished [. . .]'. On the consequential drafting changes (to 'a statement of legal principle or a more definite legal rule, and not merely one of an exhortatory or descriptive character'), see Rosenne, *Legislative History* ...above, note 5, at 34, 35). The decision of the Commission was later endorsed by the General Assembly on the basis of the approval of a great majority of representatives in the Sixth Committee (see GAOR 17th Session, Annexes, Vol III, agenda item 76, at 13, § 19; and GA Resolution UN Doc A/Res/1765 (XVII)).

[70] YILC 1961, Vol I, 620th-621st meetings, in particular § 46 of the 621st meeting; see also that year's Report, YILC 1961, Vol II, § 39 at 128.

[71] Presented and discussed at the 1962 Session; YILC 1962, Vol II, 27–83.

[72] 'General provisions', II 'The Rules Governing the Conclusion of Treaties by States', III 'The Entry into Force and Registration of Treaties' and IV 'The Correction of Errors and Functions of depositaries'.

particular rules peculiar to organizations.'[73] The draft's general provisions maintained a reference to subjects of law other than states. Article 1 (*Definitions*) reads:

> (a): '*International agreement*' means an agreement intended to be governed by international law and concluded between two or more States *or other subjects of international law* possessing international personality and having capacity to enter into treaties under the rules set out in article 3 below.
>
> (b): 'Treaty' means any international agreement in any written form [. . .].[74]

In his commentary the Rapporteur explains that the phrase 'other subjects of international law' was inserted 'to leave no doubt as to the right of entities such as the Holy See to conclude treaties' and 'to admit the possibility of international organizations being parties to international agreements'. He adds that:

> 'the number of international agreements concluded by international organizations in their own names [. . .] is now very large, so that inclusion in the general definition [. . .] seems really to be essential'.[75]

The draft also contained a renewed attempt to formulate a general provision on treaty-making capacity. The formula was much more elaborate than the one proposed by Brierly ten years before[76] but did not truly offer a general rule. Paragraph 1 seems circular with regard to non-state entities, whereas paragraph 4 ultimately relegates treaty-making capacity to the constituent instruments of the organisation.

> Article 3(1): Capacity in international law [. . .] to become a party to treaties is possessed by every independent State, whether a unitary state, a federation or

[73] Introduction to the first report (YILC 1962, Vol. II, at 30, § 11). But see the oral introduction by Sir Humphrey Waldock to the Commission: having made "some progress on that Chapter", the Rapporteur "was finding it less easy to align with Chapter II [. . .] and Chapter III [. . .] than he had expected." By consequence, "he would suggest that the Commission leave that particular subject in abeyance until it saw what progress had been made on the remainder." (YILC 1962, Vol. I, 637th meeting, § 10); cf. also the ILC Report of that year's session, YILC 1962, Vol. II, at 161).

[74] YILC 1962, Vol II, at 31. Otherwise, only paragraphs 1(c) on the definition of 'Party' and 1(h) on the definition of 'Signature' refer to 'a State or other Subject of international law', whereas paragraphs (i), on 'Ratification', (j), on 'Accession', (k), on Acceptance', and (l), 'Reservation', refer solely to states. § 1 of Art 2, entitled 'Scope of the Present Articles', reads: 'Except to the extent that the particular context may otherwise require, the present articles shall apply to every international agreement which under the definitions laid down in article 1, §§ (a) and (b), constitutes a treaty for the purpose of these articles'. As in the draft provisionally adopted by the Commission in 1959 (see above, note 65), the conjunction of Art 1(a) and (b) with Art 2(1) leaves way for the draft covering treaties concluded by international organisations.

[75] YILC 1962, Vol II, at 32, § 3.

[76] See above, note 10.

other form of union of States, and by other subjects of international law invested with such capacity by treaty or by international custom.[77]

Article 3(4): International capacity to become a party to treaties is also possessed by international organizations and agencies which have a separate legal personality under international law if, and to the extent that, such treaty-making capacity is expressly created, or necessarily implied, in the instrument or instruments prescribing the constitution and functions of the organization or agency in question.[78]

However, the question of IGO treaty-making capacity again proved to be an obstacle.[79] An unchallenged statement by the Chairman to the effect that 'the Commission would discuss the present draft on the understanding that treaties entered into by international organizations were not within its scope'[80] assumed the status of a Commission decision, as appears from that year's report. Thus the Commission 'reaffirmed' the 1951 and 1959 decisions to preliminarily exclude organisations from the draft, 'until it had made further progress with its draft on treaties concluded by States'; but not without recognising at the same time 'that international organizations may possess a certain capacity to enter into international agreements and that these agreements fall within the scope of the law of treaties'.[81]

That same year the Commission adopted 29 articles as Part I of a provisional draft, entitled 'Conclusion, entry into force and registration of treaties'.[82] As in the approach adopted by the Special Rapporteur, the substantive provisions of the draft were confined to treaties concluded by states, whereas the broadly formulated draft Articles 1 (*Definitions*) and 3 (*Capacity to conclude treaties*) and the commentary thereto made clear that 'the international agreements to which organizations are parties' were considered 'to fall within the scope of the law of treaties'.[83] Discussion on

[77] YILC 1962, Vol II, at 35; the commentary stressed again that the phrase on 'other subjects of international law' was 'designed primarily to cover the cases of international organisations and agencies and other entities like the Holy See' (*ibid*, § 2 at 36).

[78] *Ibid.*, 35–37; according to the Commentary "[p]aragraph 4 of this article seeks to state the general rule in regard to the treaty-making capacity of international organizations and agencies. [. . .] it is based upon principles analogous to those laid down by the International Court of Justice in [the Reparations case] for determining the capacity of the United Nations to present an international claim." (§ 6).

[79] See observation by Mr Tunkin (YILC 1962, Vol I, 637th meeting, § 6), and by the Special Rapporteur (§ 10).

[80] § 28.

[81] ILC Report, YILC 1962, Vol II, § 21 at 161.

[82] Part II, consisting of another 25 articles with regard to 'Invalidity and Termination of Treaties', was adopted by the Commission in 1963 (YILC 1963, Vol II, 189–217). The 19 articles of Part III, entitled 'Application, Effects, Modification and Interpretation of Treaties', were adopted by the Commission at its subsequent session (YILC 1964, Vol II, 177–208).

[83] YILC 1962, Vol II, § 21 at 161.

these provisions was inconclusive, oscillating between the open and the closed image of organisations, and may be summarised as follows.

Definition

With regard to Waldock's draft article on definition,[84] it was (again) suggested that the phrase 'possessing international personality' be deleted, with the argument that it was unnecessary since all subjects of international law possessed international personality.[85] The Rapporteur proposed a provision in which only the qualification 'having capacity to enter into treaties under the rules set out in article 3' would remain.[86]

Eventually the Drafting Committee submitted a new Article 1(1)(a),[87] which was adopted without changes:[88]

> Treaty means any international agreement [. . .] concluded between two or more States or any other subjects of international law and governed by international law.[89]

The commentary confirmed that this addition was meant to deal with international organisations, the Holy See and 'other international entities, such as insurgents, which may in some circumstance enter into treaties'.[90] The references to 'other subjects of international law' in the definitions of 'party' and 'signature' were dropped.[91]

Capacity

The first reading of draft Article 3[92] focused on treaty-making capacity in general. It was only at this point that the need for a general article on

[84] For the text of Art 1(1)(a) and (b) see above, note 74 and accompanying text.
[85] Mr Luna, YILC 1962, Vol I, 637th meeting, § 62; suggestion supported by Mr Ago (§ 64) and Mr Castrén (§ 80).
[86] YILC 1962, Vol I, 638th meeting, § 3; a choice at which one member expressed his regret (Mr El-Erian, § 33).
[87] 661th meeting, § 27.
[88] *Ibid*, § 30.
[89] Emphasis added – cf ILC Report, YILC 1962, Vol II, at 161. The treaties covered by this definition were again brought under the scope of the draft by the newly adopted Art 2(1): 'Except to the extent that the particular context may otherwise require, the present articles shall apply to every treaty as defined in article 1, paragraph 1(a)' (*ibid*, at 163).
[90] It goes on to state that '[t]he phrase is not intended to include individuals or corporations created under national law, for they do not possess capacity to enter into treaties nor to enter into agreements governed by public international law'; ILC Report, YILC 1962, Vol II, at 161–162, quotation from § 8.
[91] On recommendation of the Drafting Committee, a definition of 'party' as had been contained in § (c) was dropped altogether (YILC 1962, Vol I, 661th meeting, § 28). The definition of 'Signature', originally contained in § (h) was combined with that of other means of expressing consent to be bound and in the final version referred only to states (new Art. 1(1)(d); YILC 1962, Vol II, at 161).
[92] YILC 1962, Vol I, 639th and 640th meeting.

treaty-making capacity came to be questioned.[93] The Drafting Committee prepared a new Article 3 in the light of this discussion.[94] The relevant paragraphs read:

> 1) Capacity to conclude treaties under international law is possessed by States and by other subjects of international law. [. . .]
>
> 4) In the case of international organizations, the capacity to conclude treaties depends on the instrument by which the organization concerned was constituted.[95]

Some members of the Commission were of the opinion that the first paragraph should be formulated in a more restrictive manner so as to indicate that not all subjects of international law had treaty-making capacity,[96] while others held that the term 'instrument' in paragraph 4 should be substituted with a broader formula, so as to include also subsequent decisions and practice of international organisations.[97] Further discussion led to a new text with a slightly modified paragraph 4:

> In the case of international organizations, capacity to conclude treaties depends on the constitution of the organization concerned.[98]

The Special Rapporteur explained that 'constitution' had been used instead of 'constituent instrument' since the former expression was broader. He supported paragraph 4 of the article, since it gave useful information on the customary limitation by object and purpose of organisations' legal capacity, and he felt 'article 3 was the right context for the provisions of paragraph 4, because the article dealt with the capacity to conclude treaties in general and not only with the capacity of States to conclude treaties'.[99]

The paragraph on capacity was subject to much criticism in the Commission, and several members proposed its deletion for political

[93] Eg by Mr Jimenez de Aréchaga (639th meeting, § 13) and Mr Tunkin (§ 27). The majority of members, however, agreed with the Special Rapporteur on the usefulness of such a provision. In the commentary to his draft, Waldock had stated that '[c]apacity under international law to become a party to treaties has [. . .] a dual aspect, since it touches the question, what kind of legal persons are necessary as parties to an agreement if it is to be considered a treaty, as well as the question of the validity under international law of the agreement claimed to be a treaty'; he felt that, with respect to the first aspect, a general provision should be included (YILC 1962, Vol II, § 1 at 36).

[94] YILC 1962, Vol I, 640th meeting, § 91.

[95] *Ibid*, 658th meeting, § 87.

[96] Mr Castrén (658th meeting § 90); cf observation by Mr Bartoš (§ 97) who held that such a limitation should be dealt with in the commentary to Art. 3.

[97] Mr Briggs (§ 96); supported by Mr Tunkin (§ 106).

[98] Submitted by the drafting committee, discussed in the 666th meeting, § 16; emphasis added.

[99] §§ 39, 38 and 40, respectively; for discussion on this matter, see YILC 1962, Vol I, 666th meeting, §§ 16–66.

reasons,[100] because of the vagueness of the term 'international organisation'[101] or in view of the fact that the Commission did not intend to deal with international organisations in its draft in the first place.[102] The Commission eventually decided to maintain a general provision on capacity, including the reference to international organisations, and adopted an Article 3 with a first and third paragraph identical to the texts of §§ 1 and 4 quoted above.[103] The commentary in relation to organisations in particular referred to the 'implied powers doctrine' as distilled from the *Reparation* case,[104] but admitted that

> [s]ome members of the Commission were doubtful about the need for an article on capacity in international law to conclude treaties. They pointed out that capacity to enter into diplomatic relations had not been dealt with in the Vienna Convention and suggested that, if it were to be dealt with in the Law of Treaties, the Commission might find itself codifying the whole law concerning the 'subjects' of international law.

The ambivalent approach of the Commission with regard to IGO treaties seems to be reflected in the provisionally adopted Article 2(1) (*Scope of the present articles*): 'Except to the extent that the particular context may otherwise require, the present articles shall apply to every treaty as defined in article 1, paragraph 1(a)'.[105]

Other Provisions

Otherwise, only Article 4(2) as adopted by the Commission in 1962 contained a reference to IGO treaties. As this provision concerns 'full powers' of heads of diplomatic missions, and of heads of permanent

[100] Cf the observation by Mr Tunkin (§ 23), supported by Mr El-Erian (§ 27) and by Mr Bartoš, who opposed the suggestion of an effect erga omnes of a provision on treaty-making capacity in the constitution of an organisation: 'It was not advisable to make a general pronouncement which would give the impression that all states were obliged to recognize in advance that any and every international organization had treaty-making capacity' (§ 32).

[101] Which, according to Mr Briggs, even suggested treaty-making capacity of NGOs (§§ 17 and 20).

[102] Mr Yasseen, who considered the paragraph 'to be out of place in a set of draft articles dealing with treaty law in inter-state relations' (§ 48).

[103] § 65. The article in its entirety now read: '1) Capacity to conclude treaties under international law is possessed by States and by other subjects of international law. 2) In a federal State, the capacity of the member states of a federal union to conclude treaties depends on the federal constitution. 3) In the case of international organizations, capacity to conclude treaties depends on the constitution of the organization concerned.'

[104] YILC 1962, Vol II, §§ 2 and 4.

[105] YILC 1962, Vol II, at 163; for the text of Art 1(1)a see above, note 89 and accompanying text.

missions *to* international organisations (and the possible equation of these two categories), it falls outside the scope of the present discussion.[106]

The Parts of the draft articles on 'essential validity' and on 'application' submitted by Waldock to the Commission in 1963[107] and 1964[108] contained no reference to IGO treaties – with the exception of an Article 60 on treaties concluded by international organisations 'with a non-member State in the name both of the organization and of its Member States'.[109]

This draft provision constitutes the one effort to include the phenomenon of 'agency' in the codified law of treaties. That effort was complicated for two reasons in particular, and arguably remained fruitless because of them. In relation to organisations, formal agency, on the one hand, and a materially functional relation with the member states,[110] on the other, tended to be interchanged and merged into one analytical category. This made the question of legal agency seem relevant, although in reality it lies outside the law of treaties (since the principal, and not the agent, becomes bound to a legal obligation).[111] Second, 'mixed agreements' serve as one of the references for the draft Article on agency. But the very rationale for mixed agreements is an division of competences – often exclusive – between the organisation and the member states. Such a division is established at the institutional level. In other words, an organisation may be transparent but is by definition not 'open' enough to allow for a general rule in this respect. A mechanism to invoke the entire treaty vis-à-vis each member state, as envisaged by the Rapporteur, was

[106] On the initiative of Mr Rosenne (§ 73) the italicised phrase was added (§ 84); Art 4(2) now read: a) 'Heads of a diplomatic mission are not required to furnish evidence of their authority to negotiate, draw up and authenticate a treaty between their state and the state to which they are accredited; b) The same rule applies in the case of the head of a permanent mission to an international organisation in regard to treaties drawn up under the auspices of the organization in question *or between their states and the organization to which they are accredited*'.

[107] For the 28 articles constituting Part II of the draft, entitled 'The essential validity, duration and termination of treaties', see YILC 1963, Vol II, 36–94.

[108] (The concluding) Part III consisted of 21 articles and was entitled 'Application, effects, revision and interpretation of treaties'; see YILC 1964, Vol II, 5–65.

[109] '1) When a State, duly authorised by another State to do so, concludes a treaty on behalf and in the name of the other State, the treaty applies to that other State in the capacity of a party to the treaty. It follows that the rights and obligations provided for in the treaty may be invoked by or against the other State in its own name; 2) Similarly, when an international organisation, duly authorised by its constituent instrument or by its established rules, concludes a treaty with a non-member State in the name both of the organisation and of its Member States, the rights and obligations provided for in the treaty may be invoked by or against each Member State' (YILC 1964, Vol II, at 16).

[110] See section 2.3.1 above on the functional nature of organisations in general.

[111] In the definition of international agency given eg by Sarooshi – legal consequence for the principal, based on mutual consent, revocable, state exercises control over the way in which the organisation exercises its powers – see Dan Sarooshi, *International Organizations and their Exercise of Sovereign Powers*, 2005, at 36 ff; on doctrine in the inter-war period with respect to IGO treaty-making see section 3.3.2 above.

therefore problematic – the discussion is a precursor of the debate on several liability for member states in the field of international responsibility.[112] Setting a *general* norm on the division of competences and invokability of corresponding parts of the treaty obviously would have been problematic for the same reason of institutional variety.

After an inconclusive debate[113] and two referrals, the Drafting Committee informed the Commission that it was unable to find a satisfactory solution, recommending postponement of a decision on the matter.[114] Parts II and III of the Draft as provisionally adopted by the Commission in 1963[115] and 1964[116] thus no longer made reference to treaties concluded by non-state actors.

8.1.5 The Final ILC Draft Articles

In 1966 the Commission succeeded in adopting a complete set of draft articles on the law of treaties.[117] The final draft contained no reference to treaties concluded by actors other than states,[118] and it opened with a new Article 1: 'The present articles relate to treaties concluded between States'. The conceptual distinction between the scope of the draft and the (working) definition of 'treaty', earlier employed by Fitzmaurice,[119] was the fruit

[112] Cf § 5 in Catherine Brölmann, 'A Flat Earth? International Organizations in the System of International Law', in J Klabbers (ed), *International Organizations*, Series: Library of Essays in International Law, 2005, 183–206 (reprint from Nordic JIL 2001); see on responsibility of organisations section 11.3 below.

[113] See YILC 1964, Vol I, summary records of the 733rd meeting.

[114] 770th meeting, § 50; see also ILC report, YILC 1964, Vol II, § 20 at 176.

[115] 25 articles, Part II, 'Invalidity and termination of treaties' (YILC 1963, Vol II, 189–217).

[116] 19 articles, Part III, 'Application, effects, modification and interpretation of treaties' (YILC 1964, Vol II, 176–208).

[117] The section of the fourth report comprising Part I of the provisional draft articles had been discussed at the first part of the Commission's 17th session (May/July 1965). The remainder of the fourth report, the fifth report and the sixth report were disscused during the second part of the 17th session and at the 18th session. The final draft was included in Chapter II of the ILC Report (YILC 1966, Vol II, 177–274).

[118] On Art 1 (now 2) see Summary Records of the 1965 Session, 776th, 777th and 810th meeting; on Art 3 (capacity) see 779th and 780th meeting (YILC 1965, Vol I).

[119] Cf above, at 15; a distinction also supported, though in a less explicit manner, by Sir Humphrey Waldock (his arts 1(a) and 2(b) in note 74 above and accompanying text).

of intense discussion in the Commission.[120] The Commission thought it essential to 'indicate clearly the restriction of the present articles to treaties concluded between States'.[121]

The Rapporteur had drawn attention to the inconsistency of a broad definition of 'treaty' next to a limited scope of the draft,[122] and had consequently proposed deletion of the references to 'other subjects of international law'.[123] With some opposition[124] the definition of 'treaty' was eventually amended.[125] According to the Commentary:

> [t]he term 'treaty' as used in the draft articles [. . .] is not [. . .] in any way intended to deny that other subjects of international law, such as international organizations [. . .], may conclude treaties.[126]

The decision to limit also the general provisions to treaties among states bore an enlarged Article 2, now renumbered 3, designed to set the scope of the draft ('International agreements not within the scope of the present

[120] Discussion at the 776th and 777th meetings of the 1965 Session; see Mr Tunkin's observation (777th meeting, § 14), supported by Mr Ago (§ 26), Mr Elias (§ 32), Mr Rosenne (§§ 27 and 28) and by Sir Humphrey Waldock (§ 71). The new article was proposed by the Drafting Commmittee, and adopted without comment at the 810th meeting (§ 10).

[121] 1 YILC 1966, Vol II (Part Two), at 187, § 3; noteworthy was the proposal by Mr Reuter, not awarded by the Commission, to include a provision which would have brought treaties concluded by organisations under the scope of the draft after all: 'The rules which follow shall apply to agreements governed by public international law which are not treaties within the meaning of paragraph 1(a) [new article 2(a)], subject to due regard for the special nature of these agreements'. (YILC 1966, Vol I, 777th meeting, § 25; cf earlier version submitted in 776th meeting, § 66).

[122] Lastly in his introduction to the fourth report; YILC 1965, Vol II, at 10.

[123] See YILC 1965, Vol I, 776th meeting, §§ 50, 51; see in general 776th meeting, §§ 50–73 and 777th meeting on the definition of 'treaty', notably with regard to the phrase 'other subjects of international law' (see also government comments in the ILC Yearbook of that year).

[124] While some members of the Commission supported the Rapporteur's proposal (see eg observations by Mr Castrén (776th meeting, § 55); Mr Yasseen (§ 63); Mr Tunkin (§ 72)), others held the view that such a limitation should be effectuated in a different manner (Mr Ago (§ 58); supported by Mr Reuter (§ 66) and Mr Rosenne (§ 67); see also statement by Mr Rosenne that the kind of treaty concluded between a state and an international organisation 'involved a State and it would be a retrograde step to exclude it from the definition' (§ 68), supported by Mr Briggs (777th meeting, § 7).

[125] See 777th meeting, § 78. The final Article (renumbered) 2 on 'Use of terms' read: '[1) For the purposes of the present articles:] (a) "Treaty" means an international agreement concluded between States in written form and governed by international law, whether embodied in a single instrument or in two or more related instrument and whatever its particular designation'; § 1(a) was adopted informally at the 810th meeting (§ 11); the article in its entirety was adopted at the 811th meeting (§ 104). New was the definition of "'international organisation" included under paragraph (f) *quater* in draft article 1: ' "International organization" means an intergovernmental organization,' sufficient for its new function which amounted to excluding non-governmental organisations from the scope of the draft (820th meeting, §§ 17, 22).

[126] YILC 1966, Vol II, Part Two, § 5 at 188.

articles') and designed also to reserve the legal force of agreements concluded by other subjects of international law.[127] In its commentary the Commission stated:

> As such international agreements are now frequent – especially between States and international organizations and between two organizations – the Commission considered it desirable to make an express reservation in the present article regarding their legal force and the possible relevance to them of certain of the rules expressed in the present articles.[128]

Confirmed by the governments' critical comments[129] on Article 3, which mentioned the treaty-making capacity of states, the Rapporteur had expressed doubts about the value of the 'truncated treatment of the question' offered by the article and about the difficulty of 'formulating more extended provisions' that would be generally acceptable.[130] He had thus proposed to delete the provision on treaty-making capacity altogether. The final draft, however, retained an Article 3 (renumbered 5) on general treaty-making capacity – but it was trimmed considerably as the reference to international organisations in the general first paragraph was deleted, as well as the entire separate paragraph 3 on capacity of international organisations.[131] Otherwise, the 'agency' provision, on conclusion of

[127] The final draft Art 3 read: 'The fact that the present articles do not relate (a) to international agreements concluded between States and other subjects of international law or between such other subjects of international law; or (b) to international agreements not in written form, shall not affect the legal force of such agreements or the application to them of any of the rules set forth in the present articles to which they would be subject independently of these articles'; the former Art 2, on the legal force of agreements not covered by the draft, came to include a reference to 'treaties concluded between subjects of international law other than States' at the initiative of Mr Ago (777th meeting, § 59); it was discussed at the 810th meeting (§§ 12–27), and adopted unanimously at the 816th meeting (§ 2).

[128] YILC 1966, Vol II, § 2 at 190.

[129] Article 3 – cf comments by Austria (YILC 1966, Vol II, at 281); Finland (*ibid*, at 291); Japan (*ibid*, at 302); Sweden (*ibid*, at 338); on the other hand see the United States delegation, who wished to maintain the third paragraph of Art 3 but proposed to change the term 'constitution' into 'authority' (*ibid*, at 346); relating to the draft articles adopted by the Commission at its 1962, 1963 and 1964 Sessions, comments had been submitted by governments pursuant to the request of the Secretary-General (in accordance with the decisions of the Commission: YILC 1962, Vol II, at 160, § 19; YILC 1963, Vol II, at 189, § 13; YILC 1964, Vol II, at 175, § 16); along with extracts from the discussion in the Sixth Committee, these have been reproduced in UN Docs A/CN.4/175 and Add 1–5, and A/CN.4/182 and Add 1–3; the written comments have been subsequently printed in an Annex to the 1966 ILC Report (YILC 1966, Vol II, 279–361).

[130] YILC 1965, Vol II, § 2 at 18.

[131] The final Art 5 read: '1) Every State possesses capacity to conclude treaties; 2) States members of a federal union may possess a capacity to conclude treaties if such capacity is admitted by the federal constitution and within the limits there laid down;' see YILC 1966, Vol II (Part Two), at 191, § 2. For the discussion of (former) Art 3, see YILC 1965, Vol I, 779th and 780th meetings; fairly general agreement appeared to exist on the deletion of paragraph 3 (decision at the 780th meeting, § 16); see also 810th meeting, §§ 28–78; 811th meeting, §§ 2–51 (referred back to the Drafting Committee); 816th meeting, §§ 3–9; adoption of the article – without a reference to international organisations – in § 5.

treaties by international organisations on behalf of member states,[132] was abandoned.[133]

The commentary to Article 1 of the 1966 draft accounts for the eventual exclusion of international organisations from the scope of the articles with an argument reminiscent of the 1935 Harvard Draft commentary:[134]

> Treaties concluded by international organizations have many special characteristics; and the Commission considered that [inclusion of such treaties] would both unduly complicate and delay the drafting of the present articles.[135]

As in the commentary to the Harvard draft, these 'special characteristics' were not specified.

8.2 RECEPTION OF THE ILC DRAFT AND THE 1968–1969 VIENNA CONFERENCE

8.2.1 Comments of Governments and International Organisations and Discussion in the Sixth Committee

Following discussion in the Sixth Committee at the 1966 session of the General Assembly, written comments to the draft were submitted by 'Member States' and international organisations.[136] These comments were before the Sixth Committee at the 1967 session of the Assembly.[137] In 1968 further comments by international organisations[138] and additional statements by 'participating States' were sent in.[139]

[132] See above, note 109 and accompanying text.

[133] YILC 1965, Vol I, 810th meeting, § 9; brief discussion on the subject during the 781st meeting, §§ 42–58; and 810th meeting, §§ 4 and 8.

[134] Section 3.3.2 above.

[135] YILC 1966, Vol II, § 2 at 187.

[136] In Resolution 2166 (XXI) the General Assembly had decided to convene an international conference and to 'embody the results in an international convention and such other instruments as it may deem appropriate' (§ 1); it had invited 'Member States, the Secretary-General and the Directors-General of those Specialized Agencies which act as depositaries of treaties to submit their written comments and observations on the final draft articles' (§ 9). Pursuant to paragraph 9, comments were submitted by 17 member states, the Secretary-General, four specialised agencies and the IAEA. These written comments, as well as extracts from the debate in the Sixth Committee at the 21st session, were reproduced in Conference document A/CONF.39/5 (Vol I and II).

[137] Quotations from the discussion in the Sixth Committee at the 22nd session have been reproduced in Conference document A/CONF.39/5 (Vol I and II) as well.

[138] Also pursuant to Res 2166 (XXI), § 9, statements by ICAO, IBRD and four of the intergovernmental organisations invited to send observers to the Conference (Asian-African Legal Consultative Committee, Council of Europe, OAS, United International Bureaux for the Protection of Intellectual Property (UN Doc A/Conf.39/7 and Add 1 and Add 1/Corr 1; a second statement (1969) by the IBRD reproduced in UN Doc A/Conf.39/7/Add.2).

[139] Pursuant to 1967 Resolution 2287 (XXII), in which the General Assembly invites 'participating States' to send to the Secretary-General, 'for circulation to governments, any

The discussion in the Sixth Committee at the 1967 session[140] and 1968 session,[141] which focussed on the scope of the draft Articles, was indecisive as to the fate of IGO treaties. Though a majority accepted the course taken by the Commission, several states expressed their regret on the limited scope of the draft.[142] A recurring argument was the special importance of IGO treaties for developing countries.[143] Also, the question was raised whether a treaty concluded between both states and organisations would be governed by the draft convention.[144] The United States observed that '[the decision to limit the scope of the draft] could well be reviewed in order to determine whether the articles of the draft convention do, in fact, conflict with "special characteristics" of agreements to which international organizations are parties'.[145]

additional coments and draft amendments to the draft articles [. . .]' (§ 2), additional comments were submitted in 1968 by seven participating states (reproduced in UN Docs A/Conf.39/6 and Add.1 and 2).

[140] GAOR, Twenty-First Session, Sixth Committee, 902nd to 919th meetings; the discussion was summarised in the Report of the Sixth Comittee: 'The limitation of the draft to treaties concluded between States [. . .] was approved by some representatives who felt that [. . .] treaties concluded between States and other subjects of international law, or between those other subjects of international law, presented special features which fully justified the view that the International Law Commission should not consider them in the context of its draft articles'. [. . .] 'Other representatives, however, regretted that the draft articles were limited solely to treaties concluded between States. In particular, it was emphasised that [other treaties] [. . .] were playing an increasingly important role in the life of the international community today, and were of great importance, above all, to the developing countries. [. . .] Some representatives suggested that the International Law Commission should prepare a draft on treaties concluded with international organizations in time for the future conference [. . .]'. (GAOR, Twenty-First Session, Annexes, UN Doc A/6516, agenda item 84, §§ 43, 51and 52).

[141] GAOR, Twenty-Second Session, Sixth Committee, 964th, 967th, 969th, 971st, and 974th to 983rd meetings; see for introduction by Sir Humphrey Waldock to the Sixth Committee, 964th meeting, §§ 3 and 6. The – still – diverging views on the scope of the draft articles were summarised in §§ 13 and 14 of the Report of the Sixth Committee (GAOR, Twenty-Second Session, Annexes, agenda item 86, UN Doc A/6913): 'The majority of representatives who spoke on the scope of the draft articles approved the limitations adopted by the Commission. Prolonged study would be necessary before the precise extent of application of the general law of treaties to the agreements of international organizations could be determined. [. . .] On the other hand, some representatives would have preferred that the draft articles be given a broader scope. One representative stated that the omission to deal with treaty-making by international organizations might prove unfortunate in view of the growing importance and number of such treaties'. For the 1966 and 1967 debates in the Sixth Committee, see also in UN Doc A/Conf.39/5 (Vol I), the compilation of comments on the draft articles as a whole (9–51), and on Art 1 (52–63).

[142] See UN Doc A/Conf.39/5, Vol I, 52–63, in particular comments by Ceylon, Cyprus, Dahomey, Kuwait, Liberia, Sierra Leone, Sweden, UK, USA.

[143] Eg Ceylon, *ibid*, at 52.

[144] FAO (*ibid*, at 62); a question that would be brought up by Canada during the Conference (SR, CW, 3rd meeting, § 4).

[145] UN Doc A/Conf.39/5 (Vol I), at 61; this would seem a rather rhetoric observation, as at that point there was no clarity on the 'special characteristics' of treaties concluded by international organisations.

The comments of international organisations show at least two recurring elements: the undesirability of a legal regime for IGO treaties that would be different from the regime for inter-states treaties;[146] but also the desirability of a IGO treaty-making practice developing unfettered by prematurely set out legal rules. The statement by the IBRD is particularly noteworthy, as it is the first to address the notorious 'special features' of treaties concluded by international organisations:

> Without attempting to catalogue here all the special devices used by international organizations in this field, any instrument dealing with international organization treaties will have to take account, inter alia, of the following practices, which are naturally not reflected in the current [1966] draft: (a) The entry into force of an agreement occurring directly as a consequence of the separate actions of the legislative organs of the organization concerned, without the exchange of any signatures or ratifications. This procedure is customarily used in concluding relationship agreements between organizations. (b) The custom whereby international organizations frequently accept by implication (rather than expressly as foreseen in draft article 31) obligations or functions with respect to treaties to which they are not parties (but which they may have sponsored). (c) The explicit or implicit delegation by an organization to another of the power to sign agreements in its name. [. . .]. (d) The dual mechanism whereby organizations on the one hand and States on the other may become parties to a particular agreement [. . .]. (e) The general absence of any ratification procedure by organizations, even in concluding agreements with States whose representatives are only authorized to sign subject to ratification. In addition to these 'procedural' points, due consideration should be given to the application of many of the even more important 'substantive' provisions of the Draft Articles to the agreements of international organizations. While in the

[146] FAO: 'There appears to be a certain tendency towards the conclusion of treaties between States to which one or more international organizations may also be parties. [. . .] It is not clear whether international instruments of this type fall within the scope of the draft articles [. . .] this problem may well deserve further consideration prior to – and possibly during – the proposed diplomatic conference on the law of treaties. In our opinion, it would be desirable to avoid a situation in which two different sets of rules would be applied to one and the same international instrument [. . .] '. (comment to Art 1; UN Doc A/CONF.39/5 (Vol I), at 62); IBRD: 'In view of the growing number and importance of the agreements falling into the categories excluded from the present draft, the Bank anticipates that if a Convention on the law of treaties is adopted, it will be followed in the not-too-distant future by another similar instrument dealing with treaties to which international organizations are parties. [. . .] care will have to be taken that, whatever special rules may be required with respect to procedural aspects, the substantive provisions governing such treaties do not deviate more than necessary from those established in relation to treaties among States. It would be undesirable to create wholly different régimes [. . .]' (UN Doc A/Conf.39/7/Add.1 and Corr.1, at 67; see also main text). Comments on Art 4 ('Treaties which are constituent instruments of international organizations or which are adopted within international organizations") are left out of account, as such agreements fall outside the scope of the present study (comments by FAO and ILO (UN Doc A/Conf.39/5 (Vol I), at 50–51) on the draft as a whole; and comments by the FAO, ILO, ITU, WHO on draft Art 4 (*ibid*, 88–94); by the Council of Europe (UN Doc A/Conf.39/7, at 15–18).

> event it may be determined that no more than the adaptation of the text of the Articles as they relate to States will be required, no such determination can be made until a careful examination of the character and subjects of the agreements of international organizations has been undertaken [. . .].[147]

While the points advanced by the IBRD are important and go into considerable detail, it should also be noted that, as the organisation itself pointed out, they are 'procedural' issues. Moreover, these do not encroach upon the (customary) law of treaties of the time; either because the form of creating obligations lies outside the law of treaties scope (points a (parallel legislation) and c (agency)), or because they are perfectly compatible (points d ('plurilateral agreements') and e (parties using different means of expressing consent)). Only point b (implicit acceptance of treaty obligations by a 'third organisation') was relevant in that the final ILC draft Article, the fruit of long discussions, stipulated 'expressly accepted'. In the 1969 Convention Article 35 this became '...the third State expressly accepts that obligation in writing'.[148] In the corresponding 1986 Article this was to be mitigated, at least at first sight,[149] by the provision that '[a]cceptance by the third organization of such an obligation shall be governed by the rules of that organization.' It seems unsurprising that the IBRD could not immediately specify the 'substantive' provisions, which it proposed to reserve for further study. As emerged from the codification work in later years, insofar as these provisions do not amount to doctrinal statements, arguably the law of treaties is such that the substance *must* be equal for all subjects.[150]

8.2.2 The Vienna Conference (1968–1969)

At the diplomatic conference[151] it was not long before the issue of IGO treaties came up again. During the discussion of Article 1,[152] the USA tabled an amendment purporting to extend the scope of the draft to

[147] UN Doc A/Conf.39/7/Add 1 and Corr 1, at 93; in a second statement, the Bank expressed its 'satisfaction' on the 'tentative decisions' to limit the draft to treaties between states, 'because of the concern that any such regulation should only be consequent on an extensive and intensive study of the existing and developing practices' (UN Doc A/Conf.39/7/Add. 2, § 2).

[148] YILC 1966, Vol II, at 227; the additional requirement that it be 'in writing' was inserted during the Conference at the instigation of developing countries (United Nations Conference on the Law of Treaties, *Official Records*, Second Session, at 59–60).

[149] The legal significance of the added clause 'governed by the rules of the Organization' is not clear; see section 10.1.3 below on expression of consent by an international organisation.

[150] Chapter 10 below.

[151] 26 March-24 May 1968.

[152] Article 1 ('The present Articles relate to treaties concluded between States') and the amendments thereto were discussed in the Committee on the Whole at its 2nd and 3rd meetings (UN Doc A/Conf.39/11, Summary Records CW, 11–20).

'treaties concluded between two or more States or other subjects of international law'.[153] Two more amendments relevant to the issue of IGO treaties were tabled,[154] but their consideration revolved mainly around the US proposal.[155] Some representatives restated their regret on the limitation of the scope of the draft convention to inter-state treaties, in view of the fact that IGO treaties had an increasingly important role.[156] Others doubted whether it was possible to make a clear distinction between treaties concluded by states and those concluded by organisations.[157] Others underscored once more the problem of different legal regimes applying to one single treaty with both states and organisations as parties.[158]

The majority of representatives supported the decision of the International Law Commission, mainly for lack of a convincing alternative.[159]

[153] UN Doc A/Conf/39/C.1/L.15. Instead of 'The present articles relate to treaties concluded between States' the USA proposed 'The present articles apply to treaties concluded between two or more States or other subjects of international law'; the rationale – the increasing number of treaties to which organisations are parties, the assumption that '[i]n general, such treaties have the same characteristics as treaties between States', and the stability of international relations – reiterated arguments brought forward in the written comments by the USA.

[154] Hungary proposed to delete Art 1 (UN Doc A/Conf.39/C.1/L.18); the Republic of Vietnam proposed to amend draft Art 1 as follows: 'The present articles apply to treaties concluded between States and also to treaties concluded between States and other subjects of international law'. (UN Doc A/Conf.39/C.1/L.27).

[155] See the introductory statements by the representative of the USA ('At the present time, international organizations were important elements in the world community; [. . .] The exclusion of international organizations from the scope of the convention would create serious difficulties in the future. [. . .]' – CW, 2nd meeting, §§ 3–5), by the representative of Hungary ('[. . .] he saw no need to retain [article 1], since the scope of the proposed convention was already stated in the title of the draft and was perfectly clear from the definition of the term 'treaty' in article 2'. – CW, 2nd meeting, § 6) and by the representative of Vietnam who held that it was 'desirable to extend the scope of the draft articles owing to the importance, particularly to developing countries, of treaties concluded 'between two or more States or other subjects of international law" (CW, 2nd meeting, § 24).

[156] Cf statements in CW, 2nd meeting, § 14 (Cyprus), § 28 (Tanzania), § 31 (Australia); CW 3rd meeting, § 13 (United Kingdom), § 17 (Czechoslovakia), § 30 (Poland), § 32 (Sierra Leone), § 36 (Brazil), § 55 (Germany), § 62 (Japan) and § 66 (Sweden).

[157] Cf, eg, CW, 2nd meeting, § 14 (Cyprus), § 28 (Tanzania: 'Moreover it did not seem possible to draw a clear distinction between treaties concluded by those international organizations and treaties concluded between States. International organizations were subject to normal rules of international law, especially when a treaty had entered into force'.), § 31 (Australia); 3rd meeting, § 13 (United Kingdom), § 47 (Liberia), § 52 (Turkey), § 55 (Federal Republic of Germany).

[158] CW, 3rd meeting (France).

[159] See, again, CW, 2nd and 3rd meetings. A reasoned summary of the discussion in the Committee on the Whole on this matter is found in UN Doc A/CN.4/L.161/Add.1, 26–33, §§ 26–62. Note eg the statement by Finland (CW, 3dr meeting, § 38) which mentions 'many differences between treaties concluded between States and those to which international organizations were parties'; the statements by Poland (3rd meeting, § 30) and Switzerland (3dr meeting, § 43) which perceive the special characteristics rather in the differences between legal personality of states and organisations; cf also the representative of Ceylon (2nd meeting, §§ 15 and 18), who "recognized that treaties concluded between States and treaties

The idea of starting out with a convention on inter-state treaties to subsequently 'expand' the law was generally accepted as a working strategy.[160]

The American proposal, which was criticised on account of the unspecified phrase 'other subjects of international law,[161] also met with opposition on more practical grounds: that changing the draft so as to include IGO treaties in its scope would require substantial adaptations and bring an amount of work that could hamper the progress of the Conference.[162]

In a renowned démarche Swedish representative Blix then stated:

> His delegation believed that the limitation of the applicability of the draft [. . .] was a shortcoming [. . .] it was convinced, however, that it was too late to remedy that shortcoming during the present Conference. [. . .] A more practical course of action would be for the Conference to adopt a special resolution urging the International Law Commission to prepare a complement to the draft, specifying which of its rules and what additional rules might be applicable to such treaties.[163]

Eventually the US delegation announced the withdrawal of its amendment.[164] Article 1 thus retained its restrictive formula,[165] as did the definition of 'treaty' in Article 2(1)(a), which was adopted in the form proposed by the ILC.[166] The compromise proposal to include a resolution

concluded by international organizations had similar characteristics, but [. . .] hesitated to support the proposition that they should be governed by the same body of principles' (§ 15).

[160] Cf CW, 2nd meeting, § 20 (Ceylon), 3rd meeting, § 6 (Sweden) and § 24 (Iraq).

[161] CW, 2nd meeting, § 28 (Tanzania); 3rd meeting, § 10 (France), § 22 (Ghana), § 27 (Argentina), § 38 (Finland), § 42 (Switzerland); see above on similar deliberations in the Commission over the years.

[162] Cf 2nd meeting, §§ 8, 9 (India), §§ 17, 21 (Ceylon), § 22 (Jamaica), § 26 (USSR); 3rd meeting, § 15 (Romania), §§ 17, 18 (Czechoslovakia), § 22 (Ghana), § 27 (Argentina), § 29 (Afghanistan), § 41 (Switzerland).

[163] 3rd meeting, §§ 6 and 5, respectively.

[164] 3rd meeting, § 64. The amendment proposed by Vietnam (see above, note 154) was also withdrawn (§ 49).

[165] The Hungarian amendment to delete Art 1 was referred to the Drafting Committee (3rd meeting, § 76), but not accepted (CW, 11th meeting, § 6); see also CW, 3rd meeting, § 14 (United Kingdom), § 16 (Czechoslovakia), § 25 (Italy), § 28 (Argentina), § 40 (Switzerland). Text of article 1 adopted by the Drafting Committee (UN Doc A/Conf.39/C.1/L.32) introduced at the 11th meeting of the Committee on the Whole (§ 2); adopted by the Committee at the same meeting (§ 6); adopted by the Plenary Conference at its 7th meeting (§ 14); cf statement in which the British delegation stated that it 'accepted that limitation but wished to stress that it did not imply that treaty law did not govern treaties concluded between States and other subjects of international law or between such other subjects of international law, whatever their status or character' (PC, 7th meeting, § 13).

[166] Article 2(1)(a): '"Treaty" means an international agreement concluded between [two or more] States [or other subjects of international law] in written form and governed by international law, whether embodied in a single instrument or in two or more related instruments and whatever its particular designation'. The brackets indicate insertions proposed in a United States amendment (UN Doc A/Conf.39/C.1/L.16), which was subsequently withdrawn by the United States 'because its amendment to article 1 had not been accepted' (CW, 4th meeting, § 12). Text of Art 2 introduced by the Drafting Committee (UN Doc

in the Conference Final Act recommending further study of IGO treaties was unanimously accepted.[167]

The saving clause of draft Article 3 ('International agreements not within the scope of the present articles') gave rise to much discussion[168] and several amendments. Those tabled by Switzerland,[169] Gabon[170] and Ethiopia[171] deserve special mention, as they sought ingeniously to bring back IGO treaties within the scope of the draft convention by deleting the

A/CONF.39/C.1/17) and adopted without a formal vote by the Committee on the Whole at its 105th meeting (§§ 19–43); adopted by the Plenary Conference at its 28th meeting (§ 48).

[167] Proposal 3rd meeting, § 60, adopted § 75. Draft resolution as proposed by the Drafting Committee (UN Doc A/CONF.39/C.1/2), adopted by the Committee on the Whole at its 11th meeting (§ 7); adopted by the Plenary Conference at its 32nd meeting (§ 52). The operative paragraph of the 'Resolution Relating to Article 1 of the Vienna Convention on the Law of Treaties' (annexed to Final Act of the Conference; UN Doc A/Conf.39/26 and Corr.2) reads: 'Recommends to the General Assembly of the United Nations that it refer to the International Law Commission the study, in consultation with the principal international organizations, of the question of treaties concluded between States and international organizations or between two or more international organizations"; the (added) italics indicate the phrase inserted on the basis of a Swedish amendment, notwithstanding some opposition (notably from the USSR: 'Under the Swedish amendment, the Commission would be bound to consult the international organizations. [. . .] Those States [members of international organizations] would thus be in a position to exert pressure on the Commission [. . .]'; PC, 32nd meeting, § 43; cf also statement by Iraq, *ibid*, § 45). The delicate issue of the Commission's autonomy received an extra emphasis in the text of the eventual resolution in which, after the italicised phrase, was added: 'as it may consider appropriate in accordance with its practice' (UN Doc A/Res. 2501 (XXIV); see summary of debate in the Sixth Committee in GAOR, Twenty-Fourth Session, Annexes, agenda items 86 and 94(b), §§ 109–115).

[168] Text of Art 3 above, in note 127; for the initial discussion of Art 3 and amendments thereto see CW, 6th and 7th meetings; the amendment proposed by China to delete Art 3 altogether (UN Doc A/Conf.39/C.1/L.14) is left out of account; a reasoned compilation of the discussion in UN Doc A/CN.4/L.161/Add.1, §§ 93, 95 and 97.

[169] 'Delete the words "to which they would be subject independently of these articles"' (UN Doc A/Conf.3/C.1/L.26); in the introduction of the amendment the Swiss representative said that '[i]t was, moreover, desirable in the interests of the development of international law, to which the convention under discussion would make an important contribution, that the rules set forth in it could be applies to that type of agreement. On the other hand, it was redundant to state that those rules were not applicable by virtue of the convention'. (CW, 6th meeting, § 47).

[170] 'Amend article 3 to read as follows: "The present articles shall not affect either the legal force of international agreements not in written form or of agreements concluded between States and other subjects of international law or between such other subjects of international law, or the application to such agreements of the rules set forth in the present Convention"'. (UN Doc A/Conf.39/C.1/L.41); in his introduction of the amendment the representative of Gabon stated that '[t]he words 'to which they would be subject independently of these articles' had been dropped, as no mention was made of them in the Commission's commentary' (CW, 7th meeting, § 20).

[171] 'Replace article 3 by the following: "[. . .] (b) The scope of the present articles shall not affect the legal force of the agreements between States and other subjects of international law and the application to them so far as possible of the rules of the present Convention".' (UN Doc A/Conf.39/C.1/L.57 and Corr 1); the representative of Ethiopia stated in his introduction of the amendment, after having referred to the application of customary law: 'But the question remains of the application of the progressive and substantial principles

reference to '[law of treaties] rules to which they would be subject independently of these articles',[172] so that precisely the articles in question would remain to be applied.

As with the majority of states, international organisations were not keen on this development. The IBRD and other selected organisations with observer status expressed strong opposition, urging the Committee 'to retain the qualifying words at the end of the text, otherwise the scope of the convention would be indirectly extended to treaties concluded by international organizations.'[173] The ILO had already stated that '[it] was gratified at the Committee's decision to recommend that the question of agreements to which subjects of international law other than States were parties should be examined by the International Law Commission'.[174] The saving clause was eventually maintained, in an even more elaborate form.[175]

The trimmed down draft Article 5, which mentioned only states' treaty-making capacity,[176] was submitted to the Plenary Conference without amendment proposals relevant to the issue of IGO treaties.[177] The

contained in the convention. Any suggestion of a difference between the laws of inter-State treaties and other treaties should be avoided at the present stage of the law'. (CW, 7th meeting, § 22).

[172] Text of Art 3 above, in note 127.

[173] CW, 7th meeting, §§ 74 and 75.

[174] CW, 7th meeting, § 2; the ILO observer furthermore made an extensive comparison of some of the ILO's rules and practices with certain provisions of the draft articles in the context of Art 4 ('The application of the present articles to treaties which are constituent instruments of an international organisation or are adopted within an international organisation shall be subject to any relevant rules of the organization'); a subject which, however, falls outside the scope of the present chapter (*ibid*, §§ 3–19); see on constituent treaties in ch 6 above.

[175] (For reference of the Article to the Committee -see CW, 7th meeting, § 76). The new text read: 'The fact that the present convention does not apply to international agreements concluded between States and other subjects of international law or between such other subjects of international law, or to international agreements not in written form, shall not afect: (a) the legal force of such agreements; (b) the application to them of any of the rules set forth in the present convention to which they would be subject, in accordance with international law, independently of the convention; *(c) the application of the convention to the relations of States as between themselves under international agreements to which other subjects of international law are also parties'*. (UN Doc A/CONF.39/C.1/3). The (added) italics indicate the provision inserted by the Drafting Committee on its own initiative (cf introduction in CW, 28th meeting, §§ 5–7) – a rare event; after some discussion, the article was adopted without a formal vote (CW, 28th meeting, § 13) and subsequently adopted by the Plenary Conference without changes (PC, 7th meeting, § 21).

[176] For the text of the article see above, note 131.

[177] Discussion in the CW, 11th and 12th meetings, reference to the Drafting Committee, 12th meeting, § 51; text submitted by Committee (UN Doc A/Conf.39/C.1/3) at the 28th meeting; at that meeting the text, controversial because of the reference to federal states in paragraph 2, was adopted by 54 votes to 17 with 22 abstentions (§§ 33–48).

Conference rejected by a large majority paragraph 2, relating to treaty-making capacity of federal states. The lapidary Article 5, which became part of the final Convention text, reads: 'Every State possesses capacity to conclude treaties'.[178]

8.3 INTERNATIONAL ORGANISATIONS IN THE FIRST STAGE OF THE CODIFICATION PROCESS

The barriers to the inclusion of IGO treaties in the scope of the Convention eventually proved insurmountable, but, as is clear from the above, the limitation of the scope of the draft articles had not been self-evident. Throughout the years of preparatory work, the Commission wavered between inclusion and exclusion of IGO treaties. The main underlying cause is arguably the dual legal image of international organisations: a vehicle for states with an open structure, on the one hand, and an independent actor with a closed structure, on the other. This stage of the law of treaties codification process gives a first indication of how the transparent institutional veil of organisations could not be readily accommodated by the law of treaties, because the drafters had difficulty accepting the independent, equal role of organisations next to states, implied in the treaty machinery.

In the formal framework that many lawyers and policy-makers use, the process of conceiving written rules of international law is determined by two factors:[179] the descriptive aspect of codification, relating to the factor of consensus on the existence of customary law or, in any case, practice; and the normative aspect, connected to the factor of preparedness to accept 'new' legal rules. It is notoriously difficult to draw a distinction between *lex lata* and *lex ferenda* in conventional international law, and it seems equally hard to distinguish between the two corresponding factors at play during the codification process. The law of treaties is no exception in this respect.[180]

A declared motive for the cautious approach adopted by the Commission and the Conference was the scarcity of data on the treaty practice of organisations and the apprehension that an attempt to set adequate rules

[178] The article was considered at the 7th and 8th meetings of the Plenary Conference; at the 8th meeting paragraph 2 of the article was rejected (§§ 50 and 51).

[179] Reflected in Art 15 of the ILC Statute which sets out the functions of the Commission, comprising both 'codification of international law' and 'progressive development of international law' (ILC Statute in an Annex to UN Doc A/Res. 174(II) of 21/XI/1947, establishing the ILC).

[180] With regard to the first matter, a suggestion as to which provisions of the 1969 Vienna Convention were, at the time, an expression of 'codification', and which of 'progressive development' is given in Paul Reuter, *La Convention de Vienne du 29 Mai 1969 sur le droit des traités*, 1970, at 7–9.

could founder on a lack of consistent practice, or lack of knowledge of practice. Although an extensive survey of practice was not – and is not[181] –available, there was some feedback from organisations during the drafting process, with the IBRD statement reported above as an outstanding example.[182] Apart from the descriptive force of the draft Convention, a second, implicit question was whether 'special features' of IGO treaties would afterwards prove to be at odds with the normative body of the Convention. Such features were not known, either from IGO comments, or from other sources. The history of the second Vienna Convention[183] confirms that these features probably do not exist. In hindsight this is not difficult to construe, considering the content of the 'law of treaties', the subsidiary character of these rules and the fact that organisations have developed their treaty practice largely within the existing parameters of international relations.[184] Thus, the drafters of the first Vienna Convention made occasional reference to the 'special characteristics' of IGO treaties but without specifying the basis of practice or doctrinal considerations. In hindsight one may ask whether the more economic approach would have been for the Commission immediately to look into this question, rather than to hold back in the face of at that point spectral 'special features'.

The fact that the Commission did reserve the matter also points to another factor. As was noted by observers in the drafting process, and as appears from the records of the Commission and the proceedings of the Conference,[185] the question regarding the extent to which organisations *could* be governed by the classical law of treaties was inextricably linked to the question regarding the extent to which international organisations *should* be able to participate in the international legal system, through treaty-making, on an equal footing with states.[186] These questions were addressed from the perspective of doctrine – there being not much received knowledge on IGO treaty practice – blended with political and philosophical views on the role of states and organisations.[187]

[181] On the accessibility of data on IGO treaty-making practice see section 7.1 above.

[182] Above, note 147 and accompanying text.

[183] Ch 10 below.

[184] Ch 3 above.

[185] See eg quotations above; a representative picture of the doctrinal and political climate in the UN and notably the ILC through the years with regard to this particular subject, however, is obtained only from the Summary Records of the different UN bodies as a whole.

[186] Günther Hartmann, 'The Capacity of International Organizations to Conclude Treaties' in Karl Zemanek (ed.), *Agreements of International Organizations and the Vienna Convention on the Law of Treaties*, 1971, 127–163, at 129; cf also Rosenne, *Legislative History...*, above, note 5, at 44; and Richard Kearney and Robert Dalton, 'The Treaty on Treaties', 64 *American JIL* 1970, 495–561, at 496.

[187] On 'external' factors in the transparent image of organisations, see section 2.3 above and ch 11 below.

The perceived distinction between states and organisations in some way had to be expressed in relation to the law of treaties. Its first manifestation was doubt as to whether international organisations could be subject of the law of treaties at all. Doctrine was not prepared to accept this without a struggle of sorts. However, practice of the time already showed numerous examples of international organisations concluding agreements, with states and between themselves.[188] Moreover, the classic law of treaties (as the law of contract) proceeds from a concept of 'treaty' that focuses on the instrument, not on the parties. Thus, the discussion logically came to be cast in terms of whether IGO agreements qualify as 'treaties'.

There were several factors facilitating such qualification. First there was the – novel – approach in which 'treaty' was consistently defined as the *concept* 'agreement' rather than as the factual (single formal) *instrument*,[189] whereby the term lost its traditional connotation and became a generic term for all agreements in writing. This brought for example 'exchanges of notes' and 'memoranda of understanding' under the scope of the draft, and no doubt also facilitated the inclusion of treaties made by organisations.

Furthermore, a distinction *ratione materiae* as part of the definition of 'treaty' never took root. A difference between 'agreements' with an administrative purport and 'treaties' of a political nature (which would *de facto* set IGO treaties apart from inter-state treaties) thus could not be based on the formal treaty machinery. Hence IGO agreements increasingly came to be discussed in terms of one unified category of agreements, part of a general treaty-practice.

Yet another factor was the Commission's approach to the delimitation of the law of treaties as a branch of law. From the outset it was clear that 'the law of treaties' would be concerned with 'agreements' themselves, rather than with the obligations stemming from them.[190] For one thing, this enabled the Commission to leave out of account certain complex questions relating to the international responsibility of organisations and their member states.[191] Finally, this approach in turn entailed the practical necessity of creating a legal regime applicable to IGO treaties that would be compatible with – if not identical to – the regime applicable to inter-state treaties.

[188] See section 7.1.1 above on the estimates of Oscar Schachter in 1960.

[189] Cf Brierly I, comment to Art 1(b), 1950 YILC, Vol II, § 33 at 229. Followed in the definition articles proposed by the other Special Rapporteurs and in the drafts provisionally adopted by the Commission.

[190] As was pointed out in the discussions on the draft of the second Vienna Convention in 1983 (Summary Records of the General Assembly, Sixth Committee, 38th session, 32nd meeting).

[191] On international responsibility of organisations, see section11.3 below.

As a consequence, formally restricting the term and concept of 'treaty' to its traditional meaning of 'inter-state agreement' was not a viable option. But then the majority of the definitions of 'treaty' proposed by the Special Rapporteurs show an untraditional qualification *ratione personae* in that they contain references to the treaty *parties*. Only the definition proposed by Fitzmaurice is concerned purely with the 'instrument' (or the legal act it embodies) as a unified category.[192] The definitions by Brierly,[193] Lauterpacht (who omits 'for the purpose of the present draft')[194] and, later, Waldock[195] contain a reference to specific parties – be it states, organisations or both.

The Commission reached general agreement on the necessity of addressing the phenomenon of IGO treaties. However, if and when this was accepted, the drafters clearly proceeded from the preset objective to maintain a distinction between treaties concluded only by states and treaties to which international organisations are also party. On several occasions in the codification process the possibility that inter-state treaties and treaties of organisations would be governed by the same set of rules was discarded as *a priori* unacceptable.

These counteracting trends of thought – the latter most consistently maintained in the socialist doctrine of the time – prompted lengthy discussions and some complex compromises. A noteworthy example is the distinction between treaties with both organisations and states as parties, on the one hand, and treaties with only organisations as parties, on the other. This undoubtedly was inspired by the view that treaties between an organisation and a state would – and for the sake of compatibility of legal regimes, *should* – be more akin to inter-state treaties, and simultaneously by a wish to underscore the difference between states and organisations as treaty-making subjects of international law. This distinction eventually found its way into the 1986 Vienna Convention[196] but was never corroborated by a difference in legal effect.

At the end of the day the question of treaty-making capacity appears to have been the biggest obstacle. The problem with regard to capacity of organisations was twofold. First, while recognising that *some* international organisations had treaty-making capacity, the Commission was not prepared to recognise such capacity as a principle for all international organisations. The ensuing problem of how to distinguish between organisations on the basis of treaty-making capacity, and how to cast this in a

192 With the added general condition that it can be employed only by entities qualified under international law to do so; section 8.1.3 above.

193 Section 8.1.1 above.

194 Section 8.1.2 above.

195 Section 8.1.4 above.

196 See section 10.1.1 below.

general provision, remained unsolved. This parallels the doctrinal debate of that period on 'legal personality' of organisations.[197] An attempt to effect a distinction by refining the definition of 'organisation' had perished during discussions in the 1950s. The Commission would regularly state, however, that it had no doubts on the possible treaty-making capacity of certain international organisations, or on the validity of treaties concluded by international organisations in general.[198]

With regard to capacity, Brierly put states and international organisations on the same plane, and did not specify the possible limitations to which such capacity could be subject.[199] Lauterpacht's draft did not contain a general provision on treaty-making capacity, but the implication of his general approach would probably have been that capacity accrued to all international organisations.[200] While Fitzmaurice did not deal with the matter, Waldock envisaged treaty-making capacity 'if, and to the extent that, such treaty-making capacity is expressly created, or necessarily implied' in the institutional law of the organisation.[201]

This leads to the second aspect of the question of treaty-making capacity: its legal basis. The inevitability of a choice between the view that capacity must be conferred upon the organisation by its member states, on the one hand, and the view in which the organisation's capacity is 'inherent' or conferred by general international law, on the other, was signalled by Lauterpacht in his commentaries.[202] However, he did not propose an answer. The question was taken up and decided by Waldock, who clearly rejected the notion of 'inherent' or objective capacity, as appears from the quoted Article 3 above.

The Rapporteurs proposed different notions of 'international organisation'. While Brierly regarded states and organisations as separate, independent entities, Lauterpacht viewed organisations as true collectivities of states. He essentially took a classic point of view and adhered to the law of treaties paradigm that was upheld also by socialist scholars in that period, namely that organisations remain products of treaties between sovereign

[197] See section 4.2.1 above.

[198] This eventually found expression in Art 3 of the 1969 Convention: 'The fact that the present Articles do not relate: (a) To international agreements concluded between States and other subjects of international law or between such other subjects of international law [. . .] shall not affect the legal force of such agreements [. . .]'. Already the commentary to the Harvard Draft had stated that 'this is not saying that the League [of nations] cannot be a party to treaties [. . .]' (Harvard Law School, Research in International Law, III (Law of Treaties), the 36 draft Articles are reproduced in a Supplement to 29 *American JIL* 1935, pp 655–1226, at 692), and that 'it is not to be implied that a treaty between two or more such entities [ie 'persons other than a State'], and especially one between such an entity and a State, may not properly be regarded as a treaty' (as above, at 699).

[199] Section 8.1.1 above.

[200] Section 8.1.2 above.

[201] For the draft Art 3(4), see section 8.1.4 above, note 78 and accompanying text.

[202] Section 7.1.2 above.

states – perhaps to the detriment of legal and political reality. Interestingly, this opinion would ultimately lead to the conclusion – which, as seen above, was accepted by Lauterpacht to some extent – that treaties concluded by international organisations are governed by the exact same body of law as inter-state treaties. The perspective of Rapporteur Waldock, on the contrary, was a moderate one. He recognised the independent personality of (some) organisations, but relegated the power to confer such personality to member states.

The perspective on international organisations in the first stage of the law of treaties codification process was thus more set than it was to become in later years. Organisations appear as markedly transparent, and secondary to states. For the few tenets of the law of treaties that were tentatively addressed, it appears the drafters were not easily prepared to sacrifice this transparency – so the project temporarily faltered on the law of treaties system, which dictates one-dimensional, equal treaty partners. Otherwise, an organisation would be generally equated with its constituent treaty, and questions would be traced to the 'will' of the member states. Along the same line, in the grapple with the treaty-making capacity of organisations, no distinction was made between the concepts of 'capacity' and 'competence',[203] or between international law and the law of the organisation. The idea of general international law providing the legal basis, analogously to domestic legal systems, for capacity in legal subjects was not accepted. (Seyerstedt's monograph appeared in 1963.) Noteworthy in this respect is the expression 'inherent capacity' used by Lauterpacht for what later would be termed an 'objective approach'. The formula eventually proposed by Waldock and adopted by the Commission relies on the *Reparation* case, and therewith takes over also the unclear points of that decision with respect to the legal basis of personality.[204]

Finally, contradictory concerns emerge also from the written comments of states on the final draft. Developing countries especially, against the backdrop of the so-called 'assistence' agreements with international organisations, advocated a broadening of the Convention's scope. International organisations for their part appeared motivated both by the idea to bring all international agreements under one single legal regime, and at the same time by the fear they would lose their freedom of practice. This notwithstanding, the 1968–1969 Conference eventually decided – seemingly on the basis of both practical and political grounds, more so than the Commission – to maintain the limited scope of the draft Convention, and to relegate the codification of the law of treaties as applicable to international organisations to a separate codification project.

[203] See section 4.2.5 above.
[204] See sections 4.2.2 and 4.2.3 above.

When that project took off in 1971 the relation of the 1969 Convention to the prospective second Vienna Convention was all that remained of the 'scope' problem. However, the legal issues that were raised with regard to IGO treaties during the years 1950–1968 to some extent had set the tone for the preparation of the 1986 Convention, and they were to resurface in the second stage of the law of treaties codification project.

9

The 1986 Vienna Convention: Preliminary Questions and Procedural Aspects

BEFORE THE SUBSTANCE of the Second Vienna Convention and its preparatory work is addressed, it is useful to point to some methodological and procedural aspects of the process, as these reflect the status attributed to international organisations and their treaty practice. The topic at hand seemed to require a level of involvement on the part of organisations for which there was no precedent. Preliminary discussions were concerned in particular with the way in which international organisations could participate in the drawing up of legal rules and in the work of a possible diplomatic conference, and the way in which such rules should become binding on organisations.

The General Assembly had swiftly responded to the recommendation made by the 1969 Conference[1] with a resolution requesting the International Law Commission to study thc question of treaties concluded by international organisations.[2] At its 1970 Session the Commission included the question in its general programme of work and established a Sub-committee,[3] which in the same Session submitted a report on the 'preliminary problems involved with the study of this new topic',[4] adopted with some minor drafting changes by the Commission.[5] A full report was

[1] See section 8.2.2 above.

[2] UN Doc A/Res/24/2501 (12-XI-1969), 5, in which the GA 'Recommends that the International Law Commission should study, in consultation with the principal international organizations, as it may consider appropriate in accordance with its practice, the question of treaties concluded between States and international organizations or between two or more international organizations, as an important question'.

[3] YILC 1970, Vol I, SR. 1069, §§ 82–85.

[4] Report of the ILC, YILC 1970, Vol II, at 310, § 89; the preliminary report (UN Doc A/CN.4/L.155) is reproduced in this paragraph of the ILC report.

[5] YILC 1970, Vol I, SR. 1078; the report to the Commission proposed (a) to request the Secretary-General for certain working-documents (surveys) and (b) that the Chairman submit to the members of the Sub-committee a questionnaire on the matter.

submitted by the Sub-committee and approved by the Commission at the 1971 session.[6] In the same year Paul Reuter was appointed Special Rapporteur on the subject.[7]

The ILC produced a final draft in 1982. The UNGA Sixth Committee examined the draft in 1983 and 1984, while intensive 'informal consultations'[8] took place in 1984 and 1985. In large part these concentrated on the procedural role of international organisations in the drafting Conference.[9] In 1986 a diplomatic conference of five weeks was convened, which ended with adoption of the text of the Vienna Convention on the Law of Treaties Between States and International Organizations or Between International Organizations.

9.1 QUESTIONS OF METHODOLOGY

9.1.1 Drafting Method

The method employed in the drafting process is closely related to the substance of the convention.[10] Both the Special Rapporteur and the Commission had explicitly taken an approach of parallelism between the 1969 Convention and the new Articles. Notwithstanding the alleged 'special characteristics' of IGO treaties and the doubts expressed by several Commission members as to 'whether [such treaties] should be governed by the same set of principles [as treaties concluded by states]' at all,[11] the choice was made for a close connection with the 1969 Convention, in terms of both form and substance. One stated reason was the undesirability of two different, possibly conflicting, sets of rules which could apply to a single treaty (with both states and organisations as parties). The Commission thus decided to 'follow as closely as possible'[12] the first law of treaties Convention, and explicitly regarded the new draft articles as a 'further stage in the codification of the law of treaties'.[13] It thus took the

[6] UN Doc A/CN.4/250; YILC 1971, Vol I, SR.1129, § 52.

[7] YILC 1971, Vol I, SR.1129, § 53.

[8] On this strategy, see Tullio Treves, 'Innovations dans la technique de codification du droit international: la préparation de la conférence de Vienne sur les traités passés par les organisations internationales', XXXII *Annuaire FDI* 1986, 474–494.

[9] See the *Informal Summing-up by the Co-Chairman of the Informal Consultations held During the Period from 18 March to 1 May 1985* and the *Informal Summing-Up by the Co-Chairmen of the Informal Consultations Held During the Period From 8 to 12 July*, UN Doc A/C.6/40/10.

[10] Cf ch10 below.

[11] Ch 8 above.

[12] 1982 Report of the ILC, YILC 1982, Vol II (Part Two), 9–16.

[13] YILC 1982, Vol II (Part Two), at 12, § 36; and thus 'cannot be divorced from the basic text on the subject, namely the Vienna Convention'.

1969 Convention as a guide and considered on an article-by-article basis which provisions would need substantive or drafting modifications in order to become applicable to IGO treaties.

This also entailed the theoretical starting point of viewing all international agreements or 'treaties' as a single legal category – a marked difference with the hesitations on this point[14] expressed during the preparations for the 1969 Convention:

> Treaties are based essentially on the equality of the contracting parties, and this premise leads naturally to the assimilation, whenever possible, of the treaty situation of international organizations to that of States. The Commission has largely followed this principle in deciding generally to follow as far as possible the articles of the Vienna Convention referring to treaties between States for Treaties between States and International Organizations, and for treaties between International Organizations. The increasing number of treaties in which international organizations participate is evidence of the value of treaties to international organizations as well as to States.[15]

The 'new' law of treaties was drawn up in accordance with this idea.

The text, however, was to be formally independent and would no make use of *renvois* to the 1969 Convention, so that its provisions would be able to 'produce legal effects irrespective of the legal effects of the Vienna Convention'.[16] Then, as the Commission explained:

> In conformity with the general conception of the relationship which the draft articles should naturally bear to the Vienna Convention, it was decided to keep the order of that Convention so far as possible, so as to permit continuous comparison between the draft articles and the corresponding articles of that Convention[17]

This approach, which was followed by the Sixth Committee as well as the Conference, had obvious consequences for the approach to international organisations as treaty-parties. For one thing it limited the possibility of differentiating between inter-state treaties and other international agreements. The Commission, however, was to maintain a distinction between inter-organisation treaties and other agreements throughout the drafting process:[18]

> On the one hand it was held that there are sufficient differences between States and International Organizations to rule out in some cases the application of a single rule to both; on the other hand it was held that that a distinction must be

[14] See ch 8 above on the (inter-state) 'treaty' as a species of a larger class of 'agreements'.
[15] Summarised in the ILC report of 1982, YILC 1982, Vol II (Part Two), at 13, § 40.
[16] 1982 ILC Report, §§ 46, 48.
[17] *Ibid*, § 54; provisions which had no parallel in the 1969 Convention were accordingly numbered *bis* etc.
[18] Ch 8 above.

> made between treaties between States and international organizations and between international organizations and that different provisions should govern each.[19]

The economic drafting method was carried through until the final stage. In view of the limited time allotted to the Conference it was decided to refer draft Articles deemed 'unproblematic' immediately to the drafting Committee, whereas others, qualified as 'problematic' on the basis of a list prepared by the Sixth Committee,[20] would be considered by the Committee on the Whole. To this procedure was added a hotly debated safeguard mechanism for changing the designation as 'unproblematic'.[21]

Already during the informal consultations on the preparation for the Conference, it was remarked (and due consideration would be given at the Conference) that:

> examining the articles on the basis of mere parallelism with the corresponding articles of the Vienna Convention on the Law of Treaties was not enough to single out articles as 'non-problematic'.[22]

Further:

> [T]he selection process should be oriented to objective criteria such as the specific needs of international organizations or substantive debates which had taken place in the [ILC], even though a given draft article had been left parallel to the corresponding provision of the Vienna Convention.
>
> Further discussion of the singling-out process should be based on an initial list to be prepared by the co-Chairmen on the basis of objective criteria.[23]

The informal consultations resulted in a draft resolution with three annexes relating to: (i) the Rules of Procedure, (ii) a List of Draft Articles of the Basic Proposal, for which Substantive Consideration is Deemed Necessary, and (iii) a set of Draft Final Clauses,[24] proposed by the co-chairmen of the Sixth Committee, adopted without a vote by the Sixth Committee[25] and passed on the nod by the General Assembly.[26]

[19] YILC 1982, Volume II (Part Two), § 51.

[20] See UN Doc A/C.6/40/10.

[21] A list of 'problematic articles' to be referred to the Committee on the Whole for substantive consideration was contained in Annex II of Resolution 40/76. Article 28 of the Rules of Procedure provided for a safeguard mechanism to recall articles to 'substantive consideration' by the Committee on the Whole.

[22] UN Doc A/C.6/40/10, at 3, § 4(a).

[23] Safeguard mechanism (d), which became rule 28 of the RoP, was discussed again in UN Doc A/C.6/40/10, at 11. The List of 'problematic articles' (Annex II of the first informal summing-up and Annex IV of the second) was re-examined in UN Doc A/C.6/40/10, at 26; for the list, see Annex III below.

[24] UN Doc A/C.6/40/L.16.

[25] UN Doc A/C.6/ 40/SR.46, Agenda Item 139; Report of the Sixth Committee, UN Doc A/40/952.

[26] Un Doc A/Res/40/76.

9.1.2 Form

As it was decided that the law governing IGO treaties would parallel where possible the existing body of the law of treaties, the status of international organisations in the codification process became an issue.

A first point of discussion was the form in which the rules would be framed. The Commission had recommended 'the course capable of conferring the highest possible legal authority on the proposed articles, [viz] . . .to convoke a conference to conclude a convention'.[27] The international organisations of the UN system, however, as stated by the Administrative Committee on Co-ordination (ACC), favoured an expository code rather than a binding instrument, 'as a standard of reference for action destined to harden into customary law'.[28]

The ACCs arguments were: doubts as to whether the field was sufficiently crystallised to be fit for codification in binding rules, whereas 'the rules and practice of the organizations combined with references to the 1969 Vienna Convention provided an adequate legal framework, which there is no demonstrated need to supplement in the form of a convention'; avoidance of the significant costs of a diplomatic conference and avoidance of the procedural problem of representation and participation of organisations therein; and 'the complex and delicate matter of those organizations exercising the right to vote belonging to states'.[29]

The General Assembly, however, on recommendation of the Sixth Committee, decided to aim for the conclusion of a convention,[30] leaving aside for the moment the question of how this convention would become binding on international organisations.

This was not changed by a written comment of the ILO that 'this approach [of an expository code] . . . may avoid some sterile controversy about the capacity of one organization or another to participate in more formal action',[31] nor by the second statement of the ACC,[32] in which it again urged the General Assembly to consider the option of incorporating the draft Articles into a declaration, which subsequently, with added

[27] 1982 ILC Report, 1982 YILC, Vol II (Part Two), § 57, at 16; rationale §§ 60–61 (decision at 1728th meeting in June 1982, YILC 1982, Vol I); although it stressed that that the articles were 'structured in such a way as to accord with whatever solution the General Assembly may ultimately adopt' (ILC Re, § 49).

[28] ACC Decision 1982/17, UN Doc A/C.6/37/L.12 (December 1982), §§ 2 (d), 3.

[29] ACC Decision 1982/17, UN Doc A/C.6/37/L.12 (December 1982), §5.

[30] UN Doc A/Res/37/112, § 5; see Report of the Sixth Committee, UN Doc A/37/700, Agenda Item 125, and Summary Records of the Sixth Committee, 37th to 52nd and 63rd meetings.

[31] UN Doc A/38/145, at 21, § 10(d), 1983. The statement figured verbatim in the first ACC statement; UN Doc A/C.6/37/L.12, § 2(d).

[32] ACC Decision 1983/11, UN Doc A/C.6/38/4 (Oct 1983).

experience and 'crystallization of this area of law', might lead to the conclusion of a convention on the matter.[33]

9.2 THE PROCEDURAL POSITION OF INTERNATIONAL ORGANISATIONS

The 1983 debates in the UNGA Sixth Committee show two trends among the supporters of a convention. One group favoured convening a diplomatic conference; another advised preparation of the treaty text by the Sixth Committee rather than by a diplomatic conference.[34] The draft basically consisted of an adaptation of the 1969 Convention which could be handled by the Sixth Committee and the General Assembly. Notwithstanding substantive arguments – including the advisability of a low political profile in view of the topic and the fear that a conference of plenipotentiaries would bring changes to the text which could break the parallelism with the 1969 Convention – as well as economic considerations – the Assembly decided on a diplomatic conference.[35]

9.2.1 The Participation of International Organisations in the Diplomatic Conference

The decision that 'the appropriate forum for the final consideration of the draft articles' (and the adoption of a convention text) would be a conference of plenipotentiaries[36] meant that the General Assembly was willing to address the question of organisations' status as participants in the diplomatic process and as addressees of a 'law-making treaty'. It seemed fitting that organisations would become parties in their own right to the new convention,[37] and therefore that their position at the conference would go beyond the customarily accorded observer status, but these questions could not be decided on the basis of precedent. A statement by the Special Rapporteur merits quotation in full:

[33] *Ibid*, § 19.

[34] Cf the declarations of the delegates of Israel, the United States *and* the Soviet Union (UN Doc A/C.6/38/SR.70 – as referred to in Treves, above, note 8).

[35] Reconfirmed in UNGA resolution of December 1983; UN Doc A/Res/38/139.

[36] UN Doc A/Res/38/139, § 1.

[37] Cf a traditional solution in the 1946 *Convention on the Privileges and Immunities of the United Nations* (1 UNTS 15; 90 UNTS 327) and the 1947 *Convention on the Privileges and Immunities of the Specialized Agencies* (33 UNTS 261) where a status of 'semi-parties' was created for the pertinent organisations, implicitly acknowledged by the ICJ in its *Reparation* Opinion; see on this eg Shabtai Rosenne, *United Nations Treaty Practice*, RdC 1954 /II, 281–444, at 323–324.

> From the juridical standpoint every organization has features quite different from those of any other organization, and only by taking the greatest precautions can there be any hope of formulating general rules. It is not correct to consider the organization as being on a par with a State, for it is made up of States which have not ceased to be States by reason of their membership of the organization, and to regard the organization as a subject of law is no more than a technical means for reducing the will of the several member States to a single will. To give only one example of the problems which cannot be avoided, one need only consider the final phase of the work to be undertaken. The normal outcome would be to produce a series of draft articles which could be embodied in a future convention; but is it conceicable that the parties to a convention concerning treaties between organizations would be the organizations themselves? Or would States be the parties? Not to speak of the question whether the States are members of the organization concerned or not?[38]

Procedural aspects of the prospective Conference were discussed further in the Sixth Committee in 1984,[39] as well as in informal consultations which also addressed the substance.[40] Here, three problematic areas were identified, one of which related to 'a basic difference in the approach to international organisations as subjects of international law'.[41] The Polish delegate expressed a generally shared concern when he observed that '[t]he arrangements governing the participation of international organiza-tions in the conference should fully reflect the differences between such organizations and states as subjects of international law'.[42] The primary expression of this concern would be the absence of voting rights for organisations.[43]

Participants

Relatively few international organisations were invited to participate in the Conference (for logistical reasons it was felt that invitations could not be extended to 140 organisations), and even fewer actually took part.

With account taken of the informal consultations, a draft resolution proposed by Iraq,[44] which specified the invitations to the conference,

[38] See introduction to questionnaire prepared by the Chairman of the Sub-Committee, § 5 (YILC 1971, Vol II, Part Two, at 186)

[39] SR, Sixth Committee, 39th Session, 31st-33rd, 65th meetings.

[40] Pursuant to § 6 of the previous year's General Assembly resolution 38/139.

[41] UN Doc A/C.6/39/SR.31, §§ 15–23. Other points of discussion were 'the parallels between the 1969 and the new articles' and 'difficulties presented by individual articles'.

[42] Cf Poland, Sixth Committee, 38/SR.32, § 26; the matter (agenda item 132) was discussed at the 31st-33rd, the 35th and the 70th meetings.

[43] See below, note 54 and accompanying text.

[44] UN Doc A/C.6/39/L.27.

passed through the Sixth Committee[45] and the General Assembly[46] without changes. Thus it was decided that a United Nations Conference on the Law of Treaties Between States and International Organizations or Between International Organizations would be held at Vienna from 18 February to 21 March 1986; and that invitations would be extended to:

(a) 'all states';
(b) Namibia, represented by the United Council for Namibia;
(c) 'organizations with a standing invitation to participate in UN international conferences';[47]
(d) national liberation movements recognised by the Organization of African Unity; and
(e) 'international intergovernmental organizations that had been traditionally invited to participate as observers at legal codification conferences convened under the auspices of the United Nations'.

Points (a) to (d) reflected standard practice; organisations envisaged under e) would participate in a capacity that was still to be decided upon.[48] The resolution also reconfirmed an earlier appeal 'to organize consultations, primarily on the organization and methods of work of the Conference,

[45] See SR, A/C.6/39/SR.65, §§ 8–26; certain states however distanced themselves from the text of the resolution (*ibid*, §§ 27–35). See Report of the Sixth Committee (UN Doc A/39/779).

[46] UN Doc A/Res/39/86.

[47] In the capacity of observers. This paragraph refers to the Palestine Liberation Organisation (Resolution 3237(XXIX)) and to the South West Africa People's Organisation (UN Doc A/Res/31/152).

[48] The introduction to the draft resolution (UN Doc A/C.6/39, SR.65, § 14) by Iraq explains that category e) would cover Specialized and Related Agencies (IAEA, ILO, FAO, UNESCO, WHO, IMF, IDA, IBRD, IFC, ICAO, UPU, ITU, WMO, IMCO, WIPO, IFAD); international organisations with a standing invitation to participate in work of the GA (at the 39th session these were: the African, Caribbean and Pacific Group of States (UNGA Resolution 36/4)); Agency for technical and Cultural Co-operation (UNGA Resolution 33/18); Asian-African Legal Consultative Committee (UNGA Resolution 35/2); Commonwealth Secretariat (UNGA Res 31/3); COMECON (UNGA Resolution 3209 (XXIX)); EEC (UNGA Resolution 3208 (XXIX)); Latin American Economic System (SELA) (UNGA Resolution 35/3); League of Arab States (UNGA Resolution 477 (V)); OAU (UNGA Resolution 2011(XX)); OAS (UNGA Resolution 253 (III)); Organizati-on of the Islamic Conference (UNGA Resolution 3369 (XXX)); organisations 'engaged in the progressive development of international law and its codification at the regional level, with which the ILC maintained links of co-operation in accordance with article 26 of its statute and which were not covered by [the second category]' (the Council of Europe's European Committee on Legal Co-operation). A decision on the capacity in which group e) was going to participate would be postponed to the following year's Session, on the basis of the consultations held pursuant to § 8 of the same resolution.

including rules of procedure, and on major issues of substance . . .'[49] A following resolution proposed participation of the United Nations itself.[50]

The Secretary-General had been requested to invite 'all states'.[51] Ninety-seven states and Namibia represented by the United Nations Council for Namibia, participated in the Conference.[52] On the basis of the same the Palestine Liberation Organization, the African National Congress of South Africa and the Pan Africanist Congress participated. Of the organisations invited, eventually a somewhat smaller number participated.[53] While nearly all states took part in the Conference, only 19 international organisations of the 27 invitees did (of a total of over 200 treaty-making organisations). The ACC had considered it essential that 'as many international organisations as possible, be covered by any instrument in which the rules relating to treaty practices of such organizations are set out'.[54] To this end, feedback was sought by a request for written observations, to which some 20 organisations responded.

Status

As for the mode of participation, the ACC had advocated that international organisations should be granted full status, with the exception of the right to vote, and in particular that organisations should have the right to table amendments.[55] The fruit of the lengthy informal consultations[56] was a General Assembly resolution which inter alia contained an Annex with

[49] UN Doc A/Res/39/86, §§ 1, 2 and 8 (such 'consultations' had already been mentioned in resolution 38/139, § 6).

[50] In addition to the organisations mentioned in the resolution adopted at the 39th session (UN Doc A/Res/40/76).

[51] UNGA Res 39/86.

[52] Final Act, UN Doc A/Conf.129/14, § 5.

[53] Asian-African Legal Consultative Committee, Council of Europe, COMECON, EEC, FAO, IAEA, ICAO, IFAD, ILO, IMO, IMF, ITU, League of Arab States, OAS, UNESCO, UNIDO, World bank and WHO; UN Doc A/Conf.129/14, § 9; the United Nations also participated, in the same capacity (pursuant to UN Doc A/Res/40/76).

[54] UN Doc A/C.6/38/4, §§ 5, 10, 11; quotation in §10.

[55] UN Doc A/C.6/37/L.12, §§ 4(c), 5.

[56] There was ongoing discussion on participation (cf UN Doc A/C.6/37/L.12, at 6). In the Protocol, IGOs were put after states (cf §§ 18 to 20). Agreement was reached on the possibility for IGOs to submit substantive and procedural proposals, but with a mechanism 'in order to safeguard the interests of states participating in the Conference' (§§ 21, 22). Consulted parties also agreed on decision-making rights exclusively for states (§ 23), and on the presence of the UN in a dual capacity as host and participant (§ 26). Envisaged was (at 12) the possibility for IGOs to submit substantive proposals in two ways: a) if sponsored by state, b) by themselves, put to a vote only if accepted by general agreement. In a second round of consultations (where organisations were present as observers (at 13, § 50(c)), debate on the fine points of conference diplomacy continued: re quorum required for commencing a meeting: A) IGOs not counted; B) IGOs counted a) une unified enumeration formula, b) double quorum formula, c) alternative quorum formula.

the rules of procedure.[57] The consulted parties had agreed that the final rules of procedure resulting from the extensive informal negotiations would not be reconsidered at the Conference. Thus the General Assembly had (strongly) recommended[58] their adoption by the Conference, which so happened.[59]

These Rules provided for the fully-fledged participation of international organisations, with the one exception of the right to vote (Rule 34 on Decision-making). Organisations had the right to submit procedural proposals as well as substantive proposals (which was the right to amendment promoted by the ACC), which could, however, not be put to a vote unless formally supported by a state.[60]

9.2.2 Final Clauses of the Second Vienna Convention

The ILC draft Articles did not contain final clauses for the prospective Convention;[61] these had been proposed by the co-chairmen of the Sixth Committee and adopted without changes.[62]

The law of treaties essentially regulates the subject matter of final clauses, so the final clauses of this Convention are a test also of its substantive clauses.[63] But in this case they were also a test of the legal status and position of international organisations.

Becoming Bound to the Convention

A first question was how the Articles could be made binding on international organisations. The Commission had considered some aspects of this question,[64] and the ACC had more specifically pointed to three known

[57] UN Doc A/Res/40/76, based on UN Doc A/C.6/40/L.16, also included (II) a *List of Draft Articles of the Basic Proposal, for which Substantive Consideration is Deemed Necessary* (see below, Annex IV) and (III) a set of Draft Final Clauses; cf above, notes 23, 24, 25 and accompanying text.

[58] UN Doc A/Res/40/76, § 4.

[59] UN Doc A/Conf.129/SR.1, at 5; the rules of procedure are reproduced in A/Conf.129/7.

[60] Rule 60(1)(e) and Rule 60(1)(d), respectively.

[61] Ch 10 below.

[62] UN Doc A/C.6/40/L.16, Annex III; adopted without a vote by the Sixth Committee (UN Doc A/C.6/ 40/SR.46, Agenda Item 139. Report of the Sixth Committee, UN Doc A/40/952); passed on the nod in the General Assembly (UN Doc A/Res/40/76).

[63] This had been the logical objection, rather than practical considerations of the ACC (above), of Special Rapporteur Fitzmaurice to embodiment of the law of treaty rules in a convention (see citation in section 8.1.3 above).

[64] ILC Report of 1982, YILC 1982, Vol II (Part Two); see also YILC 1972, Vol II, at 192 ff.

legal constructions: a convention to which states and international organisations would become parties on the same footing;[65] a convention that would be 'approved' by the UN General Assembly and be 'accepted' by 'other international organizations' and subsequently be opened for accession by states;[66] or a convention that would be open to ratification or accession by states only, but with which international organisations would agree to comply.[67]

The last option was discarded, as the ACC considered it essential that 'no international organization be bound without its explicit consent by a convention incorporating the draft articles'.[68] Also, Annex IX of 1982 UNCLOS – designed to accommodate the European Community as a party for those parts of the treaty in relation to which it had exclusive competence – had meanwhile set an innovative precedent as to the possibility of organisations becoming parties to 'law-making treaties'.

The draft final clauses contained in Annex III provided for international organisations becoming bound as 'normal' parties to the Convention – either by the newly coined 'act of formal confirmation' or by accession.[69] This arrangement was eventually included in the Convention.[70]

Entry into Force of the Convention

A tentative discussion on the entry into force of the future Convention showed two trends of thought with respect to the possible role of international organisations: one option was to set a certain minimum number of IGO parties as a necessary condition for entry into force;

[65] Eg the 1980 Agreement Establishing a Common Fund for Commodities (UN Doc TD/IPC/CF/CONF/24). Though states and organisations could become a party to the convention at the same footing (arts 54, 56), entry into force of the convention was effectuated by the consent to be bound of states only (Art 57(1)).

[66] Eg the 1947 *Convention on the Privileges and Immunities of the Specialized Agencies* (33 UNTS 261); *in casu* the 'other international organizations' were the Specialized Agencies. Interesting is the entry into force '*inter partes*' only, in virtue of sections 37 and 44 – see also above, note 37.

[67] The 'third party approach' was used in eg the 1975 Vienna Convention on the Representation of States in their Relations with International Organizations of a Universal Character (UN Doc A/Conf.67/16); signature and ratification was possible only for states, (arts 86–88); entry into force was based on states' expressions of consent to be bound (Art 89). After entry into force, international organisations could 'communicate' their decision to 'implement' the Convention to the Host State and the Depositary of the Convention (Art 90), and thus create legal obligations and rights (!) by universal declaration. See also the reference to the IGO practice of unilaterally accepting treaty obligations in the IBRD statement on the 1966 draft Articles, under c), section 8.2.1 above.

[68] UN Doc A/C.6/38/4, § 11.

[69] *Ibid*, Annex III, draft Art 84.

[70] See ch 10 below.

another was that only states parties would be relevant for entry into force, but without impediment to organisations becoming fully fledged parties to the convention.[71]

The draft articles[72] then envisaged entry into force of the Convention on the basis of a certain number of ratifications or accessions by states (and Namibia) only.[73] The discussion on Annex III remained inconclusive during the 'informal consultations' and was 'referred to the Conference with the purpose of providing assistance in finding a generally acceptable solution'.[74] At the actual Conference, draft Article 84 (on entry into force of the Convention) was however adopted without changes – reportedly inspired by the spirit of 'general agreement' propagated by the General Assembly and the priority of other agenda items.[75]

9.3 DIPLOMATIC FORTUNE OF THE CONVENTION

The speed of adoption of the second Vienna Convention has not been matched by the speed of ratification. The 1969 Convention, considered a complex instrument with intricate implications for domestic law, took eleven years to enter into force. The 1986 Convention, its legal purport practically identical to the first Convention, by 1 September 2006 had received only 28 expressions of consent to be bound by states, of the 35 needed for entry into force. After the United Nations adopted two exhortative Resolutions,[76] several organisations have become party to the Convention.[77]

Why the project resulted in a diplomatic failure is undocumented. The reference to *jus cogens* in Articles 53 and 64 of the two Conventions has been a known obstacle for states, such as France, which has a political culture that is strongly sovereignty-oriented. Reportedly this was also a

[71] UN Doc A/C.6/40/10, at 6, § 14, at 12, § 43.

[72] See above, notes 62, 63 and 64.

[73] UN Doc A/C.6/38/4, Annex III, draft Art 84.

[74] See UN Doc A/C.6/40/SR.46, § 48–50. Cf UN Doc A/Res/40/76, §§ 5 (Annex II referred to the Conference for 'its consideration and action') and 6 (Annex III referred to the Conference for 'its consideration').

[75] The 'General agreement' had been propagated by UNGA Res. 40/76; cf section 9.4 below.

[76] UN Doc A/Res/52/153 (1998), § 5 and UN DocA/Res/53/100 (1999), § 7.

[77] As of 1 Sept 2006: UN (formal confirmation 21–12–1998); ILO (formal confirmation 31–7-2000); WHO (formal confirmation 22–6-2000); UNESCO (23–6-1987); FAO (29–6-1987); ICAO (formal confirmation 24–12–2001); ITU (29–6-1987); IMO (formal confirmation 14–2- 2000); WMO (30–6-1987). International Criminal Police Organization, accession 3-1-2001; IAEA, accession 26–4–2001; OPCW, accession 2–6-2000; Preparatory Commission for the Comprehensive Nuclear Test-Ban Treaty Organization, accession 11–6-2002; UNIDO accession 4–3-2002; WIPO 24–10–2000; UPU, accession 19–10–2004. FAO, ITU, UNESCO and WMO are signatories only, and have not yet submitted an 'act of formal confirmation'. See http://untreaty.un.org.

ground for the European Community, a prominent presence in the drafting process, not to become a party to the 1986 Convention.[78] In this respect it may be noted also that the European Court of Justice, when relying on the international law of treaties, always refers to the 1969 Convention and not to the 1986 Convention.[79]

Otherwise, why by 1 September 2006 had only 28 of the 107 state parties to the first Convention become party to the second one? This question can only be explained from the equal position allotted to organisations by the Convention, since the substance of the rules is essentially the same as in the 1969 Convention. While the equal and independent status of organisations is the most likely cause for the reluctance of states to bind themselves to the 1986 Convention, for organisations this would rather be the apprehension that the Convention will curtail IGO treaty-making practice.[80]

Whatever may have been the balance between 'codification' and 'progressive development' at the time of drafting, it is safe to say that ultimately most rules are considered to have (acquired) the status of custom. One example appeared from the reference made by the International Court of Justice already in the WHO Advisory Opinion of 1980 as to the applicable legal principles and rules on the period of notice that should be given for the termination of an agreement.[81]

9.4 CONCLUSION: THE STATUS OF ORGANISATIONS IN METHOD AND PROCEDURE

Whereas the relation of the 1982 draft to the 1969 Convention could be elegantly and rightly described as 'one of material dependence and formal

[78] This information has been given on an informal basis.

[79] Which can be inferred *a contrario* from the study by Pieter Jan Kuijper, 'The Court and the tribunal of the EC and the Vienna Convention on the Law of Treaties 1969', 25 *Legal Issues of European Integration* 1999, 1–23; cf section 6.2 above.

[80] See eg section 10.1.4 below on draft Art 36*bis*; this apprehension was voiced on several occasions during the drafting process.

[81] *Interpretation Of The Agreement Of 25 March 1951 Between the WHO and Egypt*, Advisory Opinion, 20 December 1980, ICJ Re 1980, at 96, para 49: 'Precisely what periods of time may be involved in the observance of the duties to consult and negotiate, and what period of notice should be given, are matters which necessarily vary according to the requirements of the particular case. In principle, therefore, it is for the parties in each case to determine them. Some indications as to the possible periods involved can be seen in provisions of host agreements including Section 37 of the Agreement of 25 March 1951, as well as in Article 56 of the Vienna Convention on the Law of Treaties and in the corresponding article of the International Law Commission's draft articles on treaties between States and international organizations or between international organizations. The paramount consideration for both the WHO and the host State in every case must be their obligation to co-operate in good faith to promote the objectives and purposes of the WHO'.

independence',[82] this certainly does not characterise the drafting process as such. The Commission explicitly regarded the drafting process for the second Vienna Convention as a 'further stage in the codification of the law of treaties', and by methodological implication took the 1969 Convention as a point of departure, deciding on an article-by-article basis which provision needed substantive or drafting modifications in order to become applicable to IGO treaties,[83] and adhering as closely as possible to 'the spirit, forms and structure' of the 1969 Convention.[84] The drafting process with regard to the new law of treaties thus essentially revolved around the extent to which international organisations could be equated with states. The main obstacle posed to such equation by the Commission's method was arguably the *a priori* distinction between inter-organisation treaties and other treaties, maintained throughout the drafting process.[85]

The question as to the equation of organisations and states also has a procedural dimension, which appears from the drafting process. The Rules of Procedure employed at the 1986 Conference differed in at least three respects from the Rules customarily applied by (UN hosted) codification conferences:[86] first, they introduced the division between rules requiring substantive consideration by the Committee on the Whole and rules that to be examined directly in plenary meeting and by the Drafting Committee; second, they contain an emphatic provision on 'the promotion of general agreement' (Rule 63) (mitigating to some extent the voluntarist spirit of classic inter-state negotiations); and third, they contain specific provisions with regard to participation of representatives of invited international organisations (Rule 60).

The adjustment of procedural rules to the new class of participants resulted in a participatory status for organisations in the conference which included the right to table amendments, but not the right to vote. Likewise, the 1986 Convention accepts organisations as full-fledged parties (something which – although relatively unproblematic given the substance of the Convention – for political reasons was not self-evident at the time of drafting), but it does not take them into account for the entry into force.

The procedural role of international organisations in the drafting of the Convention and in the subsequent treaty-creating procedure may thus be

[82] Egbert Vierdag, 'Some Problems Regarding The Scope of International Instruments on the Law of Treaties', 23 *Archiv des Völkerrechts* (1985), 408 at 439.

[83] YILC 1982, Vol II (Part Two), at 12 (§ 36).

[84] Reuter II, YILC 1973, Vol II, at 77 (§ 9); cf the report of the Sub-Committee, YILC 1971, Vol II, Annex, at 347–348. This approach was reflected in the rules of procedure of the 1986 Vienna Conference (UN Doc A/Conf.129/7); draft Articles whose 'adaptation' was considered uncontroversial were classified as 'non-problematic' and were meant, after scrutiny by the Drafting Committee, to be adopted by the Conference as a formality. See eg Treves, above, note 8, at 474.

[85] Above, notes 18 and 19 and accompanying text.

[86] Shabtai Rosenne, 'International Conferences and Congresses', EPIL, I, 1992, 739–746.

summarised as more important than ever before, but nonetheless secondary with regard to states – and thereby as transparent in the sense that the functional and serviceable aspect of organisations is reflected next to their role as independent treaty-making actors.

10

The 1986 Vienna Convention on the Law of Treaties Between States and International Organizations or Between International Organizations

THE VIENNA CONVENTION on the Law of Treaties Between States and International Organizations or Between International Organizations, which was opened for signature on 21 March 1986, turned out to be very similar to the Vienna Convention on the Law of Treaties of 1969.[1] Because of this likeness,[2] the 'second Vienna Convention'[3] has elicited lukewarm comments. And arguably, after the references to the 'sui generis characteristics' of IGO treaties, which at the time of drafting the 1969 Convention summed up the ground for separate treatment[4] but which were never specified, the final text could appear as an anti-climax. In addition, as a diplomatic effort the Convention has been less than successful, and it has still not entered into force.[5]

The 1986 Convention is, however, an important instrument in several respects. On a general note, the Convention serves the same communal goal as all 'codification treaties', even if the black-and-white model of codification and sources only partially captures the diffuse processes of international law-making.[6] Second, the Convention and the story of its

[1] More similar still than the draft Articles submitted by the International Law Commission in 1982; see the Annexes.

[2] Cf Giorgio Gaja, 'A 'New' Vienna Convention on Treaties Between States and International Organizations or Between International Organizations: A Critical Commentary', LVIII *British YIL*, 1987, 253–269.

[3] In accordance with common parlance this leaves out the *Vienna Convention on Succession of States in Respect of Treaties* of 1978. *The Vienna Convention on the Law of Treaties Between States and International Organizations or Between International Organizations* (UN Doc A/Conf.129/15; 25 ILM 543) hereinafter will be referred to as the 'second Vienna Convention' or the '1986 Convention'.

[4] Ch 8 above.

[5] Section 9.3 above.

[6] It is considered to have codified and, in turn, generated international customary law; see ch 9 above, note 81 and accompanying text.

development shed some light on important points of law. It has been a catalyst in the conceptualisation of organisations as legal actors, and a gauge of the degree of equation of organisations with states, and of the – limited – flexibility of the legal system.

The drafters' objective was to produce a text that would stay as close as possible to the 1969 Convention.[7] Unsurprisingly therefore, the substantive issues of discussion during the drafting process revolved around the question of the extent to which organisations could be equated with states. In the words of the Commission, 'The question to be decided came down to whether the same regime should be applicable to international organizations as to States'.[8]

A commentary to the law of treaties of international organisations thus amounts to a comparison with the classic, inter-state law of treaties.[9] This

[7] Section 9.1.1 above.

[8] YILC 1982, Vol II (Part Two), at 50, § 3. The comment was made in relation to draft Art 45, but holds valid for the entire drafting process.

[9] As appears also, sometimes implicitly, from the commentaries to the 1986 Convention, which include: Ingolf Pernice, 'Völkerrechtlige Verträge internationaler Organisationen', 48 *ZAöRV* 1988, 229-250; in the same vein Felice Morgenstern, 'The Vienna Convention on the Law of Treaties between States and International Organizations or between International Organizations' in Yoram Dinstein (ed), *International law at a Time of Perplexity*, 1989, 435-447. A commentary, with perhaps more than due reference to the 1969 Vienna Convention, in PK Menon, *The Law of Treaties Between States and International* 1992 (reprint of 'International Organizations: With Special Reference to the Vienna Convention of 1986', *Révue de Droit International, de Sciences Politiques et Diplomatiques*, annuaires 1987, 1–46, and 1988, 1-50). A commentary to the draft articles prepared by the ILC in Eckhart Klein and Meinhart Pechstein, *Das Vertragsrecht internationaler Organisationen*, 1985, 64 pp; Meinhard Schröder, 'Die Kodifikation des Vertragsrechts internationaler Organisationen', 23 *Archiv des Völkerrechts* 1985, 385-408. Otherwise, see: Michael Bothe, 'Die Wiener Konvention über das recht der Verträge zwischen Staaten und internationalen Organisationen und zwischen internationalen Organisationen', *Neue Juristische Wochenschrift*, 1991, 2169–2174; Geraldo Do Nascimento e Silva, 'The 1969 and the 1986 Conventions on the Law of Treaties: A Comparison', in Yoram Dinstein (ed) *International Law at a Time of Perplexity*, 1989, 461–487; Karl Zemanek, 'The United Nations Conference on the Law of Treaties Between States and International Organizations or Between International Organizations: The unrecorded history of its 'general agreement"', *Völkerrecht, Recht der Internationalen Organisationen, Weltwirtschaftsrecht (Festschrift für Ignaz Seidl-Hohenveldern)*, 1988, 665–680; Hubert Isak and Gerhard Loibl, United Nations Conference on the Law of Treaties between States and International Organisations or between International Organisations, *Österreichisches Zeitschrift für öffentliches Recht und Völkerrecht*, 1987, 49–78; Philippe Manin, 'The European Communities and the Vienna Convention on the Law of Treaties between States and International Organizations or Between International Organizations,' *Common Market Law Review*, 1987, 457–481; Willem Riphagen, 'The Second Round of Treaty Law', in Francesco Capotorti et al (eds), *Du droit international au droit de l'intégration: Liber Amicorum Pierre Pescatore*, 1987, 565–581; Philippe Manin, 'La Convention de Vienne sur le droit des traités entre états et organisations internationales ou entre organisations internationales', *Annuaire français de droit international*, 1986, 454–473; Geraldo Do Nascimento e Silva, 'The 1986 Convention and the Treaty-Making Power of International Organizations,' *German Yearbook of International Law*, 1986, 68–85; Neri Sybesma-Knol, 'The New Law of Treaties: The Codification of the Law of Treaties Concluded between States and International Organizations or Between Two or More International

chapter hence aims to analyze the 1986 Convention, in particular the way in which its regime equates international organisations with states *vel non*. In view of the above these two endeavours largely cover the same ground.

The *travaux* of the Convention confirms the propositions made in Parts One and Two above. Apart from the political reticence *a priori* in putting organisations and states on the same footing, there is an obstacle endemic to the law of treaties. This branch of law is strictly geared to equal actors and by consequence accommodates (in a vertical sense) one-dimensional and (in a horizontal sense) unitary subjects of the law only. International organisations, on the other hand, are not perceived in such a manner – a condition that has been referred to in the previous chapters as the 'transparency' of the 'institutional veil' that clothes the organisation as a legal entity. As it turns out, this transparency – sometimes expressed as the problem of putting states and organisations on the same footing, and sometimes as the problem of the role of member states within organisations – has been a central factor in the drafting process.

This chapter is structured on thematically grouped provisions, rather than an article-by-article commentary. These groups of provisions – which cover the main questions that were cause for discussion and sometimes resulted in a (even if unsubstantive) deviation from the inter-state law of treaties of the 1969 Convention – are divided into issues of doctrine, issues of practice and issues of principle.

The first are issues that pose a problem primarily from a doctrinal perspective. This is taken to cover both the system of prevailing legal ideas and the system of existing legal rules. The story of draft Article 36*bis*, which exemplifies the dilemma posed by the transparency of organisations in the most literal manner (and which, significantly, took up the most time in the drafting process), is taken as a showcase of sorts, and is recounted in special detail. The second section includes issues brought up by practice, be they related to 'social reality', such as the fact that most organisations do not have territory, or to legal reality, such as the given that organisations have no standing before the International Court of Justice. It may also look to elements of international practice which the drafters felt needed to be reflected in the text.[10] The last category relates to issues which do not primarily relate to practice, and essentially go beyond doctrine and systemics. They therefore amount to a choice of principle – such as

Organizations,' *Georgia Journal of International and Comparative Law*, 1985, 425–452; Renata Sonnenfeld, 'International Organizations as Parties to Treaties', *Polish Yearbook of International Law*, 1982, 177–200.

[10] As known eg from comments of IGOs. As organisations are not represented in the International Law Commission, nor in the Sixth Committee of the General Assembly, they did not take part in the drafting process via institutionalised channels. After finalisation of the draft, Organizations' comments, along with those of states, were formally sought by the UN Secretary-General; cf ch 9 above.

questions regarding whether organisations as such can be established to have been negligent; whether organisations are capable of coercion; or whether they are part of the 'international community'. Obviously there is an element of principle in all doctrinal and practice-oriented solutions, as there is the other way round. One perspective, however, is generally predominant in the drafters' approach to a particular issue. The different headings set apart these perspectives and can thus be helpful in interpreting the Convention.

The final clauses, as a reflection of the procedural status of organisations in relation to the 1986 Convention itself, have been discussed in Chapter 9 above. An exhaustive list of Articles compared to provisions in the 1969 Convention and the 1982 draft Articles can be found in the Annexes.

10.1 ISSUES OF DOCTRINE

10.1.1 The Classification of Treaties by Party

The 1986 Convention consistently distinguishes between treaties on the basis of parties. It is a prominent distinction (albeit not corroborated by legal effect), since in all cases where the 1969 Convention mentions 'states' as contracting or negotiating participants, the 1986 Convention refers to 'states and organizations,' and in the majority of cases connects this to the treaty instrument. Only those provisions of the 1969 Convention that proceed entirely from treaty instruments or the treaty relation without making specific mention of the parties, have entered in the 1986 Convention in an unchanged form, an example being Article 26 stating the *pacta sunt servanda* rule.[11]

Article 1 (*Scope of the present Convention*) uses 'agreement' to refer to all agreements concluded by parties other than the ones addressed by the Convention.[12] In so doing the drafters abandoned the meaning implicitly

[11] The other articles are 28 (*Non-retroactivity of treaties*); 31 (*General rule of interpretation*); 32 (*Supplementary means of interpretation*); 33 (*Interpretation of treaties authenticated in two or more languages*); 41 (*Agreements to modify multilateral treaties between certain of the parties only*); 55 (*Reduction of the parties to a multilateral treaty below the number necessary for its entry into force*) and 56 (*Denunciation of or withdrawal from a treaty containing no provision regarding termination; denunciation or withdrawal*); 58 (*Suspension of the operation of a multilateral treaty by agreement between certain of the parties only*) and 59 (*Termination or suspension of the operation of a treaty implied by conclusion of a later treaty*); 64 (*Emergence of a new peremptory norm of general international law* (jus cogens)); 71(*Consequences of the invalidity of a treaty which conflicts with a peremptory norm of general international law*); 72 (*Consequences of the suspension of the operation of a treaty*), and 81 (*Registration and publication of treaties*).

[12] The elaborate wording of Art 1 also serves to convey that the 1986 Convention is not intended to subsume and replace the 1969 Convention. Treaty relations between states parties

attached to the term in the 1969 Convention,[13] namely an 'agreement' concluded by an international organisation, as opposed to a 'treaty' concluded by states.

While the 1986 Convention thus makes no *terminological* distinction between 'treaties' on the basis of parties, it does – as is clear from its title – distinguish treaties between states and organisations from treaties between organisations only.[14] One example is **Article 9** (*Adoption of the text*), which specifies 'all the States and international organizations or, as the case may be, all the organizations participating in its drawing up'. According to the Commission the text was worded in such a manner that 'the capacity of the "participants" in the drawing up of the text of the treaty has been clarified by distinguishing between the *two categories of treaty* that are the subject of the draft articles'.[15]

Likewise, **Article 10** (*Authentication of the text*) follows the corresponding Article in the 1969 Convention, except for, as put by the Commission, 'differences in presentation reflecting *the two particular kinds of treaty* with which it is concerned'.[16] However, the two separate paragraphs that result – one on 'the text of a treaty between one or more states and one or more international organizations' and one on 'the text of a treaty between international organizations' – are textually identical.

Generally, in the course of the drafting process provisions became less, rather than more, differentiated. Several times the cautionary approach of

to a treaty that also counts one or more IGOs as a party, will continue to be governed by the 1969 Convention – such as ex Art 73 of the 1986 Convention; cf Egbert Vierdag, 'Some Remarks on the Relationship between the 1969 and the 1986 Vienna Convention on the Law of Treaties', *Archiv des Völkerrechts*, 1987, 82–91.

[13] Cf Art 2(1)a and Art 3 of the 1969 Convention and commentary to the corresponding draft articles (YILC 1966, Vol II, at 8–10).

[14] Article 2 (*Use of terms*) 2(1)a; Art 9 (*Adoption of the text*); Art 10 (*Authentication of the text*); Art 12 (*Consent to be bound by a treaty expressed by signature*); Art 13 (*Consent to be bound by a treaty expressed by an exchange of instruments constituting a treaty*); Art 15 (*Consent to be bound by a treaty expressed by accession*); Art 16 (*Exchange or deposit of instruments of ratification, formal confirmation, acceptance, approval or accession*); Art 17 (*Consent to be bound by part of a treaty and choice of differing provisions*); Art 20 (*Acceptance of and objection to reservations*); Art 24 (*Entry into force*); Art 25 (*Provisional application*); Art 77 (*Depositaries of treaties – cf VCLT I Article 76*). Art 37 (*Revocation or modification of obligations or rights of third States or third organizations*) is an example of a provision that was gradually simplified, at the cost of methodic purity, and to the benefit of reader-friendliness. In the draft article both the modification of rights and obligations and states and organisations as consenting parties, were separated. This resulted in four paragraphs, plus a fifth safeguarding 'the rules of the organization'. During the Conference this was trimmed down to three paragraphs, thus equating states and organisations to a further degree.

[15] YILC 1982, Vol II (Part Two), at 28 (emphasis added).

[16] *Ibid*, at 29 (emphasis added).

the drafters[17] resulted in such long and unwieldy texts (in the words of the Special Rapporteur: 'they are hard to read and, hence, hard to follow')[18] that these were simplified in the final Draft or during the Conference primarily for reasons of reader-friendliness.[19] Draft **Article 12** (*Consent to be bound by a treaty expressed by signature*) put signature as the expression of consent of states and signature by organisations in separate paragraphs, necessitated if only by the distinction at that point still maintained, between the 'full powers' of the state representative and the 'powers' of the representative of an organisation.[20] Convention **Article 12** then maintains a stylistically lighter version of the distinction between treaties, with the formula of 'the negotiating States and negotiating organizations, or, as the case may be, the negotiating organizations'.[21] Likewise, draft **Article 17** (*Consent to be bound by part of a treaty and choice of differing provisions*) envisaged separate treatment of consent and of the choice of provisions, each in turn addressing separately treaties between states and organisations and treaties between organisations; the four paragraphs were brought back to two during the Conference.[22]

The distinction between treaties on the basis of parties is an interesting feature of the Convention. It is consistently maintained, but nowhere in the Convention does it has legal consequences attached to it. Nonetheless, in his final proposal the Special Rapporteur stated that '[s]uch a distinction is necessary in terms of principle. It also suits the purposes of the draft articles'.[23] The Commission couched the matter in terms of descriptive accuracy, rather than doctrinal or normative necessity: 'this distinction will sometimes have to be made *in the treaty regime* to which the draft articles apply'.[24]

Leaving aside such case-by-case application, the fact remains that at a general level the – customary or conventional – law of treaties offers tools to establish whether an agreement constitutes a 'treaty', but after that, it has no means for further differentiation. Rather it operates on the concept

[17] A consequence, as pointed out by the Special Rapporteur (Reuter X, at 48, § 15), of the 'dual position of principle' that a difference exist between states and organisions, as well as a difference between treaties between states and organisations on the one hand, and treaties between organisations only, on the other.

[18] The rapporteur made this observation in relation to the draft provisions on reservations; Reuter X, at 60, § 67.

[19] Other examples are Art 22 (*Withdrawal of reservations and of objections to reservations*); Art 25 (*Provisional application*); Art 35 (*Treaties providing for obligations for third States or third organizations*).

[20] See also below, in section 10.1.3 on Art 7.

[21] Paragraphs 12(1)(b) and 12(2)(a). See also section 10.1.3 below on Article 46, note 61 and accompanying text.

[22] Adopted, on proposal of the Drafting Committee (UN Doc A/Conf.129/DC/R.3 and R.21), at the 5th Plenary Meeting (UN Doc A/Conf.129/16, at 12, 13).

[23] Reuter X, YILC 1981, Vol II (Part One), at 49, § 20 (emphasis added).

[24] YILC 1982, Vol II (Part Two), at 17, Section D (italics added).

of a single legal instrument and strict equality of parties. This seems logical, as the law of treaties has developed as a unified system (which moreover the drafters of the new Convention expressly aimed to 'extend' to organisations).[25]

The distinction based on (*types* of) parties appears as a remnant of a doctrinal distinction – in part terminology and in part substance – between states' 'treaties' and organisations' 'agreements', which was upheld by a number of writers well into the 1950s.[26] It is also reminscent of the doctrinal approach – present in the drafting process especially of the first Vienna Convention – that deduces the status of the legal instrument from the status of the parties.[27]

Finally, mention should be made of a question brought up by the Special Rapporteur in relation to **Article 2(1)a,** as this amounted to a tentative enquiry into the transparency of organisations. The point was whether the Convention definition should explicitly cover treaties concluded between organisations and member states ('to investigate whether some agreements are of an "internal" nature ..., whether they are governed by rules peculiar to the organization in question'),[28] and treaties concluded by organs of international organisations ('does...a subsidiary organ of the United Nations conclude treaties which ... are not United Nations treaties?').[29] There was no follow-up, if only because 'the Special Rapporteur addressed inquiries on this point to various international organisations without receiving any conclusive replies'.[30] From the drafting history of some following Articles, notably draft Article 36*bis*, it would seem that if the drafters had decided to deal with the matter, the Convention would have had either to reserve its operation in regard of such 'internal agreements', or to treat them as regular treaties – thereby piercing the institutional veil completely.

10.1.2 Treaty-Making Capacity

The design of a general provision on treaty-making capacity had proven an obstacle to the inclusion of organisations in the first Convention.[31] However, in view of the chosen drafting method it was clear that the new

[25] See ch 9 above, and note 8 of this chapter.

[26] Sections 3.3.1 and 7.2.1 above; a proponent of this view was Clive Parry (cf 'UN Treaty Making Power', *British YIL* 1949, at 131).

[27] Cf section 8.3 above; on the construction of the relation between legal personality and treaty-making capacity, see section 4.2.2 above.

[28] Reuter X, at 50, § 20.

[29] Reuter X, at 50, § 24.

[30] *Ibid.*

[31] See ch 7 above.

Convention would have to contain some reference to the treaty-making capacity of organisations as a counterpart to the 1969 Article 6 on states.[32]

The draft Article adopted in first reading, based on a proposal of the Special Rapporteur who had taken into account the doctrinal division existing in this regard, read: 'The capacity of an international organization to conclude treaties is governed by the [relevant] rules of that organization.'[33]

Discussions in the Commission[34] and in the Sixth Committee indeed showed strongly divergent views on the subject.[35] These generally covered the entire range of doctrinal viewpoints which has been discussed above.[36] As no agreement could be reached, the final Article, after omission of the word 'relevant',[37] remained:

> **Article 6** (*Capacity of international organizations to conclude treaties*)
>
> The capacity of an international organization to conclude treaties is governed by the rules of that organization.'

This provision can be read in two ways: as referring to the legal foundation of an organisation's treaty-making capacity, or as referring to the factual exercise of such capacity, which would logically be delimited by the constitution that sets out the functions and notably the 'area of competence' of the organisation.[38] The Commission explained that the final draft Article 6 was:

> the result of a compromise based essentially on the finding that this article should in no way be regarded as having the purpose or effect of deciding the question of the status of international organizations in international law; that question remains open, and the proposed wording is compatible both with the concept of general international law as the basis of international organizations' capacity and with the opposite concept.[39]

[32] The lapidary Art 6 of the 1969 Vienna Convention reads: 'Every State possesses capacity to conclude treaties.' On the preliminary discussions about the inclusion of such a provision, see eg Do Nascimento e Silva, 'The 1969 and the 1986 Conventions…' above, note 9, at 468–469.

[33] YILC 1974, Vol II (Part One), at 298, 299.

[34] Eg 1646th meeting of 7 May 1981; YILC 1981 Vol I, at 17.

[35] See eg UN Doc A/9897 of 11 December 1974, Agenda item 87, at 17. The item was discussed in GAOR, 29th Session, Sixth Committee, 1484th to 1496th, 1507th, 1509th and 1519th meetings; GAOR, Fifth Committee, 1692nd meeting; GAOR, Plenary Meetings, 2319th meeting; see also YILC 1982, Vol II (Part One), at 23, 24.

[36] See section 4.2 above.

[37] See section 10.1.6 below.

[38] Chapter 4 above deals extensively with these two approaches. The second would be an equivalent of the concept of 'functional limitation', delimiting the actual exercise of legal personality, as proposed by White.

[39] YILC 1982, Vol II (Part Two), at 24.

However, even if Article 6 is interpreted as founding legal capacity on the internal law of the organisation (in classic terms, traced to the 'will' of the member states), the result is that an IGO constitution has the final say in defining and delimiting such capacity. In that sense the provision differs from others which make reference to the 'rules of the organisation', as these generally lack not only normative force but also normative effect on the general level.[40] Arguably this is because the organisation's functional nature[41] raises one preliminary question which does not play a role in the case of states: that is whether an organisation can conclude a treaty on a particular subject *at all*. The answer necessarily depends on the organisation's area of competence, which is defined in the constituent treaty.

The Commission stated:

> It should be clearly understood that the question how far practice can play a creative part, particularly in the matter of international organizations' capacity to conclude treaties, cannot be answered uniformly for all international organizations. This question, too, depends on the 'rules of the organization;' indeed, it depends on the highest category of those rules – those which form, in some degree, the constitutional law of the organization and which govern in particular the sources of the organization's rules.[42]

Thus, as the reservation clause in Article 6 looks to the very existence of the organisation (the basis of which undeniably lies with the constituent states), the normative effect on the general level is considerable, as it may deny an organisation the ability to conclude a treaty. All the same, the Article does not take a doctrinal stance in a long-time debate, for which it has been strongly criticised.[43]

10.1.3 Expressing the Juridical Will

Several instances in the life of a treaty involve expression of the juridical will of a (prospective) party. This includes the central legal moment of 'expression of consent to be bound', but also 'acceptance' in the context of reservations. In the case of states, the construction of this will has been formalised and stylised by international law (cf the rule codified in Article

[40] Cf section 10.1.3 below on an organisation's expression of juridical will.

[41] See section 2.3.1 above.

[42] YILC 1974, Vol II (Part One), at 299, § 5.

[43] Cf Klein and Pechstein, above, note 9; Gaja, above, note 9; Do Nascimento e Silva, above, note 9. Particularly critical was Finn Seyersted ('Treaty-Making Capacity of International Organizati-ons: Article 6 of the International Law Commission's Draft Articles on the Law of Treaties Between States and Internati-onal Organizations or Between International Organizations,' 34 ÖZöRV 1983, 261–267), who since his monograph in 1963 had consistently advocated objective (attribution and foundation of) legal personality for organisations. See section 4.2.3 above.

7(1) stating that the 'big three' can represent a state in the treaty-making process without the need to produce full powers), while the internal law of the state is entirely left out of account. There is less general agreement on how to construe the will of an international organisation. This seems to mirror the general lack of clarity and conviction regarding the *volonté distincte* of an international organisation – notwithstanding the fact that it is a central element in the formal definition'.[44]

These doubts are reflected in either of two ways: some provisions set the requirement of an explicit, as opposed to tacit, expression of will on the part of the organisation. Others make a reference to the internal legal order of the organisation. Often the drafters (that is, the Commission and all other parties involved in the process) started out with a transparent, state-based image of organisations, but in the process came to parallel the expression of will by organisations entirely to that of states.[45] On occasion symmetry was abandoned to stipulate a particular form of expression for the organisation or to add a reference to institutional requirements. The latter may relate to a particular ('competent') organ of the organisation, or to 'the rules of the organization,'[46] and as such raise the question of the organisation's transparency.

Consent, Assent and Acquiescence

Article 7 (*Full powers*) deals with the representation of states (in paras 1 and 2) and organisations (in paras 3 and 4) for the purpose of expressing agreement at various stages of the treaty-making process. The first question was whether the concept of a representative proving by document his competence to represent the state could be transposed to international organisations. In the end this was decided to be the case.[47] However, the drafters found no counterpart in organisations for the 'big three' state representatives earmarked by international law to possess such competence *ex officio*.

[44] See section 2.2.1 above on the definition of 'international organisation'.
[45] See in this section below on the acceptance of reservations (Art 20).
[46] See 10.1.5 below on the '[relevant] rules of the organization.'
[47] Otherwise, minor adaptations with respect to the 1969 Convention were inspired by the work of the International Law Commission on 'the representation of States in their relations with international organizations,' such as the change of 'state representatives' into 'heads of delegations of states'. The draft Arts had been completed in 1971 with the adoption of the draft articles; see YILC 1971, Vol II (Parts One (draft articles) and Two (ILC Report 1971, cf §§ 57–60, with the recommendation for the convening of a conference of plenipotentiaries to study the draft articles and to conclude a convention on the subject). The 1975 *Convention on the Representation of States in their Relations with International Organizations of a Universal Character* has not yet entered into force.

The representation of organisations[48] then raised doubts about the notion of 'expression' of consent. The argument now clearly turned to an institutional, or transparent, perspective. It was felt that 'expression' might not be the proper term, as 'the representatives of organizations, who are, more often than not, members of international secretariats, might declare a consent that had never been formulated by the competent organs of the organization.'[49] The provisions which dealt with such expression therefore initially used the formula 'communicate' – 'the use of the term ... implying the consent is given by an organ other than the one which declares it'[50] – but on second reading this was changed into 'express' to match the provision on states.

Articles 11–17 enumerate and specify the means of expressing consent to be bound by a treaty.[51] The first paragraph of Article 11 reproduces the corresponding Article of the 1969 Convention. This was the result of a much praised amendment tabled during the 1969 Conference by the Polish representative Nahlik, laying out the general *systematique* of the section on consent, and bringing flexibility into the system by allowing for 'any other means if so agreed'.[52] Here the Commission was of the opinion that 'practice has shown ... that the considerable expansion of treaty commitments makes this flexbility necessary...'[53] and 'saw no reason not to extend' this flexibility to organisations.

Article 15 (*Consent to be bound by a treaty expressed by accession*) in its paragraph b implies the possibility (examples from practice do not currently abound) that a treaty between organisations could have a state acceding at a later stage – a reason for one member of the Commission to abstain from voting in the adoption of the text, as he considered such possibility unacceptable and unrealistic.[54]

The Convention regime for rights and obligations for non-parties[55] at several moments requires expression of juridical will. **Article 35** (*Treaties*

[48] Possibly the only gender issue in the Vienna Conventions: during the Conference the wording was changed to a neutral formula ('that person').

[49] YILC 1982, Vol II (Part Two), at 26, 27.

[50] *Ibid*, at 27.

[51] See also section 10.1.6 below on terminology.

[52] Introduced by amendment UN Doc A/Conf.39/C.1/L.88; adopted at 9th Plenary Meeting (UN Doc A/Conf.39/13, at 60–74); see otherwise the detailed *The Law Of Treaties: A Guide To The Legislative History of the Vienna Covnention*, 1970, by Shabtai Rosenne. Cf also the analysis of Alexander Bolintineanu, 'Expression Of Consent To Be Bound By A Treaty In The Light Of The 1969 Vienna Convention', 68 *American JIL*, 1974, 672–686.

[53] YILC 1982, Vol II (Part Two), at 29, § 2 to Art 11.

[54] 1681th meeting, YILC 1981, Vol I, at 203, § 47.

[55] As laid down in arts 35 and 36 and 37. Obligations for third parties (Art 35) have to be accepted 'in writing' by the addressees, and rights (Art 36) are conditional upon their 'assent', which is presumed so long as the contrary is not indicated. In case these categories are too closely linked for separation, the stricter regime applies. See further section 10.1.4 below on third party regimes and member states in relation to draft Art 36*bis*.

providing for obligations for third States or third organizations) was reproduced literally from the 1969 Convention. **Article 36** (*Treaties providing for rights for third States or third organizations*), identical to draft Article 36, proceeds from the beneficiary, not from the contracting parties (to the main treaty), and requires a form of agreement. It reproduces the rule for states from the 1969 Convention and adds a second paragraph on the creation of rights for third organisations. The necessary 'assent' (the commentary does not follow this subtlety and speaks of 'consent') of an organisation cannot be 'presumed', as with states, but has to be given explicitly. This is justified by 'the fact that the international organization has not been given unlimited capacity and that, consequently, it is not possible to stipulate that its consent shall be presumed in respect of a right'.[56] Rather than tacit agreement, the text provides for an expression of assent on the part of the organisation which 'shall be governed by the rules of the organization.' This is an interesting example of the transparent image of organisations; but arguably it is a safeguard of limited value on the general international plane, since in this case international law does not pose formal requirements as to the expression of assent to begin with. Moreover, as exemplified by Articles 27 and 46, the rules of an organisation – like the rules of a state – are not in principle presumed to be known to the co-contractors of the organisation.

Similar to Article 36, **Articles 37** (*Revocation or modification of obligations or rights of third States or third organizations*) and **39** (*General rule regarding the amendment of treaties*) contain a new paragraph, specifying that an organisation's consent in the context of that provision is governed by the rules of that organisation.

The drafting of a new **Article 45** (*Loss of a right to invoke a ground for invalidating, terminating, withdrawing from or suspending the operation of a treaty*) gave rise to ample discussion. Some Commission members held that 'the unity of the state [...] meant that the State could be regarded as bound by its agents who possessed a general competence in international relations'.[57] But for organisations – the transparent image now being linked to their functional, rather than territorial, design[58] – this was not considered to be the case. Addressing 'the organisation' as such then was problematic, and reference to 'the competent organ' was made instead.

[56] YILC 1982, Vol II (Part Two), at 43 § 2 of the commentary to Art 36.
[57] Report of the ILC, commentary to the final draft articles, YILC 1982, Vol II (Part Two), at 50.
[58] On functionality of organisations, see section 2.3.1 above.

Article 45(2)(b) reads: '[the organization] must by reason of the conduct of the competent organ be considered as having renounced the right to invoke that ground'.[59]

The perceived lack of unitary character on the part of organisations also led to doubts as to the applicability of the construct of acquiescence. While states may 'acquiesce' in the validity of the treaty, this was not considered an appropriate legal notion for organisations: their presumably diverse and diffuse institutional structures would make it difficult to ascertain such acquiescence. The term 'renounce' was chosen to provide greater certainty, although the wording is still reminiscent of 'tacit consent': 'it must by reason of the conduct of the competent organ be considered as having renounced the right to invoke'.

On second reading the specific formula '*communicate* consent to be bound' in **Article 46** (*Provisions of internal law of a State and rules of an international organization regarding competence to conclude treaties*), as in Article 7,[60] was abandoned and changed to the traditional '*express* consent to be bound'. Reduced to one paragraph, the final draft nonetheless maintaned a systematic distinction between the notification (of the pertinent 'special instructions') 'to the other negotiating states and negotiating organizations' on the one hand, and that 'to the other negotiating organizations and negotiating states' on the other. In the Convention this implicit distinction between the representative of a state and the representative of an organisation was abandoned: '[notification] to the negotiating States and negotiating organizations.'[61]

Articles 58 (*Suspension of the operation of a multilateral treaty by agreement between certain of the parties only*) and **59** (*Termination or suspension of the operation of a treaty implied by conclusion of a later treaty*) were adopted unchanged from the corresponding articles in the 1969 Convention.[62] Interestingly, in its commentary the Commission dedicated a separate paragraph to the less than affirmative statement that 'there is no reason for not extending the provisions of Article 58 ... to treaties to which international organizations are parties'.[63] The Commission observed that the two Articles 'lay down rules which derive from a

[59] Article 45(1)(b) reads: '[the state] must by reason of its conduct be considered as having acquiesced in the validity of the treaty or in its maintenance in force or in operation, as the case may be'. The reference to 'the competent organ', included already in the ILC draft article, also figures in eg Art 7.

[60] Above, note 49 and accompanying text.

[61] Above, note 21 and accompanying text.

[62] The Commission noted that the incongruity between the title of the article and the text (which speaks of 'suspension of provisions of a treaty' rather than of 'the treaty' as a whole) has been reproduced (YILC 1982, Vol II (Part Two), at 58, § 1).

[63] YILC 1982, Vol II (Part Two), at 58, § 2.

straightforward consensuality approach and may therefore be extended without difficulty to the treaties which are the subject of the present draft articles...'.[64]

Reservations

The provisions on reservations in the 1986 Convention are very similar to the section in the first Vienna Convention. This similarity hides lengthy discussions and numerous attempts to make some sort of distinction between states and organisations on this point.

Article 19 (*Formulation of reservations*) states the right of contracting parties to make reservations when becoming bound by a treaty. A substantive question was whether the freedom to make reservations – traditionally linked to the tenet, and rhetoric, of sovereignty and free will of the state – was to be extended to international organisations, or whether, on the contrary, the Convention should set a *prohibition* for organisations to make reservations. This point animated discussion in the Commission for extended periods of time.[65]

The Special Rapporteur had started out with a 'very liberal position',[66] extending the rules of the 1969 Article 19 to organisations, with paragraph c (on the compatibility of the reservation with the object and purpose of the treaty) as the only safeguard.[67] This was not acceptable to the Commission.

One reason was that the drafters were concerned about existing practice.[68] In general the practice of organisations filing reservations existed but was scant (incidentally, none of the organisations party to the 1986 Convention have filed a reservation).[69] In addition there was the possibility of complications arising for instance from agreements to which both the organisation and member states are parties (the main examples being mixed agreements in EEC practice).[70]

[64] *Ibid.*

[65] YILC 1982, Vol II (Part Two), at 34, § 7.

[66] YILC 1977, Vol II (Part Two), at 96, § 69.

[67] Reuter IV, at 36, 37.

[68] YILC 1982, Vol II (Part Two), at 33, 34, general commentary to section 2, §§ 3–5.

[69] As of 1 Sept 2006: UN (formal confirmation 21–12–1998); ILO (formal confirmation 31-7-2000); WHO (formal confirmation 22–6-2000); UNESCO (23–6-1987); FAO (29–6-1987); ICAO (formal confirmation 24–12–2001); ITU (29–6-1987); IMO (formal confirmation 14–2- 2000); WMO (30–6-1987). International Criminal Police Organization, accession 3–1-2001; IAEA, accession 26–4–2001; OPCW, accession 2–6-2000; Preparatory Commission for the Comprehensive Nuclear Test-Ban Treaty Organization, accession 11–6-2002; UNIDO accession 4–3-2002; WIPO 24–10–2000; UPU, accession 19–10–2004. FAO, ITU, UNESCO and WMO are signatories only, and have not yet submitted an 'act of formal confirmation' – see http://untreaty.un.org.

[70] Cf Reuter X, at 57, § 58 and footnotes.

An arguably more persistent reason for the reluctance to equate organisations with states in the field of reservations was the perceived uncertainties around the independent legal commitments of organisations. As pointed out by the Special Rapporteur, it:

> involves what might be described as the constitutional nature of international organizations. It is argued that the constitutional status of such organizations is fraught with uncertainties; their constituent instruments contain only sketchy provisions concerning their international commitments (when they contain any at all); it would be difficult to find one constituent instrument that includes a provision on reservations to treaties concluded by the organization.'[71]

The Articles adopted in first reading then aimed to establish a compromise between the opposing views. An elaborate Article 19*bis* stated a right for an organisation to make a reservation in case of a treaty between organisations, or in case of a treaty between states and organisations, provided the participation of the organisation is *not* essential to the object and purpose of a treaty.[72] Otherwise, an organisation may formulate a reservation only if this is expressly authorised by the treaty.[73] An Article 19*ter* stated a similar rule for the right of organisations to make objections to reservations.[74]

Critical discussion in the Commission and in the UNGA Sixth Committee, as well as (few) comments by international organisations, led in the second reading to the adoption of an Article 19 that took the opposite approach, 'in accordance with the wishes of . . . organizations and ... with a number of pointers from the realm of practice'.[75] The new article conferred on organisations the same freedom to make reservations as states, and incorporated both states and organisations also in regard to the conditions set out in the Article. Articles 19*bis* and *ter* were removed. During the diplomatic conference Article 19 was trimmed down further by merging the separate paragraphs on states and organisations. An additional safeguard as to the admissibility of reservations in draft paragraphs 19(1)(a) and (b) ('when the reservation is prohibited by the treaty *or it is*

[71] Reuter X, at 58, § 59.

[72] Article *19bis*(3). An example in which this, on the contrary, would be the case, would be a treaty on nuclear safety measures in which the consistent participation of the IAEA and Euratom may count as crucial (cf YILC 1977, Vol II (Part Two), at 108, § 4).

[73] Article *19bis*(2). Report ILC twenty-ninth session, YILC 1977, Vol II (Part Two), at 107–109.

[74] Report ILC 29th session, YILC 1977, Vol II (Part Two), at 107–109.

[75] YILC 1982, Vol II (Part Two), at 34, § 14. The response of organisations to the regime for reservations proposed earlier had not been entusiastic: cf YILC 1981, Vol II. (Part Two), Annex: UN (at 198); ILO (at 199–200); EEC ('It is not clear why the Commission has adopted the position international organizations should not be able to avail themselves of commonly agreed principles concerning the right to formulate reservations and especially the right to object to reservations formulated other contracting parties to a treaty'. (at 202, § 10). Later comments of states and organisations in UN Doc A/Conf.129/5.

otherwise established that the negotiating States and organizations were agreed that the reservation is prohibited...') was deleted.[76]

Parallel to the merger of the provisions on formulation of reservations, the matter of acceptance of and objection to reservations on the second reading was combined in one **Article 20.** A point of contention had been and remained application to organisations of the notion of tacit acceptance of reservations, that is, presumed acceptance if no objection were raised after twelve months. The Special Rapporteur had proposed such tacit acceptance for any 'contracting entity'.[77] After 'protracted discussion' inter alia on the twelve-month period (too short for organisations whose competent bodies do not always have annual meetings) and on the reference to organisations as such (which should rather be the 'competent organs'), the Commission decided on a final draft Article 20(5) which reproduced the text from the 1969 Convention and therefore only mentioned tacit acceptance by states.[78] During the Conference, international organisations were added to the provision,[79] so that a complete parallel with the corresponding 1969 Article 20 was secured.

Article 23 (*Procedure regarding reservations*) was the result of minor drafting changes only. The required expression of will by organisations was not an issue, arguably because the original Article 23 envisaged concrete and active expression ('...only when notice of it has been received').

10.1.4 Member States and Third States

The transparency of the institutional veil and the dilemmas that it poses for the drafters – member states versus an organisation, or an organisation as an open versus a closed legal structure – presented itself in the most litteral manner in relation to the rule on third states or non-parties. It is not surprising that **Article 36*bis*** was 'unquestionably the one [Article] that has aroused most comment, controversy and difficulty, both in and outside the Commission'.[80] For that reason the drafting story of Article 36*bis* will be addressed in more detail, as will the main topics which came up during the drafting process.

[76] Discussed at the 11th, 12th and 27th Meetings of the Committee of the Whole UN Doc A/Conf.139/16 s.v.); adopted at the 5th Plenary Meeting (*ibid* at 13).

[77] Reuter X, at 61–63.

[78] YILC 1982, Vol II (Part Two), at 36, commentary to article 20, § 6.

[79] Discussed at the 12th, 13th,14th and 27th Meetings of the Committee of the Whole (UN Doc A/Conf.139/16 s.v.); adopted at the 5th Plenary Meeting (*ibid* at 13).

[80] YILC 1982, Vol II (Part Two), at 43, commentary to article 36, § 1. Section 10.1.4 is partly based on "The 1986 Vienna Convention on the Law of Treaties: The History of Draft Article 36bis" in: Jan Klabbers & René Lefeber (eds.), *Essays on the Law of Treaties*, 1998, 121–140.

The third states regime laid down in Articles 34–38 of the 1969 Vienna Convention represents a rather strict adherence to the *pacta tertiis* rule: obligations for third parties (Article 35) have to be accepted 'in writing' by the addressees, and rights (Article 36) are conditional upon their 'assent', which is presumed so long as the contrary is not indicated. If these two categories cannot be readily separated, the stricter regime applies.[81]

The question of the applicability of this regime to the member states of a contracting international organisation had been singled out at the outset.[82] Transposition of these clauses to the new Convention would equate the member states of a contracting organisation with regular third states vis-à-vis the treaty, with the concomitant requirement of express consent in writing for any obligations to arise.

The Drafting History of Article 36bis

In accordance with practice the Special Rapporteur considered it desirable that member states be 'associated with the obligations of the organization,' and held that 'the premise [. . .], the affirmation of the legal personality of the organization, must be modified by *factual* considerations.'[83] As it was clear that the 'excessively formal terms of Articles 34–38'[84] did not leave room for an intermediate position, he accordingly proposed an Article '36*bis*':

> *Effects of a treaty to which an international organization is party with respect to States members of that organization*

[81] In his Tenth Report the Special Rapporteur stated that '[a]t all events, one thing is certain: the utility of Article 36*bis* has to be considered in the light of the rules laid down to cover the establishment of obligations' (Reuter X, above, note 23, at 67, § 89; emphasis in the original). In the version of the draft Article proposed on the same occasion, the reference to rights was omitted (*ibid*, above, note 23, at 69, § 104). The present discussion will be mostly limited to the question of obligations.

[82] See § 17 of the questionnaire on 'preliminary questions' with regard to IO treaties (YILC 1971, Vol II (Part Two), at 188).

[83] Reuter VI, YILC 1975, Vol II (Part One), at 126 (emphasis added).These 'considerations' were specified as the 'weaknesses' of the legal capacity of organizations, the uncertainties surrounding their competence to conclude treaties in specific cases, and the fact that in practice the 'effective performance' of their obligations often could be secured only through resources of the member states. Earlier, Reuter had stated that '[o]ne would be tempted to say that States members of an organization may be "more or less" third States in relation to the treaties concluded by the organization' (Reuter I, at 197 (§ 85); see also Reuter VI, at 125 (§ 30)).

[84] Rosenne as quoted in Chinkin, *Third Parties in International Law*, 1993, at 37 (see on the third party-regime of the Vienna Conventions 29–44, 134–140). The text prepared by the Commission, in itself the result of long discussions, had stipulated 'expressly accepted' (YILC 1966, Vol II, at 227); the additional requirement that it be 'in writing' was inserted during the Conference (United Nations Conference on the Law of Treaties, Official Records, Second Session, at 59–60).

1. A treaty concluded by an international organization gives rise directly for States members of an international organization to rights and obligations in respect of other parties to that treaty if the constituent instrument of that organization expressly gives such effects to the treaty.

2. When, on account of the subject-matter of a treaty concluded by an international organization and the assignment of areas of competence involved in that subject-matter between the organization and its member states, it appears that such was indeed the intention of the parties to that treaty, the treaty gives rise for a member State to: (i) rights, which the member State is presumed to accept, in the absence of any indication of intention to the contrary; (ii) obligations when the member State accepts them, even implicitly.[85]

The provision envisages two situations in which a treaty may give rise to 'direct' rights and obligations of member states in respect of the co-contractors of the organisation: first, the case in which the constituent instrument of an organisation stipulates that any treaty concluded by the organisation will have that effect, regardless of the intention of the treaty-partners, who are presumed to be cognisant of the constitution of the organisation with which they are dealing; second, the case in which the division of (areas of) competence between the organisation and its member states with regard to the subject matter regulated by the treaty will produce such an effect. In the latter case, however, such a result is conditional upon the intention of the treaty-partners and on the acceptance of the member states, presumed in the case of rights, and at the least implicit in the case of obligations.[86]

Of the discussion that followed,[87] only the major point of criticism and debate is mentioned here, namely the fact that the article seemed to be moulded solely on the example of the then EEC.[88]

At the subsequent session, the Special Rapporteur submitted a modified text to the Drafting Committee, which notably reinforced the independence of organisations – through the addition of the subjective element between brackets in the first paragraph – as well as the position of member states – through the requirement of explicit acceptance of an obligation.[89]

[85] Reuter VI, at 128.

[86] See Reuter VI, at 126, and his commentary to Art 36bis, in particular at 129–133; cf the introduction of the Article at the 1440th meeting; YILC 1977, Vol I, at 134–135 (§§ 32–35).

[87] See 1440th-1442nd meetings (YILC 1977, Vol I, at 134 ff).

[88] See eg Schwebel, who stated that 36bis 'dealt with an exceptional case in a largely unexceptional manner' (*ibid*, at 141, § 36) and Quentin-Baxter who held that the Article could also be viewed 'as a genuine glimpse of the reality of the future' (*ibid*, at 139, § 21).

[89] '1. A treaty concluded by an international organization gives rise directly for States members of an international organization to rights and obligations in respect of other parties to that treaty if the constituent instrument of that organization [as interpreted within the organization,] expressly gives such effects to the treaty. 2. A treaty concluded by an international organization, where, by reason of the distribution as between the organization and its members of the competences affected by the object of the treaty, it appears that such

The Drafting Committee then proposed a text ('to convey more clearly and succintly the meaning of the rules embodied in the Article')[90] which to a higher degree respected the internal structure of the international organisation as such. While the Rapporteur had proposed to subject the creation of obligations for member states to the stringent test of the constituent instrument,[91] the Committee had opted for the more flexible 'relevant rules of the organization'.[92] The notions of 'assent' and 'acceptance' in the second paragraph had made way for the rather vague – and much criticised[93] – term 'acknowledged'. The specification 'directly' with regard to the rise of obligations was now omitted. In view of the numerous questions raised in this respect, the addition of 'third' in the title can be interpreted as a statement on the status of member states.

Inconclusive debates in the Commission came to revolve around the question of whether the article was applicable to the EEC only, or whether it could also be used for a more traditional kind of international organisation.[94] The meetings of the Sixth Committee in that same year[95] brought out more or less the three trends present within the Commission as well. A first group opposed the inclusion of Article 36*bis* altogether – either because it was considered impossible to formulate rules that would apply to all international organisations, or because of opposition to the particular case of the EEC, both for legal and political reasons. A second group favoured inclusion of the provision in the draft. Some members accepted the view, presented with perseverance by the Special Rapporteur,[96] that the provision applied to organisations other than the EEC, as in the case of headquarters agreements and customs unions; others valued the provision

was in fact the intention of the parties to the treaty, gives rise for a member state to: (a) rights, which the member State, in the absence of any indication of a contrary intention, is presumed to accept; (ii) obligations when the member State accepts them explicitly' (YILC 1978, Vol II (Part Two), at 134, note 620).

[90] 'Effects of a treaty to which an international organization is party with respect to third States members of that organization: Third States which are members of an international organization shall observe the obligations, and may exercise the rights, which arise for them from the provisions of a treaty to which that organization is a party if: (a) the relevant rules of the organization, applicable at the moment of the conclusion of the treaty, provide that the States members of the organization are bound by the treaties concluded by it: or (b) the States and organizations participating in the negotiation of the treaty as well as the States members of the organization acknowledged that the application of the treaty necessarily entails such effects' (YILC 1978, Vol I, at 193, § 28).

[91] See eg Reuter VI, above, note 81, at 130 (§7).

[92] See section 10.1.6 below on terminology.

[93] Eg Francis (YILC 1978, Vol I, at 138 (§13). Cf report ILC on its 30th session, YILC 1978, Vol II, at 135 (§ 6).

[94] For discussion and provisional adoption of the Drafting Committee's version of Art 36*bis*, see 1510th-1512th meetings, YILC 1978, Vol I, at 194–203. See also Report of the ILC on its 30th session, YILC 1978, Vol II (Part Two), at 134–135.

[95] A topical summary of the observations of delegations is contained in the 1978 Report of the Sixth Committee (UN Doc A/33/419, §§ 233–247).

[96] See egReuter's comments at the 1704th meeting (YILC 1982, Vol I, at 37 (§§44–48)).

as a statement of principle, possibly with an outlook on future developments. A third group advocated careful further study of the legal intricacies with regard to, mainly, the status of international organisations and their member states, before taking any decision.

Yet another draft version of Article 36*bis* was submitted by the Special Rapporteur at the 33rd session of the Commission. This text differed from the previous one mainly in the formally stated requirement of 'assent', duly emphasised by the drafting style. The controversial term 'third states' was omitted.[97]

Discussions on the provision during the next session[98] acquired an increasingly political character.[99] The need to protect developing countries that are members of an international organisation from being bound by obligations they had perhaps not voted for, was extensively underscored (Chief Akinjide: 'The consequences of article 36bis were far greater than its words indicated and could even be devastating. The real impact would be greatest in economic matters, and there could be no political independence without some degree of economic independence').[100] So was the particularity of the EEC as a Western European institution (Mr Ushakov: 'Personally, he had nothing against supranational organizations . . .').[101] The proposals made during that session by Commission members for yet two other versions of Article 36*bis* strongly emphasised the sovereignty of the member states[102] and no longer contained a reference to the 'intention' or the 'acknowledgment' of the contracting parties.

[97] '[Assent to the establishment of obligations for the States members of an organizations] – The assent of States members of an international organization to obligations arising from a treaty concluded by that organization shall derive from: (a) the relevant rules of the organization applicable at the moment of the conclusion of the treaty which provide that States members of the organization are bound by such a treaty; or (b) the acknowledgement by the States and organizations participating in the negotiation of the treaty as well as the States members of the organizations that the application of the treaty necessarily entails such effects', Reuter X, above, note 23, at 69. Introduced at the 1675th meeting (YILC 1981, Vol I, at 172, §§ 23–29), discussed during the 1676th-1679th meetings (*ibid*, at 176 ff.).

[98] See 1704th-1707th and 1718th and 1719th meetings (YILC 1982, Vol I, at 36 ff.). The Special Rapporteur re-submitted his last proposal for Art 36*bis*, which the Drafting Committee had not been able to consider at the previous session.

[99] Cf eg Reuter: 'Some States, then, opposed the article, while others, because they were members of the EEC, felt that it must be defended at all costs. That was a very bad situation, and it proved that the article under examination was bad [. . .]' (YILC 1982, Vol I, at 39 (§ 5).

[100] Chief Akinjide (YILC 1982, Vol I, at 53 (§ 2).

[101] Introductory words of Mr Ushakov (*ibid*, at 121 (§7).

[102] Sucharitkul: 'Obligations arising from a treaty concluded by an international organization shall have effects on the States members of that organization if: (a) the constituent instrument of the organization applicable at the moment of the conclusion of the treaty expressly provides that the States members of the organization are bound by such a treaty; or (b) the States members of the organization expressly undertake to assume those obligations'. (YILC 1982, Vol I, at 32 (§13); a stronger formulation still by McCaffrey: 'A treaty to which an international organization is a party does not create obligations with respect to States

In spite of the pessimistic tenor of the discussion,[103] the article was referred to the Drafting Committee. The text subsequently proposed by the Committee became the final version of Article 36*bis*, which reads as follows:

> Obligations and rights arise for States members of an international organization from the provisions of a treaty to which that organization is a party when the parties to the treaty intend those provisions to be the means of establishing such obligations and according such rights and have defined their conditions and effects in the treaty or have otherwise agreed thereon, and if:
>
> (a) the States members of the organization, by virtue of the constituent instrument of that organization or otherwise, have unanimously agreed to be bound by the said provisions of the treaty; and
>
> (b) the assent of the States members of the organization to be bound by the relevant provisions of the treaty has been duly brought to the knowledge of the negotiating States and the negotiating organizations.'

The position of the member states was now safeguarded through the requirement of their unanimous agreement to be bound, while the position of the co-contracting parties was strengthened by the proviso regarding their intention in all cases. The Article thus no longer envisaged the possibility of rights and obligations for member states arising out of the constitution of an organisation on their own accord. As this is precisely what happens in a supranational organisation, the case of the EEC seemed to be no longer covered. This was clear also from the expressly stated rule of unanimity, conflicting with Article 228(2) of the Rome Treaty.[104] The new compromise Article 36*bis* contented also the Commission members who had consistently opposed earlier versions, and could thus be uninanimously adopted.[105]

That theoretical problems had not been solved became clear from observations in the UNGA Sixth Committee. One delegate recapitulated the central problem of qualifying member states as 'third states' and convincingly expounded on the view that the situation covered by Article 36*bis* in reality involved two sets of relations: an 'internal' (between the

members of that organization without their consent/assent. States members will be considered to have given such consent/assent where (a) The constituent instrument of the organization applicable at the moment of the conclusion of the treaty expressly provides that States members of the organization are bound by such a treaty; or (b) States members of the organization expressly undertake to assume such obligations'. (YILC 1982, Vol I, at 47 (§15)).

[103] See eg the observations by Reuter, YILC 1982 , Vol I, at 119–120 (§§ 40–46).

[104] The Article, later amended by Art G(80) of the TEU, read: 'Agreements concluded under the conditions laid down above shall be binding on the institutions of the Community and on Member States'.

[105] Discussed and adopted at the 1740th meeting (YILC 1982, Vol I, at 261–263 (§§ 21–40).

organisation and its member states) and an 'external' (between the organisation and its co-contractors) treaty-relationship – the question was how these were to be linked.[106] This dualist view is reminiscent of the construct of a 'collateral agreement' between member states and co-contractors of an organisation – a concept which was advanced by the Special Rapporteur at an early stage, but which never caught on in the drafting process.[107] It seems, however, to have – rightly – found its way into the commentary of the Commission to the final draft articles.[108]

A general reserve with regard to Article 36*bis* was equally clear from the numerous comments of states and organisations.[109] It is noteworthy that the comments of international organisations in particular were lukewarm at best. They moreover seemed to defy the premise that traditional intergovernmental organisations were particularly familiar, or concerned, with direct rights and obligations between member states and co-contractors of the organisation that were envisaged in Article 36*bis*.[110]

When the conference started, 'the fate of the provision was doomed even before the formal discussion [. . .] started in the Committee of the Whole'.[111] Nonetheless, Article 36*bis* again gave rise to what another participant has described as 'débats longs et souvent confus'.[112] These largely dealt with the same questions that had come up in the later stages of the preparatory work in the Commission. Presumably because of the active participation of some international organisations, practice came to play a more prominent role in the discussion, which led on the whole to unfavourable conclusions. While some organisations held that the topic was simply not ripe for codification,[113] others stated that the rules which

[106] Netherlands (Riphagen); UN Doc A/C.6/37/SR.40 (§§ 50–67); see also the observations made by Mr Riphagen in the previous year (UN Doc A/C.6/36/SR.40 (§ 54)); and his remarks as a member of the Commission ('when two treaties met'; YILC 1982, Vol I, at 39, § 9 ff).

[107] Reuter VI, at 126 (§ 38).

[108] 1982 Report of the Commission, YILC 1982, Vol II (Part Two), at 43 ff.

[109] Cf the observations by Canada on the risk that the 'rule of unanimity' would hamper the conclusion of eg headquarters agreements by organisations that take decisions by majority (UN Doc A/Conf.129/5, at 161).

[110] See comments on earlier drafts of the article reproduced in YILC 1981, Vol II (Part Two), Annex II (Section B for International organisations); eg ILO ('no experience that could shed light on the problematique of Article 36bis'); FAO (affirming only the existence of indirect obligations for member states); IAEA (declaring the article to be 'virtually irrelevant to the IAEA'). For comments on the final draft Articles see UN Doc A/Conf.129/5; eg UNESCO (stating that the Article 'will give rise to more problems than it will solve in the future') at 177; EEC (supporting the inclusion in the draft of 'the principle that an international organization may have the ability to bind its member States through the conclusion of a treaty') at 178.

[111] Gaja, above, note 2, at 264.

[112] Manin, above, note 9, at 470. For these debates see UN Doc A/Conf.129/C.1/SR.19, SR.20 and SR.25.

[113] Cf ILO (Un Doc A/Conf.129/C.1/SR.19, at 5) and UNESCO (*ibid*, at 8).

the Article sought to establish, and especially the rule of unanimity, ran counter to the practice of the organisations and were therefore unacceptable.[114] The representative of the EEC remarked that the system proposed in Article 36*bis* 'differed considerably' from the Community system, but since relations between the Community and its members states 'derived from a provision, Article 228, of its constituent instrument, [. . .] the Community did not consider itself as concerned by the provisions of article 36 *bis*'.[115]

Several amendments were tabled – representing some well-known shifts in perspective – ranging from deleting Article 36*bis*, or specifying the means of assent by the member states and removing the rule of unanimity, to adding a condition clause that would make the procedural rules of the Article (already of a subsidiary nature) 'subject to the rules of the organization[. . .]' or a requirement that member states agree to be bound '*ad hoc* and in a definite manner'.[116] The amendment tabled by ILO, IMF and UN[117] contained a drastic proposal to make the creation of rights and obligations for member states *solely* dependent on the 'rules of the organization', as well as a saving clause for the case in which Article 36*bis* would not be included in the Convention. When, on the basis of consultations held by the President of the Conference among delegations, it was indeed agreed that the article would be deleted,[118] this saving clause, after minor drafting changes, was inserted in Article 74(3) and came to be all that remained of Article 36*bis*:

> The provisions of the present Convention shall not prejudge any question that may arise in regard to the establishment of obligations and rights for States members of an international organization under a treaty to which that organization is a party.[119]

Issues of Article 36bis

A few of the focal points in the drafting process of Article 36*bis* will now be summarised.[120]

The Special Rapporteur had at the outset clearly stated the problem:

[114] Cf Council of Europe (*ibid*, at 10) and FAO (SR.20, at 6).

[115] UN Doc A/Conf.129/C.1/SR.20, at 6; the speaker was referring inter alia to Art 5 of the draft, which makes the convention applicable to IO constituent instruments 'without prejudice to any relevant rules of the organization'. The E(E)C for now has not become a party; see also section 9.3 above.

[116] Austria and Brazil (UN Doc A/Conf.129/C.1/L.49); The Netherlands (L.50); Switzerland (L51); and the USSR (L.62), respectively.

[117] UN Doc A/Conf.129/C.1/L.56 and L.65.

[118] UN Doc A/Conf.129/C.1/SR.28, at 2.

[119] Cf below, notes 160–162 and accompanying text.

[120] The problem of separating rights and obligations, as well as the concern about incongruencies with the regime of Art 37 ('Revocation or modification of obligations or

> Having noted the need arising in practice to associate member States with agreements concluded by international organizations, the question arises as to how far it is possible to go in taking that into account while at the same time remaining faithful to the fundamental principle of the relative effect of treaty undertakings as viewed in the light of the distinctive legal personality of international organizations.'[121]

His statement reflects the dilemma that emerges from the drafting history of Article 36*bis*. Whereas in some respects it would be practical to adhere to the image of international organisations as transparent, in the law of treaties such stratification cannot exist. If an organisation (having distinctive legal personality) is party to a treaty, the member states, in view of the principle of relativity of treaties, by definition are not, and they will have to give their consent for any collateral rights and obligations *under general international law* to arise in their regard.

With a view to safeguarding the system and simultaneously obtaining some of the required transparency for organisations, the idea was to observe the relativity of treaties, but to make the ensuing condition of consent by member states subject to a more flexible regime than that of Articles 35 and 36. This principle has been a point of departure for all versions of Article 36*bis*[122] – albeit the concept of consent was stretched to its limits, as in the case of consent *ex ante*, through adherence to the constituent instrument of the organisation, or in the case of 'acknowledgement', a notion that one commentator observed contained an element of estoppel rather than consent proper.[123]

An interesting element in the discussions was the nature of the rights and obligations at stake. On this point some confusion seemed to subsist until the final stage of the draft. As the Special Rapporteur had emphasised on more than one occasion, the article was not concerned with *de facto* consequences for member states, nor with *de jure* consequences in the relations between an organisation and its member states ('that depends on the relevant rules of each organisation, not on general international law'),[124] but with *direct* rights and obligations between member states and co-contracting parties of an organisation. In the discussions, however, this distinction often seemed to get blurred.

rights . . .'), is left out of account, as it is of less importance in the present context, and arguably less central in the drafting process leading up to the final version of Art 36*bis*.

[121] Reuter VI, at 126, (§ 37; italics added).

[122] The representation, eg by Professor Gaja, that '[. . .] up to the discussion within the ILC in 1982, the text provided that member States of an international organisation could become bound by the treaty without giving their specific consent' does perhaps not do justice to this endeavour (Gaja, above, note 2, at 263).

[123] Cf Francis, (YILC 1978, Vol I, at 138 (§ 13).

[124] Reuter X, at 66 (§ 95).

There may be several reasons for this. First, a separation between primary and secondary obligations, ie direct obligations and obligations arising out of liability, is in practice not always easy to maintain.[125] In this particular case the distinction was also precarious because the test case for obligations on the part of member states is often envisaged as responsibility or liability, rather than the more abstract enforceability, and responsibility or liability may arise very well secondarily (although no agreement has yet been reached on the precise form and conditions)[126] in the absence of any direct obligation on the part of a member state. While the law of (state) responsibility clearly lies outside the scope of the law of treaties as it was being studied for the purposes of codification, some elements, presumably because of the complex relationship between these two branches of law, on occasion would sneak in.[127]

There is, however, yet another reason why the distinction between direct and other obligations on the part of member states could easily become blurred. Both direct and other institutional obligations involve intrusion into the internal legal order of organisations. Whatever the precise nature of a possible obligation on the part of a member state under a treaty to which it is formally not a party, in all cases it involves the relationship between the organisation and its member states, and hence the internal institutional structure of the organisation. This may be the most important reason why truly direct obligations between member states and their organisation's co-contractors, defined *in abstracto* by the Special Rapporteur, are difficult to envision. The one exception is the case of a supranational organisation which has divided competences between itself and its member states in a mutually exclusive way – that is, the case of an organisation which, in a sense, has opened up towards the general legal order on its own accord. The comments of the international organisations that participated in the drafting process seem to confirm this assumption.

[125] Cf the rhetorical question by Mr Francis: 'Could the Commission suggest, for example, that states should not be liable to the creditor when, as in the case of the Caribbean Development Bank, they dissolved a regional bank that they themselves had formed and had authorized to enter into an agreement to obtain the major part of its capital from a source other than themselves?' (YILC 1978, Vol I, at 198, § 26). On a formalist note we may refer to the 1990 Rainbow Warrior case, in which France successfully relied on 'circumstances precluding wrongfulness' to justify non-compliance *and* termination under Art 60 of the Vienna Convention (*Rainbow Warrior Arbitration (New Zealand v France)* 82 *International Law Reports* 1990, 499). In contrast the ICJ in the 1997 *Gabčikovo-Nagymaros* case (paras 46–59) drew a clear line between the law of treaties and the law of responsibility.

[126] Now under study in the ILC, with professor Gaja as Special Rapporteur. Cf Rosalyn Higgins (Rapporteur), 'The Legal Consequences for Member States of the Non-Fulfilment by International Organizations of their Obligations Toward Third Parties', 66 AIDI 1995, Vol I, 251 (Final Report at 461-465)—see section 11.3 below.

[127] See eg Reuter in YILC 1977, Vol I, at 136, § 45, and the discussion during the 1511th meeting (YILC 1981, Vol I, at 194–199).

The recurring doubts expressed on the possibility of defining member states of a contracting organisation as 'third states' are another clear expression of the tension between the requirements of practice, as the Special Rapporteur put it, and the dictates of the legal system. The awkwardness of qualifying member states as 'third states' stems from the fact that, as the Commission had stated in a slightly different context:

> [a]s a composite structure, an international organization remains bound by close ties to the States which are its members; admittedly, analysis will reveal its separate personality and show that it is 'detached' from them, but it still remains closely tied to its component states.[128]

This political reality notwithstanding, it is beyond doubt that member states are to be considered 'third states' in the formal-juridical sense – ie they cannot be associated with the treaty in their quality of component elements within the IO's internal legal order. In view of the (at present) binary principle of 'being a party to a treaty', an intermediate position is moreover difficult to conceive, as confirmed by the fact that member states inescapably fit the definition of 'third party' as laid down in Article 2(h) of the draft convention.[129]

The larger part of the discussion was dedicated to the problem of the then EEC, allegedly the only organisation that could give rise to a clear-cut Article 36*bis* situation. Comments over the years, also from international organisations themselves, show that the Special Rapporteur had not been able to convince a majority of the contrary. The legal and political doubts voiced on this matter seem justified in that the practical effect of earlier versions of the draft article is indeed difficult to envision without the Rome Treaty in mind.[130]

Without entering into the controversy about whether in general supranational organisations may be studied alongside intergovernmental organisations,[131] it is fair to say that the EEC indeed represents a special case. Why this is so was not elaborated upon. In the present context it would seem that when an organisation has taken on certain (areas of) competence(s) from its member states to the exclusion of these member states – that is, either the organisations or the member states are competent to deal with certain matters under *general* international law – the transparency or

[128] 1982 Report of the Commission, YILC 1982, Vol II (Part Two), at 13, §40.

[129] Article 2(h) states: '"Third State" [. . .] mean[s] [. . .] not a party to the treaty' (identical provision in the Convention). Interesting in this respect is Reuter's – unrewarded – proposal to substitute 'third party' with the presumably less rigid term 'non-party' (Reuter VI, at 124–125, §§ 27–32).

[130] Cf Schröder, above, note 9, at 404.

[131] See section 2.2.1 above.

stratification which is a central problem in the case of traditional international organisations, essentially no longer exists.[132]

The drafting history of Article 36*bis* contains interesting aspects of an essentially political nature, such as the role of supranationality and the shifts in emphasis between the three actors – member states, an organisation and its co-contracting parties. It is an example, moreover, of the incompatibility of the two views of the international organisation: a closed, independent subject versus an open, or at least transparent, structure. While complete legal impermeability was considered undesirable, in view of the fact that in practice organisations are in many ways dependent on their member states, and while complete openness was not in question either, since this would deny the independent legal personality of international organisations altogether, an effort was made to obtain a transparency of sorts.

The principle of the relativity of treaties, and hence the legal independence of the contracting organisation, was observed. But at the same time an attempt was made to access the legal order of organisations, by formulating a general rule on the relationship between organisations and their member states. That this general rule was concerned with *direct* rights and obligations for member states vis-à-vis co-contractors of an organisation, does not alter the problem that rights and obligations for member states by definition are created by the law of the organisation, as they are determined by the relation between the organisation and its member states.[133] Whether such institutional law can be traced more or less emphatically to the constituent treaty, ie, to the will of the member states, is not relevant.

The earlier versions of the article were only applicable to supranational organisations (ie the EEC). As has been mentioned above, precisely in the case of such organisations the typical stratification or transparency has ceased to exist, since these institutions have of their own accord opened up to general international law. This implies that penetration of their institutional legal order is no longer necessary. Such a provision may have value as a description of practice or a statement of principle. But the more substantive arguments advanced at the time – enhancing clarity for the co-contracting parties of international organisations and at the same time

[132] Cf Paul Reuter, *Introduction to the Law of Treaties*, 1995: (with regard to the access of international organisations to certain multilateral treaties) 'In all those cases it is restricted to organizations enjoying powers transferred to them by their member States, essentially in fact the European Communities. *As the Communities do not exactly fit the mould of international organizations, such precedents carry little weight*'. (at 77, italics added).

[133] Cf the observations of Mr Riphagen (Netherlands) in the Sixth Committee (UN Doc A/C.6/37/SR.40, paras. 50–67) and as a member of the Commission ('when two treaties met'; YILC 1982, Vol I, at 39), who convincingly argued that the situation covered by Art 36*bis* in reality involved an 'internal' treaty-relationship (between the IGO and its member states) and an 'external' one (between the IGO and its co-contractors).

protecting member states from unwittingly incurring legal obligations – would not hold, precisely in the case of a supranational organisation. Thus, the earlier versions of the provision conveyed the impression of connecting general international law with the internal structure of organisations, whereas in reality this was not the case. In this view it is significant but not surprising that the EEC is recorded to have been opposed to the earlier drafts of the Article in which the direct character of the obligations was explicitly mentioned.[134]

The final draft version of Article 36*bis* took a different approach. The text manifestly was *not* moulded on the EEC and took into account, as stated by the Commission:

> the impossibility of formulating a general rule concerning the rights and obligations thus established and the correlative need to regulate by treaty, case-by-case, the solutions adopted and to inform the co-contracting parties of the organization concerned of the conditions and effects of the relations established.[135]

This version of the article, from which all hints to supranationality had been cleared (by including the conditions of unanimous consent and notification, and in general the requirement of consent of all three categories of actors), was welcomed as a (political) compromise, but met with opposition as well, this time on the part of the 'traditional' international organisations. While the EEC – rightly – no longer considered itself concerned with the provision, the other organisations now strongly criticised Article 36*bis* on account of the procedural conditions, which, slender as they were, were perceived as an imposition on the internal law and an intrusion into the institutional order that could hamper IGO treaty-making practice.

The difficulties of what seems like a no-win situation were evidenced also by the arguments of the proponents of the article. While in the first years the creation of a special third-party regime for member states of a contracting organisation was proposed with the rationale of clarity for the co-contracting parties, combined with respect for the sovereignty of the member states,[136] later the emphasis came to be on the value of the provision as a 'statement of principle', involving the concern for a balance between codification and progressive development of international law.[137]

[134] Philippe Manin, 'The European Communities and the Vienna Convention on the Law of Treaties between States and International Organizations or Between International Organizations" in 24 CMLRev 1987, 457 at 470.

[135] 1982 Report of the Commission, YILC 1982, Vol II (Part Two), at 46 (§ 10).

[136] Cf Reuter VI, at 130, § 5.

[137] Cf Francis, YILC 1978, Vol I, at 197 (§ 25). Several delegates in the Sixth Committee during the 35th session of the UNGA (1980) were however of the opinion that the ILC's work should reflect existing international practice rather than anticipate it (see Topical summary of the discussion in UN Doc A/CN.4/L.326, §§ 180–184).

The ILC commentary to the final draft articles eventually explained the insertion of Article 36*bis* in relatively technical terms: the incompatibility of existing practice with the regimes of Articles 35 and 37.[138] Elsewhere it was nonetheless presented as a vehicle for 'flexible solutions'.[139]

The series of draft Articles 36*bis* confirms the assumption made above, namely that it is not possible to accommodate both views of an international organisation, or a little of both, at the same time. Such an effort will founder on the inability of general law to enter into the legal sub-system of a subject or, in the case at hand, the inability of general law to provide rules on the internal practice of international organisations that have a general value. The increasingly political overtones of the debate on this provision, which subsisted during the Conference, cannot obscure the fact that the lack of enthusiasm and the consequent inglorious fate of Article 36*bis* was in large part due to the inherent theoretical problems of the provision and to the ensuing sense of lack of clarity surrounding it.

10.1.5 'Internal Law'

Other than in relation to the expression of juridical will, the 1986 Convention contains several references to the 'rules of the organization', often without a matching reference to states. One example is **Article 65**, which provides for non-judicial means of dispute settlement. For that reason the article was uncontroversial and could be adapted with a light edit of the last paragraph (the addition of 'organizations') and an insertion of a fourth paragraph, which again specifies that notifications or objections made by an international organisation are to be governed by 'the rules of that organization': 'Invoking a ground ... and making an objection ... are sufficiently important acts ... to have considered it necessary ... to specify that ... they are governed by the relevant rules of the organization.' The Commission specifies that 'the rules in question are, of course, the relevant rules regarding the competence of the organization and its organs'.[140]

References to the rules of the organisation may take the form of a reference to the internal law parties seek to rely on, or of a general

[138] YILC 1982, Vol II (Part Two), at 44 (§§ 4–9).

[139] YILC 1982, Vol II (Part Two), at 47, commentary to Art 37.

[140] YILC 1982, Vol II (Part Two), at 64, § 5. Similar references in arts 6; 7(3)b; 35; 36(2); 37(3); 39.

reservation clause, reserving the operation of the organisation's institutional rules in a particular legal situation.[141]

Invoking the Rules of the Organisation

The classic international rules on the relation between internal law and international treaty obligations are laid down in Articles 27 (*Internal law of States, rules of international organizations and observance of treaties*) and 46 (*Provisions of internal law of a State and rules of an international organization regarding competence to conclude treaties*). These provisions take a classic dualist approach and in principle do not allow for a party to rely on its internal law as a ground for non-compliance (Article 27) or for challenging the validity of its consent to be bound (Article 46).

It took the Commission comparatively little time to agree on the basic form of **Article 27**. However, application of the 'Alabama rule' to organisations proved controversial. Again, discussion hinged on the transparency of organisations, as the preliminary question was to what extent the legal order of an international organisation is separate, and to what extent it is part of general international law. In accordance with the now well-tried division of schools, commentators can roughly be divided in two groups. One was of the opinion that organisations are bound by treaties in the same way as states and may not modify their obligations in any way. The other held the view that the rules of an organisation are part of general international law and cannot be equated in any way with the 'internal law of the state'.

The latter assumption would have as a consequence that the organisation is able to unilaterally change its performance duties under a treaty by modifying the institutional rule (for instance in the UN by a Security Council decision) on which the treaty was based.[142] Put differently, this argument takes the vertical or centralising dynamic out of the problem and reduces it to a conflict of co-ordinated treaty obligations. Along the same lines there was discussion on the viewpoint that organisations provide a clear example of a breach of internal rules which justify non-performance of a treaty in case of a member state breaching its obligations under the law of the organisation.[143]

Finally, the debate on the question of treaties concluded by organisations outside their (as the International Court of Justice would later put it)[144]

[141] On the notion of 'rules of the organization' see also section 10.1.6 below.

[142] The Commission adds: 'The subordination of a treaty to a unilateral act of the organization can only arise in practice for States whose status as members of an organization renders them substantially subject to 'the rules of the organization' (YILC 1982, Vol II (Part Two), at 39, 40, § 8 to Art 27).

[143] YILC 1982, Vol II (Part Two), at 39, § 4 to Art 27.

[144] See section 4.2.5 above.

area of competence,[145] moved between two poles. In the case of IGO treaties concluded *ultra vires*, either Article 27 would be irrelevant (since this provision only deals with treaties of undisputed validity), or the internal rules of the organisation would be irrelevant (as the treaty would bind the organisation as such or, as the Commission put it, in 'an autonomous manner'.)[146]

On first reading the Commission had adopted a text that aimed to capture both the rule and the exception at the general level of international law:

> 2. An international organization party to a treaty may not invoke the rules of the organization as a justification for its failure to perform the treaty, unless performance of the treaty, according to the intention of the parties, is subject to the exercise of the functions and powers of the organization.[147]

As is clear also from the story of Article 36*bis*, this is problematic in view of the autonomy of the IGO institutional order. Unsurprisingly, at the second reading the attempt was abandoned for the classic dualist approach of the 1969 Convention, applied to both states and organisations. The Commission explains that the answer to the question concerning which of the two above-mentioned views to take, must be found – always subject to Article 46 – in the field of interpretation – that is, Article 31 of the Vienna Convention(s).[148] Interestingly, this means the decision on whether a treaty binds an organisation autonomously or not (or, in the present context: whether an organisation is open or closed), is ultimately deferred to the interpreters of a particular treaty, on a case-by-case basis. According to the commentary, therefore, Article 27(2) does not provide a general rule of international law but rather a procedural reference rule.[149]

Article 46 (*Provisions of internal law of a State and rules of an international organization regarding competence to conclude treaties*)[150] deals with the effect of a breach of the internal law of a party on the validity of expressed consent. The 1969 Convention recognises internal law as a lawful ground for invalidating such consent, on the stringent condition (using the formula of a negation plus exception) that the internal

[145] The Commission said: 'Each organization has certain limits to the treaties it may conclude concerning the exercise of its functions and powers' YILC 1982, Vol II (Part Two), at 39, § 5.

[146] YILC 1982, Vol II (Part Two), at 39, § 6 (emphasis in the original).

[147] YILC 1977, Vol II, at 118–120.

[148] YILC 1982, Vol II (Part Two), at 39, § 7 to Art 27.

[149] This appears as a procedural variant of 'the strategy of referral' (cf Martti Koskenniemi, *From Apology to Utopia: The Structure of International Legal Argument,* 2006, 439 ff. (on UNCLOS) which has a rule defer the material decision to another rule; see also David Kennedy, *International Legal Structures*, 1987, 201–245; and Philip Allott, 'Mare Nostrum: A New International Law of the Sea', 86 *American Journal of International Law*, 1992, 764–787).

[150] Above, notes 21 and 61 and accompanying text.

rule at issue be 'fundamental' and that the breach be 'manifest'. Application of this rule, as with those of Article 27 and draft Article 36*bis*, touches directly upon the question concerning if and to what extent the internal rules of organisations are to be equated with that of states. As can be seen from the history of eg Article 45, drafters would generally start with the idea that such equation was not possible, and that the organisation was to some extent an open structure. In the Article 46 adopted on first reading, the criterion of the 'fundamental rule' was deleted in relation to organisations,[151] with the argument that international organisations deserve legal protection against manifest breach of any 'rule of the organization.' On second reading the qualification was reinserted.[152]

Otherwise, the required 'manifest' character of the breach was cause for discussion. As to the breach of state law, on first reading the Commission had adopted a provision identical to 46(2) of the 1969 Convention. On second reading, the Commission felt that, since such manifest character would be conveyed also to international organisations, this provision should be modified so as to make clear that the reference was to the 'practice' (regarding representatives who may express consent) of states only.[153]

The final draft Article 46, with many provisions trimmed down in the discussion process, stipulated the criterion 'manifest' for both states and organisations. It added that breach of the rules of an organisation qualifies as manifest 'if it is or ought to be within the knowledge of any contracting State or any contracting organization.'[154] During the Conference, that subjective factor was taken out. The reference to the practice of international organizations, however, now includes the qualification 'where appropriate'.[155]

Article 47 (*Specific restrictions on authority to express the consent of a State or an international organization*) is concerned with a slightly different situation, namely the legal effect of a representative with full powers who expresses consent in contravention of ('internal') instructions. Such legal effect is appreciated similarly for states and organisations. The *ultra vires* character of acts by a representative can be relied on for invalidating the expression of consent only if such instructions have been notified to the negotiating partners in advance, thus raising in a sense the domestic obligation to the international plane. The emphasis lies on legal certainty and the cognisance of the co-contractors, and no reference is made to the internal law of organisations.

151 YILC 1979, Vol I, 1576th meeting.
152 YILC 1982, Vol II (Part Two), at 52, § 3.
153 YILC 1982, Vol II (Part Two), at 52, § 6.
154 Draft Article 46(4); YILC 1982, Vol II (Part Two), at 51.
155 UN Doc A/Conf.129/16, 17th and 18th meeting, at 129–139.

Reserving the Rules of the Organisation

Although the formula may look similar to the frequent references in relation to the expression of juridical will by organisations,[156] the two provisions mentioned below are different in that they genuinely delimit the operation of international law and demarcate a boundary between the law of treaties and the institutional law of organisations.

Article 5 of the 1969 Convention was the 'without prejudice' clause expressly reserving the right of international organisations to maintain their own rules with regard to their constituent treaties and to the treaty-making process in their framework. Considering the – still – scant practice of organisations functioning in the framework of other organisations,[157] the Special Rapporteur had been of the opinion that '[i]t is obvious that there can be no article in the draft articles similar to article 5 of the 1969 Convention'.[158]

The Commission thought differently. On second reading a parallel **Article 5** (*Treaties constituting international organizations and treaties adopted within an international organization*) was inserted in the draft; it is not entirely symmetrical to its counter-provision in the 1969 Convention. It secures 'no prejudice' to 'any relevant rules of the organization' where it comes to 'any treaty *between one or more States and one or more international organizations* which is the constituent instrument of an international organization and to any treaty adopted within an international organization' (emphasis added). Constituent treaties which have only organisations as parties were not taken into consideration, with no further explanation on the part of the Commission.[159]

Article 74 (*Questions not prejudged by the present Convention*) is the provision that parallels the clause of Article 73 of the 1969 Convention.[160] Article 74(3) – the first two paragraphs will be discussed below[161] – contains a saving clause, which is the remainder of Article 36*bis*, reserving questions 'of obligations and rights for States members of an international organization under a treaty to which that organization is a party'.[162]

The paragraph states a principle of complete respect for the internal legal order of international organisations. Its practical significance within

[156] Section 10.1.3 above, note 46 and accompanying text.

[157] See, on contemporary practice in this respect, Henry Schermers and Niels Blokker, *International Institutional Law*, 2003, §§ 81–84.

[158] Reuter III, YILC 1974, Vol II (Part One), at 145.

[159] YILC 1982, at 23; the Joint Vienna Institute is an example of such an organisation; it came into being on 29 July 1994, established by the BIS, the EBRD, the IBRD, the IMF and the OECD; see above, ch 2.

[160] Parallelism of the 1986 Convention with the 1969 Convention is abandoned from Art 73 (*Relationship to the [1969] Vienna Convention on the Law of Treaties*) onwards.

[161] Section 10.3.1 below.

[162] Section 10.1.4 above.

the system of the law of treaties is not entirely clear, however, especially in view of Articles 27 and 46. The residue of Article 36*bis* essentially amounts to a delimitation of the law of treaties (in the same way as international law operates in regard of the legal order of states), and, as mentioned in relation to, for example, Articles 36*bis* and 45, it is difficult to see how this could have been otherwise.

10.1.6 Terminology

The 1986 Convention has introduced several terminological novelties to mark a distinction between states and organisations as subjects of the law of treaties. As to legal effect these changes are mostly cosmetic, but they always have a relevant conceptual component. One example is the 'expression of consent' by states' representatives versus the 'communication of consent' by the representatives of organisations. This terminological distinction, which ultimately was not maintained in the Convention text, has already been addressed in the context of expression of juridical will.[163]

Another example is the provision in **Article 2** *(Use of terms)* on 'the rules of the organization', which is the only newly added paragraph in respect of the 1969 Convention. 'Rules of the organization' figure regularly in the 1986 Convention, in some cases as the counterpart of a reference to the 'internal law' of states (Articles 2(2); 27; 46(2)), and in some cases as a specifying remark in relation to organisations only (Articles 6; 7(3)b; 35; 36(2); 37(3); 39; 65(4)).[164] As with the references to 'the competent organ' in lieu of the organisation as such, which is discussed above,[165] the legal effect may vary according to the context.

The choice of terms for a reference to the institutional law of an organisation does not entail practical legal consequences, but obviously touches upon a question of principle regarding the nature of organisations and their institutional order. The formula 'rules of the organization'[166] is noteworthy for the absence of the notions 'internal' (present in earlier versions) and 'law'. In its commentary to the final draft, the Commission takes a clear stance and maintains the transparency of the institutional veil:

[163] In relation to arts 7 and 46; section 10.1.3 above.

[164] The reservation clause in Art 5 refers to '*relevant* rules of the organization,' but this is because of the similar wording in the parallel article of the 1969 Convention.

[165] Eg in Art 45; see above, note 59 and accompanying text.

[166] Which are defined as: ' . . . in particular, the constituent instruments, decisions and resolutions adopted in accordance with them, and established practice of the organization.' (Art 2(1)j).

'[t]here would have been problems in referring to the "internal law" of an organization, for while it has internal aspect, this law also has in other respects an international aspect'.[167]

Ex abundante cautela the final draft Articles in all cases refer to 'relevant rules of the organization' – according to the Commission, 'to underline the fact that it is not all "decisions" or "resolutions" which give rise to rules, but only those which are *of relevance* in that respect'.[168] However, the condition of 'relevancy' was dropped during the Conference.[169]

Otherwise, Article 2 mostly follows the 1969 Convention. Of some interest is the definition of 'party' in sub-paragraph g. In the final version 'party' was defined similarly for states and organisations, but the term had raised questions in relation to organisations and their (transparent) institutional order. The Commission in its commentary to the final draft articles then stressed the strict, one-dimensional meaning of the words 'to be bound by the treaty', which would not, for instance, envisage an organisation being bound by collateral rights or obligations stemming from a treaty to which the member states are party.[170]

For reasons of clarity the economic formula of **Article 3** of the 1969 Convention *(International agreements not within the scope of the present Convention)* was not followed. The Commission resorted to a somewhat 'cumbersome' phrasing (its own words), which spells out the different treaties on the basis of parties.[171] Here the reference in the 1969 Convention to 'other subjects of law' constituted a minor issue of terminology. To avoid implications about the legal personality of creatures other than states or organisations, the draft articles until the second reading referred to 'entities other than states and organizations';[172] it was then replaced by the 1969 Convention formula 'other subjects of international law'.[173] According to the Commission this wording 'is, as things stand, far narrower in scope and the area of discussion which it opens up is very limited'.[174] The discussion that the Commission thus – rightfully – avoided is whether an agreement is a treaty only when concluded by a subject of international

[167] YILC 1982, Vol II (Part Two), at 21, § 25.

[168] *Ibid* (emphasis in the original).

[169] Discussed at the 2nd, 3rd, 4th and 27th (decision) Meetings of the Committee of the Whole UN Doc A/Conf.139/16 s.v.); adopted at the 5th Plenary Meeting (*ibid* at 13).The wording of Art 5 is an exception, in order to maintain symmetry with the parallel provision in the 1969 Convention, which is the only onc referring to the rules of the organisation.

[170] YILC 1982, Vol II (Part Two), at 20, § 17.

[171] Report of the International Law Commission on its thirty-fourth session, YILC 1982, Vol II (Part Two), at 22; cf section 10.1.1 above.

[172] Changed at the 26th session; YILC 1974, Vol I, discussed at the 1291st meeting (paras 31–40).

[173] Report of the International Law Commission on its thirty-fourth session, YILC 1982, Vol II (Part Two), at 22, § 6.

[174] YILC 1982, Vol II (Part Two), at 22, § 6.

law, or whether, on the contrary, apparent treaty-making acitvity may lead to attribution of treaty-making capacity.[175] Differently put, it is the question of whether legal personality is to be considered a consequence of, or a threshold to, treaty-making – or both, as seems to be the case in prevailing doctrine.[176]

Article 7 (*Full powers*) (and in its wake Articles 14(2)d and 67) originally envisaged 'powers' to designate the credentials of an organisation and 'full powers' the credentials of a state. A cosmetic distinction, it is also a doctrinal statement about the functional basis of organisations. The Commission held that '[i]t seemed inappropriate to use the term "full powers" for an organization, for the capacity of such a body to bind itself internationally is never unlimited'.[177] During the Conference, inter alia because of the lack of legal substance of this distinction (Riphagen: 'Furthermore, the "powers", even of representatives of States, were never in fact "full"'), the term was brought in line with the 'full powers' of states.[178]

Articles 11 (*Means of expressing consent to be bound by a treaty*) and **14** (*Consent to be bound by a treaty expressed by ratification, act of formal confirmation, acceptance or approval*)[179] introduce a 'new verbal expression describing an operation which has not so far had any generally accepted term bestowed on it in international practice'.[180] This is the term 'formal confirmation', used to denote the expression of consent to be bound by organisations as an 'analogous means'[181] for ratification. It is a distinction with doctrinal weight (and reportedly a compromise gesture toward states with strongly sovereignty-oriented systems).[182] The Commission stated that the term (international) 'ratification' is reserved for states, 'since in accordance with a long historical tradition it always denotes an act emanating from the highest organs of the State [...] and there are no corresponding organs in international organizations.'[183]

175 Cf section 4.2.2 above.

176 *Ibid.*

177 YILC 1982, Vol II (Part Two), at 19, § 10.

178 Discussed at the 7th, 8th (Riphagen, § 54), 10th and 14th Meetings of the Committee of the Whole.

179 Cf above, on arts 11–17 in section 10.1.3; a reference to the 'act of formal confirmation' is included also in Art 77(1)f.

180 YILC 1982, Vol II (Part Two), at 31, § 1 to Art 14.

181 YILC 1982, Vol II (Part Two), at 29, § 3 to Art 11.

182 Richard Kearney and Robert Dalton, 'The Treaty on Treaties', 64 *American JIL* 1970, 495–561, at 532.

183 YILC 1982, Vol. II (Part Two), at 19, § 8 to article 2.

10.2 ISSUES OF PRACTICE

The issues brought under this heading were primarily approached by the drafters from the perspective of (f)actual[184] practice with regard to organisations, although such a perspective is inevitably bound up with doctrinal premises.

10.2.1 Territory

Article 29 (*Territorial scope of treaties*) constitutes a clear break of symmetry between states and organisations. The inclusive territorial rule for state parties is extended to treaties which also have organisations as parties, but the provision does not refer to territorial application for organisations. An obvious reason is that 'we cannot speak in this case of "territory" in the strict sense of the word'.[185] Two observations may be made. These revolve around the differing parameters of territoriality and functionality.

To note the obvious, the drafters have not envisaged territorial application for organisations, such that a treaty would be applicable to the entire territory covered by its member states.[186] But, although organisations are not territorially defined in the way of states, territorial application would have been possible given that the functional design or 'functional limitation'[187] of an organisation provides its own boundaries on the basis of (the area of) competence. This is especially clear in an organisation with a supranational set-up, where the organisation assumes tasks and competences which i) in substance are not limited to the functioning of the organisation itself; and ii) rest with the organisation to the exclusion of the member states.

On the other hand, the commentary raises a point which is surprising because it does make an analogy between territoriality and functionality: 'the question of the extension of treaties ... to all the entities, subsidiary organs, connected organs and related bodies which come within the orbit of that organisation and are incorporated in it to a greater or lesser extent'[188] is put as '[a] problem comparable to that affecting States, ... which might ... arise for ... organizations *in different yet parallel terms*'.[189]

On a general note it may be added that while the 'internal scope' of a treaty in the case of a state party is not addressed by the Convention, in the

[184] Objectivity of legal phenomena mentioned in section 2.2.1 above.
[185] YILC 1982, Vol II (Part Two), at 40, § 2 to Art 29.
[186] *Ibid*, §§ 1–2 to Art 29.
[187] See section 4.2.2 above.
[188] YILC 1982, Vol II (Part Two), at 40, § 3 to Art 29.
[189] *Ibid;* emphasis added.

case of an organisation the drafters considered it necessary to take up the question. It had no follow-up, mainly because theory and practice on this point were not considered sufficiently settled.

The gist of **Article 62** (*Fundamental change of circumstances*), which had been the subject of extensive debate during the preparations for the first Vienna Convention,[190] was smoothly incorporated in the new Convention. Questions arose only as to the second paragraph, which states the exceptions to the rule. One of these exceptions is boundary treaties, which are per se not affected by the *rebus sic stantibus* clause. The Convention specifies that such boundary treaties have at least two states as parties. The drafters considered, but eventually did not include, situations of IGO treaties having territorial components – an example of existing practice being a treaty concluded by the United Nations establishing a territorial regime: 'The article has been worded from the traditional standpoint that only States possess territory and that only delimitations of territories of States constitute boundaries'.[191]

Apart from descriptive accuracy, the article also seems to make a doctrinal point.[192] Rather than leaving the rule unspecified to allow further development of law and practice,[193] the drafters chose to include a limiting specification (which obviously had no counterpart in the 1969 Convention).

10.2.2 Dispute Settlement

When it comes to the settlement of disputes, organisations seem to be taken as actors in their own right, with no sign of transparency. The controversial Article 66 of the 1969 Convention (not drafted by the ILC but by the Conference)[194] constitutes an important exception to the basic rule of acceptance of jurisdiction by states, as it provides for compulsory jurisdiction of the International Court of Justice in disputes arising out of matters relating to *jus cogens*. In the 1982 draft article the 1969 provision was adapted (for the obvious procedural reason that organisations do not have *locus standi* before the Court) to stipulate compulsory arbitration in case of a dispute regarding *jus cogens* (Articles 53 or 64), and compulsory conciliation in case of other disputes arising out of the provisions of Part V.

[190] Summary in the commentary to draft Art 59, YILC 1966, Vol II, at 76–79.

[191] YILC 1982, Vol II (Part Two), at 61, § 11.

[192] *Ibid*, at 60, 61, §§ 8–11.

[193] A frequently taken approach – for example in Art 60.

[194] A reference guide and analysis in Shabtai Rosenne, *Developments in the Law of Treaties (1945–1986)*, 1989, at 296–317 (see in particular Chapter 5.6 : 'The Legislative History of Articles 65 and 66 of the Vienna Conventions').

During the Conference this solution was rejected.[195] The new Article 66, then, provides for different categories. An inter-state dispute gives compulsory jurisdiction to the International Court, as in the corresponding article of the 1969 Convention (which would prevail in any case: Article 73 of the 1986 Convention). For the settlement of disputes to which an organisation also is a party, the formula of a 'binding' advisory opinion was chosen. This had been considered but rejected in the second reading by the Commission,[196] 'in view of all the imperfections and uncertainties of such a procedure',[197] but at a later stage appeared as the best option. Somewhat awkwardly, Article 66(2)d provides that such opinion 'shall be accepted as decisive by all the parties to the dispute concerned'.

10.2.3 Descriptive Force

International law codification *sensu lato* famously has the dual function of.developing new rules and writing down existing rules.[198] The degree of accuracy of the latter aspect may be referred to as the descriptive force of a codification project. The descriptive force of the new Convention was a general concern throughout the drafting process (linked to the – apparently justified – concern about political support for the new Convention). However, the following provisions seem to have been approached by the drafters with a particular view to existing practice.

Draft **Article 9** (*Adoption of the text*) in its second paragraph stated that a diplomatic conference is to be interpreted as 'an international conference of States in which organizations participate.' Here the Commission aimed for an adequate description of practice and chose not to leave the provision unspecified. The commentary explains that although 'an international conference consisting only of international organizations is conceivable, ... *each organization would possess such specific characteristics* ... that there would be little point in bringing such a "conference" within the scope of article 9'.[199] During the Conference, this qualification was taken out.[200]

[195] Adoption at the 7th Plenary Meeting, UN Doc A/Conf.139/16, §§ 11–31. Discussion at the 24th, 26th, 27th, 28th, 29th, 30th meeting of the Committee of the Whole (UN Doc A/Conf.139/16 s.v.)

[196] YILC 1980, Vol II (Part Two), at 87, § 9.

[197] YILC 1982, Vol II (Part Two), at 65, § 4.

[198] Pursuant to article 13(1)a of the UN Charter, Art 1(1) of the 1947 ILC Statute provides: 'The International Law Commission shall have for its object the promotion of the progressive development of international law and its codification'.

[199] YILC 1982, Vol II (Part Two), at 28, § 3 to Art 9 (emphasis added). For reasons of symmetry Art 10(2) maintained an implicit reference to a conference existing only of organisations, notwithstanding the above-quoted comment in relation to Art 9.

[200] Discussed at 8th, 9th, 10th, 28th Meetings of the Committee of the Whole (UN Doc A/Conf.139/16 s.v.), decided at the 5th Plenary Meeting (*ibid* at 13).

Incidentally, the provision of Article 9 is of interest also because it constitutes one of the few instances in which the drafters of the second Convention set aside the principle of not amending the first Vienna Convention. The 1969 Article 9(2) had been criticised from the outset as it stipulated a two-thirds voting rule (which was inspired by UN practice) for adoption in a diplomatic conference, whereas formerly this had been at the discretion of the conferencing states. The draft of 1982 reproduced this controversial provision. A redraft during the Conference provided for the choice of procedure to remain with the conference participants.

Article 63 (*Severance of diplomatic or consular relations*) provides that severance of diplomatic relations between states does not affect the legal relation established between those states under a treaty to which one or more organisations are also party (if not, a treaty would be governed by the 1969 Convention). During the preparatory work the practice of 'diplomatic relations' between states and organisations did come up. However, ultimately the Commission was of the view that 'it was not necessary to burden the text of Article 63 with a provision concerning that case', also because in most cases the source of diplomatic relations between an organisation and its member states is the constituent treaty.[201] Organisations as diplomatic partners are thus not included in the scope of the article. Alternatively, in the view of the drafters, the relations with states maintained by organisations are not considered as 'diplomatic', '[f]or diplomatic and consular relations exist between states alone'.[202] The article is thus asymmetrical, and basically a restatement of the rule on relations between states, which would already have effect on the basis of 1986 Article 73.

Article 75 (*Diplomatic and consular relations and the conclusion of treaties*) addresses the capacity of states to conclude treaties while diplomatic relations have already been severed. Proceeding from the premise that 'diplomatic and consular relations exist between states alone',[203] the provision applies only to multilateral treaties 'between two or more of those states and one or more international organizations' – a restrictive formula used also in relation to boundary treaties.[204]

In the present context **Article 77** (*Depositaries of treaties*) is of interest because it opens up the institutional order of the organisation. While the state may perform the depositary function only as a unitary actor, in the case of organisations this may also be an organ: Article 77(1): 'The

[201] YILC 1982, Vol II (Part Two), at 62, § 3 to Art 63.

[202] ILC Commentary to draft article 74, YILC 1982, Vol II (Part One), at 70, § 2. After discussion, the Article was adopted at the 6th Plenary Meeting of the Conference, UN Doc A/Conf.129/16, at 18, § 5.

[203] YILC 1982, Vol II (Part Two), at 70, § 2.

[204] See above, note 191 and accompanying text.

depositary may be one or more States, an international organization or the chief administrative officer of the organization.' This is firmly based in practice, considering the depository tasks of the UN Secretary-General in his own name (although the legal meaning of this is not entirely certain).[205] In contrast, the possibility of 'multiple depositories' (famously employed for the 1968 Anti-nuclear Proliferation Treaty, which was deposited in Moscow, Washington and London) is envisaged only for state depositories.

In the same vein **Article 78** (*Functions of depositaries*), which provides that a conflict with the depository may be brought 'to the attention of: ... (b) where appropriate, the competent organ of the international organization concerned' (Para 2).

10.3 ISSUES OF PRINCIPLE

10.3.1 The International Organisation as a Moral Person

The meaning of 'moral person', in the civil law tradition, is a 'legal person'[206] as opposed to a physical person. This particular term has been chosen for the title of the present section, as it goes to underscore the sentient aspect of the fiction of legal personality: it refers to an entity that possesses an understanding and will peculiar to itself, and is susceptible to obligations and rights.

Obviously the very project of canonising international organisations as subjects of the law of treaties depends to some extent on the recognition of their moral personality. For instance the notion of an organisation being able to express its juridical will[207] proceeds from such recognition.[208] At the same time, as appears at various points in the drafting process and sometimes in the actual Convention, lawyers do not seem prepared to go all the way. Organisations are considered to have an independent will, but one which only goes so far and may not quite extend to international relations in general; organisations may entertain international relations with other subjects, but these do not count as true 'diplomatic' relations;

[205] Cf 'Status of Multilateral Treaties Deposited with the Secretary-General' (http://untreaty.un.org/English/treaty.asp).

[206] On the notion of 'moral personality' eg Frederic Maitland, 'Moral Personality and Legal Personality', 6 *Journal of Comparative Legislation and International Law* 1905, 192–200; Evelyne Pisier-Kouchner, 'La notion de personne morale dans l'oeuvre de Léon Duguit', 11/12 *Quaderni fiorentini per la storia del pensiero giuridico moderno*, 667.

[207] Section 10.1.3 above.

[208] Whether the state is a 'moral person' is of course connected to the acknowledgment of its corporate nature. As has been discussed above (section 3.1), for at least an extended period of time around the turn of the 19th century, this was not the case as the state had assumed the status of a 'natural person'.

an organisation may be negligent or fraudulent in its international relations, but the institution is not sufficiently organic for this to be ascertained, so recourse is sought in its internal structure, and hence, in its member states. As the Commission commented in relation to an early version of the Draft Articles on State Responsibility, 'it must not be forgotten that, by their very nature, international organizations *normally behave in such a manner as not to commit internationally wrongful acts*'.[209] This ambivalent and functionalist approach, compared to the moral personality attributed to states, is closely tied in with the transparent image of organisations, as it is the member states who are perceived as the real actors.

The right of organisations to formulate reservations, in connection to **Article 19** (*Formulation of reservations*), was discussed above[210] in the context of expression of juridical will. However, the division among the drafters on this right – which is a classic expression of the freedom of contract of an independent entity – may be recalled here. A right to conclude treaties without a right to make reservations, as was extensively considered during the drafting process, neatly reflects the ambiguous approach to organisations as moral persons.

The question of moral personality also presents itself for example in relation to practices as coercion, aggression and use of force. An organisation is deemed capable of 'good faith,[211] but does it have sufficient independent legal identity for such classic wrongful acts to be attributed to it – or is this reserved to states?

From **Articles 48** and **49** it appears that the mental state necessary for error and fraud can be attributed to organisations. The articles give one rule for both states and organisations, but as the Commission points out, the effect for organisations is different. Because – and this touches upon the issue raised first in relation to Article 7 on full powers – 'international organizations do not have an organ equivalent to the Head of state ... which can fully represent them in all their treaty commitments and determine the organization's "conduct" by its acts alone', it is necessary to look into the institutional order of organisations for establishing proof of, for instance, negligence.[212]

[209] YILC 1975, Vol II, para.3, at 87 (emphasis added); both the article and the commentary were adopted in an unaltered version in 1996. Allott's argument of the 'unmoral state' – it is the people that act – would provide a counter-argument to both the image of the state as a 'moral person' (also in the literal sense), and to the view of the Commission (Philip Allott, 'State Responsibility and the Unmaking of International Law', 29 *Harvard Journal of International Law*, 1988, 1–26).

[210] Section 10.1.3.

[211] Cf arts 26; 46(3); and 69(2)b of the 1986 Convention.

[212] YILC 1982, Vol II (Part Two), at 53, § 2 (in relation to Art 48(2)).

The equation of organisations and states in **Articles 50** (*Corruption of a representative of a State or of an international organization*) and **51** (*Coercion of a representative of a State or of an international organization*) is unproblematic, as these provisions do not so much raise the issue of the corporate identity of the organisation – as being composed by states – as pierce the very fiction of legal personality for any legal entity other than a physical person.

As to corruption committed *by* an organisation, the Commission points out that corruption by a (usually) collective organ of an organisation is less likely than by a (usually) individual organ of a state – less likely, but not impossible: for example through 'the power of nomination to high posts and missions'.[213]

Article 52 (*Coercion of a State or of an international organization by the threat or use of force*) raised the question of coercion against and *by* an organisation (the latter not having been addressed in the commentary to Article 51). As the provision does not refer to the parties, but to the treaty, it could be included without change in the 1986 Convention. The main point of discussion was the desirability of extending the prohibition of force in the conclusion of treaties to organisations in view of their limited, functional nature: 'Is it really conceivable that ... organizations may suffer, or even employ, the threat or use of force?'[214] While some Commission members felt the whole discussion was academic and did not need to be covered, a majority found that organisations both as objects (organisations forced to conclude a headquarters agreement) and as subjects (certain organisations, such as NATO, with powers and means to use force) could be imagined as involved with coercion.

To be sure, the Commission substantiated its decision with a reference to a formula used by the UN General Assembly when on several occasions it has condemned the use of force by 'a State or group of States'. The Commission concludes that 'the General Assembly provides sufficient authority for recognizing that an ... organization may in theory be regarded as making unlawful use of armed force'.[215] This is because 'group of states' is taken to include an 'international organization'.[216] However, in a legal sense this is not necessarily so. Rather, it expresses a functionalist, 'open' view of organisations as vehicles for states, which precisely does not proceed from the organisation as an independent moral person.

Article 76 (*Case of an aggressor State*) contains a no-prejudice clause for treaty obligations stemming from measures taken under the UN Charter

213 YILC 1982, Vol II (Part Two), at 54, § 2 commentary to Art 50.

214 YILC 1982, Vol II (Part Two), at 55, § 2.

215 YILC 1982, Vol II (Part Two), at 56, § 6; such regardless of the definition and scope of 'coercion', an old point of discussion that was revived but not entirely resolved.

216 YILC 1982, Vol II (Part Two), at 56 § 6.

vis-à-vis an aggressor state.[217] Corresponding Article 75 of the 1969 Convention for purposes of the diplomatic Conference had been earmarked as 'problematic'.[218] That the text, apart from an editorial change ('a treaty between one or more states and one or more organizations'), is identical to the 1969 Article 75, implies a substantial distinction between states and organisations. As they are not considered to be a likely candidate, organisations are not mentioned as a potential aggressor.

The Commission specifies two reasons for its decision. First, if need be organisations *are* covered by the provision, since in the 1974 UNGA Resolution on the definition of aggression 'State' is known also to cover a 'group of States', which in turn is taken to include international organisations.[219] The second argument is that, if organisations were potential aggressors to be reckoned with, the 1969 Convention would have included them, since such aggression would primarily affect inter-state treaties.[220] All the same, this provision may also be taken as a statement of principle on the monopoly of force resting with states, as the visible component element of any international organisation.

Article 74 (*Questions not prejudged by the present Convention*) parallels the reservation clause of the 1969 Article 73. The provision repeats from the 1969 Convention the 'questions not prejudged' which relate to states: succession, responsibility and the outbreak of hostilities. In regard to organisations, it refers to international responsibility, and it adds 'the termination of the existence of the organization ... [and] ... the termination of participation by a State in the membership of the organization' as circumstances which are precluded from the operation of the 1986 Convention. The third paragraph, on the relation between the organisation and its member states, has been addressed above.[221]

The list in Article 74(1) and (2) reflects the transparency of the institutional veil, or the transparent image of organisations. The Commission was divided on whether organisations could be involved in hostilities, but ultimately decided to maintain the formula 'hostilities between States'. This decision was 'unconnected with the question of principle', but rather inspired by traditional law of treaties which deals with the effect of war on treaties, not war in general.[222] As to 'succession of international organizations', the Commission held that this did not need to be covered, as it was 'entirely artificial and arbitrary, unlike the case of a succession of States, in

[217] A provision inspired by the experience with the 'peace treaties' ending WW I and WW II; see also YILC 1966, Vol II, at 87, commentary to draft Art 70.

[218] In UNGA Resolution UN Doc A/40/76 (11 December 1985); see Annex IV below.

[219] The same argument was used in relation to Art 52; see above, note 216 and accompanying text.

[220] YILC 1982, Vol II (Part Two), at 70, § 2.

[221] On Art 74(3) see section 10.1.5 above.

[222] YILC 1982, Vol II (Part Two), at 68, § 5.

which it is the change in sovereignty over a territory that ... constitutes the actual basis for a transfer of obligations and property'.[223]

Thus the Convention does not envision hostilities or succession by organisations in relation to treaties. On the other hand, it explicitly reserves 'termination of the existence' of an organisation (an eventuality unmentioned in relation to states) and 'termination of participation by a State' in an organisation. The commentary adds that 'these are delicate issues which require detailed study and on which the Commission has taken no position'.[224]

Of the new **Article 62** (*Fundamental change of circumstances*) only the second paragraph, which states the exceptions to the *rebus sic stantibus* rule, was a substantive point of discussion. The exceptions are boundary treaties,[225] and concern changes in circumstances that are due to the action of an invoking party itself. The latter gave rise to interesting musings on the transparency of organisations: 'a number of fundamental changes can result from acts which take place *inside* and not *outside* the organization; these acts are not necessarily imputable to the organisation as such (although in some cases they are) but to the States members of the organization.'[226]

The issue of legally relevant 'fundamental changes' originating in the institutional order of an organisation does not quite belong to the sphere of the law of responsibility (note also the word 'imputable' rather than 'attributable'), or at least it belongs partly to the sphere of the law of treaties. A secondary role for member states – as in the tenet of 'secondary responsibility', which is *subsequently* triggered once the organisation itself cannot meet its obligations – is therefore not at issue.[227] The law of treaties is about the *Normadressat* of the primary norm, and this must be either the organisation or the member states. The set-up of the law of treaties is such that it cannot be both at the same time. Arguably, the *Normadressat* is equally indivisible when it comes to invoking a ground for unilateral termination of the tie to that primary norm. The drafting of Article 62(2) thus had the potential for posing a conundrum in the same way as draft Article 36*bis*,[228] as the legal system would dictate a choice for either the organisation or the member states, or for the organisation as either entirely closed or entirely open.

223 YILC 1982, Vol II (Part Two), at 68, §§ 6–11, quotation in § 6.

224 YILC 1982, Vol II (Part Two), at 69, § 10.

225 Discussed above – see section 10.2.1, notes 191 and 192 and accompanying text.

226 YILC 1982, Vol II (Part Two), at 60, § 2 (emphasis added); the Commentary gives the example of an organization which cannot meet its external financial obligations for the reason that member states fail to pay contribution.

227 See section 11.3 below.

228 See section 10.1.4 above.

The matter was, however, reserved by the Commission.[229] This was done partly because the element of responsibility fell outside the scope of the law of treaties Convention(s) as stated in Article 74; and partly – the commentary mentions this important point in passing – because an attempt to state a general rule on the legal effect of obstructive acts by member states would cause an incongruency with Article 27 (providing that organisations, similar to states, cannot invoke their 'internal' rules as a ground for non-compliance).

10.3.2 The International Community of States

The 1986 Vienna Convention contains a few provisions that implicitly or explicitly rely on the notion of an international (legal) community. Here, the status of international organisations within such a community had to be addressed. This section considers the way in which the drafters conceptualised international organisations in that context. Questions regarding the value and validity of a constitutional discourse on international law lie outside the scope of this book.

Article 30 (*Application of successive treaties relating to the same subject-matter*) reproduces the basic rules for conflicting treaty obligations of the 1969 Article 30. The provision appears as a classic instance of law of treaties doctrine, and the 'without prejudice' clause in § 1, which reserves the operation of Article 103 of the UN Charter, as a traditional conflict clause – albeit the most prominent one in modern treaty practice. However, the transposition of this conflict clause, and its possible application to international organisations, raised a question of substance. Discussions in the Commission neatly illustrate the two perspectives on organisations, as well as their mutual exclusiveness.

Some members thought that organisations came under Article 103 automatically, since organisations were vehicles for collective state action and nearly all states in the world were parties to the UN Charter. Others held the opposite view, that organisations were not members of the UN, and therefore were not addressed by Article 103.[230]

In order to accommodate both viewpoints, the final draft Article 30(6) used 'terms which are deliberately ambiguous'[231] and 'without prejudice to Article 103 of the Charter of the United Nations'. During the Conference this was changed[232] to a bolder statement of precedence for the UN Charter: 'without prejudice to the fact that, in the event of a conflict

[229] YILC 1982, Vol II (Part Two), at 60, § 2.
[230] *Ibid*, at 41, § 1 to Art 30.
[231] *Ibid*.
[232] Discussed at the 15th Meeting of the Committee on the Whole (UN Doc A/Conf.139/16, at 119, §§ 4–47). Adopted at the 5th Plenary Meeting (*ibid* at 15).

between obligations under the Charter ... and obligations under a treaty, the obligations under the Charter shall prevail'. Rather than a reservation clause, as was the draft Article 30(6) quoted above, this is a normative statement in its own right. However, as it is conditional upon obligations under the Charter – while the question of whether organisations may have such obligations is not answered – it ultimately amounts to a restatement of Article 103 of the Charter.

Article 38 (*Rules in a treaty becoming binding on third States or third organizations through international custom*) equates organisations with states in that both are considered (susceptible) to be bound by international customary law. The commentary to the identical draft Article concedes that 'the ... Article does not prejudge in one way or another the possibility that the effects of the process of formulation of customary law might extend to international organizations'.[233] As the provision does not explicitly address the formation of custom, the commentary is silent on the possible *participation* of organisations in that process.

This is different when it comes to higher norms of law. The Vienna Convention, otherwise a tribute to consensual obligation and freedom of contract, famously contains two non-subsidiary rules on *jus cogens*. These are **Articles 53** (*Treaties conflicting with a peremptory norm of general international law* (jus cogens)) and **64** (*Emergence of a new peremptory norm of general international law* (jus cogens)). The Articles were transposed from the first to the second Convention without change. This means that the definition of *jus cogens* contained in Article 53 refers to an international community of states only:

> ... a peremptory norm of general international law is a norm accepted and recognized by the international community of States as a whole...

In response to the question whether organisations should be added as a component of the 'international community', the Commission made a statement of principle which summarises the transparent image of organisations, and which by way of a concluding statement may be quoted in full:

> But in law, this wording adds nothing to the formula used in the Vienna Convention, since organizations necessarily consist of States, and it has, perhaps, the drawback of needlessly placing organizations on the same footing as States. Another possibility would have been to use the shorter phrase 'international community as a whole.' On reflection, and because the most important rules of international law are involved, the Commission thought it worthwhile to point out that, in the present state of international law, it is States that are called upon to establish or recognize peremptory norms.[234]

[233] YILC 1982, Vol II (Part Two), at 48, § 4 to Art 38.
[234] *Ibid*, at 56, § 3 to Art 53.

Concluding Remarks to Part Three

IN THE COURSE of the preparation for the 1969 Convention on the Law of Treaties, the drafters eventually decided that treaties concluded by international organisations possessed 'special characteristics' which warranted treatment in a separate instrument. When going through the *travaux préparatoires*, however, it is hard to escape the impression that inclusion of IGO treaties in the first Convention foundered prematurely on one particular problem: the attempt to devise a general provision on the treaty-making capacity of international organisations which would somehow distinguish between organisations that possessed such capacity and those that did not. This involves an element of stratification. An attempt was made to open up the internal legal order of organisations and to have international law capture the institutional varieties in a general rule.

That this is a difficult thing to do follows from the propositions in Parts One and Two above, and it is confirmed by the records of the second stage of the codification process. This began formally in 1971 when the ILC started its study for a second law of treaties Convention, which would cover IGO treaty-making by incorporating it in the *existing* body of rules.

Apart from a few givens, such as the absence of territorial sovereignty or the lack of *locus standi* before the International Court, it appears that all points of controversy in the preparation of the 1986 Vienna Convention involve the transparent image of organisations. This may be expressed as a question about the equality of organisations and states as legal subjects, or as an attempt to link the general norm to the institutional order of organisations. That institutional order at times equals the member states, and at times the 'competent organ' or the 'rules of the organisation'.

While the *travaux préparatoires* go to show the powerful presence of the transparent image of organisations, the final outcome of the process also shows something else. Every attempt to accommodate this image is ultimately blocked by the system of the law of treaties. Thus it seems inevitable that, while the 1986 Convention is textually similar to the 1969 Convention, in terms of legal effect it is practically identical.

For instance, the Convention distinguishes between treaties between states and organisations on the one hand, and treaties between organisations only on the other. This seems to have taken the place of the earlier preoccupation with the status of IGO treaties as such. The distinction is consistently maintained, but no legal consequences are attached to it –

arguably this would not have been possible, if only because the law of treaties was perceived by the drafters as a unified system.

Otherwise, distinctions in the 1986 Convention between states and organisations generally take one of the following patterns:

(a) Some changes are purely terminological, as in 'formal confirmation' by organisations, which is the equivalent of 'ratification' by states (Articles 11 and 14).
(b) There are references to the 'rules of the organisation' which defer a substantive decision to the actual treaty parties on a case-by-case basis. An example of such a procedural rule is Article 27(2), according to the interpretation given by Commission in its commentary.
(c) There are references to the rules of the organisation which reserves the operation of the institutional law of organisations, similar to the limitation in regard of the internal law of states. An example of such auto-limitation of international law is the reservation clauses in Articles 5 and 74(3).
(d) Some references to the rules of the organisation may have normative effect, but no normative force *per se* at the level of international law. One of several examples is Article 65(4). The specification that '[t]he notification or objection made by an international organization shall be governed by the rules of that organization' in a sense is empty, as it relates to the institutional procedure governing the expression of juridical will which binds the organisation at the international plane. But this is an expression to which international law in any event does not put any formal requirements. Thus the phrase does not encroach upon the general rule, but does not add normative substance to it either.

There are a few references to the institutional law of organisations in the 1986 Convention which possibly move through the institutional veil. That is to say, they have effect at the level of general international law – the level at which treaties are concluded and at which the law of treaties operates. Article 6 provides that the treaty-making capacity of an organisation is governed by the rules of the organisation. Although different interpretations of this (deliberately ambiguous) phrase exist, it probably should be taken as a reference to the competence, and especially the 'area of competence' or the 'functional limitation' of the organisation.[1] That is, a reference to the very boundaries of existence of the organisation – *ultra vires* therefore does not seem an appropriate term – which in practice are different in each case because of the organisation's functional, rather than sovereign-territorial, basis. Thus, if an organisation concluded a treaty on a

[1] See section 10.1.2 above.

subject outside its area of competence this would amount to a breach of the Convention. However, the effect of these provisions is limited. Neither Article 6 nor the Convention as a whole provide for a sanction of such breach, and Articles 27 and 46 in any event make it unlikely that contravention of institutional rules could be successfully invoked.

The same holds for Article 45(2)(b), which stipulates that the 'conduct' of the 'competent organ' be examined, rather than the conduct of the organisation as such. Another piece of distinctive wording in Article 45(2)(b) could also have practical weight: the condition that for an organisation to lose its right to invoke invalidity of consent '[it] must be considered as having renounced...', '*by reason of . . . conduct*'. All the same, this does come very close to the notion of 'acquiescence' for states.

Finally, there is the reverse situation, where the drafters made an attempt to set forth a general rule that would be operational in the institutional order of organisations. Examples are an early version of Article 27, of Article 62(2)[2] – which involved the (soon abandoned) possibility of acts by the *member states* constituting a 'fundamental change of circumstances' for the organisation – and, most importantly, draft Article 36*bis* on obligations for member states stemming from a treaty concluded by an organisation. As illustrated by the fate of these provisions, the effort was unsuccessful. The drafting history of Article 36*bis* – which is the lengthiest and perhaps the most intricate of all provisions – in particular makes clear why this is so. While organisations are transparent legal entities, the law of treaties is one-dimensional. It is geared to equal parties and to one-dimensional and indivisble *Normadressaten*. It therefore cannot accommodate layered subjects. Hence, in the law of treaties organisations appear as closed subjects, similar to states. Its rules do not have normative force within the legal order of organisations, and the institutional law of organisations does not have normative force at the level of the regular law of treaties.

[2] *Ibid.*

General Conclusions

11

The Invisible Continent: Concluding Remarks

INTERNATIONAL ORGANISATIONS, as they are not territorial entities, have been called 'the invisible continent'.[1] The metaphor can be used in addition to refer to the legal sphere within international organisations, which is partly visible but which also eludes general international law.

This book sets out to examine the role and position of international organisations as actors in international law. This is a pertinent inquiry, one reason being the prominent presence of organisations in international life and the need for a regular review of the way in which this presence is expressed legally. Another reason is the role of the state, which according to common contention is put under pressure by the rise of international bodies. Yet another reason is the new actors which are brought within the ambit of international law. Since international organisations are undoubtedly the non-state actors to have most successfully entered the international law system since the seventeenth century, it may give us some insight on how this process of inclusion works.

This book has chosen a formal perspective, in order to bring to light the phenomenon of the 'institutional veil'. It analyses the way in which, within the framework of positive international law, international organisations are conceptualised as legal entities *per se* and as subject of international law. It does so in a purposely rational manner, staying strictly within the positivist framework and proceeding from the classic voluntarist premises.[2] From this examination emerges a complex picture. The institutional veil of organisations turns out to be less impermeable than the sovereign veil of states. Organisations are transparent legal entities, with member states and component organs showing through to varying degrees. This may be in line with contemporary phenomena of multi-level governance, but it is at odds

[1] Johan Galtung, 'Non-Territorial Actors: The Invisible Continent (towards a typology of international organizations)', in Georges Abi-Saab (ed), *The Concept of International Organisation,* 1981, 67–75.

[2] Premises which on occasion are somewhat overdrawn for the sake of analytical stability; see section 2.1 above.

with the voluntarist setup of classic international law. This then is problematic for several reasons, ranging from practical questions of accountability to conceptual lacunae in the debate on the development of international law and its actors.

The choice of a positivist and formalist approach to the institutional veil means leaving unexplored various perspectives which may further explain its functioning. What is the social dynamic behind the oscillation between the open and closed image of international organisations? How does the organisation negotiate identity? What is the pull for lawyers and policy-makers to favour the open, functional view of organisations? What are the (geo)politics of the institutional veil? And what are its implications for non-state actors? These are questions which remain to be addressed. Such may be done by different approaches, ranging from functionalist and realist to 'disaggregationist'[3] theories to critical perspectives. The latter especially could be rewarding, as in our time the pertinent questions about international organisations undoubtedly revolve around power. International organisations have an ambiguous role in international life: they are part of the international establishment in a way that is unlike any other non-state actor, but they are also separate sources of political power competing with states. Organisations may be considered to sustain current Western liberal ideologies, but some will see them also as the best option for challenging these ideologies. Clearly an analysis of the multi-layered and elusive appearance of organisations and their bearing on international life would ultimately go beyond historical factors such as the state-based origin of organisations and realist accounts of the desire of states to remain 'masters of the treaty'.

This book, however, takes the approach of an immanent critique and aims to address the international law system on its own terms. The present chapter, in combination with the summarising remarks to Parts One, Two and Three, proposes some concluding observations on international organisations as legal entities and as subjects of international law – in the present context epitomised by the law of treaties. The first section focuses on the basic propositions of the book. The second section briefly recapitulates the way in which these propositions are confirmed by the legislative history of the Vienna Conventions on the law of treaties. The two sections that follow seek to place these findings in a broader framework: the third contains an excursus on the operation of the institutional veil in relation to legal responsibility of organisations, currently under study in the ILC; the fourth touches upon implications for general international law. Section Five concludes with some reflections on the systemic shortcomings brought

[3] See José Alvarez, *International Organizations as Law-Makers*, 2005, at 32–39.

out by the analysis, and on the value of the 'institutional veil' as an analytical tool to confront the challenges laid bare.

11.1 PROPOSITIONS ON THE INSTITUTIONAL VEIL

Our inquiry first leads to the conclusion, as described in Part One, that international organisations are in themselves transparent legal entities. Organisations constitute separate legal organisms, but they do not possess the notorious *impermeabilité* of states. Their legal image oscillates between 'open' and 'closed', with a dialectic relation between the two. Partly as a result organisations are to some extent legally transparent, and appear as layered structures – that is, the institutional order and member states remain visible[4] behind the institutional veil. The process of bringing organisations within the system of international law is marked by a tension between their layered character on the one hand and the one-dimensional character of the law, especially in branches based on 'procedural' equality such as the law of treaties, on the other. Ultimately the legal system prevails, as the legal order of necessity sets the terms for participation of legal subjects. All this becomes clear from the legislative (hi)story of the 1986 *Vienna Convention on the Law of Treaties Between States and International Organisations or Between International Organisations*, which is recounted in Part Three. This may be summarised by the following propositions.

Organisations are Semi-closed

International organisations are thus not legally impermeable in the way of states[5], but neither are they entirely open structures, in which case they would amount to an instance of classic, 'horizontal' international relations. Organisations may be called 'semi-closed' in that they, at least since the League era, have been attributed some sort of *separate* legal identity. This attribution generally revolves around the institutional feature of autonomy or *volonté distincte* of organisation vis-à-vis member states. It also entails an element of centralisation, a notion used already by Kelsen in the context of organisations, which distinguishes the institutional framework of an organisation from general international law. The institutional design of the organisation, then, lies in the hands of its founders, whose powers in this respect may be traced to the freedom of contract.

From this separate identity follows the idea that organisations possess a separate institutional legal order. This is not a daring conclusion, and it

[4] Or they are perceived as such, which in law is to a considerable extent the same thing.

[5] With all due qualification; see section 2.1 on the use of 'classical' premises.

seems undisputed in legal writing, or in positive international law, which in various instances accords an autonomous status to the internal law of organisations.[6] The separate character of the institutional order entails that the institutional rules and norms of themselves have no normative force in general international law – although they may have normative *effect*, ie legal consequences if international law so provides (for example by construing a state's contribution to the formation of custom on the basis of decisions taken in the organisation). Conversely, general international law, even if we assume the existence of a hierarchy of sorts,[7] does not automatically have normative force within the legal order of an organisation.

Organisations are Semi-open

Organisations are thus not entirely open structures, but they are neither entirely closed-off from general international law, as is the classic legal image of states. This accessibility, for which organisations may be called 'semi-open', is expressed for example in the observation of the International Law Commission that '...the internal law of an international organisation cannot be sharply differentiated from international law....'.[8] There are several interrelated reasons for this feature, which is not shared by other legal subjects.[9] One main factor is the composition of international organisations and their functional design. The component elements of organisations are eminent legal persons in their own right. More specifically, it is the nineteenth- century state, conceived as an 'original' subject of law analogous to the individual in domestic law (rather than the eighteenth-century state, perceived as a corporate entity itself and still in need of legitimation) that is the basis of contemporary international organisations.[10] Especially as state sovereignty has been taken as the foundation of modern international law, this creates a tension with the legal identity of organisations as such. Such may be visible in the institutional structure of an organisation,[11] but also in the political conviction that organisations are vehicles for states (as expressed in the

[6] See section 2.3.2 above.

[7] The discussion on 'dualism' and 'monism' lies outside the scope of this book, but it seems fair to say that at this point general international law, mostly construed on a voluntarist basis, does not provide for 'compulsory reception' in another legal order of whatever nature.

[8] Quoted more at length below, see note 58 and accompanying text.

[9] See Part One and Concluding Remarks to Part One.

[10] Section 3.1.

[11] Viz from the fact that modern international organisations are firmly state-based; eg decision-making competence with regard to matters not strictly related to the internal functioning of the organisation usually lies with the organ composed of state representatives, which often takes decisions by unanimity (cf Henry Schermers and Niels Blokker, *International Institutional Law*, 2003, § 379).

statement by Professor Alvarez, cited in Chapter 1 above, that '...IOs are not intended to be proto-states or governments in the making. They were and are established for limited purposes ..... They are institutions of limited and delegated powers, lacking the plenary rights of sovereigns under international law ...').

Moreover, organisations are established on a functional, rather than territorial basis.[12] That is, they have specific (fields of) competence without *a priori* territorial boundaries, rather than a general competence within specific territorial boundaries. Thus states and organisations do not overlap – witness for example the prominence of the 'implied powers doctrine' and the 'principle of speciality'.[13] An organisation's legal sphere is sectoral, and its actual competences or functions limited to a particular area of human action – be it food, disarmament or the internet. Its legal sphere is thus less inclusive and self-contained than that of a state, and is consequently conceptualised as more legally permeable.

The Inherent Transparency of Organisations

This particular doctrinal and systemic setup of organisations, coupled with their dual image – as vehicles for states and as independent actors – means that international organisations as legal creatures have a transparent quality. This is an essential but elusive trait. It means that member states and other institutional components to some extent are legally visible. Being 'legally visible' means that the component parts of an organisation are addressed from, and involved in, the general international plane. Put differently, organisations are layered creatures, 'conducting ... multilevel operations'.[14] The dual imagery and the transparency of the institutional veil appear in the social reality of international life (organisations *de facto* appear in two roles, as fora for states and as independent actors); in the legal-institutional structure of organisations (for example in the contrast between the functions and powers of an expert body and those of a state representative body); in institutional law and in international law doctrine (for one, because doctrine hinges on the tenet of state sovereignty); and in the minds of lawyers and policy-makers (who may have an interest in addressing member states directly). Doctrine is an especially powerful factor, as it is first of all a mind-set, and all the more complex because of the mixture of descriptive and normative arguments.

[12] Cf the sociological analysis by Nicholas Luhmann (*Das Recht der Gesellschaft* 577 paperback edn, 1995) who sees a shift from territoriality to functionality.

[13] Section 2.3.1.

[14] ILA Committee on Accountability of International Organisations (Third Report, 2002, New Delhi (70th) Conference, at 2)

The transparency of organisations is called 'inherent' because, in our time, it is part of the legal phenomenon of organisations themselves, as has been elaborated above. Whether it can actually be maintained depends on external factors. As argued below, the degree of transparency of the institutional veil varies according to the legal context in which the organisation finds itself.

The One-dimensional Character of International Law

International law so to speak *imposes* a one-dimensional mould on entities that act on their own accord. Of course it is perfectly possible for states (and organisations, if they are included in the norm-setting process) to agree on differing substantive rules for different legal subjects – compare for instance the *right* of a state to waive the immunity of an agent[15] with the *duty* of the United Nations Secretary-General to do so[16] – but international law will not be able to pierce the institutional veil and cover, by way of a general rule, the variety of institutional arrangements within the subject category of 'organisations'.

The basic mechanisms of international law (such as a formal, consensual law-making process) or branches of international law (such as the law of treaties) which are based on equality of subjects, are yet a different thing. These proceed from the idea of a one-dimensional contracting party (be it through 'express' or 'tacit consent'), and from the fiction of a unitary *Normadressat* or subject 'bearing' rights and duties after it has consented to be bound by those. The *Normadressat* of a primary norm is construed as indivisible[17] and thus must be either an organisation or the member state. It cannot be half or both at the same time, unless both are bound independently. Obviously this is different to the case in which an organisation and a member state both are addressee of a norm in their own right – as in the case of mixed agreements or in the application of customary law. Thus, if a rule is addressed to the organisation, it binds also the member states, but only in their quality of – and to the extent that they are – organic parts of the contracting party. For states this is traditionally construed in the same way.[18]

[15] Art 32 of the 1961 Vienna Convention on Diplomatic Relations (500 UNTS 95).

[16] Art V, s 20 of the 1946 Convention on the Privileges and Immunities of the United Nations (1 UNTS 15 and 90 UNTS 327).

[17] On the indivisibility of the subject in relation to international responsibility, see also note 40 below and accompanying text.

[18] Cf the statement in relation to states in the Blaskič case 'Each sovereign State has the right to issue instructions to its organs [...] and also to provide for sanctions or other remedies in case of non-compliance with those instructions. The corollary of this exclusive power is that each State is entitled to claim that acts or transactions performed by one of its organs in its official capacity be attributed to the State, so that the individual organ may not be held accountable for those acts or transactions'. (ICTY, *Prosecutor v Blaskič*, Case No

The inability of the law to accommodate a transparent, layered subject is illustrated by the hapless fate of draft Article 36*bis*,[19] which was meant somehow to include member states in the treaty obligations incurred by organisations. As it turned out, the organisation as a semi-closed structure constituted a final barrier to the operation of general international law – even if the institutional veil is more transparent than the ultimately corporate sovereign veil of the state.

Organisations as Independent Actors

Organisations of themselves are not monadic, one-dimensional legal creatures, and this feature seems crucial to the complexities of their participation in the international legal order. It has been a central issue in the conceptualisation of organisations as independent legal actors (see Part One), and as subjects of the law of treaties in particular (see Part Three), although it has never quite been rendered explicit.

The International Law Commission observed on several occasions during its preparatory work that 'the general principle of consensualism which constitutes the basis of any treaty commitment necessarily entails the legal equality of the parties'.[20] The reason why equality of organisations and states was an issue, can in turn be traced to the transparent image of organisations. As argued above, the law of treaties is geared to equal subjects. It follows that these must also be one-dimensional subjects, whose divergent, internal features cannot play a role. With the preliminary questions settled – the treaty-making capacity as a general disposition attributed by international law, and the 'area of competence' delimited by the constituting states – treaty-making organisations therefore cannot appear as anything but closed legal entities.

The International Law Commission gave an indication of the problem in its commentary to the 1982 final articles, when it observed:

> The source of many of the substantive problems encountered in dealing with this subject lies in the contradictions which may arise as between *consensuality* based on the equality of the contracting parties and the differences between States and international organisations.[21]

IT-95–14-AR108*bis*, Judgment on the request of the Republic of Croatia for review of the Decision of Trial Chamber II of 18 July 1997, Appeals Chamber, 29 October 1997, § 41. But see, for a contrary assumption, Ward Ferdinandusse, 'Out of the Black-box? The International Obligation of State Organs', 29 *Brooklyn Journal of International Law* 2003, 45–127.

[19] See section 10.1.4 above.

[20] Tenth Report on the Question of Treaties Concluded between States and International Organisations or Between Two or More International Organisations, YILC 1981, Vol II (Part Two), at 46.

[21] YILC 1982, Vol II (Part One), at 13, § 42 (italics in the original text).

The Special Rapporteur had stated earlier that '[i]nternational organizations are neither sovereign nor equal; all their powers are strictly at the service of their member states . . .'[22] These statements succinctly summarise the problem, but they leave implicit the structural tension which lies at the base. As argued above, the entry of organisations into the international scene has not simply added another subject to the catalogue of legal subjects, but also a new legal dimension. It is this dimension that the law of treaties – as any consensual law-making process or branch of law – has difficulty accommodating.

The Legal Order Overrides the Setup of the Subject

This difficulty is ultimately decided in favour of international law, as the legal order of necessity overrides the individual disposition of its subjects (as any set would 'determine' its elements). Organisations are therefore 'flattened out' when they act as independent subjects, as is exemplified – though not articulated – by the law of treaties codification process. One of the points this book seeks to make is that its transparent nature is denied when an organisation acts independently in the context of a consensual norm-setting process, or when a general international norm seeks to capture the internal institutional variety of organisations. Organisations are then reduced to one-dimensional entities, and thereby equated to states. And the operation of, for example, the law of treaties is delimited to the normative level of general international law. Perhaps the only exception is the 'area of competence' or the 'functional limitation' of the organisation[23] – that is, the very boundaries of its existence (which are different in each case because of the functional, rather than sovereign-territorial, basis of organisations). This, by definition, has normative effect on the plane of general international law. As the functional limitation of an organisation is located in the intersection between general international law and the law of the organisation, it could be even considered to amount to normative *force*.

All this is visible in practice, as described in Part Two on the basis of various forms of organisations' involvement in treaty practice. Although of themselves transparent, the legal manifestation of international organisations is flexible. The degree to which we are allowed to see through the institutional veil is dependent on the legal context in which an organisation finds itself.

[22] Sixth Report on the Question of Treaties Concluded between States and International Organisations or Between Two or More International Organisations, YILC 1977, Vol II (Part One), at 120, § 6.

[23] See section 10.1.2 above.

When serving as a forum for treaty-making[24] – ie when the IGO in a formal sense is not the author of a legal act – the organisation presents a predominantly open structure, in which (member) states and their legalised relations are largely governed by general international law. The institutional framework of the organisation, however, is never entirely open to general international law in the way of a classic inter-state diplomatic forum would be: the law of treaties is to some degree influenced by the institutional law of the organisation, or is barred from application altogether.[25]

When an organisation itself is at issue in that its constituent treaty is reviewed by international law,[26] its institutional order appears as partly screened off by the institutional veil. In comparison to regular international agreements a constituent treaty is less accessible to general international law, *in casu* the law of treaties.

When organisations then conclude treaties on their own accord,[27] which is where they themselves become subjects of the law of treaties, they manifest as closed legal structures. This is dictated by the formal treaty-making mechanism, as the institutional order and the member states cannot play a formal role at the general level. From a formal perspective (in the law of treaties essentially the only perspective) therefore the treaty-making practice of organisations turns out to be similar to that of states.

The dialectic between the open and closed conceptions of international organisations, and the tension between the transparency of organisations on the one hand and the one-dimensionality of international law on the other, have shaped legal doctrine on several points of debate: the attribution theory versus the implied powers theory with regard to the competences of international organisations;[28] the sovereign 'will' of the member states versus general international law as the source of legal personality and capacity of international organisations;[29] the constitutive instrument of an organisation as a treaty versus the constitutive instrument as a constitution;[30] and subjective legal personality versus objective legal personality for international organisations.[31] As stated before, it has also been

[24] Illustrated, notably by the United Nations system, in ch 5.

[25] Compare Arts 9(2) (a general rule for adoption of text which stems from UN institutional practice) and 5 (a no prejudice clause for inter alia 'treaties adopted within an international organisation') of the 1969 Vienna Convention.

[26] See ch 6.

[27] See section 7.1.

[28] See section 4.2.2.

[29] See section 4.2.3.

[30] See ch 6.

[31] See section 4.2.4.

a central, albeit implicit, element in the process of conceptualising organisations as subjects of the law of treaties.

Because of the overriding force of the setup of international law, the end result is something of a paradox. Voluntarist branches of the law, such as the law of treaties, are geared to unitary, one-dimensional actors. On the basis of that machinery, states create legal actors that are transparent, but whose layered character is subsequently flattened out, in order to once again fit the system.

11.2 THE INSTITUTIONAL VEIL IN THE CONVENTIONAL LAW OF TREATIES

The above propositions are confirmed by the drafting history of the two Vienna Conventions, which is discussed in Part Three above. Nearly all issues under discussion during the codification process were related to an effort, inspired by the image of organisations as transparent legal actors and functional vehicles for states, to connect the general law of treaties with the institutional order of organisations. However, as has been argued, this is a difficult thing to do. Hence the preliminary obstacle to inclusion of international organisations in the scope of the first Vienna Convention – the aim to have treaty-making capacity determined by the organisation's constituent treaty and at the same time by a general rule. And hence the predominantly cosmetic changes in the second Vienna Convention with respect to the provisions of the first Convention – a terminological distinction; a reference to the institutional law of organisations that adds no normative content to the general rule; or a rule of reservation, withholding the operation of international law at the borders of the institutional order of organisations. A genuine link between the law of treaties and the institutional law of organisations, with reciprocal normative effect, does not seem possible. This is epitomised by the story of draft Article 36*bis*.[32]

As the law of treaties is geared to one-dimensional and unitary actors, a substantive distinction between states and organisations cannot be made. Combined with the drafters' aim to create a unified body of rules (with a view to governing treaties between states on the one hand and between organisations on the other), this made it inevitable that the *dispositifs* of the two Conventions would end up as identical.[33]

One proposition already made is that the law of treaties is not capable of accommodating layered subjects. A second point is that, although in

[32] See section 10.1.4.

[33] '*Mutatis mutandis* identical…' – Karl Zemanek, International Organisations, Treaty-Making Power, in Rudolf Bernhardt (ed), *Encyclopedia of Public International Law*, Vol II, 1995, at 1346.

contemporary international life this is arguably an important weakness in the legal system, the transparent image of organisations and its uneasy union with the consensual legal setup has not been rendered explicit. While potentially a central analytical tool, it appears from the *travaux préparatoires* that this image has not been a factor in the conceptualisation of organisations as law of treaties subjects.

Meanwhile, the point is not that the 1986 Convention would be unable to cover the practice of international organisations. Apart from the fact that all provisions except for those on *jus cogens* are subsidiary norms to begin with, the Convention appears adequate both in its descriptive and its normative aspect. This means that no features of IGO treaty-making have surfaced which would require additional regulation; either because they would otherwise be left to customary law or because they would clash with existing conventional rules. A particular piece of practice, such as parallel decision-making by organisations comparable to parallel legislation by states, is a (by definition unilateral) law-making device which lies outside the scope of the law of treaties.

Genuine problems in IGO treaty practice seem to exist only where the institutional division of competences is concerned, notably the treaty-making activity of IGO organs which are not formally independent, such as the UNHCR or the UNEP.[34] For both such an organisation and its treaty partners this raises questions of bindingness, capacity and competence, and ultimately international responsibility. International relations would indeed benefit from some general rules on this issue. But, as has been argued, the law of treaties, operating at a general level, is precisely not the tool for such regulation. Within the classic international law paradigm, IGO institutional traits would have to be made uniform from the bottom up. This would be classic 'harmonisation' on a voluntary basis, subsequently formalised in, undoubtedly, a treaty.

With the benefit of hindsight we can say that the more economical approach would have been to include organisations right away in the scope of the 1969 Vienna Convention. The general reason why this did not happen is arguably that doctrinal developments – which originate with the open image of organisations as functional vehicles for states in the political as well as legal sense – had not reached a point where this was self-evident. Indeed, from the *travaux* of the first Convention (1950s and 1960s) emerges a more unbending doctrinal climate than from the *travaux* of the second Convention (1970s and 1980s), notably as regards the role of the state.

But the drawn-out process also has a strength. Because it was undertaken as a separate project, the codification of the law of treaties for

[34] See section 7.1.1.

organisations became a conscientious exploration of the legal nature of organisations and of the limits of the law of treaties system. It is all the more valuable as the procedural equality which lies at the root of the law of treaties mechanism brought this exercise to a head – while for instance the law on immunities, or on representation of states with organisations could not have that effect, although the feature of transparency is a helpful analytical tool here as well.[35] The 1986 Convention and its *travaux* are a valuable record of theoretical and doctrinal development, and also an example of some very subtle and ingenious drafting, notably on the part of the Special Rapporteur. While not a diplomatic success, the Convention is arguably as yet[36] the most important contribution to the formation of theory and doctrine on the subject. In formal terms it relates to the intersection of international institutional law and general international law; in a general sense, to the legal image of intergovernmental organisations.

11.3 THE INSTITUTIONAL VEIL AND INTERNATIONAL RESPONSIBILITY

New insights, however, may come from the process of including organisations in the other 'procedural' branch of international law: the law of international responsibility. The secondary norms triggered in the case of breach and budding doctrine on the responsibility of organisations, currently under study in the ILC, are outside the scope of this book. But in the present context one aspect must be addressed briefly, which is the position of the member states vis-à-vis that of the organisation. In the field of responsibility the connotation of the 'corporate veil' is particularly strong. Regarding the position of member states, clearly there is an analogy with the law of treaties,[37] albeit not a complete one.

Doctrine proceeds from the assumption that international organisations can be responsible for breaches of obligation in their own right, consistent with the idea that they can be the 'bearers' of a right or obligation. In addition, the default rule appears to be that such responsibility is not

[35] Cf the 1947 *Convention on the Privileges and Immunities of the Specialized Agencies* (33 UNTS 261) and its many annexes, and the 1975 *Vienna Convention on the Representation of States in their Relations with International Organisations of a Universal Character* (UN Doc A/Conf.67/16, not yet in force); see above notes 15 and 16 and accompanying text.

[36] This may change as the law of responsibility of international organisations is now under study in the ILC – see section 11.3 below.

[37] Cf Rosalyn Higgins, *Problems and Process*, 1994, at 278 et seq (on the question of the member states and draft Art 36*bis* as compared to responsibility of member states: 'in my view the analogy is precise').

coupled with *concurrent* responsibility on the part of the member states,[38] unless this is provided for in the organisation's constitution.[39] In other words, the organisation appears primarily as a closed legal entity, in the same way as when it independently assumes primary obligations under the law of treaties. In both cases doctrine maintains the principle of indivisibility of the subject,[40] although the law of responsibility does not *impose* the one-dimensional mould in the same way as the law of treaties, which turns on the equality of subjects. The reason there is no legal rule stating that member states are responsible alongside an organisation may be summarised, rather, as one of legal policy. A rule of primary responsibility for organisations fits the practice of several organisations, such as the United Nations which has on several occasions borne the cost of compensation for damages to third parties in the course of an operation.[41] The ILC has also adopted this line.[42]

The difference with the law of treaties context is that member states may assume a part in the responsibility of the organisation at a later stage through the mechanism of 'secondary responsibility', which is triggered once the organisation itself cannot meet its obligations. As for the position of member states, discussion appears to focus on this mechanism, which is the classic case of 'piercing' the legal veil of a corporate body. The

[38] 'Concurrent liability' in the sense of 'joint and several liability' is not covered here. Transposed to the context of creation of primary norms such as the law of treaties, this would amount to an organisation and its member states being party to a treaty separately and simultaneously. Moreover, the relation between the concepts of 'liability' and 'responsibility' is complex. 'Concurrent liability' would not necessarily imply simultaneous attribution of the wrongful act. Likewise the concept of 'dual or even mutual attribution' is not taken into account. Concurrent attribution of an *act*, on the other hand, would not necessarily mean that the obligation under international law – the breach of which leads to the wrongfulness – rests on both the organisation and the member states (see on attribution the 2004 ILC Report, UN Doc A/59/10, at 101, quote in § 4).

[39] See Schermers and Blokker, above, note 11, § 1585; an example would be the 1972 *Convention on International Liability for Damage Caused by Space Objects* which provides for joint and several liability of the organisation and its member states in case of damage caused by space activities of the organisation (UN Doc Res 2777 (XXVI), Art XXII.3).

[40] Referred to by the arbitral tribunal in the 1984 *Westland Helicopters Ltd* Award in relation to *international* responsibility: '[a] widespread theory, deriving from Roman law ('*Si quid universitati debetur, singulis non debetur, nec quod debet universitas singuli debent*': Digest 3, 4, 7, 1), excludes cumulative liability of a legal person and of the individuals which constitute it, these latter being party to none of the legal relations of the legal person'. (80 ILR 600, at 612); on indivisibility of the subject in relation to primary (treaty) norms, see also note 17 above and accompanying text.

[41] Cf Paul Szasz, 'The United Nations Legislates to Limit its Liability', 81 *American Journal of International Law* (1987), 739–744; and Schermers and Blokker, above, note 11, para 1583, citing the UN Office of Legal Affairs on the matter (UNJY 1980, at 184–185). Cf NATO which has compensated approx. $40,000 to a Bulgarian family for damage to their house by a deflected missile during the Kosovo campaign (*Trouw* 3-VIII-2000).

[42] Cf Art 3 (*general principles*) of the ILC draft articles on responsibility of international organisations, which applies the 'Chorzow factory principle' to organisations (2003 ILC Report, UN Doc A/58/10, at 45–49).

mechanism of the subsidiary piercing of the veil has been at issue also outside the hard and fast context of responsibility – for instance in relation to the exercise of diplomatic protection (*in casu* of a private company) in the 1970 *Barcelona Traction* case.[43] In a conceptually similar vein, the veil of an organisation or one of its organs may be pierced in a non-formal process, as in the opening up of the UN Security Council[44] or the General Assembly[45] to detect signs of *opinio juris* of individual states on the basis of voting behaviour.

In the formal sphere of international responsibility the existence of a general norm piercing the institutional veil, ie imposing secondary responsibility for member states, is doubtful at this point. Such was the conclusion of Professor Higgins in her 1989 Report for the *Institut de droit international.*[46] Such is also the approach of the ILC Special Rapporteur on Responsibility of Organisations, who in his 2006 Report proposed a draft provision stating that a member state is *not* affected by the responsibility of the organisation, 'unless: (a) it has accepted with regard to the injured third party that it could be held responsible; or (b) it has led the injured third party to rely on its responsibility'.[47]

The law of treaties does not have a mechanism of this kind, as it deals with primary norms only.[48] The contracting party and the *Normadressat* are one and the same. There is no such thing as 'secondary boundness'. The law of responsibility, on the other hand, is more flexible because of its subsidiary mechanism, and because it is less inherently at odds with the transparent nature of organisations as it does not stipulate equality of parties. The institutional veil in the law of responsibility therefore does not

[43] International Court of Justice, *The Barcelona Traction, Light and Power Company, Ltd (Belgium v Spain)*, Second Phase – Judgment, 5 February 1970, § 57 '...hence, the lifting of the veil is more frequently employed from without...'.

[44] Cf Walter Schilling, 'Der Schutz der Menschenrechte gegen Beschlüsse des Sicherheitsrats – Möglichkeiten und Grenzen', in 64 *Zeitschrift für ausländisches öffentliches Recht und Völkerrecht* 2004, 343–362.

[45] Cf. International Court of Justice, *Military and Paramilitary Activities in and Against Nicaragua (Nicaragua v United States of America)*, Judgment – Merits, 27 June 1986, §§ 188, 203, 204.

[46] 1989 Report for the *Institut de droit international* (with the IDI final report of 1994 in 'The Legal Consequences for Member States of the Non-Fulfilment by International Organisations of their Obligations Toward Third Parties', in 66 *Yearbook of the Institute of International Law* 1995, 251–469), at 284–285: '...there is no principle of general international law beyond this'. As for (scant) judicial practice, it may also be recalled that, in the absence of a pertinent provision in the 1981 Sixth International Tin Agreement, the majority of the UK Court of Appeal dismissed the claim of secondary liability on the part of the member states of the Tin Council (*MacLaine Watson v Dept of Trade*, (Kerr LJ) [1988] 3 All ER; 80 ILR (1989) 49).

[47] Article 29 – 'Responsibility of a State that is a member of an international organization for the internationally wrongful act of that organisation' (UN Doc A/CN.4/564 Add 2, at 14).

[48] Cf above note 40 and accompanying text.

have the same theoretical urgency – but its doctrinal and practical urgency may well exceed that of the law of treaties.[49]

While there are thus some differences in how the law of treaties and the law of responsibility are able to operate in regard to the institutional order of organisations, there is of course an important parallel: the difficulty in addressing the IGO legal order from the plane of general international law. As said above, for now there is no evidence of a general rule of responsibility which can be seen to override the institutional law of organisations or, alternatively, capture its variety. This is a general factor: organisations being semi-closed (see section 11.1 above), their institutional order poses to some degree a barrier to the operation of general international law. In the framework of the law of treaties this factor lies hidden behind the condition of procedural equality that is inherent in the contractual instrument. Already for that condition the internal legal order of organisations cannot play a role. But the result is the same in both the law of treaties and the law of responsibility: attempts to give expression to the layered structure of international organisations by way of a rule of general international law have not been successful. This raises the (familiar) question of whether public international law is even *capable* of prescribing a general rule in this regard.[50] The answer, as has been argued above, must be in the negative.

What then happens is that general international law can be seen to clear the way for the institutional law of the organisation, whether it be by a reservation clause, as in the law of treaties, or by a (doctrinal) practice to resort to the constitutional treaty of an organisation, as in the law of

[49] It is noteworthy that since the Tin Council crisis many commodity agreements are found expressly to exclude liability of member states (cf Catherine Brölmann, 'A Flat Earth? International Organisations in the System of International Law', in J Klabbers (ed), *International Organisations* (Library of Essays in International Law), 2005, 183–206 (reprint from Nordic JIL 2001), § 5).

[50] An in-depth study is Rosalyn Higgins' report of 1989 for the *Institut de droit international* (251–469), with annexed comments and the IDI final report of 1994 (above, note 46; see also CF Amerasinghe, 'Liability to Third parties of member States of International Organisations: Practice, Principle and Judicial precedent', 85 *American Journal of International Law* (1991), 259–280; Moshe Hirsch, *The Responsibility of International Organisations Towards Third Parties: Some Basic Principles*, 1995 – on the responsibility of organisations (chs 1–3) and on the responsibility of member states (notably chs 4, 5). A very broad scope was envisaged by the ILA Committee on Accountability of International Organisations (Second Report, 2000, London (69th) Conference, § 4 at 2); on the scope of the Committee's work and the notion of accountability see also the Third Report, above, note 14, at 4–6. The 2006 Report by the ILC Rapporteur (UN Doc A/CN.4/564 Add. 2) provides a good survey of doctrine on the issue of member state responsibiity; it incidentally also shows the complexity of the issue by the fact that it has to rely on the same cases and materials as the final Report of the IDI twelve years before.

international responsibility.[51] In either case the normative moment is transposed to the institutional order of the organisation, with the obvious consequence that there is no general legal rule for international actors to rely on.[52]

A saving principle, which perhaps will become part of 'the law of international organisations', would be the obligation for international organisations to make their respective institutional designs fully accessible to other actors on the international plane. This would have been one effect of the final version of draft Article 36*bis* on treaty obligations for member states of a contracting organisation, and it is also the purport of the 1995 proposals of the *Institut de droit international* on the liability of member states. Streamlining the cognisance of an organisation's institutional law by third parties appears to approximate the creation of a general international norm, but it is not quite the same. It means that international actors must familiarise themselves with the internal law of an international legal co-actor in each individual case. This is legally unproblematic (or so it seems from the lack of judicial decisions on this point), but it defeats the positivist objective of a general rule and indeed is perceived as burdensome in practice – as appears for instance from the treaty relations of the EC/EU.[53]

The work of the ILC on the responsibility of organisations for now addresses the institutional veil in a few instances. Apart from the issue of secondary responsibility on the part of member states,[54] the draft articles cover the 'Responsibility of a State in connection with the act of an international organization' – here no distinction is made between third states and member states.[55] The intricate draft provision on 'Use by a State that is a member of an international organization of the separate personality of that organization' does involve the institutional veil of the

[51] See the 1984 *Westland Helicopters Ltd* interim arbitral award (23 ILM 1071; 80 ILR 600); cf also draft Art 29(a) proposed by Special Rapporteur Gaja in his 2006 Report, quoted above (note 47 and accompanying text).

[52] Cf Brölmann, 'A Flat Earth?..'., above, note 49, § 5.

[53] On the cumbersome practice of EC and EU treaty partners requiring 'safeguard provisions', which is not pre-empted by the current law of treaties regime as laid down in the Vienna Conventions, see the study by Delano Verwey, *The European Community, The European Union and the International Law of Treaties*, 2004. The author proposes certain clarifying amendments to the text of the Vienna Conventions, especially in relation to mixed agreements (*ibid* at 262–268); while this would be useful and advisable for streamlining international treaty practice, it seems less urgent on theoretical grounds. The internal division of competences in an organisation and the ensuing division of competences as to adoption and reservations in essence follow from the law of treaties as it currently stands; likewise, the obligation for member states not to defeat object and purpose of a treaty to which an organisation is a party, exists automatically, insofar as the member state is an component part of the organisation and has 'transferred sovereignty' for a particular area of competence; see also below, note 61 and accompanying text.

[54] See above, note 47 and accompanying text.

[55] UN Doc A/CN.4/564 Add 1, paras 53–63.

organisation but essentially refers to the responsibility of member states independently, on the basis of pre-existing obligations, in the constellation of eg the 1999 ECHR *Waite and Kennedy* case.[56]

From the work of the ILC – in which references to the role of member states in the IGO law of treaties are scarce – it appears that the question of how to tackle the layered aspect of organisations is as yet unresolved. Thus, in its commentary to the general provision of Article 3,[57] the Commission emphasised the transparency of the institutional veil:

> ...the internal law of an international organisation cannot be sharply differentiated from international law. At least the constituent instrument of the international organisation is a treaty or another instrument governed by international law; some further parts of the internal law of the organisation may be viewed as belonging to international law.

But at the same time it noted the separate or *closed* aspect of the IGO institutional order:

> ... the relations between international law and the internal law of an international organisation appear too complex to be expressed in a *general* principle.[58]

11.4 THE INSTITUTIONAL VEIL IN GENERAL INTERNATIONAL LAW

In a general vein, the findings about international organisations and about their strained relation with the law of treaties contribute to our understanding of organisations and international law in several ways.

International Organisations and International Law

In the voluntarist vision of international law, an analysis of organisations and their place in the law of treaties has general explanatory force. As long as according to prevailing sources doctrine international law has a consensual basis – reflected in the practice of 'codification treaties' and the doctrinal emphasis on 'tacit consent' in the formation of custom – the law of treaties can serve as a test case for organisations and their potential for fully-fledged participation in formal norm-setting processes.

Moreover, many legal 'system rules' stipulate the equality and one-dimensionality of subjects because of the need to bring them into one category. The debate on the attribution of legal personality is a case in point. Thus, the account on the formal legal image of organisations in the UN era in Chapter 4 provides a background for the codification history of

[56] *Waite and Kennedy v Germany* [GC], No 26083/94, ECHR 1999-I.

[57] Stating that the characterisation of an act as wrongful under international law 'is not affected by the characterization of the same act as lawful by internal law'.

[58] 2003 ILC Report, UN Doc A/58/10, at 48 (emphasis added); cf section 10.1.5 above.

the IGO law of treaties recounted in Part Three, but it is also in itself an illustration of the legal transparency of organisations and the binary mould imposed by international law.

Finally, when equality of subjects is not at issue and *specific* norms may be designed to apply to international organisations – as for instance in the field of immunities[59] – the semi-closed character of the institutional order of organisations remains, with concomitant difficulties for access from the general international level. Here as well the notion of the institutional veil is a valuable tool in gaining the necessary awareness of the layered character of organisations and of the complexities of law and legal policy which it entails.

The Nature of International Law

As argued above, the way in which the law of treaties imposes a one-dimensional, closed mould on its subjects, provides an understanding of the binary and dualist setup of international law and formal law-making mechanisms (no reference intended to the different constitutional designs in states for the reception of international law).

This calls for two additional remarks. To refer to the dualist setup of international law is not to say that the gap between national and international law is not being bridged. However, in the positivist framework maintained in this book, the dynamic is geared upwards, not top-down. States are opening up their legal orders, but ultimately they are doing so of their own accord, for instance by assuming obligations under human rights treaties, or by designing their constitutions in an international law-friendly way.[60] A traditional case of the sovereign veil opening up is when a state unit is accorded competence to maintain (part of the) 'external relations' on its own accord to the exclusion of the federal state.

Supranational organisations present an analogous situation. This is why 'supranationality' is not of special interest in the context of this book, and has not been given separate attention in the previous chapters. In contrast to regular organisations, supranational organisations have taken on from their member states specific competences with an external dimension. That is, either the organisation or the member states are on the basis of *internal* rules predisposed, often exclusively, to deal with certain matters under *general* international law. Such a division of competences comes out for example in the conclusion of mixed agreements – the result is precisely that the individual treaty norms have only one *Normadressat*: either the organisation or the member states. In that case, as became implicitly clear from the intricate debate on Article 36*bis*, the institutional veil is lifted

[59] Above, note 35 and accompanying text.
[60] See above, note 34 and following text.

from within. Although in practice it may be problematic for an organisation's treaty partners to gain information on a division of competences,[61] on a formal level the problem of a transparent or layered legal actor no longer exists.[62]

Other Legal Subjects

Finally, the conceptualisation of international organisations has general relevance because, as part of the trend of 'New Medievalism'[63] or transnationalism, or any perspective that brings out the growing participation of non-state actors, international law is called upon to include ever more 'subjects'. Some of these will be legally transparent or layered in some way. This goes in particular for actors which are, in turn, component elements of another legal actor. As we have seen, such a constellation exists in the case of states that are both independent subjects and member states. But it also holds for individuals, as both independent actors and component parts of states, which in the context of international responsibility can give rise to *concurring* international obligations of states and individuals.[64]

11.5 THE POSITIVIST PERSPECTIVE ON THE INSTITUTIONAL VEIL

The aim of this book in the broadest sense is to give an analysis of the way in which the classic system of international law has incorporated and expressed the phenomenon of international organisations. This is done by way of a critique of the international law 'system', with the consequence that perspectives outside the positivist framework are omitted. The choice of method has been inspired by the fact that the paradigm of positive, consent-based and state-based law – for instance when it comes to the creation of legal rules and the creation of 'derived' legal subjects – is the daily bread of most international lawyers. Even where multifaceted practice is difficult to contain, it is within this paradigm that most scholars, law-makers and practitioners move about, develop their thoughts and seek legally to capture their social reality. Paradigms then have not only

[61] On the 'safeguard provisions' in treaties concluded by the EC or EU see above, note 53.

[62] Cf Paul Reuter, *Introduction to the Law of Treaties*, 1995: (with regard to the access of international organisations to certain multilateral treaties) 'In all those cases it is restricted to organizations enjoying powers transferred to them by their member States, essentially in fact the European Communities. *As the Communities do not exactly fit the mould of international organisations, such precedents carry little weight*' (at 77, emphasis added).

[63] Jörg Friedrichs, 'The Meaning of New Medievalism', 7 *European Journal of International Relations* 2001, 475–502.

[64] Cf André Nollkaemper, 'Concurrence between individual responsibility and state responsibility in international law', in 52 *International and Comparative Law Quarterly* 2003, 615–640.

descriptive, but also normative force, as they tend to press experience into a pre-existing mould. It is thus useful to address the system in itself, and to examine its ability to accommodate new phenomena of social and political organisation.

When that capability is lacking, it is problematic for more reasons than just theoretical comprehensiveness. But why is the particular legal setup of organisations a problem? Is not the state at the same time a self-contained entity and part of a larger whole, an organisation? To be sure, the open and the closed image of organisations can exist side by side, and make their appearance depending on the perspective one takes. What is problematic is the oscillation between these two images, the ensuing transparent legal setup of organisations and the difficulty of international law in accommodating that transparency.

In legal practice, this difficulty leads first of all to a problem that can be summarised as one of accountability. Because of the different layers involved in the organisation's 'external relations', the locus of accountability is not always clear. In a formal-legal framework, as discussed in section 11.3 above, this is visible in the field of legal responsibility, where the role and position of the member states next to the organisation continue to be an uncertain factor.

But the institutional veil also complicates the broader mechanisms of accountability and prerequisites thereto. For example it may be uncertain whether member states are bound by the obligations of the organisation (an intensely debated and unresolved question in the process of fine-tuning the *pacta tertiis* rule for organisations in the law of treaties); or whether the organisation is bound by the obligations of the member states (a question in the 1999 *Matthews* case before the ECHR);[65] or whether an organ incurs legal obligations in its own right or on behalf of the organisation (a recurring question in relation to UN organs such as the UNHCR); or whether stakeholders have to address the organisation or the member states on the implementation of an agreement (which may be at issue for a host state regarding an organisation's observer or peace-keeping mission) or on reparation (as was the question in the Tin Council cases). These examples have relatively formal settings, but the complex dynamic that comes with the involvement of a layered legal actor essentially remains at any degree of (in)formality. Or, approached from a different angle, the institutional veil is a factor also when law is not taken as a set of 'rules' or past decisions, but as 'a continuous process of authoritative decision-making'.[66]

[65] *Matthews v The United Kingdom* Application No 24833/94 [1999] ECHR 12 (18 February 1999).

[66] Cf the perspective of the New Haven School as articulated by Rosalyn Higgins, *Problems & Process, International Law And How We Use It*, 1994, 1–12.

Classic international law is not equipped to deal with this complexity. In the words of the ILA Committee on Accountability of International Organisations, '[t]he variety of legal layers providing flexibility for IOs when conducting their multilevel operations has to be matched by a comprehensive set of yardsticks leaving no loopholes at each individual legal level'.[67] It is telling that the Committee did not resort to the discourse of *lex lata* and *ferenda*, but concluded its impressive study with 'recommended rules and practices'.

This book has argued that international organisations are dynamic and layered legal creatures, but that their particular nature does not have full play in positive international law. This tends to impose a crude division on the legal landscape. Law is either municipal law or international law. Treaty-making subjects are unitary, one-dimensional legal actors or they are not subjects at all. These may seem mundane considerations – as if international law consisted only of technicalities, as if the view of law as an autonomous system of constraining rules had not come to be superseded, and as if the formalist, binary view of law-making had not come under pressure. But it is important to keep in mind that this is the framework used by many in theory and practice. On a dramatic note it could be said that in those respects where international law cannot accommodate the transparency of international organisations, it also lacks the ability to accommodate developments of multilevel governance and the involvement of non-state actors in the international community at large.

In order to legally involve and address 'each individual legal level' mentioned by the ILA Committee, the formal legal framework also will ultimately need to be reconstituted. For this to be possible a theoretical awareness of the transparent setup of organisations is indispensable. This leads to the second problematic aspect of the legal conceptualisation of international organisations – one that does not have an immediate bearing on international practice, but carries equal weight. The layered aspect of organisations – symbolised in this book by the transparent institutional veil – is elusive. It has for the most part not been articulated and does not seem to be part of the analytical tools used in the debate on the development of international law. By examining this stratification and its role in international law, this book aims to make a contribution to the debate on the reconstitution of the international law system. The open–closed framework and the notion of the institutional veil allow us more sharply to conceptualise international organisations as legal entities and thereby as international players in an increasingly multilevelled international life.

[67] ILA Third Report 2002, above, note 14, at 2.

Annexes

THE TABLES OF comparison in Annexes I and II use three categories of text qualification: ID (identical), ED (editorial change) and SUB (substantive change).

'Identical' are the articles which adopt the corresponding provision of the 1969 Convention, whether or not with a distinction between states and organisations (see below). 'Editorial' indicates changes that are textual in nature, whether they relate to drafting in general (eg Article 3) or to terminology (eg 'formal confirmation' as the equivalent of 'ratification' in Article 11).[1] The category of 'substantive changes' includes Articles which differ from the corresponding provisions in the 1969 Convention as to their substance. This includes eg provisions which refer to 'the rules of the organisation' without a parallel reference to the law of states in the 1969 Convention, such as Article 6. As is argued in Chapter 9, such difference in legal substance does not necessarily imply a difference in legal *effect* for states and organisations respectively. Conversely, an identical wording such as in Articles 53 and 62, may imply a substantial difference in effect, at least on the doctrinal plane.

In principle provisions are referred to in their entirety; where appropriate, the paragraph which is the basis for a specific qualification is indicated between square brackets.

Annex III contains the list of 1969 Convention articles earmarked by the ILC and the UNGA Sixth Committee as potentially 'problematic' when transposed to a new convention on the law of treaties for organisations. During the Vienna Conference these provisions were referred to the Committee on the Whole (rather than to the Plenary Conference straight away) for more extensive discussion.

Annex IV, by way of illustration of Chapter 9, puts some provisions of the 1969 Convention next to their counterparts of the 1986 Convention.

[1] Cases in which the 1969 provision (eg Art 20(4)a) refers to '*another* contracting state', while the corresponding 1986 provision mentions 'contracting state' rank under 'identical' (+ or ++). Omission of the word 'another' is not ground for listing under 'editorial'. Neither is the reference to a changed article number.

Annex I. TABLE OF COMPARISON: ARTICLES 1986 CONVENTION AND ARTICLES 1969 CONVENTION

An additional classification is made of i) provisions which do not distinguish between parties; ii) provisions which, next to 'states', mention 'international organisations' [+]; and iii) provisions which make a distinction between treaties between states and IGOs, on the one hand, and treaties between IGOs only, on the other [++].

1986 Convention Articles

ID	2(1)b; 26; 28; 31; 32; 33; 41; 53; 55; 56; 58; 59; 61; 64; 68; 71; 72; 81
ID+	2(1)d; 2(1)b*ter*; 2(1)c, e-i; 2(2); 8; 19; 21; 22; 23; 34; 38; 40; 42 [§1]; 43; 44 [§4]; 47; 48; 49; 50; 51; 52 [title]; 54; 57; 60; 63; 69 [§4]; 70 [§2]; 76; 78; 79; 80
ID++	2(1)a; 4; 10; 12; 13; 15; 16; 17; 20; 24; 25; 77
ED	
ED+	11; 14[§§2, 3]; 18; 27; 62 [§2]
ED++	3
SUB	1; 2(1)*bis*; 2(1)j; 5; 6; 7; 9 [§b]; 29; 30; 35; 36 [§2]; 37 [§3]; 39; 45; 46; 65 [§4]; 66; 67; 73; 74; 75; [final clauses] 82; 83; 84; 85; 86; Annex

Annex II. TABLE OF COMPARISON: ARTICLES 1986 CONVENTION AND DRAFT ARTICLES 1982

An additional classification is made on the basis of degree of differentiation between states and organisations. Here [+] means that the 1986 provisions are 'more differentiated' than the draft Articles, and [-] that they are 'less differentiated'. Omission of 'relevant' in 'the rules of the organisation' is taken to count as an editorial change. Note that the draft Articles contained no final clauses (82–86).

1986 Convention Articles

ID	1; 2(1) a, b, d-I; 2(2); 4; 8; 10; 11; 13; 14; 15; 16; 18; 21; 23; 24; 26; 27; 28; 29; 31; 32; 33; 34; 36; 38; 39; 40; 41; 42; 43; 44; 45; 48; 49; 50; 51; 53; 55; 56; 58; 59; 60; 61; 62; 63; 64; 67; 68; 69; 70; 71; 72; 75; 76; 77; 79; 80; 81
ID-	12; 17; 22; 35; 37; 54; 57; 78
ED	52 [title]

ED- 6; 25; 47; 65 [§4]
SUB 3; 5; 7; 9; 19; 20 [§5]; 30 [§6]; 46; 66; 73 [added at Conference]; 74

Annex III. ARTICLES OF THE 1969 CONVENTION MARKED AS 'PROBLEMATIC' FOR THE PURPOSE OF THE 1986 VIENNA CONFERENCE

By UNGA Resolution UN Doc A/40/76 (11 December 1985), Annex II, the following articles of the 1969 Convention were marked as 'problematic' in the transposition to a new convention:[2]

List of draft articles of the basic proposal, for which substantive consideration is deemed necessary (a)

1. Article 2(b) 'Use of terms'
2. Article 3 'International agreements not within the scope of the present articles'
3. Article 5 'Treaties constituting international organisations and treaties adopted within an international organisation'
4. Article 6 'Capacity of international organizations to conclude treaties'
5. Article 7 'Full powers and powers'
6. Article 9 'Adoption of the text'
   - paragraph 2

   a) It is understood that if certain changes to the articles listed above were approved by the Conference, consequential changes might have to be introduced in other draft articles.

   b) It is noted that since draft article 2 sets out definitions, its provisions should not be considered separately but in conjunction with the substantive consideration of other articles to which those definitions are closely related.
7. Article 11 'Means of expressing consent to be bound by a treaty'
   - paragraph 2 (arts 14.3, 16, 18 and 19.2 are closely related to this paragraph)
8. Article 19 'Formulation of reservations'
9. Article 20 'Acceptance of and objection to reservations'
10. Article 27 'Internal law of States, rules of international organizations and observance of treaties'
11. Article 30 'Application of successive treaties relating to the same subject-matter'
    - paragraph 6

[2] Cf the 1971 preliminary report on the topic which proposed (on the basis of a questionnaire prepared by the sub-committee) an informal list of provisions needing special consideration: arts 6, 7–17, 34–38, 47 ff, 54, 63, 66 (YILC 1971, Vol II (Part Two), at 188, §§ 14–22).

12. Article 36*bis* 'Obligations and rights arising for States members of an international organization from a treaty to which it is a party'
13. Article 38 'Rules in a treaty becoming binding on third States or third organizations through international custom'
14. Article 45 'Loss of a right to invoke a ground for invalidating, terminating, withdrawing from or suspending the operation of a treaty'
15. Article 46 'Provisions of internal law of a State and rules of an international organization regarding competence to conclude treaties'
    - paragraph 2
    - paragraph 3
    - paragraph 4
16. Article 56 'Denunciation of or withdrawal from a treaty containing no provision regarding termination, denunciation or withdrawal'
17. Article 61 'Supervening impossibility of performance'
18. Article 62 'Fundamental change of circumstances'
19. Article 65 'Procedure to be followed with respect to invalidity, termination, withdrawal from or suspensions of the operation of a treaty'
    - paragraph 3
20. Article 66 'Procedures for arbitration and conciliation'
21. Article 73 'Cases of succession of States, responsibility of a State or of an international organization, outbreak of hostilities, termination of the existence of an organization and termination of participation by a State in the membership of an organization'
22. Article 75 'Case of an aggressor State'
23. Article 77 'Functions of depositaries'
24. Annex 'Arbitration and conciliation procedures established in application of Article 66'

Annex IV. SOME PARALLEL PROVISIONS OF THE 1986 CONVENTION AND THE 1969 CONVENTION

1969 Convention	1986 Convention
Article 2 (*Use of terms*) 1. 'For the purposes of the present Convention:' [—-]	Article 2 (*Use of terms*) 1. 'For the purposes of the present Convention:' [...] (b *bis*) 'act of formal confirmation' means an international act corresponding to that of ratification by a State, whereby an international organisation establishes on the international plane its consent to be bound by a treaty;
Article 6 (*Capacity of States to conclude treaties*) 'Every State possesses capacity to conclude treaties.'	Article 6 (*Capacity of international organisations to conclude treaties*) 'The capacity of an international organisation to conclude treaties is governed by the rules of that organisation.'
Article 27 (*Internal law and observance of treaties*) A party may not invoke the provisions of its internal law as justification for its failure to perform a treaty. This rule is without prejudice to article 46.	Article 27 (*Internal law and observance of treaties*) 1. 'A State party to a treaty may not invoke the provisions of its internal law as justification for its failure to perform the treaty. 2. An international organisation party to a treaty may not invoke the rules of the organisation as justification for its failure to perform the treaty. 3. The rules contained in the preceding paragraphs are without prejudice to article 46.'

1969 Convention	1986 Convention
Article 30 (*Application of successive treaties relating to the same subject-matter*) 'Subject to Article 103 of the Charter of the United Nations, the rights and obligations of States parties to successive treaties relating to the same subject-matter shall be determined in accordance with the following paragraphs. ... [—]	Article 30 (*Application of successive treaties relating to the same subject-matter*) 1. 'The rights and obligations of States and international organisations parties to successive treaties relating to the same subject-matter shall be determined in accordance with the following paragraphs. ... 6. The preceding paragraphs are without prejudice to the fact that, in the event of a conflict between obligations under the Charter of the United Nations and obligations under a treaty, the obligations under the Charter shall prevail.'
Article 34 (*General rule regarding third States*) A treaty does not create either obligations or rights for a third State without its consent.	Article 34 (*General rule regarding third States and third organisations*) A treaty does not create either obligations or rights for a third State or a third organisation without the consent of that State or that organisation.
Article 35 (*Treaties providing for obligations for third States*) An obligation arises for a third State from a provision of a treaty if the parties to the treaty intend the provision to be the means of establishing the obligation and the third State expressly accepts that obligation in writing.	Article 35 (*Treaties providing for obligations for third States or third organisations*) An obligation arises for a third State or a third organisation from a provision of a treaty if the parties to the treaty intend the provision to be the means of establishing the obligation and the third State or the third organisation expressly accepts that obligation in writing. Acceptance by the third organisation of such an obligation shall be governed by the rules of that organisation.

1969 Convention	1986 Convention
Article 36 (*Treaties providing for rights for third States*)	Article 36 (*Treaties providing for rights for third States or third organisations*)
A right arises for a third State from a provision of a treaty if the parties to the treaty intend the provision to accord that right either to the third State, or to a group of States to which it belongs, or to all States, and the third State assents thereto. Its assent shall be presumed so long as the contrary is not indicated, unless the treaty otherwise provides.	1. A right arises for a third State from a provision of a treaty if the parties to the treaty intend the provision to accord that right either to the third State, or to a group of States to which it belongs, or to all States, and the third State assents thereto. Its assent shall be presumed so long as the contrary is not indicated, unless the treaty otherwise provides.
2. A State exercising a right in accordance with paragraph 1 shall comply with the conditions for its exercise provided for in the treaty or established in conformity with the treaty.	2. A right arises for a third organisation from a provision of a treaty if the parties to the treaty intend the provision to accord that right either to the third organisation, or to a group of international organisations to which it belongs, or to all organisations, and the third organisation assents thereto. Its assent shall be governed by the rules of the organisation.
[—]	3. A State or an international organisation exercising a right in accordance with paragraph 1 or 2 shall comply with the conditions for its exercise provided for in the treaty or established in conformity with the treaty.

1969 Convention	1986 Convention
	Article 36 *bis* (*Obligations and Rights arising for States members of an international organisation from a treaty to which it is a party*) 'Obligations and rights arise for States members of an international organisation from the provisions of a treaty to which that organisation is a party when the parties to the treaty intend those provisions to be the means of establishing such obligations and according such rights and have defined their conditions and effects in the treaty or have otherwise agreed thereon, and if: (a) the States members of the organisation, by virtue of the constituent instrument of that organisation or otherwise, have unanimously agreed to be bound by the said provisions of the treaty; and the assent of the States members of the organisation to be bound by the relevant provisions of the treaty has been duly brought to the knowledge of the negotiating States and the negotiating organisations.'
Article 73 (*Cases of State succession, State responsibility and outbreak of hostilities*) The provisions of the present Convention shall not prejudge any question that may arise in regard to a treaty from a succession of States or from the international responsibility of a State or from the outbreak of hostilities between States.	Article 74 (*Questions not prejudged by the present Convention*) 1. The provisions of the present Convention shall not prejudge any question that may arise in regard to a treaty between one or more States and one or more international organisations from a succession of States or from the international responsibility of a State or from the outbreak of hostilities between States.

1969 Convention	1986 Convention
	2. The provisions of the present Convention shall not prejudge any question that may arise in regard to a treaty from the international responsibility of an international organisation, from the termination of the existence of the organisation or from the termination of participation by a State in the membership of the organisation. 3. The provisions of the present Convention shall not prejudge any question that may arise in regard to the establishment of obligations and rights for States members of an international organisation under a treaty to which that organisation is a party.

Select Bibliography of Authors

ABBOTT, KENNETH W, 'International Relations Theory, International Law, and the Regime Governing Atrocities in Internal Conflicts', in Steven Ratner and Ann-Marie Slaughter (ed), *American Journal of International Law: Symposium on Method in International Law,* 1999, 361–378

ABEYRATNE, RUWANTISSA IR, 'Law Making and Decision Making Powers of the ICAO Council – A Critical Analysis', 4 *Zeitschrift fur Luft-und Weltraumrecht* 1992, 387–394

ABI-SAAB, GEORGES (ed), *The Concept of International Organisation,* Paris, UNESCO, 1981

AKANDE, DAPO, 'The Jurisdiction of the International Criminal Court over Nationals of Non-Parties: Legal Basis and Limits', 1 *Journal of International Criminal Justice* 2003, 618–650

ALEXANDROWICZ, CHARLES H, *The law-Making Functions of the Specialised Agencies of the United Nations,* Sydney, Angus and Robertson, 1973

ALLOTT, PHILIP, 'Language, Method and the Nature of International Law', 45 *British Yearbook of International Law* 1971, 79

——, 'State Responsibility and the Unmaking of International Law', 29 *Harvard International Law Journal* 1988, 1–26

——, 'Mare Nostrum: A New International Law of the Sea', 86 *American Journal of International Law* 1992, 764–787

——, 'The Concept of International Law', 10 *European Journal of International Law* 1999, 31–50

——, *The emerging universal legal system* (2002), Amsterdam Center for International Law seminar on theoretical approaches to the relationship between international and national law, 20 September 2002, Amsterdam

——, *The Health of Nations: Society and Law beyond the State,* Cambridge, Cambridge University Press, 2002

ALVAREZ, JOSÉ E, *International Organisations as Law-Makers,* Oxford, OUP, 2005

AMERASINGHE, CF, 'Liability to Third parties of member States of International Organisations: Practice, Principle and Judicial precedent' 85 *American Journal of International Law* 1991, 259–280

——, 'International Legal Personality Revisited', 47 *Austrian Journal for Public International Law* 1995, 123–145

——, *Principles of Institutional Law of International Organisations,* Cambridge, Cambridge University Press, 1996

——, 'Review of "The responsibility of International Organisations toward Third Parties"', 45 *International and Comparative Law Quarterly* 1996, 752–754

ANZILOTTI, DIONISIO, *Corso di diritto internazionale,* Rome, Athenaeum, 1928

——, *Corso di Diritto Internazionale,* Padova, CEDAM, 1955

——, *Scritti di Diritto Internazionale Pubblico,* Padova, CEDAM, 1956

ARANGIO-RUIZ, GAETANO, 'The "Federal Analogy" and UN Charter Interpretation: A Crucial Issue', 8 *European Journal of International Law* 1997, 1–28

——, 'Dualism revisited: international law and interindividual law', LXXXVI *Rivista di Diritto Internazionale* 2003, 909–999

ARCHER, CLIVE, *International Organisations,* London, Routledge, 1992

AUST, ANTHONY, *Modern Treaty Law and Practice,* Cambridge,Cambridge University Press, 2000

AVINERI, SHLOMO, *Hegel's theory of the modern state,* Cambridge, Cambridge University Press, 1972

BARBERIS, JULIO, 'Nouvelles questions concernant la personnalité juridique internationale', I79/I *Recueil des Cours de l'Academie de droit international* 1983, 145–304

——, 'Los Limites del Tratado Internacional', in (ed), *Pensamiento Juridico y Sociedad Internacional (Estudios en honor del professor Antonio Truyol Serra),* 1986, 173–192

BARTON, JOHN H, 'Two Ideas of International Organisation', in Michigan Law Review Association: *The Art of Governance (Festschrift zu Erven Eric Stein),* Baden Baden, Nomos Verlag, 1987, 382–394

BASDEVANT, JULES, 'La Conclusion et la Rédaction des Traités et des Instruments diplomatiques autres que les Traités', in 15 *Recueil des Cours de l'Academie de droit international,* 1926, 535–643

BEAULAC, STÉPHANE, 'The Westphalian Legal Orthodoxy – Myth or Reality?' *Journal of the History of International Law* 2000, 148–177

BEDERMAN, DAVID J, 'The Souls of International Organisations: Legal Personality and the Lighthouse at Cape Spartel', 36 *Virginia Journal of International Law* 1996, 275–377

——, 'I Hate International Law Scholarship (Sort of)', 1 *Chicago Journal of International Law* 2000, 75–84

——, *The Spirit of International Law,* University of Georgia Press, 2002

BEKKER, PIETER, *The Legal Position of Intergovernmental Organisations: A Functional Necessity Analysis of Their Legal Status and Immunities,* Dordrecht, Martinus Nijhoff, 1994

BERNÁRDEZ, SANTIAGO TORRES, 'Interpretation of Treaties by the International Court of Justice Following the Adoption of the 1969 Vienna

Convention on the Law of Treaties', in Gerhard Haffner and Gerhard Loibl et al (eds), *Liber Amicorum Professor Seidl-Hohenveldern,* The Hague, Kluwer Law International, 1998, 721–748

BERNHARDT, RUDOLF, 'Treaties', 7 *Encyclopedia of Public International Law* 1984, 459–464

——, 'Evolutive Treaty Interpretation, especially of the European Convention on Human Rights', 42 *German Yearbook of International Law* 1999, 11–25

BINDSCHEDLER, RUDOLF L, 'International Organisations: General Aspects', 5 *Encyclopedia of Public International Law* 1983, 119–140

BLECKMANN, ALBERT, *Grundprobleme und Methoden des Völkerrechts,* Freiburg/München, Verlag Karl Alber, 1982

BLIX, HANS, 'The requirement of Ratification', XXX *British Yearbook of International Law* 1953, 352–380

——, *Treaty-making power,* London/New York, Stevens and Sons/ Frederick A Praeger, 1960

BOLINTINEANU, ALEXANDER, 'Expression of Consent to be bound by a treaty in the light of the 1969 Vienna Convention', 68 *American Journal of International Law* 1974, 672–686

BOTHE, MICHAEL, 'Die Wiener Konvention über das recht der Verträge zwischen Staaten und internationalen Organisationen und zwischen internationalen Organisationen', 44 *Neue Juristische Wochenschrift* 1991, 2169–2174

BOWETT, DEREK, *The Law of International Institutions,* London, Stevens and Sons, 1982

BOYLE, JAMES, 'Is Subjectivity Possible? The Postmodern Subject In Legal Theory', 62 *University of Colorado Law Review* 1991, 489

BRÖLMANN, CATHERINE, 'The Legal Nature of International Organisations and the Law of Treaties', 4 *Austrian Review of International and European Law* 2000, 85–125

——, 'A Flat Earth? International Organisations in the System of International Law', in J Klabbers (ed), *International Organisations*, Series: Library of Essays in International Law, Ashgate, 2006, pp 183–206 (reprint from Nordic JIL 2001)

BROWNLIE, IAN, *Principles of Public International Law,* Oxford, Clarendon Press, 2003

CAFLISCH, LUCIUS, 'Unequal Treaties', 35 *German Yearbook of International Law* 1993, 52–80

CANFORA, LUCIANO ET AL, *I trattati nel mondo antico,* Roma, 1990

CANSACCHI, GIORGIO, *Istituzioni di diritto internazionale pubblico,* Torino, G Giappichelli, 1983

CAPOTORTI, FRANCESCO, *La Convenzione di Vienna sul Diritto dei Trattati,* Padova, CEDAM, 1984

CAPPS, PATRICK, 'The Kantian Project in Modern International Legal Theory', 12 *European Journal of International Law* 2001, 1003–1025

CARTY, ANTHONY, 'Critical International Law: Recent Trends in the Theory of International Law', 2 *European Journal of International Law* 1991, 66–96

CASS, DEBORAH, 'Navigating the Newstream: recent critical Scholarship IN INTERNATIONAL LAW', 65 *Nordic Journal of International Law* 1996, 341–383

CASSESE, ANTONIO, 'Remarks on Scelle's Theory of 'Role Splitting': (*dedoublement fonctionel*) in International Law', 1 *European Journal of International Law* 1990, 210–231

CASTRO RIAL, JUAN MANUEL, 'States, Sovereign Equality', in (ed), *Encyclopedia of Public International Law,* Heidelberg, Max Planck Institut, 1981, 477–481

CHARLESWORTH, HILARY, and CHRISTINE CHINKIN, *The Boundaries of international Law: A Feminist Analysis,* Manchester University Press, 2000

CHAUMONT, CHARLES M, 'La signification du principe de spécialité des organisations internationales', in (ed), *Melanges offerts à Henri Rolin,* Paris, Pedone, 1964,

CHAYES, ABRAM, and ANTONIA HANDLER CHAYES, *The New Sovereignty: Compliance with International Regulatory Agreements,* Cambridge Massachusetts, Harvard University Press, 1995

CHINKIN, CHRISTINE, *Third Parties in International Law,* Oxford, Clarendon Press, 1993

CHIU, HUNGDAH, *The Capacity of International Organisations to Conclude Treaties, and the Special Legal Aspects of the Treaties so Concluded,* The Hague, Martinus Nijhoff, 1966

CHOATE, JOSEPH H, *The Two Hague Conferences,* Princeton, Princeton University Press, 1913

CHURCHILL, ROBIN R and GEIR ULFSTEIN, 'Autonomous Institutional Arrangements in Multilateral Environmental Agreements: A Little-Noticed Phenomenon in International Law', 94 *American Journal of International Law* 2000, 623–659

CLAUDE, INIS L, *Swords into Ploughshares: The Problems and Progress of International Organisation,* New York, Random House, 1971

CONFORTI, BENEDETTO, 'Le Rôle de l'accord dans le système des Nations Unies', in 142 *Recueil des Cours de l'Académie de droit international,* 1974-II, 203–288

CORBETT, PERCY, 'What is the League of Nations?' V *British yearbook of International Law* 1924, 119–148

CRAVEN, MATTHEW, 'Legal differentiation and the concept of the human rights treaty in international law', 11 *European Journal of International Law* 2000, 489–519

CULLET, PHILIPPE, 'Differential Treatment in International Law: Towards a New Paradigm of Inter-state Relations', 10 *European Journal of International Law* 1999, 549–582

DALTON, RICHARD KEARNEY and ROBERT, 'The Treaty on Treaties', 64 *American Journal of International Law* 1970, 495–561

D'AMATO, ANTHONY (ed), *International Law Anthology,* Cincinnati Oh, Anderson Publishing Company, 1994

DANILENKO, GENNADY, 'Sources of International Law in a Changing International Community: Theory and Practice', in William Butler (ed), *Perestroika and International Law,* The Hague, Kluwer Academic Publishers, 1990, 61–79

DANILENKO, GENNADY, *Law-Making in the International Community,* Dordrecht, Martinus Nijhoff, 1993

DEGAN, VLADIMIR, *Sources of International Law,* Dordrecht, Martinus Nijhoff, 1997

DEKKER, GUIDO DEN, 'De beproeving van de Comprehensive Test Ban Treaty', 16 *Merkourios* 1996, 7–13

DEKKER, IGE and RAMSES WESSEL, 'Van CVSE naar OVSE: De sluipende institutionalisering en onvermijdelijke juridisering van een internationale conferentie', 31 *Vrede En Veiligheid* 2002, 425–438

DENDIAS, MICHEL, 'Les principaux services internationaux administratifs', in (ed), *Recueil des Cours de l'Academie de droit international,* 1938, 247–366

DIXON, MARTIN, *Textbook on International Law,* Oxford, Oxford University Press, 2000

DO NASCIMENTO E SILVA, GERALDO, 'The 1986 Convention and the Treaty-Making Power of International Organisations', 29 *German Yearbook of International Law* 1986, 68–85

——, 'The 1969 and the 1986 Conventions on the Law of Treaties: A Comparison', in Yoram Dinstein (ed), *International law at a Time of Perplexity,* Dordrecht/London, Martinus Nijhoff, 1989, 461–487

DOBBERT, JP, 'Evolution of the Treaty-Making Capacity of International Organisations', in (ed), *The Law and The Sea: Essays in Honour of Jean Carroz,* Rome, FAO, 1987, 21–102

DOMINICÉ, CHRISTIAN, 'La personnalité juridique dans le systeme du droit de gens', in Jerzy Makarczyk (ed), *Theory of International Law at the Threshold of the 21st Century; Essays in Honour of Krysztof Skubiszewski,* Dordrecht, Kluwer Law International, 1996, 147–171

DUPUY, RENÉ-JEAN, *Le droit international,* Paris, Presses universitaires de France, 1963

——, 'L'application des règles du droit international général des traités aux accords conclus par les Organisations internationales', 55 *Annuaire de l'Institut de Droit international* 1973, 214–415

——, *Manuel sur les organisations internationales / A handbook on international organisations,* Dordrecht, Martinus Nijhoff, 1998

EDWARDS, RICHARD, 'Reservations to Treaties: The Belilos Case and the Work of the International Law Commission', 31 *The University of Toledo Law Review* 2000, 195–207

ELIAS, TASLIM, *The Modern Law of Treaties,* Leiden, Sijthoff, 1974

EYFFINGER, ARTHUR CLÉMENT GUILLAUME MARIE (ed), *Compendium Volkenrechtsgeschiedenis,* Deventer, Kluwer, 1991

FELD, WERNER, and ROBERT JORDAN, *International Organisations: A Comparative Approach,* New York, Praeger, 1994

FERRARI BRAVO, LUIGI, *Lezioni di Diritto Internazionale,* Napoli, Editoriale Scientifica, 1986

FIORE, PASQUALE, *Il diritto internazionale codificato,* Rome, Unione tipografico-editrice, 1890

——, 'L'organisation juridique de la société internationale', *Rivista di Diritto Internazionale* 1899

FITZMAURICE, MALGOSIA, 'Modifications to the Principles of Consent in Relation to Certain Treaty Obligations', 2 *Austrian Journal of International and European Law* 1997, 275–317

——, 'Actors (and Factors) in the Dynamic Evolution of Treaty Norms (An Empirical Study)', 4 *Austrian Journal of International and European Law* 1999, 1–84

FITZMAURICE, GERALD, 'Do Treaties Need Ratification?', XIV *British yearbook of International Law* 1934, 113–137

FLAESCH-MOUGIN, CATHERINE, *Les accords externes de la CEE: essai d'une typologie,* Bruxelles (diss), 1979

FRANKOWSKA, MARIA, 'De la prétendue présomption en faveur de la ratification', 69 *Revue générale de droit international public* 1973, 62–88

FRID, RACHEL, *The Relations Between the EC and International Organisations: Legal Theory and Practice,* Kluwer Law International, 1995

FRIEDRICHS, JÖRG, 'The Meaning of New Medievalism', 7 *European Journal of International Relations* 2001, 475–502

FULLER, LON, *The morality of law,* New Haven, Yale University Press, 1964

GAJA, GIORGIO, 'A 'New' Vienna Convention on Treaties Between States and International Organisations or Between International Organisations: A Critical Commentary', 58 *British yearbook of International Law* 1987, 253–269

——, 'Positivism and Dualism in Dionisio Anzilotti', 3 *European Journal of International Law* 1992, 123–138

GALTUNG, JOHAN, 'Non-Territorial Actors: The Invisible Continent (towards a typology of international organisations)', in George Abi-Saab (ed), *The Concept of International Organisation,* Paris, UNESCO, 1981, 67–75

GECK, WILHELM, 'Treaties: Registration and Publication', 7 *Encyclopedia of Public International Law* 1984, 490–496

GEISER, HANS-JÖRG, *Les Effets des Accords conclus par les Organisations Internationales (Etude en Droit des Traités des Organisations Internationales à la lumiere de la Convention de Vienne de 1969),* Publications Universitaires Europeènnes, 1977

GERBET, PIERRE, 'Rise and Development of International Organisation: a Synthesis', in Georges Abi-Saab (ed), *The Concept of international Organisation,* Paris, UNESCO, 1981, 27–49

GIERKE, OTTO VON, (A Black (ed) and M Fischer (trans)), *Community in Historical Perspective (Das Deutsche Genossenschaftsrecht, 1868),* 1990

GIERKE, OTTO VON, (trans Bernard Freyd), *The development of Political Theory,* New York, 1966

GILSON, BERNARD, *The Conceptual System of Sovereign Equality,* Leuven, Peeters, 1984

GOODMAN, RYAN, 'Human Rights Treaties, Invalid Reservations, and State Consent', 96 *American Journal of International Law* 2002, 531–560

GOWLLAND-DEBBAS, VERA (ed), *Multilateral Treaty-Making: The Current Status of Challenges to and Reforms Needed in the International Legislative Process,* The Hague, Nijhoff, 2000

GREIG, DON, *International law,* London, Butterworths, 1976

——, 'Reflections on the Role of Consent', 12 *Australian Yearbook of International Law* 1992, 125–176

——, 'Reservations: Equity as a Balancing Factor', 16 *Australian Yearbook of International Law* 1995, 21–172

GREWE, WILHELM, *Epochen der Völkerrechtsgeschichte,* Baden Baden, Nomos Verlag, 1984

——, 'Treaties: Revision', 7 *Encyclopedia of Public International Law* 1984 (sv)

GROOM, ARTHUR, 'The Advent of International Institutions', in Paul Taylor, and Arthur Groom (ed), *International Organisation: A Conceptual Approach,* London, Frances Pinter Ltd, 1978, 11–27

GROOM, ARTHUR, and MARGOT LIGHT (ed), *Contemporary International Relations: A Guide to Theory,* London, Pinter Publishers, 1994

GUARDIA, ERNESTO, DE LA and MARCELO DELPECH, *El Derecho de los Tratados y la Convención de Vienna de 1969,* Buonos Aires, La Ley, 1970

GUGGENHEIM, PAUL, *Lehrbuch des Völkerrechts,* Basel, Verlag für Recht und Gesellschaft, 1948

HAN, HENRY, 'The UN Secretary-General's Treaty Depository Function: Legal Implications', XIV *Brooklyn Journal of International Law* 1988, 549–572

HANDL, GÜNTHER, 'The Legal Mandate of Multilateral development Banks as Agents for Change toward Sustainable Development', 92 *American Journal of International Law* 1998, 642–665

HARASZTI, GEORGY, *Some fundamental problems of the law of treaties,* Budapest, 1973

HARRIS, JAMES WILLIAM, *Legal Philosophies,* London, Butterworths, 1980

HART, HERBERT, *The Concept of Law,* Oxford, Clarendon Press, 1961

HARTMANN, GÜNTHER, 'The Capacity of International Organisations to Conclude Treaties', in Karl Zemanek (ed), *Agreements of International Organisations and the Vienna Convention on the Law of Treaties,* New York/Vienna, Springer Verlag, 1971, 127–163

HEGEL, GEORG FRIEDRICH, *Grundlinien der Philosophie des Rechts (1821),* Berlin, Suhrkamp, 1986

HIGGINS, ROSALYN, (Rapporteur) 'The Legal Consequences for Member States of the Non-Fulfilment by International Organisations of their Obligations Toward Third Parties', in (ed), *Yearbook of the Institute of International Law,* IDI Fifth Commission, Session of Lisbon, 1995, 251–469 (Final Report, pp 461–465)

——, *The development of international law through the political organs of the United Nations,* Oxford, Oxford University Press, 1963

——, *Problems and process: International Law And How We Use It,* Oxford, Clarendon Press, 1994

HIRSCH, MOSHE, *The Responsibility of International Organisations Towards Third Parties: Some Basic Principles,* Dordrecht, Martinus Nijhoff, 1995

HOHFELD, WESLEY NEWCOMB, *Fundamental Legal Conceptions,* New Haven Connecticut, Yale University Press, 1919

HOLLOWAY, KAYE, *Modern Trends in Treaty Law,* London, Stevens and Sons, 1967

HUBER, JEAN, *Le droit de conclure des traités internationaux,* Lausanne, Librairie Payot, 1951

HUTCHINSON, DAVID, 'The Juridical Nature of Article 7 of the Vienna Convention on the Law of Treaties', 17 *Australian Yearbook of International Law* 1996, 187–225

IMBERT, PIERRE HENRI, 'Le consentement des états en droit international: Reflexions à partir d'un cas pratique concernant la participation de la CEE aux traités du Conseil de l'Europe', 89 *Revue générale de droit international public* 1989, 382

ISAK, HUBERT, and GERHARD LOIBL, 'United Nations Conference on the Law of Treaties between States and International Organisations or between International Organisations', 38 *Österreichisches Zeitschrift für öffentliches Recht und Völkerrecht* 1987, 49–78

JANIS, MARK, 'Jeremy Bentham and the Fashioning of "International Law"', 78 *American Journal of International Law* 1984, 405–418

——, *An Introduction to International Law,* New York, Aspen Law and Business, 2003

JELLINEK, GEORG, *Die Lehre von den Staatenverbindungen,* Aalen, Scientia Verlag, 1882

——, *Allgemeine Staatslehre,* Berlin, Springer Verlag, 1914

JENKS, WILFRED, 'Les instruments internationaux à caractère collectif', 69/III *Recueil des Cours de l'Académie de droit international* 1939, 447–552

JENKS, WILFRED, 'The Legal Personality of International Organisations', XXII *British yearbook of International Law* 1945, 267–275

——, 'Some Constitutional problems of International Organisations', XXII *British Yearbook of International Law* 1945, 11–72

JENNINGS, ROBBERT, and ARTHUR WATTS (ed), *Oppenheim's International Law,* London, Longman, 1992

JOHNSTON, DOUGLAS, 'Theory, Consent, and the Law of Treaties: a Cross-Disciplinary Perspective', 12 *Australian Year Book of International Law* 1992, 109–124

JOYNER, CHRISTOPHER and OSCAR SCHACHTER (eds), *United Nations Legal Order,* ASIL / Cambridge University Press, 1995

KANT, IMMANUEL, 'Perpetual Peace: A Philosophical Sketch (1799)', in Ted Humphrey (ed), *Perpetual Peace and Other Essays on politics, History and Morals,* Indianapolis, Hackett Publishing Company, 1983,

KARL, WOLFRAM, *Vertrag und spätere Praxis im Völkerrecht,* Berlin, Springer Verlag, 1983

KARUNATILLEKE, KESERA, 'Essai d'une classification des accords conclus par les organisations internationales, entre elles ou avec des états', LXXV *Revue générale de droit international public* 1971, 16–91

KASME, BADR, *La capacité de l'organisation des Nations Unies de conclure des traités,* Paris, Pichon and Durand-Auzias, 1960

KAZANSKY, PIERRE, 'Théorie de l'administration internationale', IX *Revue générale de droit international public* 1902, 366

KELSEN, HANS, *Das Problem der Souveränität und die Theorie des Völkerrechts,* Tübingen, Mohr, 1928

——, *General Theory of Law and State,* Cambridge-Massachusetts, Harvard University Press, 1945

——, *The Law of the United Nations : A Critical Analysis of its Fundamental Problems,* London, Stevens, 1950

——, *Principles of International Law,* New York, Rinehart and Company, 1952

KENNEDY, DAVID, *International Legal Structures,* Baden Baden, Nomos Verlag, 1987

——, 'The Move to Institutions', 8 *Cardozo Law Review* 1987, 841–988

——, 'International Law and the Nineteenth Century: History of an Illusion', 65 *Nordic Journal of International Law* 1996, 385–420

KIRGIS, FREDERIC, 'Specialized Law-Making Processes', in Christopher Joyner (ed), *The United Nations and International Law,* Cambridge University Press – ASIL, 1997, 65–94

KLABBERS, JAN, 'Informal Agreements in International Law; Towards a Theoretical Framwork', 5 *Finnish Yearbook of International Law* 1994, 267–387

——, *The Concept of Treaty in International Law,* Kluwer Law International, 1996

——, 'Over het leerstuk van de impliciete bevoegdheden in het recht der internationale organisaties', in JDM Steenbergen (ed), *Ongebogen Recht,* Den Haag, SDU Uitgevers, 1998, 1–11

——, 'Presumptive Personality: The European Union in International Law', in Martti Koskenniemi (ed), *International Law Aspects of the European Union,* The Hague, Kluwer Law International, 1998, 231–253

——, 'Accepting the Unacceptable? A New Nordic Approach to Reservations to Multilateral Treaties', 69 *Nordic Journal of International Law* 2000, 179–193

——, 'The Changing Image of International Organisations', in Jean-Marc Coicaud and Veijo Heiskanen (ed), *The Legitimacy of International Organisations,* Tokyo, UN University Press, 2002, 221–255

——, *An Introduction to International Institutional Law,* Cambridge, Cambridge University Press, 2002

KLEIN, ECKART, 'United Nations, Specialized Agencies', 5 *Encyclopedia of Public International Law* 1983, 349–368

KLEIN, ECKART, and MATTHIAS PECHSTEIN, *Das Vertragsrecht internationaler Organisationen,* Berlin, 1985

KOHONA, PALITHA TB, 'Implementing Article 102 of the Charter of the United Nations and the Depositary Function of the Secretary General', 1 *Romanian Journal of International Law* 2003, 141–171

KOOIJMANS, PETER, *The Doctrine of the Legal Equality of States: An Enquiry into the Foundations of International Law,* Leiden, Sijthoff, 1964

KORKELIA, KONSTANTIN, 'New Challenges to the Regime of Reservations Under the International Covenant on Civil and Political Rights', 13 *European Journal of International Law* 2002, 437–478

KOROWICZ, MARC-STANISLAS, *Organisations Internationales et souveraineté des états-membres,* Paris, Pedone, 1961

KOSKENNIEMI, MARTTI, *From Apology to Utopia: The Structure of International Legal Argument,* Cambridge, CUP, 2005

——, 'The Politics of International Law', 1 *European Journal of International Law* 1990, 2–32

——, 'The Pull of the Mainstream', 88 *Michigan Law Review* 1990, 1946–1962

——, 'The Future of Statehood', 32 *Harvard International Law Journal* 1991, 397–410

——, 'Breach of Treaty or Non-Compliance? Reflections on the Enforcement of the Montreal Protocol', 3 *Yearbook of International Environmental Law* 1992, 123–162

——, 'International Law in a Post-Realist Era', 16 *Australian Year Book of International Law* 1995, 1–19

——, 'The Wonderful Artificiality of States', in *ASIL Proceedings 1994,* ASIL, 1995, 22–29

——, 'The Limits of International Law: Are There Such?' *Institute of International Public Law and International Relations of Thessaloniki* 1999, 19–50

——, *The Gentle Civilizer of Nations,* Cambridge, Cambridge University Press, 2002

KRATOCHWIL, FREDERIC, and JOHN RUGGIE, 'International Organisation: A state of the Art on an Art of the State', in Frederic Kratochwil, and Edward Mansfield (eds), *International Organisation: A Reader,* New York, Harpers and Collins Publishers, 1994, 4–19

KUIJPER, PIETER-JAN, 'The Court and the tribunal of the EC and the Vienna Convention on the Law of Treaties 1969', 25 *Legal Issues of European Integration* 1999, 1–23

LACHS, MANFRED, 'Le développement et les fonctions des traités multilateraux', in (ed), *Recueil des Cours de l'Académie de droit international,* 1957, 228–341

LANDAUER, CARL, 'Antinomies of the United Nations: Hans Kelsen and Alf Ross on the Charter', 14 *European Journal of International Law* 2003, 767–799

LAUTERPACHT, ELIHU, 'The development of the Law of International Organisation by the Decisions of International Tribunals', in 152-IV *Recueil des Cours de l'Academie de droit international,* 1976, 377–478

LAVRANOS, NIKOLAOS, *Legal Interaction between Decisions of International Organisations and European Law,* Groningen, Europa Law Publishing, 2004

LAWSON, RICK, *Het EVRM en de Europese Gemeenschappen,* Deventer, Kluwer, 1999

LEFEBER, RENÉ, 'The Gabcíkovo-Nagymaros Project and the Law of State Responsibility', 11 *Leiden Journal of International Law* 1998, 609–623

LESSNOFF, MICHAEL (ed), *Social Contract Theory,* NY, New York University Press, 1991

LIM, CHIN and OLUFEMI ELIAS, 'The Role of treaties in the Contemporary International Legal order', 66 *Nordic Journal of International Law* 1997, 1–21

LINK, ARTHUR, ET AL (eds), *The Papers of Woodrow Wilson,* Princeton University Press, 1984

MANIN, PHILIPPE, 'L'article 228, paragraphe 2, du traité CEE', in (ed), *Melanges Henri Teitgen,* 1984, 289–310

——, 'La Convention de Vienne sur le droit des traités entre états et organisations internationales ou entre organisations internationales', XXXII *Annuaire français de droit international* 1986, 454–473

——, 'The European Communities and the Vienna Convention on the Law of Treaties between States and International Organisations or Between International Organisations', 24 *Common Market Law Review* 1987, 457–481

MARCHEGIANO, GIUSEPPE, 'The Juristic Character of the International Commission of Cape Spartel Lighthouse', 25 *American Journal of International Law* 1931, 339–347

MAREK, KRYSTYNA, 'Contribution à l'étude de l'histoire du traité multilateral', in Emanuel Diez et al (eds), *Festschrift fuer Rudolf Bindschedler,* Bern, Verlag Staempfli and Cie AG, 1980, 17–39

MARTINES, FRANCESCA, 'Legal Status and Powers of the Court', in Antonio Cassese, and Paolo Gaeta, John Jones (eds), *The Rome Statute of the International Criminal Court: A Commentary,* Oxford, Oxford University Press, 2002

MARTINEZ, MAGDALENA MARTIN, *National Sovereignty and International Organisations,* Kluwer Law International, 1996

MCNAIR, ARNOLD, 'The Function and the Differing Legal Character of Treaties', XI *British yearbook of International Law* 1930, 100–118

——, *The Law of treaties,* Oxford, Clarendon Press, 1961

MENG, WERNER, 'Zollverein (German Customs Union)', *Encyclopedia of Public International Law* 1984, 542–544

MENON, PK, *The Law of Treaties Between States and International Organisations,* New York, Lewiston, 1992

——, 'The Legal Personality of International Organisations', *Sri Lanka Journal of International Law* 1992, 79–97

MENSAH, THOMAS A, 'The Practice of International Law in International Organisations', in Bin Cheng (ed), *International Law: Teaching and Practice,* London, Stevens and Sons, 1982, 146–163

MERVYN JONES, J, 'International Agreements other than 'Inter-State Treaties' – Modern Developments", XXI *British yearbook of International Law* 1944, 111–122

MEULEN, JACOB TER, *Der Gedanke der internationalen Organisation in seiner Entwicklung,* Dordrecht, Martinus Nijhoff, 1917

MORGENSTERN, FELICE, *Legal Problems of International Organisations,* Cambridge, Cambridge University Press, 1986

——, 'The Vienna Convention on the Law of Treaties between States and International Organisations or between International Organisations', in Yoram Dinstein (ed), *International law at a Time of Perplexity,* Dordrecht / Boston, Martinus Nijhoff, 1989, 435–447

MOSLER, HERMANN, 'The International Society as a Legal Community – Part 3: Institutionalised International Co-operation', in (ed), *Recueil des Cours de l'Académie de droit international,* 1974, 11–320

——, 'Völkerrecht als Rechtsordnung', in Hermann Mosler (ed), *Völkerrecht als rechtsordnung: Grundlagen und Quellen (ZAörV),* 1976, 6–46

——, 'Subjects of International Law', 7 *Encyclopedia of Public International Law* 1984, 442–459

MULLER, ALEXANDER, *International Organisations and Their Host States: Aspects of Their Legal Relationship,* Dordrecht, Kluwer Law International, 1995

MURPHY, ALEXANDER, 'The Sovereign State System as Political-Territorial Ideal: Historical and Contemporary Considerations', in Thomas Biersteker and Cynthia Weber (eds), *State Sovereignty as Social Construct,* Cambridge, Cambridge University Press, 1996, 81–120

MURPHY, CORNELIUS, *The Search for World Order,* Dordrecht, Martinus Nijhoff, 1985

MYERS, DENYS P, 'The Names and Scope of Treaties', 51 *American Journal of International Law* 1957, 574–605

MYJER, ERIC, 'The Organisation for the Prohibition of Chemical Weapons: moving closer towards an International Arms Control Organisation? A Quantum Leap in the Institutional Law of Arms Control', in Eric Myjer (ed), *Issues of Arms Control and the Chemical Weapons Convention,* The Hague, Kluwer Law International, 2001, 61–139

NEKAM, ALEXANDER, *The Personality Conception of the Legal Entity,* Cambridge – Massachusetts, Harvard University Press, 1938

NIJMAN, JANNE, *The Concept of International Legal Personality: An Inquiry into the History and the Theory of International Law,* The Hague, TMC Asser Press, 2004

NOLLKAEMPER, ANDRÉ, 'Concurrence between individual responsibility and state responsibility in international law', 52 *International and Comparative Law Quarterly* 2003, 615–640

NUSSBAUM, ARTHUR, *A Concise History of the Law of Nations,* New York, The MacMillan Company, 1961

O'CONNELL, DANIEL, *International Law,* London, Stevens and Sons, 1965

O'CONNELL, MARY ELLEN, 'New International Legal Process', in Steven Ratner, and Ann-Marie Slaughter (ed), *American Journal of International Law: Symposium on Method in International Law,* 1999, 334–350

OKEKE, CHRISTIAN, *Controversial Subjects of Contemporary International Law: An Examination of the New Entities of International Law and Their Treaty-Making Capacity,* Rotterdam University Press, 1974

ONUF, NICHOLAS, 'Sovereignty: Outline of a conceptual history', 16 *Alternatives* 1991, 425–446

OPPENHEIM, LASSA, *International Law: A Treatise,* London, Longmans, Green and co, 1905

OPPENHEIM, LASSA, and ARNOLD MCNAIR, *International Law: A Treatise* (4th edn), London, Longmans, 1928

OPPENHEIM, LASSA, and HERSCH LAUTERPACHT, *International Law: A Treatise* (8th edn), London, Longmans, 1955

OSAKWE, CHRIS, 'The Concept and Forms of Treaties Concluded by International Organisations', in Karl Zemanek (ed), *Agreements of International Organisations and the Vienna Convention on the Law of Treaties,* New York / Vienna, Springer Verlag, 1971, 165–193

PARRY, CLIVE, 'The Treaty-Making Power of the United Nations', 26 *British yearbook of International Law* 1949, 108–150

PARRY, CLIVE, and JOHN GRANT, *Encyclopaedic Dictionary of International Law,* New York, Oceana Publications, 1986

PELLET, ALLAIN, 'Normative Dilemma: Will and Consent in International Law-Making', 12 *Austrian Journal of International and European Law* 1988, 22–54

PERNICE, INGOLF, 'Völkerrechtlige Verträge internationaler Organisationen', 48 *Zeitschrift für Ausländisches öffentliches recht und Völkerrecht* 1988, 229–250

PETMAN, JARNA, 'The Problem of Evil and International Law', in Jarna Petman and Jan Klabbers (ed), *Essays in International Law for Martti Koskenniemi,* Leiden / Boston, Martinus Nijhoff Publishers, 2003, 111–140

PISIER-KOUCHNER, EVELYNE, 'La notion de personne morale dans l'oeuvre de Léon Duguit', 11/12 *Quaderni fiorentini per la storia del pensiero giuridico moderno* 1983, 667

POEGGEL, WALTER, *Zur Wiener Konvention über Verträge zwischen Staaten und internationalen Organisationen von 1986: Konzeptionelle Probleme der beiden Wiener Staatennachfolgekonventionen von 1978 und 1983* (1987), Vorträge vor dem Europa-Institut in Saarbrücken am 25 und 26 Juni 1987

POLITAKIS, GEORGE, 'Enforcing International Humanitarian Law: The Decision of the Appeals Chamber of the War crimes Tribunal on the Duško Tadic Case (Jurisdiction)', 52 *Zeitschrift für Ausländisches öffentliches recht und Völkerrecht* 1997, 283–329

POTTER, PITMAN, 'Origin of the term international organisation', 39 *American Journal of International Law* 1945, 803–806

POUND, ROSCOE, *Philosophical Theory and International Law,* Leiden, Bibliotheca Visseriana – Brill, 1923

PUISSOCHET, JEAN-PIERRE, *Organisation de coóperation et de développement économiques,* Paris, École Nationale d'Administration, 1983

RAIC, DAVID, *Statehood and the Law of Self-Determination,* Dordrecht, Kluwer Law International, 2002

RAMA-MONTALDO, MANUEL, 'International Legal Personality and Implied Powers of International Organisations', XLIV *British yearbook of International Law* 1970, 111 – 155

RAPISARDI-MIRABELLI, ANDREA, 'Theorie générale des unions internationales', 1 *Recueil des Cours de l'Academie de droit international* 1925, 345–391

REDGWELL, CATHERINE, 'Reservations to Treaties and Human Rights Committee General Comment No 24(52)', 46 *International and Comparative Law Quarterly* 1997, 390–412

REINISCH, AUGUST, *International Organisations before National Courts,* Cambridge, Cambridge University Press, 2000

REUTER, PAUL, *Institutions internationales,* Paris, Presses universitaires de France, 1962

——, *La Convention de Vienne du 29 mai 1969 sur le droit des traités,* Paris, Librairie Armand Colin, 1970

——, 'L'ordre juridique internationale et les traités des organisations internationales', in *Völkerrecht als Rechtsordnung: Internationale Gerichtsbarkeit: Menschenrechte (Festschrift für Hermann Mosler),* Springer Verlag, 1983, 745–757

——, *Introduction to the Law of Treaties,* Geneva, Graduate Institute of International Studies, 1995

RIETBERGEN, PETER, *Europe: A Cultural History,* London, Routledge, 1998

RIPHAGEN, WILLEM, 'The Second Round of Treaty Law', in Francesco Capotorti et al (eds), *Du droit international au droit de l'intégration: Liber Amicorum Pierre Pescatore,* Baden Baden, Nomos Verlag, 1987, 565–581

ROHN, PETER, 'A Legal Theory of International Organisation', 5 *Turkish Yearbook of International Relations* 1964, 19–53

——, *Registration and Publication of Treaties,* American Society of International Law, 1967

——, 'The United Nations Treaty Series Project', 12 *International Studies Quarterly* 1968, 174–195

——, *Institutions in Treaties: A Global Survey of Magnitudes and Trends From 1945 to 1965,* Syracuse – New York, Syracuse University, 1970

——, *Treaty Profiles,* California, ABC-CLIO Inc, 1984

ROSENNE, SHABTAI, 'United Nations Treaty Practice', 86/II *Recueil des Cours de l'Academie de droit international* 1954, 281–444

——, 'The Depository of International Treaties', 61 *American Journal of International Law* 1967, 923–945

——, *The Law of Treaties: A Guide to the Legislative History of the Vienna Convention,* Leiden, Sijthoff, 1970

——, *League of Nations Conference for the Codification of International Law (1930),* NY, Dobbs Ferry, Oceana Publications, 1975

——, *Breach of Treaty,* Cambridge, Cambridge University Press, 1985

——, 'Treaties: Conclusion and Entry into Force', 6 *Encyclopedia of Public International Law* 1985, 464–467

——, *Developments in the Law of Treaties, 1945–1986,* Cambridge, Cambridge University Press, 1989

——, 'International Conferences and Congresses', I *Encyclopedia of Public International Law* 1992, 739–746

——, *An International Law Miscellany,* Dordrecht, Martinus Nijhoff, 1993

ROSENZWEIG, FRANZ, *Hegel und der Staat*, Aalen, Scientia Verlag, 1921

ROSS, ALF, *A Textbook of International Law : General Part,* London, Longmans, Green and co, 1947

ROUSSEAU, CHARLES, *Droit International public,* Paris, Pedone, 1953

ROUSSEAU, FRANCOIS, ''Joint Vienna Institute': brèves remarques relatives à la creation de l'institut commun de Vienne', 99 *Revue générale de droit international public* 1995, 639–650

RUDDY, FRANCIS STEVEN, *International Law in the Enlightenment,* New York, Oceana Publications, 1975

SAMSON, KTH, 'International Labour Organisation', II *Encyclopedia of Public International Law* 1995, 1150–1159

SANDS, PHILIPPE, and PIERRE KLEIN, *Bowett's Law of International Institutions,* London, Sweet and Maxwell, 2001

SAROOSHI, DAN, INTERNATIONAL ORGANISATIONS and THEIR EXERCISE OF SOVEREIGN POWERS, OXFORD, OUP, 2005

SATO, TETSUO, *Evolving Constitutions of International Organisations,* The Hague, Kluwer Law International, 1996

SCHACHTER, OSCAR, 'Review of : JW Schneider, Treaty-making Power of International Organisations', 54 *American Journal of International Law* 1960, 201–202

——, *Towards wider acceptance of UN Treaties,* New York, Arno Press, 1971

——, 'Recent Trends in International Law Making', 12 *Australian Year Book of International Law* 1988, 1–16

——, 'The UN Legal Order: An Overview', in Christopher Joyner (ed), *The United Nations and International Law,* Cambridge University Press – ASIL, 1997, 3–26

——, 'The Decline of the Nation-State and its Implications for International Law', 22 *Colombia Journal of Transnational Law* 1998, 7–24

SCHERMERS, HENRY, 'International Organisations as Members of Other International Organisations', in *Volkerrecht als Rechtsordnung: Internationale Gerichtsbarkeit: Menschenrechte (Festschrift für Hermann Mosler),* Springer Verlag, 1983, 823–837

SCHERMERS, HENRY, and NIELS BLOKKER, *International Institutional Law,* Boston / Leiden, Martinus Nijhoff, 2003

SCHINDLER, DIETRICH, *Recht, Staat, Völkergemeinschaft,* Zürich, Schulthess and Co, 1948

SCHNEIDER, JAN WILLEM, *Treaty-Making Power of International Organisations,* Genève, Librairie Droz, 1959

SCHREUER, CHRISTOPH, 'The Waning of the Sovereign State: Towards a New Paradigm for International Law?' 4 *European Journal of International Law* 1993, 447–471

SCHRÖDER, MEINHARD, 'Die Kodifikation des Vertragsrechts internationaler Organisationen', 23 *Archiv des Völkerrechts* 1985, 385–408

SCHWARZENBERGER, GEORG, *The Frontiers of International Law,* London, Stevens and Sons, 1962

SCHWEISFURTH, THEODOR, 'The Treaty-Making Capacity of the CMEA in Light of a Framework Agreement between the CEE and the CMEA', 22 *Common Market Law Review* 1985, 615–647

SEIDL-HOHENVELDERN, IGNAZ, 'Danube River', 12 *Encyclopedia of Public International Law* 1990, 80–83

SEIDL-HOHENVELDERN, IGNAZ, and GERHARD LOIBL, *Das Recht der Internationalen Organisationen einschliesslich der Supranationalen Gemeinschaften,* Köln, Carl Heymans Verlag, 2000

SEIDL-HOHENVELDERN, IGNAZ, and TORSTEN STEIN, *Völkerrecht,* Vienna, Carl Heymans Verlag, 2000

SETEAR, JOHN, 'An Iterative Perspective on Treaties: A Synthesis of international Relations Theory and International Law', 37 *Harvard International Law Journal* 1996, 139–229

SEYERSTED, FINN, *Objective International Personality of Intergovernmental Organisations: Do Their Capacities Really Depend upon Their Constitutions?,* Copenhagen, Krohns Bogtrykkeri, 1963

——, 'Treaty-Making Capacity of International Organisations: Article 6 of the International Law Commission's Draft Articles on the Law of Treaties Between States and International Organisations or Between

International Organisations', 34 *Österreichisches Zeitschrift für öffentliches Recht und Völkerrecht* 1983, 261–267

SHAW, MALCOLM, *International Law,* Cambridge, Cambridge University Press, 2003

SHELTON, DINAH, 'International Law and 'Relative Normativity'', in Malcolm Evans (ed), *International Law,* Oxford, Oxford University Press, 2003, 145–172

SIBERT, MARCEL, 'Quelques aspects de l'Organisation et de la technique des conferences internationales', 48/II *Recueil des Cours de l'Académie de droit international* 1934, 387–457

SIMMA, BRUNO, 'Consent: Strains in the Treaty System', in Douglas Johnston and Ross St Macdonald (eds), *The Structure and Progress of International Law,* The Hague, Martinus Nijhoff, 1983,

——, *The Charter of the United Nations: A Commentary,* Oxford, Oxford University Press, 2002

SIMMA, BRUNO, and ANDREAS PAULUS, 'The 'International Community': Facing the Challenge of Globalization', 9 *European Journal of International Law* 1998, 266–277

SIMMONDS, KENNETH, 'International Maritime Organisation', II *Encyclopedia of Public International Law* 1995, 1262–1267

SIMON, DENYS, *L'interpretation judiciaire des traités d'organisations internationales: morphologie des conventions et fonction jurisdictionelle,* Paris, Pedone, 1981

SIMPSON, GERRY, 'The Situation on the International Legal Theory Front: The Power of Rules and the Rule of Power', 11 *European Journal of International Law* 2000,

SINCLAIR, IAN, *The Vienna Convention on the Law of Treaties,* Manchester, Manchester University Press, 1984

——, *The International Law Commission,* Cambridge, Grotius Publications, 1987

SKUBISZEWSKI, KRYSZTOF, 'International Legislation', II *Encyclopedia of Public International Law* 1995, 1255–1261

SOHN, LOUIS, and THOMAS BUERGENTHAL (eds), *International Protection of Human Rights,* Indianapolis, Bobbs-Merrill, 1973

SONNENFELD, RENATA, 'International Organisations as Parties to Treaties', XI *Polish Yearbook of International Law* 1982, 177–200

STEINBERGER, HELMUT, 'Sovereignty', 10 *Encyclopedia of Public International Law* 1987, 397–418

STONE, JULIUS, *Legal System and Lawyers' Reasonings,* London, Stevens and Sons, 1964

STRUPP, KARL, 'Les règles générales du droit de la paix', 47 *Recueil des Cours de l'Académie de droit international* 1934, 259–595

SYBESMA-KNOL, NERI, 'The New Law of Treaties: The Codification of the Law of Treaties Concluded between States and International Organisations or Between Two or More International Organisations', 15 *Georgia Journal of International and Comparative Law* 1985, 425–452

SZASZ, PAUL, 'The united nations Legislates to Limit its Liability', 81 *American Journal of International Law* 1987, 739–744

——, 'General Law-Making Processes', in Christopher Joyner (ed), *The United Nations and International Law,* Cambridge University Press – ASIL, 1997, 27–64

TABORY, MALA, 'Recent developments in United Nations Treaty registration and Publication Practices', 76 *American Journal of International Law* 1982, 350–363

TAMMES, ARNOLD, *Hoofdstukken van Internationale Organisatie,* The Hague, Martinus Nijhoff, 1951

——, 'The status of consent in International Law', II *The Netherlands Yearbook of International Law* 1971, 2–28

TESON, FERNANDO, 'The Kantian Theory of International Law', 92 *Columbia Law Review* 1992, 53–102

TEUBNER, GÜNTHER, *Law as an Autopoietic System,* Oxford, Blackwell, 1993

THIERRY, HUBERT, 'The Thought of Georges Scelle', 1 *European Journal of International Law* 1990, 193–209

TIETJE, CHRISTIAN, 'The Changing Legal Structure of International Treaties as an Aspect of an Emerging Global Governance Architecture', 42 *German Yearbook of International Law* 1999, 26–55

TOMUSCHAT, CHRISTIAN, '*Obligations for States*', in (ed), *Recueil des Cours de l'Academie de droit international,* Nijhoff, 1993, 195–374

TOSCANO, MARIO, *The history of Treaties and International Politics,* Baltimore, The Johns Hopkins Press, 1966

TREVES, TULLIO, 'Innovations dans la technique de codification du droit international: la preparation de la conference de Vienne sur les traites passes par les organisations internationales', XXXIII *Annuaire français de droit international* 1986, 474–494

TRIEPEL, HEINRICH, *Völkerrecht und Landesrecht,* Leipzig, Hirschfeld, 1899

TRIMBLE, PHILIP, 'International Law, World Order and Critical Legal Studies', 42 *Stanford Law Review* 1990, 811–845

——, 'The Plight of Academic International Law', 1 *Chicago Journal of International Law* 2000, 117–124

TRUYOL Y SERRA, ANTONIO, *Histoire du droit international public,* Paris, Editions Economica, 1995

UNGER, ROBERTO MANGABEIRA, *Knowledge and Politics,* New York, Free Press, 1975

VERDROSS, ALFRED, *Die Verfassung der Völkerrechtsgemeinschaft,* Vienna, Springer Verlag, 1926

VERWEY, DELANO, *The European Community, The European Union and the International Law of Treaties,* The Hague, TMC Asser Press, 2004

VERZIJL, JOHANNES HW, *International Law in Historical Perspective,* Leiden, Sijthoff, 1973

VIERDAG, EGBERT, 'The law governing treaty relations between parties to the Vienna Convention on the Law of Treaties and states not party to the Convention', 76 *American Journal of International Law* 1982, 779–801

——, 'Some Problems Regarding The Scope of International Instruments on the Law of Treaties', 23 *Archiv des Völkerrechts* 1985, 408–499

——, 'Some Remarks on the Relationship between the 1969 and the 1986 Vienna Convention on the Law of Treaties', 25 *Archiv des Völkerrechts* 1987, 82–91

——, 'The time of 'conclusion' of a multilateral treaty: art 30 of the Vienna Convention on the Law of Treaties and related provisions', 59 *British Yearbook of International Law* 1988, 75–111

——, *Spanningen tussen recht en praktijk in het verdragenrecht (Preadvies),* Nederlandse Vereniging voor Internationaal Recht, 1989

VILLIGER, MARK, *Customary International Law and Treaties,* Dordrecht, Martinus Nijhoff, 1985

VIRALLY, MICHEL, *L'organisation mondiale,* Paris, Librairie Armand Colin, 1972

——, 'La notion de fonction dans la théorie de l'organisation internationale', in Susanne Bastid (ed), *Mélanges offerts à Charles Rousseau : la communauté internationale,* Paris, Pedone, 1974, 277–300

——, 'Definition and Qualification: A Legal Approach', 29 *International Social Science Journal* 1977, 58–72

VISSCHER, CHARLES DE, *Theory and Reality in Public International Law,* Princeton University Press, 1968

WALKER, DAVID, *The Oxford Companion to Law,* Oxford, Clarendon Press, 1980

WEIL, PROSPER, *Le droit international en quête de son identité : cours général de droit international public,* 237-IV Recueil des Cours de l'Académie de droit international 1992, 9–370

WESSEL, RAMSES, 'Revisiting the International Legal Status of the EU', 5 *European Foreign Affairs Review* 2000, 507–537

WETZEL, RALF, and DIETRICH RAUSCHNING, *The Vienna Convention on the law of treaties – Travaux Préparatoires,* Frankfurt am Main, Alfred Metzner Verlag, 1978

WHITE, GILLIAN, 'Treaty Interpretation: The Vienna Convention 'Code' as Applied by the World Trade Organisation Judiciary', 20 *Australian Year Book of International Law* 1999, 319–342

WHITE, NIGEL, *The Law of International Organisations,* Manchester, Manchester University Press, 1st edn (1996), and 2nd edn (2005)
——, 'Discerning Separate Will', in Wybo Heere (ed), *From Government to Governance: The Growing Impact of Non-State Actors on the International and European Legal System (ASIL/NVIR Proceedings of the Hague Joint Conference 2004),* The Hague, TMC Asser Press, 2004, 31–38
WIDDOWS, KELVIN, 'What is an agreement in international law?' 50 *British Yearbook of International Law* 1979, 117–149
WILCOX, FRANCIS, *The ratification of international conventions: A study of the relationship of the ratification-process to the development of international legislation,* London, George Allen and Unwin, 1935
WILLOWEIT, DIETMAR and ULRIKE SEIF (eds), *Europäische Verfassungsgeschichte,* München, Beck, 2003
ZEMANEK, KARL, *Das Vertragsrecht der internationalen Organisationen,* Vienna, Springer Verlag, 1957
——, 'International Organisations: Treaty-Making Power', 5 *Encyclopedia of Public International Law* 1983, 168–171
——, 'The United Nations Conference on the Law of Treaties Between States and International Organisations or Between International Organisations: The unrecorded history of its 'general agreement'', in Karl-Heinz Böckstiegel, et al (eds), *Völkerrecht, Recht der Internationalen Organisationen, Weltwirtschaftsrecht (Festschrift für I Seidl-Hohenveldern),* Köln, Carl Heymans Verlag, 1988, 665–680
ZIECK, MARJOLEINE, 'UNHCR's 'Special Agreements'', in Jan Klabbers, and René Lefeber (eds), *Essays on the Law of Treaties,* The Hague, Martinus Nijhoff, 1998, 171–187
——,*UNHCR's World-Wide Presence in the Field: A Legal analysis of UNHCR's Cooperation Agreements,* Nijmegen, Wolf Legal Publishers 2006
ZOLLER, ELISABETH, 'The 'Corporate will' of the United Nations and the Rights of the Minority', 81 *American Journal of International Law* 1987, 610–634
ZWANENBURG, MARTEN, *Accountability under International Humanitarian Law for UN and NATO Peace Support Operations,* Leiden, Meijers instituut, 2003

Index

Accountability 5, 6, 252, 270, 271
Administrative Committee on Coordination (now the United Nations System Chief
Executives Board (CEB) for Coordination 127, 185
Ambatielos case (1952), ICJ 117
Anglo-Iranian Oil Co. case (1952), ICJ 116
Anzilotti, Dionisio 41, 55, 59, 62
Application for Review of Judgment N. 273 of the United Nations Administrative Tribunal (Advisory Opinion, 1982), ICJ 120

Bederman, David 51, 57, 59, 67, 72

Case C-327/91 (*France v Commission*), ECJ 122
Case concerning certain German interests in Polish Upper Silesia (1926), PCIJ 29
Case concerning Questions on Interpretation and Application of the 1971 Montreal Convention Arising from the Aerial Incident at Lockerbie (Provisional Measures 1992), ICJ 110
Case of the S.S. Wimbledon (1923), PCIJ 135
Centralisation of International Organisations 27–9
  autonomy, and 27
  Certain Expenses case 28
  degree of 28
  meaning 27
  pacta tertiis principle 28
  sources, and 29
  World Bank Tribunal 29
Certain Expenses of the United Nations (Article 17, Paragraph 2, of the Charter) (Advisory Opinion, 1962), ICJ 28, 117, 120
Codification 1, 49, 63, 67, 133, 143, 146, 155, 168, 173, 175, 176, 177, 179, 182, 185, 188, 193, 194, 197, 218, 221, 224, 235, 245, 258, 260, 261, 267
Codification of law of treaties for international organisations 143–79
  International Law Commission 144–65, *see also* International Law Commission
  international organisations in first stage 173–9
    capacity 176–7
    classical law of treaties, and 174
    contradictory concerns 178
    delimitation of law of treaties as branch of law 175
    descriptive aspect 173
    differing notions of 'international organisation' 177–8
    legal basis of capacity 177
    normative aspect 173
    perceived distribution between states and organisations 175
    traditional meaning of 'treaty' 176
    transparency 178
Conditions for Admission of a State to Membership in the United Nations (Advisory Opinion, 1947), ICJ 119
Conference on Disarmament 23, 106–7
Constitution of the Maritime Safety Committee of the Inter-Governmental Maritime Consultative Organization (Advisory Opinion, 1960), ICJ 119
Constitutive treaties of international organisations 113–23
  constitutionalist view 114
  inter-state treaties 113–14
  interpretation 115
  law of treaties applied to 116–23
    amendment 116
    competences, and 118
    European Community 122
    European Court of Justice 122–3
    functional interpretative framework 119–20
    guiding principle in choice of interpretative methods 118–19
    International Court of Justice 122
    interpretation 116–17
    normative value of practice of organisation 120
    'systemic approach' 121
    teleological approach 119
    transparency in relation to organs 121–2
    WHO constitution 117
  law of treaties doctrine, and 114
  'objective regime' 115
  treaty or constitution, whether 113–15

Dedoublement fonctionnel 32, 55
Difference relating to Immunity from Legal Process of a Special Rapporteur of the Commission on Human Rights (Advisory Opinion, 1999), ICJ 120

Effect of Awards of Compensation made by the United Nations Administrative Tribunal (Advisory Opinion, 1954), ICJ 119
Exchange of Greek and Turkish Populations (Advisory Opinion, 1925), PCIJ 62, 135
European Community 22, 24, 26, 84, 85, 92, 110, 122, 129, 132, 191, 193, 266
European conference system 40
European Union 24, 25, 84 see also European Community
  functionality 25

Food and Agricultural Organization 116, 129, 130
  treaty-making practice 129–30
Functionality of international organisations 25–6
  distinction between 'capacity' and 'competence' 25–6
  European Union 25
  'powers', and 25–6
  territoriality, and 26

Gierke, Otto von 45, 58

Hegel, Georg Wilhelm Friedrich 38

IGO treaties 1
  law of treaties, and 2–3. *See also* Law of treaties
IGO treaties in doctrine 132–7
  qualitative perspective 128–32
    distinctive factors of legal nature 131–2
    European Community 129
    FAO 129–130
    formal-legal criteria 131
    'gentleman's agreements' 128–9
    OECD 129
    OPCW 130–1
  quantitative perspective 125–8
    data 125–6
      estimates of number of treaties 127–8
      micro-perspective 128
      UNTS 126–8
  status of IGO Agreements 132–4
    'amity and goodwill' 133–4
    content, and 133–4
    'instruments of another nature' 132–3
    terminology 133
  treaty-making powers 134–7
    agency 136–7
    capacity 134–6
    decentralisation 136–7
    in the 1969 Vienna Convention on Law of Treaties 136
    IGO treaties in practice 125–32
International Arbitral Tribunal, *Texaco Overseas Petroleum Company v Libyan Arab Republic*, 1977 132
International Arbitral Tribunal, *Westland Helicopter*, 1984 263, 266
Institutional law 4, 12, 13, 16, 18, 22, 25, 29, 31, 67, 76, 81, 86, 92, 104, 115, 121, 131, 135, 177, 223, 229, 230, 246, 247, 255, 259, 260, 262, 265, 266. *See also* Rules of the organisation
Institutional veil 5, 6, 23, 30, 32, 61, 93, 101, 143, 173, 199, 203, 212, 240, 246, 251, 252, 253, 255, 256, 257, 258, 259, 260, 261, 262, 263, 264, 265, 266, 267, 268, 269, 270, 271
  conventional law of treaties, in 260–2
    institutional division of competences, and 261
    layered subjects, and 260–1
    theoretical and doctrinal development 262
  dialectic between open and closed conceptions of international organisations 259–60
  drafting history of Vienna Conventions 260
  fiction of unitary *Normadressat* 256
  flexibility of legal manifestation of international organisations 258–9
  formalist approach 252
  general international law 267–9
    international organisations and international law 267–8
    nature of international law 268–9
    'New Medievalism' 269
  international responsibility, and 262–7
    accessibility of institutional designs 266
    default rule 262–3
    general international law, and 265
    general norm piercing institutional veil 264
    ILC, and 266–7
    primary norms 264
    'secondary responsibility' 263–4
  legal order overrides setup of subject 258–60

nature of 251–2
one-dimensional character of international law 256–7
organisations as independent actors, on 257–8
organisations as semi-closed 253–4
organisations as semi-open 254–5
positivist approach 252
positivist perspective 269–71
accountability 270
capability, and 269–70
reconstitution of formal legal framework 271
treaty-making subjects 271
propositions 253–60
transparency of organisations 255–6
International Bank for Reconstruction and Development 128, 167, 168, 172, 174
International Civil Aviation Organisation (ICAO) 108, 109
'standards' 108
International Commission for the Cape Spartel Lighthouse 47, 51, 54, 58–9
International Commission of the Danube 54
International community 12, 45, 55, 56, 72, 83, 90. 109, 200, 242, 243, 271
International Congo Association 46–7
International Institute of Intellectual Co-operation 53
International Labour Organisation (ILO) 2, 48, 49, 50, 51, 102, 103, 108, 109, 146, 172, 185, 219
institutional structure 50
treaties, and 49–50
treaty-making capacity 63
International law
binding force of 54–5
International Law Commission 144–65
ILC Special Rapporteur on Responsibility of Organizations (Gaja) 19
ILC Special Rapporteur on the Law of State Responsibility (Crawford) 23
ILC Special Rapporteur on the Law of Treaties between States and Organizations or Between Organizations (Reuter) 2, 42, 89, 115, 143, 182
ILC Special Rapporteur on the Law of Treaties (Brierly) 144, 145, 156, 176, 177
ILC Special Rapporteur on the Law of Treaties (Fitzmaurice) 133, 144, 152, 162, 176, 177
ILC Special Rapporteur on the Law of Treaties (Lauterpacht) 133, 144, 150, 151, 155, 176, 177, 178
ILC Special Rapporteur on the Law of Treaties (Waldock) 144, 155, 158, 161, 176, 177, 178
involving law of organisation:1961–1966 155–62
'agency' 161
'application' 161
capacity 158–60
'constitution' 159
definition 158
'essential validity' 161
first Waldock report 155–6
formulation of general provision 156–7
'implied powers doctrine' 160
international agreement, meaning 156
'mixed agreements' 161–2
law of treaties, and 144–65
'organisation of states':1953–1954 150–1
functional view on organisations 151
'organisations of states' 151
treaty, definition 150–1
Vienna Conference 1968–1969, *and see* Vienna Conference 1968–1969
International organisation as a legal person 68–77. *See also* Legal personality
International organisations
actors in international law, as 6
Anzilotti on 54, 55
area of competence 26, 92, 93, 95, 139, 204, 205, 227, 233, 246, 247, 257, 258
assumptions 96–7
autonomy 97
basic criteria 18–19
'bureau' 40–1
capacity of 149, 164, 245, 259, 277
centralisation, and *see* Centralisation
classification 22–4
Conference on Disarmament 23
European Union 24
Human Rights Committee 24
institutional competences 22
legal consequences 22–3
Nauru 23
Ozone Secretariat 23–4
treaty regimes, and 23
collective diplomacy, system of 39–40
competence 21, 22, 24, 25, 26, 43, 51, 53, 60, 67, 81, 90, 91, 92, 93, 94, 95, 102, 103, 114, 118, 119, 120, 121, 129, 131, 134, 139, 144, 161, 162, 178, 191, 204, 205, 206, 208, 209, 214, 221, 222, 225, 226, 227, 233, 146, 247, 255, 257, 258, 259, 261, 268, 269, 276
conceptual laguna 5–6

core definition 17
definition 13–22
'agreement' 17–18
Article 24, LON Covenant 18
Article 71, UN Charter 14
autonomous will 19
autonomy, criterion of 17
Bowett on 18
Brownlie on 20
cooperative function 16
core aspects 20–1
courts, and 15
criteria 16
descriptive 14
Henry Schermer and Niels Blokker on 17, 20–1, 23–4
identification of existing legal actors 19–20
ILC draft Articles on Responsibility of International Organisations 19
institutional autonomy as central factor 21–2
International Law Commission 15
Klabbers on 17
legal personality 19
membership 18
Michael Virally on 16
normative 14
objective of common interest 16–17
Special Rapporteur Gaja on 19–20
treaty basis 18–19
volonté distincte 21
Yearbook of International Organisations 15
doctrinal division between primary and secondary legal persons 59
European conference system 40
European Congress 45
external perspective 5
formal aspects 13–24
formal characteristics of 11, 61
functional delimitation 3
functionality 25–6, *see also* Functionality
general international law, and 12–13
German positivist school 46
history until era of United Nations 35–64
implied powers 26, 29, 86, 160, 255, 259
independent will 17, 21, 45, 237
inequality with states 2–3
'institutional veil' 3–4
International Commission for the Cape Spartel Lighthouse 47, 51, 54, 58–9
International Congo Association 46–7
Jellinek on 45
Kazansky 45, 55
layered character 2, 4, 253, 260, 268
legal images 44–8
legal independence 96
legal subjects, as 1–2
material aspects 24–33
material characteristics 6, 11
nature of 11–33
nineteenth century 39–48
notion of 55
'objective theory' of attribution 62–3
organs of 16, 17, 24, 28, 32, 44, 45, 55, 56, 60, 61, 75, 77, 95, 102, 103, 104, 107, 120, 121, 127, 136, 137, 145, 151, 153, 167, 203, 207, 212, 225, 232, 233, 251, 261, 264, 270
origin of notion 44
Otto von Gierke on 45
Pitman Potter on 44
powers 134–137
public institutions concerned with administration of technical matters 42
public unions 40
rise of 39–48
River Commission 41–2, 43
role in international law 1
supranational 22, 43, 131, 216, 217, 221, 222, 223, 224, 233, 268
territoriality principle 47–8
transparency *see* Transparency
transparent character of 95
treaty-making, involvement with 6
unanimity, principle of 42–3
*volonte distincte*21, 23, 27, 76, 206, 253
Zollverein 43–4, 46–7

Jellinek, George 45, 55, 56, 57
Jurisdiction of the Courts of Danzig (Advisory Opinion 1928), PCIJ 62

Kant, Immanuel 37
Kelsen, Hans 36, 56, 253

Law of treaties 4–5
legal scholarship 4–5
treaties concluded by international organisations, and 6–7. *See also* IGO treaties
League of Nations 48–64
catalyst in conceptualisation of legal personality, as 59–60
legal images 54–64
legal personality 56–8
Mandates 52–3
minority protection 52–3
new phenomenon, as 61–2

pacta tertiis, precept of 61
performance of independent legal acts 62
separate identity at institutional level 56–7
subject of international law, as 60
treaties, and 49–50
treaty-making practice 52
valuation 56
Legal personality
range of opinions on 57–8
Legal personality in international law 68–71
definition 68–9
idea of 70–1
inference of 69–70
'real personality theory' 70–1
rigid framework, as 71
theory of presumptive personality 87
threshold approach 70
Legal personality in relation to international organisations 71–7
attribution 78–82
autonomy, and 76
Brownlie on 72–3
capacities 90–4
legal basis 93
treaty-making 91
competences 90–4
doctrinal debate 93–4
legal basis 93
meaning 92
core element of international organisations, and 75–6
David Bederman on 72
division between 'original' and 'secondary' subjects 73
effects 78–82
Finn Seyerstedt on 85–6
foundation 83–8
'open' and 'closed' manifestation 83
'function approach' 81–2
'functional limitation' 82
Jan Klabbers on 87
legal order, and 72
'material approach' 80–1
objective legal personality 88–90. *See also* Objective legal personality
'objective material approach' 81–2
Rama-Montaldo classification 80
Reparation case 1949 73–4, 75, 78–9
Repertory of United Nations Practice 74–5
Schermens and Blokker on 86–7
self-declared international personality 84
self-proclaimed lack of personality 85
'status approach' 81
transparent image of organisations, and 76–7
WHO Advisory Opinion 1980 74
Legality of the Use by a State of Nuclear Weapons in Armed Conflict (Advisory Opinion 1996), ICJ 26, 92, 117
Loizidou v Turkey (Judgment - Preliminary Objections, 1995), ECHR 115

Mavrommatis Palestine Concession case (1924), PCIJ 53
Minority Schools in Albania (1935), PCIJ 53

Namibia case (Advisory Opinion, 1971), ICJ 119, 120, 122,
Nansen International Refugees Office 53
Nicaragua case (Jurisdiction and Admissibility, 1984), ICJ 117
Non-governmental organisations 14, 22
North Atlantic Treaty Organization 239

Objective legal personality 88–90
constitutive instrument as constitution rather than treaty 89
internal and external perspective 88–9
Reparation Opinion 89–90
Opinion 1/91 [1991], ECJ
Opinion 1/94 [1994], ECJ
Organization for Economic Cooperation and Development 129
Organization for Security and Cooperation in Europe 85
Organization for the Prohibition of Chemical Weapons 130
treaty practice 130–1
Organization of American States 148
Ozone Secretariat 23–4

Permanent Court of International Justice 54
Polydor case, 270/80 [1982], ECJ 123
Positivism 5, 38, 54. *See also* Positivist
Positivist 5, 12, 13, 29, 37, 46, 67, 83, 251, 252, 266, 268

Reparation for Injuries Suffered in the Service of the United Nations (Advisory Opinion, 1949), ICJ 119, 144
Responsibility 6, 15, 19, 21, 23, 66, 76, 137, 162, 175, 221, 238, 240, 241, 242, 252, 261, 262, 263, 264, 265, 266, 267, 269, 270, 2786, 280, 281
River Commissions 41–2, 43
Rules of the organisation 61, 105, 114, 116, 118, 121, 205, 225, 226, 227, 229, 245, 273, 274, 277, 279

Saar Governing Commission 53
Selmouni v France (Judgment 1999), ECHR 115
Serbian Loans case (1929), PCIJ 132
Seyerstedt, Finn 85, 87, 178
  legal personality, on 85–6
South West Africa cases (Preliminary Objections 1962), ICJ 60
South West Africa cases (Second Phase 1966), ICJ 60
Sovereignty 3, 5, 27, 30, 36, 37, 38, 42, 51, 54, 62, 74, 83, 135, 150, 192, 210, 216, 224, 232, 241, 246, 254, 255
State 35–9
  advent of 35
  closed character of 12
  Hegel on 38
  Kant on 37
  natural law, and 36–7
  'personality' 36
  'real personality theory' 38
  sovereignty 36–8. See also Sovereignty
  Vattel on 37

Territorial Jurisdiction of the International Commission of the River Oder (1929), PCIJ 72
The Interpretation of the Agreement of 25 March 1951 between the WHO and Egypt; (Advisory Opinion, 1980), ICJ 31, 66
Transparency of International Organisations 29–33
  back-coupling between organisations and member states 33
  dual imagery 30–1
  forum for activities and actions of states 32
  interbellum, and 31
  meaning 32
  systemic factors 30
  UN Security Council 32–3
  WHO Advisory Opinion 1980 31
Treaty-making 101–11, 125–37
  centralisation in technical organisations 107–11
    binding character of regulatory acts 10
    concept of treaty, and 110
    ILO system 108
    International Civil Aviation Organisation 108
    Montreal Protocol on Substances which Deplete the Ozone Layer 1987 109
    Vienna Convention for the Protection of the Ozone Layer 1985 109
  centralisation in UN practice 102–7
    Conference on Disarmament 106–7
    decentralisation, and 103–4
    institutional framework 105–6
    objective of 'sponsored' conventions 107
    rationalisation 102–3
    text of treaties adopted, where 104–5
    traditional unanimity rule 105
  international organisations as forum for 101–11
Triepel, Heinrich 46, 54
Tyer v UK (1978), ECHR 115

United Nations
  centralisation in treaty-making practice 102–7
United Nations Charter
  Article 57 18
  Article 62(3) 102
  Article 63 121, 130–1
  Article 63(1) 54
  Article 102 126
  Article 103 242
  Article 108 116
United Nations Convention on the Law of the Sea 191
United Nations Educational, Scientific and Cultural Organization 53, 108, 116
United Nations era 65–94
  centralised framework of organisation 139
  competences 139–40
  IGO treaty-making practice 140
  increased prominence of international organisations 66
  institutions 65–7
  interpretive practice of International Court 140
  legal images 67–94
  role of international organisations 139–40
  Yearbook of International Organisations 66
United Nations High Commissioner for Refugees 128, 136, 261, 270
United Nations Human Rights Committee 24
UN Security Council
  transparency, and 32–3
UNTS 126–128

Versailles Treaty 54
Vienna Conference 1968–1969 168–73
  ILC, and 168–73
  saving clause of draft Article 3, and 171–2
Vienna Convention on the Law of Treaties 1969

Article 2 (use of terms) 277
Article 6 (capacity of states to conclude treaties) 277
Article 27 (internal law and observance of treaties) 277
Article 30 (application of successive treaties relating to the same subject-matter) 278
Article 34 (general rule regarding third states) 278
Article 35 (treaties providing for obligations for third States) 278
Article 36 (treaties providing for rights for third States) 279
Article 73 (cases of State succession, State responsibility and outbreak of hostilities) 280
Brierly draft articles (1950–1952) 145–50
'informalisation' 147
International Court of Justice, and 148
ratione personae limitation 147–8
states only 149–50
status of organisations 146–7
treaty, use of term 145
Final draft Articles (1966) 162–5
'agency' 164–5
comments on 165–8
IBRD statement 167–8
importance of IGO treaties for developing countries, and 166–7
procedural issues 168
reception of 165–73
'special features' of IGO treaties 167–8
treaty, definition 163–4
Fitzmaurice draft articles (1955–1960) 152–5
international organisation, meaning 153
'other subjects of international law' 154–5
'scope' 152
treaty, meaning 153
Lauterpacht draft articles (1953–1954) 150–1
Vienna Convention 1986 181–95, 197–43
ACC arguments 185
Article 36 bis (obligations and rights arising for States members of an international organisation from a treaty to which it is a party) 212–25
amendments tabled 219
'debats longs et souvent confus' 218
distinction between direct and other obligations 221
drafting history 213–19
EEC, example of 214–15
final draft version 224
final version 217
general international law, and 220
general reserve with regard to 218
internal structure of organisation, and 215
issues of 219–25
nature of rights and obligations at stake 220–2
political character of discussion 216
relativity of treaties 223
separation between primary and secondary obligations 221
UNGA Sixth Committee 217–18
Articles of 1969 Convention marked as 'problematic' 275–6
classification of treaties by party 200–3
'agreement' 200–1
Article 9 (adoption of the text) 201
Article 10 (authentication of the text) 201
Article 12 (consent to be bound by treaty expressed by signature) 202
tentative enquiry into transparency 203
'conduct' of 'competent organ' 247
descriptive force 235–7
adoption of text 235–6
depositions of treaties 236–7
diplomatic and consular relations and conclusion of treaties 236
function of codification, and 235
functions of depositaries 237
severance of diplomatic or consular relations 236
diplomatic fortune of 192–3
dispute settlement 234–5
jus cogens 234
distinction between inter-state treaties and other international agreements 183–4
distinctions between states and organisations 246
doctrinal perspective 199–200
doctrine, issues of 200–32
drafting methodology: role of 1969 Convention 182–4
economic drafting method 183–4
expressing judicial will 205–12
acquiescence 206–10
Article 7 (full powers) 206–7

Article 15 (consent to be bound by treaty expressed by accession) 207–8
Article 37 (revocation or modification of obligations or rights of third States or third organizations) 208
Article 39 (general rule regarding the amendment of treaties) 208
Article 45 (loss of a right to invoke a ground for invalidating, terminating, withdrawing from or suspending the operation of a treaty) 208–9
Article 46 (provisions of internal law of a State and rules of an international organization regarding competence to conclude treaties) 209
Article 58 (suspension of the operation of a multilateral treaty by agreement between certain of the parties only) 209–10
Article 59 (termination or suspension of the operation of a treaty implied by conclusion of a later treaty) 209–10
Articles 11–17 207–8
assent 206–10
consent 206–10
'express consent to be bound' 209
means of expressing consent 207
perceived lack of unitary character on part of organisations 209
final clauses 190–2
becoming bound to Convention 190–1
entry into force 191–2
form 185–6
importance of 197–8
informal consultations 184
institutional veil, and 245–7
'internal law' 225–30
international community of states 242–3
application of successive treaties relating to same subject-matter 242
Article 38 (rules in a treaty becoming binding on third States or third organizations through international custom) 243
Article 53 (treaties conflicting with a peremptory norm of general international law) 243
Article 64 (emergence of a new peremptory norm of general international law) 243
jus cogens, definition 243
'terms which are deliberately ambiguous' 242–3
international organisation as moral person 237–42
aggressor state 239–40
coercion 239
corruption 239
error, and 238
fraud, and 238
fundamental change of circumstances 241
questions not prejudged 240
reservations 238
transparency of institutional veil 240–1
member states and third states 212–25
EEC, and 222–3
pacta tertiis rule 213
'third states' 222
methodology, questions of 182–6
moral personality 237–42
objective of drafters 198
organisations as closed subjects 247
parallel provisions of 1969 Convention 277–81
participation of international organisations in diplomatic conference 186–90
participants 187–9
status 189–90
preliminary questions 181–95
principle, issues of 237–43
procedural aspects 181–95
procedural position of international organisations 186–92
reservations 210–12
acceptance of 212
Article 19 (formulation of reservations) 210–12
existing practice 210–11
formulation 210
objection to 212
'rules of the organisation' 225–30
'Alabama rule' 226
Article 27 (internal law of States, rules of international organizations and observance of treaties) 226
Article 46 (provisions of internal law of a State and rules of an international organization regarding competence to conclude treaties) 227–8
Article 47 (specific restrictions on authority to express the consent of a State or an international organization) 228

autonomy, and 227
invoking 226–8
reserving 229–30
'special characteristics' of IGO treaties, and 182–3
status of organisations in method and procedure 193–5
adjustment of procedural rules 194
equation of organisations and states 194
procedural role 194–5
table of comparison with Articles of 1969 Convention 274
table of comparison with draft Articles of 274–5, 1982
terminology 230–3
'communication of consent' 230
'expression of consent' 230
'formal confirmation' 232
full powers 232
'other subjects of law' 231–2
'party' 231
powers 232
'ratification' 232
'relevant rules of the organisation' 231
'rules of the organisation' 230–1
territorial scope of treaties 233–4
territory 233–4
fundamental change of circumstances 234
transparent image of organisations, and 245
travaux préparatoires 199, 245
treaty-making capacity 203–5
Article 6 204–5
rules of organisation, and 204–5

Virally, Michel
international organisations, on 16

von Gierke, Otto
international organisations, on 45

World Bank Tribunal 29

World Bank Tribunal, *Holidays Inns v Morocco* 89/1, 1979 29

World Health Organization 31, 50–1, 53, 74, 108, 117, 120, 121, 193

Zollverein 43–4, 46–7